SPSS-X™ Introductory Statistics Guide

for SPSS-X Release 3

NORUŠIS/SPSS INC.

SPSS Inc.
444 N. Michigan Avenue
Chicago, Illinois 60611
312.329.3500

SPSS International B.V.
P.O. Box 115
4200 AC Gorinchem
The Netherlands
Tel. +31.1830.36711
Twx.: 21019 (SPSS NL)
Fax +31.1830.35839

For more information about SPSS-X and other software produced and distributed by SPSS Inc., please write or call

Marketing Department
SPSS Inc.
444 North Michigan Avenue
Chicago, IL 60611
Tel: (312) 329-3500
Fax: (312) 329-3668

In Europe and the Middle East, please write or call

SPSS International BV
P.O. Box 115
4200 AC Gorinchem
The Netherlands
Tel: +31.1830.36711
Twx: 21019
Fax: +31.1830.35839

ISBN 0-918469-54-6

Library of Congress Catalog Card Number: 87-062352

Preface

Through and through the world is infested with quantity: To talk sense is to talk quantities. It is no use saying the nation is large—How large? It is no use saying that radium is scarce—How scarce? You cannot evade quantity. You may fly to poetry and music, and quantity and number will face you in your rhythms and your octaves.

—Alfred North Whitehead

Quantity is as inescapable today as it was in Whitehead's time. Even those outside technical professions face a plethora of numbers when they look at a newspaper. The purpose of data analysis is to make it easier to deal with quantity—to simplify and summarize data and to illuminate patterns that are not immediately evident.

THE SPSS-X SYSTEM

SPSS-X™ is a comprehensive tool for managing, analyzing, and displaying data. A broad range of statistical analyses and data modification tasks are accomplished with a simple, English-like language. Results can be easily obtained with minimal understanding of computer intricacies.

This manual is intended for novice users of SPSS-X Release 3.0 and introduces the basic features and procedures: descriptive statistics, measures of association for two-way tables, tests for equality of means, nonparametric procedures, and bivariate and multiple regression. It also contains an overview of four commonly used multivariate procedures: discriminant analysis, factor analysis, cluster analysis, and multivariate analysis of variance. Detailed discussion of the multivariate procedures is found in the *SPSS-X Advanced Statistics Guide.*

While this text includes instructions for entering and defining data for analysis, for managing data files, and for transforming, selecting, sampling, and weighting data, it does not attempt to cover the full range of data and file management facilities available in SPSS-X. For those who want to extend their use of the system beyond the scope of this introduction, documentation can be found in the *SPSS-X User's Guide,* 3rd ed., (SPSS Inc., 1988). The computational methods used are described in *SPSS Statistical Algorithms.*

The system and its documentation are continually being extended. Before obtaining other manuals, check with your computation center or with SPSS Inc. for information about the current release of SPSS-X being used at your site and the documentation for that release.

USING THIS TEXT

This manual is designed to be a supplement in courses that integrate the teaching of statistics and computing. The first two chapters discuss preparation of a data file and the fundamentals of an SPSS-X job. Each subsequent chapter describes a problem and the SPSS-X output useful for its solution, followed by information about the SPSS-X commands needed to obtain the analysis.

Exercises at the end of each chapter reinforce and extend the material in three main areas: syntax, statistical concepts, and data analysis. Answers for selected questions on syntax and statistical concepts are given in Appendix A. The data analysis exercises provide an opportunity to formulate hypotheses, create the SPSS-X commands needed to carry out the analysis, and run those jobs using one of four data files distributed with the SPSS-X system. Those data files are described in Appendix B. Consult the SPSS Coordinator at your installation for information about using the files.

The last chapter contains a brief guide to the features of the SPSS-X system described in this manual, including instructions for running the elementary procedures. For additional information about running the more complex procedures, consult the *SPSS-X Advanced Statistics Guide* or the *SPSS-X User's Guide*, 3rd ed.

ACKNOWLEDGMENTS Most of the SPSS Inc. staff have participated either in designing and preparing this manual or in creating and maintaining the system it documents. I am grateful for their advice.

I am also grateful to the reviewers and users of the early editions of this book for many helpful comments and suggestions, and to Harry Roberts, Harry Davis, and Richard Shekelle for permission to use and distribute the data files. Finally, I wish to thank the members of my family, who advise me on everything.

—Marija J. Norušis

Contents

Chapter 1   From Paper into a File

Statistical software packages such as SPSS-X are used to analyze information. This information, called data, has many sources, such as public opinion surveys, laboratory experiments, and personnel records. Sometimes the information to be analyzed is already stored in a form that can be processed by a computer—for example, on a disk or magnetic tape. Data from large-scale studies, such as those done by the United States Census Bureau or the National Opinion Research Center, are distributed in machine-readable form. In these situations, all that is required to analyze the data is a directory which describes the way in which the data are recorded and stored and the necessary commands to access the data.

However, often the information does not reside on a machine-readable medium. Instead, the data are stored in file folders in personnel offices, in patient medical charts, or in some other form that a computer cannot read. Before this information can be analyzed by a computer program, it must be entered onto cards, disk, or tape. This chapter examines the steps necessary to prepare data for analysis.

1.1
CASES, VARIABLES, and VALUES

Consider Table 1.4, which contains data for five cases from a study designed to identify factors associated with coronary heart disease. In the Western Electric study, 2,017 men with no history of coronary heart disease were followed for 20 years, and the occurrence of coronary heart disease was monitored (see Appendix B for further information about this study). Much information was obtained for each participant at the beginning of the study and at various points during it. Table 1.4 contains only a very small subset of the data available for each man. Each name in the table represents a *case,* or observation, for which *values* are available for a set of *variables*.

For the first case, employee John Jones, the value for the age variable is 40 and the value for the height variable is 68.8 inches. The same variables—age, family history, first cardiac event, height in inches, day of death, cholesterol level—are recorded for all cases. What differs are the actual values of the variables. Each case has one and only one value for each variable. "Unknown" and "missing" are acceptable values for a variable, although these values require special treatment during analysis.

The case is the basic unit for which measurements are taken. In this analysis, the case is an employee of Western Electric. In studies of political opinion or brand preference, the case is most likely the individual respondent to a questionnaire. A case may be a larger unit, such as a school, county, or nation; it may be a time period, such as a year or month in which measurements are obtained; or it may be an event, such as an auto accident.

For any single analysis, the cases must be the same. If the unit of analysis is a county, all cases are counties, and the values of each variable are for individual counties. If the unit is a state, then all cases are states and the values for each variable are for states.

1.2
Identifying Important Variables

A critical step in any study is the selection of variables to be included. For example, an employee can be described using many variables, such as place of residence, color of hair and eyes, years of education, work experience, and so forth. The variables that are relevant to the problem under study must be chosen from the vast array of information available. If important variables are excluded from the data file, the results will be of limited use. For example, if a variable such as years of work experience is excluded from a study of salary discrimination, few—if any—correct conclusions can be drawn. All potentially relevant variables should be included in the study since it is much easier to exclude unnecessary variables from analysis than to gather additional information.

1.3
Recording the Data

Once the variables have been selected, you must decide how they will be recorded. Do you need to record the actual date of birth or can you simply record the age in years? Is it sufficient to know if someone is a high-school or college graduate or do you need to know the actual number of years of education? It is usually a good idea to record the data in as much detail as possible. For example, if you record actual ages, cases can be grouped later into age categories. But if you just record each case as over 50 years or under 50 years of age, you can never analyze your data using any other age categories.

1.4
Coding the Variables

To enter observations into a data file, the values of the variables must be typed onto punched cards using a keypunch or entered directly into a disk file using a terminal. Punched cards are rectangular pieces of stiff paper on which 80 characters of information can be entered. Each character is represented by the position of holes in the card. Figure 1.4 shows a typical punched card. A terminal is like an electric typewriter; the information entered with it is directly stored on a disk.

Figure 1.4   A punched card

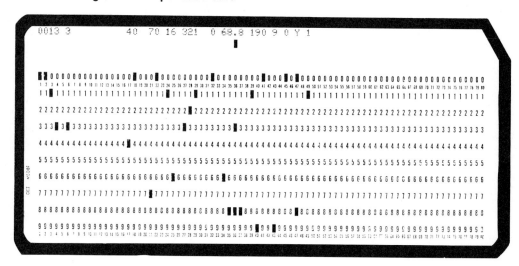

One way to simplify data entry is to assign numbers or symbols to represent responses. This is known as *coding* the data. For example, instead of typing "Yes" or "No" as the values for the family history variable, the codes *Y* and *N* can be used. If only numbers are included in a coding scheme it is called *numeric*. If letters or a mixture of numbers, letters, and special symbols are chosen, the code is termed *alphanumeric*. By coding, you substantially decrease the number of symbols that you need to type, especially for variables whose values are originally recorded as words (such as state names).

Coding schemes are arbitrary by their very nature. The family history variable could also be coded 0 for no and 1 for yes. All that is necessary is that each possible response have a distinct code. For example, coding the states by their first letter is unacceptable since there are many states that begin with the same letter. Maine, Massachussetts, Michigan, Maryland, Minnesota, Mississippi, Missouri, and Montana would be indistinguishable.

It is usually helpful to have one variable that uniquely identifies each case. For the Western Electric employee data, that variable could be the name of the individual. But, since names are generally long and not always unique, an ID number can be used as an identifier. This identifier can help you easily locate the records for cases with unusual values or missing information. Without the identifier, there is no quick way to find the correct age for an employee with a value of 12 in the data file.

Table 1.4 Excerpt from uncoded data for Western Electric study

Name	First event	Age	Diastolic BP	Education	Cholesterol	Cigarettes
John Jones	Nonfatal MI	40	70	B.A.	321	0
Clark Roberts	Nonfatal MI	49	87	11th grade	246	60
Paul Buttons	Sudden death	43	89	High school	262	0
James Smith	Nonfatal MI	50	105	8th grade	275	15
Robert Norris	Sudden death	43	110	Unknown	301	25

Height	Weight	Day of week	Vital10	Family history	Incidence of CHD
68.8	190	None	Alive	Yes	Yes
72.2	204	Thursday	Alive	No	Yes
69.0	162	Saturday	Dead	No	Yes
62.5	152	Wednesday	Alive	Yes	Yes
68.0	148	Monday	Dead	No	Yes

1.5
An Example

Consider the coding scheme in Table 1.5. Figure 1.5a contains data for the first three cases from Table 1.4 coded according to this scheme. Once the data are coded, a format for arranging the data in a computer file must be determined. Each punched card or line of type (if data are entered from a terminal) is known as a *record*. Each record is composed of columns in which the numbers or characters are stored. Punched cards have a maximum record length of 80 columns. Records stored on tape or disk can be longer. Two decisions that must be made are how many records will be needed for each case and in what column locations each variable will be stored.

Table 1.5 Coding scheme for employee data form

VARIABLE	CODING SCHEME
ID	no special code
FIRST CHD EVENT	1=No CHD 2=Sudden death 3=Nonfatal myocardial infarction 4=Fatal myocardial infarction 6=Other CHD
AGE	in years
DIASTOLIC BP	in mm of mercury
EDUCATION	in years
CHOLESTEROL	in milligrams per deciliter
CIGARETTES	number per day
HEIGHT	to nearest 0.1 inch
WEIGHT	in pounds
DAY OF WEEK	1=Sunday 2=Monday 3=Tuesday 4=Wednesday 5=Thursday 6=Friday 7=Saturday 9=Unknown
VITAL10	status at 10 years 0=Alive 1=Dead
FAMILY HISTORY OF CHD	N=No Y=Yes
CHD	0=No 1=Yes

Figure 1.5a Coded data

```
CASEID FIRSTCHD AGE DBP58 EDUYR CHOL58 CGT58   HT58 WT58 DAYOFWK VITAL10 FAMHXCVR CHD
    13       3    40    70    16    321     0   68.8  190      9       0       Y     1
    30       3    49    87    11    246    60   72.2  204      5       0       N     1
    53       2    43    89    12    262     0   69.0  162      7       1       N     1
```

Figure 1.5b shows a listing of a file in which one record is used for each case. The column locations for the variables are also indicated. The ID number is in columns 1–4; first event in column 6; age in columns 17–18; diastolic blood pressure in columns 20–22; years of education in columns 24–25; cholesterol level in columns 27–29; number of cigarettes smoked per day in columns 31–32; height in columns 34–37; weight in columns 39–41; day of death in column 43; status at 10 years in column 45; family history of coronary heart disease in column 47; and incidence of coronary heart disease in column 49. The numbers are positioned in each field so that the last digit is in the last column of the field for the variable. For example, an ID number of 2 would have the number 2 in column 4; leading blanks or zeros occupy the beginning columns. This is known as *fixed-column format*. (Freefield input is discussed in Chapter 12.) The decimal point for the height variable is included in the file. However, it does not need to be included since SPSS-X commands can be used to indicate its location. If the decimal point is included, it occupies a column like any other symbol.

Figure 1.5b   One record file

```
0   0   1   1   2   2   3   3   4   4   5
1   5   0   5   0   5   0   5   0   5   0      Columns

    13 3        40  70 16 321  0 68.8 190 9 0 Y 1
    30 3        49  87 11 246 60 72.2 204 5 0 N 1
    53 2        43  89 12 262  0 69.0 162 7 1 N 1
                        .
                        .
                        .
```

When there are many variables for each case, more than one record may be necessary to store the information. In Figure 1.5c the first case (CASEID 13) occupies two records. The first record contains codes for first cardiac event, age, diastolic blood pressure, education, cholesterol, and cigarettes smoked. The second record contains codes for height, weight, day of death, status at 10 years, family history of coronary heart disease, and incidence of coronary heart disease. Each record contains the case ID number in columns 1–4 and a record identification number in column 50. It is usually recommended that you enter the identification number and record number onto all records for a case. You can then easily locate missing or out-of-order records.

Figure 1.5c   Two record file

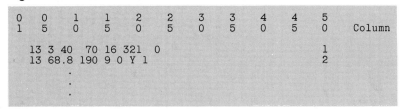

```
0   0   1   1   2   2   3   3   4   4   5
1   5   0   5   0   5   0   5   0   5   0      Column

    13 3 40  70 16 321  0                            1
    13 68.8 190 9 0 Y 1                              2
                .
                .
                .
```

It is important to allocate a sufficient number of columns for each variable. For example, if only two columns are used to record a weight variable, only weights less than 100 pounds will fit. Always allocate the maximum number of columns that you might need. Don't worry if your observed data do not actually require that many columns.

All data files considered in this manual are *rectangular*. That is, all cases have the same variables and the same number of records per case. Some data files are not rectangular. The same variables may not be recorded for every case. For example, in a study of adverse drug reactions, cases that are alive will not have a record detailing autopsy findings. Or a case might not be defined as the same unit, as in a file containing some records with data about families and some records with data about individual members within families. SPSS-X contains facilities for handling these kinds of files. See the *SPSS-X User's Guide* for more information.

1.6
DESIGNING FORMS

When a study is based on data already gathered, there is not much that can be done about the forms on which data reside or how the information is recorded. For example, if education is recorded in categories, the actual number of years cannot be entered into the data file. However, when a study is planned in advance, special forms can be designed that indicate both the type of information to be collected and where it will reside on the computer file. This type of form makes data entry much easier. You can enter the information directly from the form onto a punched card or directly onto a disk using a terminal.

Sometimes data collection forms are designed with space for miscellaneous comments. These comments can be analyzed only if they are coded. For example, if undergraduate major is listed in the comments section it must be coded into a variable. A coding scheme such as 1=physical sciences, 2=social sciences, 3=humanities, 4=engineering, and so forth could be used. Unless the comment section has specific codable information, it cannot be analyzed in any reasonable manner.

1.7
THE DATA FILE

The data file is the most crucial component of any analysis. Unless the data have been carefully gathered, recorded, and entered, all subsequent analyses will be of limited use. Always try to obtain as much of the necessary information as possible for all of the cases that are to be included in a study. A special code standing for missing information should be reserved only for cases where it is impossible to ascertain a certain value. Once the data have been coded and entered, make sure to check the values. Any suspicious values should be confirmed. They may be the result of coding or data-entry errors. Subsequent chapters show how you can use SPSS-X to help you locate errors in a data file.

EXERCISES

Data Analysis

1. a. What is wrong with the following coding scheme for the number of restaurant meals eaten per week?

    1 = One per day
    2 = Two or more per week
    3 = Three or more per week
    4 = Seven or fewer per week

    b. How would you recode this information?

2. The following coding scheme and data file layout is proposed for the variables age, occupation, and favorite color:

Variable	Code	Column location
Age	Number of years 40 is the missing value	3
Occupation	No code Occupation is spelled out in full	4–10
Color	First letter of color	9

What are the problems and how would you remedy them?

3. A survey was conducted to examine voter preference in a mayoral campaign. The three viable candidates are Jane, Harry, and Rich. The following table contains responses for six of the persons interviewed:

Person	Sex	Age	Candidate	Registered to vote	Employment status
Rogers	male	52	Harry	yes	looking
Boyd	male	25	Rich	doesn't remember	full time student
Paul	female	38	Jane	no	not on market
Kelley	male	no answer	Marija	yes	employed
Shoot	female	45	Rich	no	laid off
Harman	female	68	undecided	yes	retired

   a. What is a case in this study?
   b. What are the variables?
   c. Devise a coding scheme for any variables that need coding and indicate in which columns on the file the variables will be stored.
   d. Code the cases using your scheme from Question 3.c.

4. You wish to evaluate the satisfaction of undergraduate social science students with their required Statistics course. Select three questions you might include on a questionnaire. Write the questions and the coding scheme you would use for recording the information.

5. Devise coding schemes for the following variables:
   a. Miles driven to school each day
   b. Hobbies
   c. Attitude toward the use of animals in experiments
   d. Calories consumed per day
   e. Father's education
   f. Godfather's income
   g. Birth order in family

6. Here are some questions. Suggest coding schemes for them.
   a. Are you happily married?
   b. How many hours a week do you study?
   c. What is your favorite activity?
   d. How satisfied are you with your life?
   e. What are the characteristics of a good instructor?
   f. What would you change about your life?

Chapter 2   The SPSS-X Job

Once the data file has been prepared, you are ready to run an SPSS-X job. The usual SPSS-X job consists of three main parts: data definition, data transformation, and procedure specification. The data definition commands provide information about the variables and their location in the data file. The data transformation commands are used to restrict analyses to a subset of cases, create new variables, and modify existing variables. The procedure commands indicate what statistics, reports or tables are to be produced. This chapter will focus primarily on the first part of the SPSS-X job: data definition. The remaining chapters describe procedure commands, while information about the data transformation commands is presented as needed within the discussions of procedures and systematically in Chapter 18.

2.1
PREPARING SPSS-X COMMANDS

You can run SPSS-X in either *batch mode,* where you submit a file of SPSS-X commands for execution, or in *interactive mode,* where you submit commands one at a time for immediate execution. The rules, or *syntax,* for writing SPSS-X commands in each mode are the same. However, in batch mode, every SPSS-X command begins in the first column of a new line, and all continuation lines of the command are indented at least one column. In interactive mode, continuation lines from the command can begin in any column, and all commands must end with a *command terminator* (a period, for example).

Examples in this manual are shown in batch mode.

2.2
Batch Processing

In batch mode, you first assemble your SPSS-X commands in a file using your operating-system editor. After creating this *command file,* you submit it for execution to your operating system.

Batch processing might be the preferred way to run SPSS-X for a number of reasons. It can be a very efficient way to do the same analysis over and over on a regular basis, like for a weekly report. Batch processing can also be less tedious and error prone when you are doing long analyses involving commands with many specifications.

2.3
Interactive Processing

In interactive mode, each command is executed as soon as you've finished entering it, and the system prompts you for another specification. The prompt

```
SPSS-X>
```

means SPSS-X is ready for the first line of a command. If a command takes more than one line, hit the return key at the end of the line and you'll get the

```
CONTINUE>
```

prompt. Interactive SPSS-X will repeatedly give you the CONTINUE> prompt when you hit the return key until you enter a command terminator. By default, either a period or a blank line serves as a command terminator.

If you are entering data along with your commands, you get the prompt

```
DATA>
```

after you enter the BEGIN DATA command. The system goes back to giving you the SPSS-X> prompt after you enter the END DATA command.

You terminate an interactive session by entering the FINISH command. The command terminator is not required after FINISH.

Interactive processing can have several advantages over batch processing. Some types of data analyses are inherently interactive; feedback from initial analyses is required before you proceed with further analyses, which in turn might be followed by more analyses. An interactive computing system is more efficient in helping researchers with these kinds of iterative analyses. In addition, an extensive HELP system is available in interactive mode. For information on using the HELP command, see Chapter 18.

2.4
Commands and Specifications

Each command begins with a *command keyword* (which may contain more than one word). The command keyword is followed by at least one blank space and then any *specifications* required to complete the command, as in:

```
LIST VARIABLES=ALL
```

The command keyword is LIST, while VARIABLES=ALL is a specification. Specifications are made up of names, keywords, numbers, literals, arithmetic operators, special delimiters, and spacing as needed to separate these elements. Except within quoted strings, such as variable labels, you can add space or break lines at any point where a single blank is allowed, such as around slashes, parentheses, or equals signs.

Many specifications include *subcommands*. For example, the LIST command above has a VARIABLES subcommand to tell the system which variables to list. The LIST command can also include a CASES subcommand to specify how many cases to list, as in:

```
LIST VARIABLES=ALL /CASES=10
```

Generally, SPSS-X command, subcommand, and keyword specifications can be truncated to a minimum of three characters. Exceptions are the reserved keyword WITH and all specifications to the INFO command. For example, the following LIST command is identical to the command just above:

```
LIST VAR=ALL /CAS=10
```

2.5
DATA DEFINITION

The data definition commands answer the following questions:

- Where is the collection of data? (See Section 2.7.)
- How many records are there for each case? (See Section 2.8.)
- What are the names of the variables, and where are they located on the data file? (See Sections 2.9 through 2.13.)
- What labels should be attached to the variables and values? (See Section 2.15.)
- What values are used to represent missing information? (See Section 2.16.)

2.6
Describing the Data File

Figure 2.6 is the file containing the SPSS-X commands that define and produce a listing of data from the Western Electric Study described in Chapter 1. The first data definition command is DATA LIST, which tells SPSS-X where to find the data and how to read it.

Figure 2.6   Command file for the Western Electric study

```
TITLE  WESTERN ELECTRIC STUDY
COMMENT  *** WESTERN ELECTRIC STUDY OF CORONARY HEART DISEASE.
             DATA DEFINITION BEGINS HERE.

DATA LIST RECORD=1 /1 CASEID 1-4 FIRSTCHD 6 AGE 17-18 DBP58 20-22
    EDUYR 24-25 CHOL58 27-29 CGT58 31-32 HT58 34-37 (1) WT58 39-41
    DAYOFWK 43 VITAL10 45 FAMHXCVR 47 (A) CHD 49
VARIABLE LABELS
    CASEID 'CASE IDENTIFICATION NUMBER'
    FIRSTCHD 'FIRST CHD EVENT'
    AGE 'AGE AT ENTRY'
    DBP58 'AVERAGE DIAST BLOOD PRESSURE 58'
    EDUYR 'YEARS OF EDUCATION'
    CHOL58 'SERUM CHOLESTEROL 58 -- MG PER DL'
    CGT58 'NO OF CIGARETTES PER DAY IN 1958'
    HT58 'STATURE, 1958 -- TO NEAREST 0.1 INCH'
    WT58 'BODY WEIGHT, 1958 -- LBS'
    DAYOFWK 'DAY OF DEATH'
    VITAL10 'STATUS AT TEN YEARS'
    FAMHXCVR 'FAMILY HISTORY OF CHD'
    CHD 'INCIDENCE OF CORONARY HEART DISEASE'
VALUE LABELS  FIRSTCHD 1 'NO CHD' 2 'SUDDEN  DEATH' 3 'NONFATALMI'
    5 'FATAL    MI' 6 'OTHER    CHD'/
    VITAL10 0 'ALIVE' 1 'DEAD'/
    DAYOFWK 1 'SUNDAY' 2 'MONDAY' 3 'TUESDAY' 4 'WEDNSDAY'
       5 'THURSDAY' 6 'FRIDAY' 7 'SATURDAY' 9 'MISSING'/
    FAMHXCVR 'Y' 'YES' 'N' 'NO'/
MISSING VALUES  DAYOFWK (9)

COMMENT A PROCEDURE COMMAND GOES HERE
LIST VARIABLES=ALL/CASES=10

COMMENT THE DATA FILE STARTS HERE
BEGIN DATA
    13 3        40   70 16 321  0 68.8 190 9 0 Y 1 0
    30 3        49   87 11 246 60 72.2 204 5 0 N 1 0
    53 2        43   89 12 262  0 69.0 162 7 1 N 1 1
    84 3        50  105  8 275 15 62.5 152 4 0 Y 1 0
    .....       Remainder of cases not shown
END DATA
FINISH
```

2.7
Locating the Data

The data can be in the same file as the SPSS-X commands or in a separate file. If the data are in a file other than the SPSS-X command file, name the file in which the data are stored with the FILE subcommand, as in:

```
DATA LIST FILE=CARDIAC
```

CARDIAC is the name SPSS-X uses to locate the file on which the data are stored. If the data are included in an SPSS-X command file, you do not need to use a FILE subcommand.

2.8
Specifying the Number of Records

The data for a single case may reside on one or more records, as indicated in Chapter 1. The RECORDS subcommand identifies the number of records for each case. Specify the total number of records per case in the data file, not the number actually used in the analysis, even if your particular problem does not use variables from all records. If there are two records per case in a data file, RECORDS=2 is specified following the FILE subcommand, as in:

```
DATA LIST FILE=CARDIAC RECORDS=2
```

2.9
Choosing Variable Names

Once the location of the data and the number of records have been specified, assign names to each of the variables along with the location of each of the variables in the data file. The variable name is used to refer to a particular variable throughout the SPSS-X job. For example, a variable that describes father's occupation might be named PAOCCUP. Keep in mind the following rules when you name variables:.

- The name must begin with a letter or the symbol @. The remaining characters in the name can be any letter, any digit, a period, or the symbols @, #, or $.
- The length of the name cannot exceed eight characters.
- Blanks and special symbols such as &, !, ?, /, ', cannot occur in a variable name.
- Each variable must have a unique name—duplication is not allowed.
- The reserved keywords in Table 2.9 cannot be used as variable names since they have special meaning in SPSS-X.

The following are all valid variable names: LOCATION, LOC#5, @2.5, X.1, A#######, and OVER$500.

You can create a set of variable names by using keyword TO. When you are assigning new names, as in DATA LIST specifications, ITEM1 TO ITEM5 is equivalent to five names: ITEM1, ITEM2, ITEM3, ITEM4, and ITEM5. The prefix can be any valid name and the numbers can be any integers, so long as the first number is smaller than the second and the full variable name, including the number, does not exceed eight characters.

Table 2.9 SPSS-X reserved keywords

ALL	EQ	LE	NOT	TO
AND	GE	LT	OR	WITH
BY	GT	NE	THRU	

It is a good idea to assign names that help you to identify the variables. For example, the names X and Z can be assigned to variables for age and sex, but the variable names AGE and SEX will give you a much better idea of the nature of each variable. When a file contains many variables, it is particularly important to be able to know what you are measuring with each variable. The variable names assigned to the Western Electric data include AGE for age at entry into the study; EDUYR for years of education at entry into the study; VITAL10 for status after ten years in the study; and FAMHXCVR for family history of coronary heart disease.

**2.10
Indicating Column Locations**

Along with variable names you must also specify the location of the variables in the data file. The record number and column locations must be specified. All variables on the same record must be identified at the same time. For example, the command

```
DATA LIST FILE=CARDIAC RECORDS=1
 /1 CASEID 1-4 FIRSTCHD 6 AGE 17-18 DBP58 20-22
```

describes four variables. Variable definition begins with the first slash. The 1 after the slash indicates the variables are found on the first record. The range of numbers after the variable name gives the location on that record of the information for the variable. For example, CASEID is in columns 1–4 while AGE is in columns 17–18.

Although variables from the same record must be defined together, they do not need to be defined in any particular sequence within that record. That is, variables at the end of a record can be defined before those at the beginning of the same record.

If several variables are recorded in adjacent columns of the same record and have the same width and format type, they can be defined on the DATA LIST in an abbreviated format. List all of the variable names followed by the beginning column location of the first variable in the list, a dash, and the ending column location of the last variable in the list. For example, in the command

```
DATA LIST FILE=HUBDATA RECORDS=3
 /1 DEPT82 19 SEX 20 MOHIRED YRHIRED 12-15
```

MOHIRED and YRHIRED form a list of variables and 12–15 is the column specification for both. The DATA LIST command divides the total number of columns specified equally among the variables in the list. Thus, MOHIRED is in columns 12–13 and YRHIRED is in columns 14–15. If the total number of columns is not an even multiple of the number of variables listed, SPSS-X prints an error message and does not read the file.

2.11
Specifying Multiple Records

Sometimes your data are located on more than one record for each case, as in Figure 1.5c. To read more than one record for each case, specify the number of records using the RECORDS subcommand (Section 2.8), define the variables on the first record and then enter a slash followed by the sequence number of the next record to be read and the variable definitions for that record. Repeat this procedure until you have defined all records for each case in your data file. For example, the following DATA LIST command defines the Western Electric data arranged with two records per case, as shown in Figure 1.5c:

```
DATA LIST FILE=CARDIAC RECORDS=2
 /1 CASEID 1-4 FIRSTCHD 6 AGE 8-9 DBP58 11-13 EDUYR 15-16 CHOL58 18-20
    CGT58 22-23 RECID1 50
 /2 HT58 6-9 (1) WT58 11-13 DAYOFWK 15 VITAL10 17 FAMHXCVR 19 (A) CHD 21
    RECID2 50
```

In this DATA LIST, variables CASEID, FIRSTCHD, AGE, DBP58, EDUYR, CHOL58, CGT58, and RECID1 are read from the first record. Variables HT58, WT58, DAYOFWK, VITAL10, FAMHXCVR, CHD, and RECID2 are read from the second record. Although the case identification number appears on both records, it is necessary to define the variable CASEID from only one of the two records.

To check your data for missing, duplicate, or wild records for each case, use the FILE TYPE GROUPED command discussed in Chapter 18.

2.12
Types of Variables

Two types of variables can be defined with SPSS-X: numeric and alphanumeric. A numeric variable contains only numbers. Numeric variables can be either decimals (such as 12.345) or integers (such as 1234). An alphanumeric, or *string,* variable contains a combination of letters, numbers, and special characters. There are two types of string variables—short strings and long strings. The actual length of short and long string variables depends on the computer used at your installation. In general, a string variable whose values contain eight characters or less is considered a short string. FAMHXCVR, coded as Y or N, is a short string, If the employee's name had been coded, that would be a long string. The difference is that short strings can be used in several data transformation and procedure commands where long strings cannot. String variables must be identified with the (A) symbol following the column specification on the DATA LIST command, as in

```
DATA LIST RECORDS=1 /1 CASEID 1-4 FIRSTCHD 6 AGE 17-18 DBP58 20-22
    EDUYR 24-25 CHOL58 27-29 CGT58 31-32 HT58 34-37 (1) WT58 39-41
    DAYOFWK 43 VITAL10 45 FAMHXCVR 47 (A) CHD 49
```

where variable FAMHXCVR is defined as a string variable.

2.13
Indicating Decimal Places

By default, DATA LIST assumes that the data format type is numeric and, if no decimal point has been recorded on the data file, that the numbers are integers. To indicate noninteger values when the decimal point is not actually coded in the data, specify the number of *implied* decimal places by enclosing the intended number in parentheses following the column specification. The specification

```
DATA LIST FILE=CARDIAC RECORDS=1
 /1 CASEID 1-4 FIRSTCHD 6 AGE 17-18 DBP58 20-22
    EDUYR 24-25 CHOL58 27-29 CGT58 31-32 HT58 34-37 (1) WT58 39-41
```

locates the variable that measures height in 1958 in columns 34 through 37 on record one. The last digit of HT58 is stored as a decimal position.

For example, if the number 1234 is stored in columns 34–37, the specification HT58 34–37(1) results in the number 123.4. The specification HT58 34–37(4) results in the number 0.1234 , while HT58 34–37(2) results in the number 12.34. If the number is stored in the data file with the decimal point, the decimal point overrides the DATA LIST specification.

2.14
The DATA LIST Table

After the DATA LIST command is processed, SPSS-X prints a table showing the variable names, column and record locations, and variable types for all of the variables defined. As shown in Figure 2.14, the variable named CASEID is found in columns 1–4 of the first record. The code F is used for numeric variables, while A designates string (alphanumeric) variables. The number of implied decimals is given in the column labeled DEC. The DATA LIST correspondence table provides a convenient reference to the data file as described on the DATA LIST command.

Figure 2.14 DATA LIST correspondence table

VARIABLE	REC	START	END	FORMAT	WIDTH	DEC
CASEID	1	1	4	F	4	0
FIRSTCHD	1	6	6	F	1	0
AGE	1	17	18	F	2	0
DBP58	1	20	22	F	3	0
EDUYR	1	24	25	F	2	0
CHOL58	1	27	29	F	3	0
CGT58	1	31	32	F	2	0
HT58	1	34	37	F	4	1
WT58	1	39	41	F	3	0
DAYOFWK	1	43	43	F	1	0
VITAL10	1	45	45	F	1	0
FAMHXCVR	1	47	47	A	1	
CHD	1	49	49	F	1	0

2.15
Variable and Value Labels

The VARIABLE LABELS and VALUE LABELS commands are optional. They supply information that is used only for labeling the output of SPSS-X jobs. Using these labels often makes the output more readable. Some variables that can take on many values, such as age or weight, do not need value labels since the values themselves are meaningful.

The VARIABLE LABELS command assigns an extended descriptive label to variables. Specify the variable name followed by at least one comma or blank and the label enclosed in apostrophes or quotation marks, as in:

```
VARIABLE LABELS
    CASEID 'CASE IDENTIFICATION NUMBER'
    FIRSTCHD 'FIRST CHD EVENT'
    AGE 'AGE AT ENTRY'
    DBP58 'AVERAGE DIAST BLOOD PRESSURE 58'
    EDUYR 'YEARS OF EDUCATION'
    CHOL58 'SERUM CHOLESTEROL 58 -- MG PER DL'
    CGT58 'NO OF CIGARETTES PER DAY IN 1958'
    HT58 'STATURE, 1958 -- TO NEAREST 0.1 INCH'
    WT58 'BODY WEIGHT, 1958 -- LBS'
    DAYOFWK 'DAY OF DEATH'
    VITAL10 'STATUS AT TEN YEARS'
    FAMHXCVR 'FAMILY HISTORY OF CHD'
    CHD 'INCIDENCE OF CORONARY HEART DISEASE'
```

This command assigns variable labels to the variables CASEID through CHD. A variable label applies to only one variable. The variable must have been previously defined on a DATA LIST or on one of the transformation commands that create new variables. The label can be up to 120 characters long and can include blanks and any other characters.

Enter an apostrophe as part of a label by enclosing the label in quotation marks or by entering the apostrophe twice with no separation. For example, the command

```
VARIABLE LABELS SALARY "EMPLOYEE'S YEARLY SALARY"
```

is the same as

```
VARIABLE LABELS SALARY 'EMPLOYEE''S YEARLY SALARY'
```

Quotation marks are entered in a label in the same manner.

The VALUE LABELS command assigns descriptive labels to values. The VALUE LABELS command is followed by a variable name, or variable list, and a list of values with associated labels. The command

```
VALUE LABELS  FIRSTCHD 1 'NO CHD' 2 'SUDDEN  DEATH' 3 'NONFATALMI'
     5 'FATAL   MI' 6 'OTHER   CHD'/
     VITAL10 0 'ALIVE' 1 'DEAD'/
     DAYOFWK 1 'SUNDAY' 2 'MONDAY' 3 'TUESDAY' 4 'WEDNSDAY'
     5 'THURSDAY' 6 'FRIDAY' 7 'SATURDAY' 9 'MISSING'/
     FAMHXCVR 'Y' 'YES' 'N' 'NO'
```

assigns labels to the values for the variables FIRSTCHD, VITAL10, DAYOFWK, and FAMHXCVR. The set of labels for each variable is separated from the labels for the preceding variable by a slash. You can assign labels for values of any variable already defined. If the variable is a string, the value must be enclosed in apostrophes, as in the value labels for variable FAMHXCVR above). Value labels can be up to 60 characters long and can contain any characters, including blanks.

2.16
Identifying Missing Values

Sometimes information for a particular variable is not available for a case. When information about the value of a variable is unknown, a special code is used to indicate that the value is missing for the variable. For example, if an employee's age is not known, this can be indicated by a code such as −1 or 99. Sometimes several codes are used to indicate missing values. The value 99 might indicate that age was not recorded on the personnel data form and -1 might indicate that an employee refused to reveal his or her age.

The MISSING VALUES command identifies values that represent missing information. Specify the variable name or variable list and the specified missing values in parentheses, as in:

```
MISSING VALUES  DAYOFWK (9)
```

This command assigns the value 9 as missing for variable DAYOFWK. For a complete discussion of the MISSING VALUES command, see Chapter 18.

User-defined missing values specified on the MISSING VALUES command are distinguished from the *system-missing* value (which is indicated on the output by a period). SPSS-X assigns the system-missing value when it encounters a value other than a number as the value for a variable declared on the DATA LIST command as numeric. For example, blanks are set to system-missing for numeric variables. System-missing values are also assigned when new variables created with data transformation commands are undefined, as when logs or square roots of negative numbers are requested or when one of the variables required in a computation has a missing value for that case.

2.17
THE LIST COMMAND

Once you have defined the data file, you are ready to specify an SPSS-X procedure. SPSS-X procedures are used to tabulate the data, to calculate statistics, or to generate reports and plots. The job in Figure 2.6 requests a listing of the data values for the first 10 cases. The LIST command for this job is as follows:

```
LIST VARIABLES=ALL /CASES=10
```

The command keyword is LIST. The subcommand VARIABLES indicates which of the variables are to be printed. The keyword ALL specifies all the variables defined on the file. The CASES subcommand indicates the number of observations for which the values are to be listed.

Figure 2.17 shows the listing of the first 10 cases. This listing is useful for spotting errors in data entry or data definition. For example, if the wrong columns are given for the AGE variable, strange values will probably appear in the listing.

Figure 2.17 Output from LIST

CASEID	FIRSTCHD	AGE	DBP58	EDUYR	CHOL58	CGT58	HT58	WT58	DAYOFWK	VITAL10	FAMHXCVR	CHD
13	3	40	70	16	321	0	68.8	190	9	0	Y	1
30	3	49	87	11	246	60	72.2	204	5	0	N	1
53	2	43	89	12	262	0	69.0	162	7	1	N	1
84	3	50	105	8	275	15	62.5	152	4	0	Y	1
89	2	43	110	.	301	25	68.0	148	2	1	N	1
102	3	50	88	8	261	30	68.0	142	1	1	N	1
117	3	45	70	.	212	0	66.5	196	9	0	N	1
132	3	47	79	9	372	30	67.0	193	1	0	N	1
151	2	53	102	12	216	0	67.0	172	3	1	N	1
153	2	49	99	14	251	10	64.3	162	5	1	Y	1

```
NUMBER OF CASES READ =      10     NUMBER OF CASES LISTED =      10
```

When you specify variables on a procedure command, you can use the TO convention to refer to them, just as you can when you create them. When you are referring to variables to be analyzed by a procedure, VARA TO VARD refers to VARA, VARD, and any variables that have been defined between VARA and VARD. For example, the command

```
LIST VARIABLES=FIRSTCHD TO CHOL58
```

requests a listing for variables FIRSTCHD, AGE, DBP58, EDUYR, and CHOL58. Refer to Figure 2.6 for the DATA LIST command that defines these variables.

2.18
IN-LINE DATA

If the data are in the same file as the SPSS-X commands, you must separate them from the other lines in the command file with the BEGIN DATA and END DATA commands. The BEGIN DATA command follows the first procedure command and precedes the data and the END DATA command follows the last record of the data. If the data are in a different file from the commands, the BEGIN DATA and END DATA commands are not used.

2.19
THE ACTIVE FILE

The active file refers to the variables that you define using the DATA LIST command. This is the file that SPSS-X creates to analyze your data. After you define a file, you display the variables you have defined. You can use the DISPLAY command to produce a display of variable names, variable and value labels, missing values, and print and write formats. See Chapter 18 for a discussion of the DISPLAY command.

2.20
THE SPSS-X SYSTEM FILE

Once you have defined your data file in SPSS-X, you do not need to repeat the data definition process. Information from the data definition commands described in this chapter can be permanently saved along with the data on a specially formatted file called the SPSS-X *system file*. Variables created or altered by data transformations and the descriptive information for these variables can also be saved on a system file. You can access the system file in subsequent SPSS-X jobs or later in the same job without respecifying variable locations, formats, missing values, or variable and value labels. You can update the system file, altering the descriptive information or modifying the data, and you can save the updated version in a new system file. The SAVE command for creating the system file and the GET command for accessing the system file are discussed in Chapter 18 and are illustrated in several examples throughout this text.

2.21
WARNINGS AND ERROR MESSAGES

When SPSS-X encounters a problem in your job, it prints a message and takes some action appropriate to the kind of problem. The message appears immediately following where the error was detected and always includes what action the system is taking.

Warnings. Misspelling a variable name on the VARIABLE LABELS command causes just the label for that variable to be skipped. For example, misspelling variable EDUYR on the VARIABLE LABELS command produces the following warning:

```
10  0         VARIABLE LABELS
11  0              CASEID 'CASE IDENTIFICATION NUMBER'
12  0              FIRSTCHD 'FIRST CHD EVENT'
13  0              AGE 'AGE AT ENTRY'
14  0              DBP58 'AVERAGE DIAST BLOOD PRESSURE 58'
15  0              EDUCYRS 'YEARS OF EDUCATION'
>WARNING 4461 LINE 15, COLUMN 4, TEXT: EDUCYRS
>An unknown variable name was specified on the VARIABLE LABELS command.  The name
>and the label will be ignored.
```

Warnings often result from "undefined" data: values encountered in the input data that do not conform to the defined type of variable, such as alphanumeric characters in data defined as numeric. In this case, SPSS-X changes the code to the system-missing value and issues a warning message:

```
>WARNING   652
>An invalid numeric field has been found.  The result has been set to the system
>missing value.

SOURCE CARD NUMBER -    4
  STARTING COLUMN NUMBER -  1, CONTENTS OF FIELD: 00B4
```

SPSS-X will terminate a job after 80 warnings.

Errors. Some errors force SPSS-X to skip an entire command but allow processing to continue for subsequent commands. Frequently this involves a procedure command, such as an error in the variable list for the LIST procedure. In the following command the variable VIDAL10 does not exist:

```
32  0         LIST CASES=10/VARIABLES=DAYOFWK FAMHXCVR VIDAL10/

>ERROR     701 LINE  32, COLUMN 42, TEXT: VIDAL10
>An undefined variable name, or a scratch or system variable was specified in a
>variable list which accepts only standard variables.  Check spelling, and
>verify the existence of this variable.
>THIS COMMAND NOT EXECUTED.
```

Errors that are likely to affect the results of later commands force SPSS-X to cease processing. For example, because the last column specification is missing on the DATA LIST command below, SPSS-X assumes that later processing would most likely be meaningless. Thus processing ends, though the system continues to check for other syntax errors that might be in the same job.

```
7  0      DATA LIST RECORDS=1 /1 CASEID 1-4 FIRSTCHD 6 AGE 17-18 DBP58 20-22
8  0           EDUYR 24-25 CHOL58 27-29 CGT58 31-32 HT58 34-37 (1) WT58 39-41
9  0           DAYOFWK 43 VITAL10 45 FAMHXCVR 47 (A) CHD
>ERROR    4130  LINE   9, (END OF COMMAND)
>The DATA LIST command contains an invalid format.
>NO FURTHER COMMANDS WILL BE EXECUTED.   ERROR SCAN CONTINUES.
```

Occasionally SPSS-X is forced to terminate a job immediately. This typically happens when errors occur in accessing files, as in:

```
120S INPUT  ERROR 003 ON ELECDATA,

>ERROR    334
>An I/O error has occurred.   The causes could include a damaged medium such as
>a tape, an improper DCB specification, an attempt to read a file which was
>never written, an attempt to read a BCD file as an SPSS system file, etc.
>THIS IS A CATASTROPHIC ERROR FROM WHICH SPSSX CANNOT RECOVER.
>SPSSX CANNOT CONTINUE.
```

No further error checking is done when this type of error is encountered.

2.22 OTHER SPSS-X COMMANDS

Now that you know how to define and list your data we can examine ways of organizing and analyzing data. The next chapters present some statistical concepts and show how to use SPSS-X to analyze data in different ways. In these chapters, we discuss the other two types of SPSS-X commands: data transformations and statistical procedures. We have not been able to discuss many of the complexities of data definition in this chapter and we will encounter similar constraints in discussing other types of SPSS-X commands. More complete discussion of all facilities and procedures discussed in these chapters is found in Chapter 18.

EXERCISES

Syntax

1. Which of the following are not valid SPSS-X variable names and why?
   a. MARITALSTAT
   b. 1AGE
   c. JOB CAT
   d. FIR#ST

2. Find the syntax error in each of the following commands:
   a. DATA LIST   FILE=SURVEY RECORDS=1 /2 LOCATION 1-2 PRODUCT 3-5
   b. DATA LIST   FILE=FAMILIES RECORDS=1/ 1 LASTNAME 1-20 (A) DADAGE
      21-22
          MOMAGE 23-24 KIDAGE1 TO KIDAGE3 30-36
   c. VARIABLE LABELS   EDUC, DADEDUC, MOMEDUC 'YEARS OF FORMAL EDUCATION'
   d. VALUE LABELS   STATE 1 'VERMONT' 2 'NEW HAMPSHIRE' 3 "MAINE" 4 NEW
      YORK
   e. VALUE LABELS   1 'CHEVROLET' 2 'PONTIAC' 3 'PLYMOUTH' 4 'FORD'
   f. MISSING VALUES   DADAGE, MOMAGE, KIDAGE1 TO KIDAGE3 -1,0

3. Consider the following job:

```
DATA LIST  FILE=INLINE RECORDS=2 /1 NAME 1-20 (A) ADDRESS 21-40 (A)
  CITY 41-60(A) STATE 61-70(A) AGE 71-72 /2 MAJOR 1 GPA 3-5(2) MOMEDUC
7-8
  DADEDUC 10-11 SIBLINGS 13-14
VARIABLE LABELS  MAJOR 'MAJOR FIELD OF STUDY'
  MOMEDUC "MOTHER'S EDUCATION IN YEARS"
  DADEDUC "FATHER'S EDUCATION IN YEARS"
VALUE LABELS  MAJOR 1 'MATHEMATICS' 2 'SOCIOLOGY' 3 'BIOLOGY' 4 'ART'
  SIBLINGS 0 'ONLY CHILD' MOMEDUC, DADEDUC -1 "DON'T KNOW"
  12 'HIGH SCHOOL GRAD' 16 'COLLEGE GRADUATE'
MISSING VALUES  MOMEDUC, DADEDUC (-1)
LIST  VARIABLES=NAME AGE MAJOR GPA
BEGIN DATA
WILLIAM JOHNSON        3218 WOODSIDE AVE   BALTIMORE           MARYLAND   19
4 376 15 14 2
CAROLYN STEVENS        427 HICKORY LANE    KANSAS CITY         MISSOURI   18
1 381 16 16 1
WAYNE ROBERTSON        1801 LINCOLN DRIVE  DALLAS              TEXAS      20
2 359 14 -1 3
LEONARD GILMORE        5500 OCEANSIDE AVE  LOS ANGELES         CALIFORNIA19
3 379 16 17 5
VIVIAN SMITHFIELD      29 E. 79TH STREET   CHICAGO             ILLINOIS   21
2 380 16 14 1
END DATA
```

a. Fill in the table below for the five cases in this file.

	Name	Age	GPA
1	_____	_____	_____
2	_____	_____	_____
3	_____	_____	_____
4	_____	_____	_____
5	_____	_____	_____

b. Which student is an art major?

c. Which student has the most siblings?   L 6

d. How many cases have a valid code for DADEDUC?

4. How many syntax errors can you find in this job?

```
DATA LIST  FILE=MYDATA RECORDS=1 / 1 NAME 1-20 A HEIGHT 21-23
WEIGHT 25-27  EYECOLOR 29 HAIRCOLOR 31
VARIABLE LABELS  WEIGH 'WIEGHT IN POUNDS'
  HEIGHT "HEIGHT IN INCHES"
VALUE LABELS  EYECOLR 1 'BROWN' 2 'BLUE' 3 'GREEN' 4 'HAZEL'/
  HAIRCOLOR 1 'BLACK' 2 'BROWN' 3 'BLONDE' 4 'RED'
MISSING VALUES  HEIGHT WEIGHT AGE (-1)
LIST  VARIABLES = EYECOLOR TO HEIGHT
```

5. What is the problem in the following job? How would you fix it?

```
DATA LIST  RECORDS=1/1 BREED 1-10(A) SEX 12(A) AGE 14-15
LIST  VARIABLES=ALL
BEGIN DATA
SHEPHERD    M   9
COLLIE      F   4
TERRIER     F  11
POODLE      M   7
SPANIEL     M   3
BULLDOG     F  12
AFGHAN      F   5
BOXER       M  DK
HUSKY       F   6
DOBERMAN    M   8
END DATA
```

6. New employees at a local factory can report to any one of four test sights for a physical examination. They are weighed and have their hearing and vision tested. They also have their pulmonary and cardiovascular systems tested. Each test has four ratings: poor, fair, good, excellent. A clinician wrote the following job on the examination results:

```
DATA LIST FILE=EXAM RECORDS=1/1 EMP 1-20 (A) WGT 21-23
   TESTA TO TESTD 24-27 LOCATION 28-35 (A)
LIST VARIABLES=EMP TO TESTD
```

   a. What is the syntax error?
   b. How can you correct the syntax error?
   c. Can you make the DATA LIST command more descriptive?
   d. What command would you add to code the four test ratings?

Data Analysis

Most of the data analysis exercises in this book use the data files distributed with the SPSS-X release tape and described in Appendix B. To access the files, consult the SPSS coordinator at your installation.

1. The following questions are based on the data set described in Chapter 1, Question 3.c.
   a. Write a DATA LIST statement to define the data set (as you described it in Chapter 1, Question 3.c).
   b. Write VARIABLE LABELS, VALUE LABELS, and MISSING VALUES commands.
   c. Run an SPSS-X job to list the data file you have created and the dictionary information.

2. Using one of the data sets from Appendix B, do the following:
   a. Use the DISPLAY command to obtain information about the variables on the system file. If you are using the marketing data file, use the following command to display information for the first three products only:

```
DISPLAY  DICTIONARY/ VARIABLES=H1S TO H3S, W1S TO W3S,
   H1O TO H3O, H1R TO H3R, W1R TO W3R
```

   Make sure to enter the letter *O* and not the number *0* for the variables named H1O and H3O.
   b. Use the following command to obtain the values for the first 10 cases in the file:

```
LIST  VARIABLES=ALL/CASES=10
```

   If you are using the marketing file, use the same specification given for Question 2.a instead of VARIABLES=ALL.

3. The following table contains ages, GPA's, places of residence, and semester hours of credit for ten students. Write an SPSS-X job to input this information into the computer. Obtain a listing of values for each case.

Student	Age	GPA	Residence	Hours of credit
Bruce	19	2.1	in-state	50
Bob	22	3.9	out-of-state	99
Liz	20	3.7	in-state	44
Jim	25	3.0	in-state	12
Sheri	18	2.9	in-state	28
Tony	17	4.0	out-of-state	130
Irene	21	3.1	in-state	50
Ausra	12	3.3	in-state	8
Daina	35	2.7	out-of-state	16
Vytautas	15	3.8	in-state	30

4. Think of four characteristics that might be used to quantify "success." Evaluate 15 of your friends (or classmates if you don't have that many friends!) on the characteristics you have selected. Code the information.

   a. Enter the data into a data file.
   b. Write the DATA LIST command needed to read your information.
   c. Write VARIABLE LABELS and VALUE LABELS commands for your variables.
   d. Run a job to list the data. Check to make sure they agree with what you entered. If not, correct your job and run it again.

5. In the following questions, do you think that code 9 should be declared a missing value? Why or why not?

   a. Do you agree or disagree with the proposed tax hike?

      1 = agree
      2 = disagree
      9 = don't know about proposed hike

   b. Do you agree or disagree with the proposed tax hike?

      1 = agree
      2 = disagree
      9 = uncertain

6. What is the advantage of being able to specify user-missing values? Think of a response to a question that would sometimes be regarded as missing and sometimes as valid.

Chapter 3   Blue Mondays: Data Tabulation

Few people would dispute the effects of "rainy days and Mondays" on the body and spirit. It has long been known that more suicides occur on Mondays than other days of the week. Recently an excess of cardiac deaths on Mondays has also been noted (Rabkin et al., 1980). In this chapter we will examine the day of the week on which deaths occurred in the Western Electric Study (Appendix B) to see if an excess of deaths occurred on Mondays.

3.1 A FREQUENCY TABLE

A first step in analyzing data on day of death might be to count the number of deaths occurring on each day of the week. Figure 3.1a contains this information.

Figure 3.1a   Frequency of death by day of week

```
DAYOFWK    DAY OF DEATH


                                                      VALID     CUM
     VALUE LABEL              VALUE   FREQUENCY  PERCENT  PERCENT  PERCENT
     SUNDAY                     1        19       7.9     17.3     17.3
     MONDAY                     2        11       4.6     10.0     27.3
     TUESDAY                    3        19       7.9     17.3     44.5
     WEDNSDAY                   4        17       7.1     15.5     60.0
     THURSDAY                   5        15       6.3     13.6     73.6
     FRIDAY                     6        13       5.4     11.8     85.5
     SATURDAY                   7        16       6.7     14.5    100.0
     MISSING                    9       130      54.2   MISSING
                                     -------   -------  -------
                          TOTAL         240     100.0    100.0

     VALID CASES    110    MISSING CASES   130
```

Each row of the frequency table describes a particular day of the week. The last row represents cases for which the day of death is not known or that have not died. For the table in Figure 3.1a, there are 110 cases for which day of death is known. The first column *(value label)* gives the name of the day, while the second column contains the *value,* which is the symbol given to the computer to represent the day.

The number of people dying on each day is in the third column *(frequency).* Monday is the least-frequent death day with 11 deaths. These 11 deaths are 4.6% (11/240) of all cases. This *percentage* is in the fourth column. However, of the 240 people, 130 had no day of death. The 11 deaths on Monday are 10.0% of the total deaths for which death days are known (11/110). This *valid percentage* is in the fifth column.

The last column of the table contains the *cumulative percentage.* For a particular day, this percentage is the sum of the valid percentages of that day and all other days that precede it in the table. For example, the cumulative percentage for Tuesday is 44.5, which is the sum of the percentage of deaths that occurred on Sunday, Monday, and Tuesday. It is calculated as

$$\frac{19}{110} + \frac{11}{110} + \frac{19}{110} = \frac{49}{110} = 44.5\%$$

Figure 3.1b is a frequency table of day of death for cases who experienced sudden coronary death. This is a particularly interesting category since it is thought that sudden death may be related to stressful events such as return to the work environment. In Figure 3.1b there does not appear to be a clustering of deaths on any particular day. Sunday has 22.2% of the deaths, while Thursday has 8.3%. Since the number of sudden deaths in the table is small, the magnitude of the observed fluctuations is not very impressive.

Figure 3.1b   Frequency of sudden cardiac death by day of the week

DAYOFWK   DAY OF DEATH

VALUE LABEL	VALUE	FREQUENCY	PERCENT	VALID PERCENT	CUM PERCENT
SUNDAY	1	8	22.2	22.2	22.2
MONDAY	2	4	11.1	11.1	33.3
TUESDAY	3	4	11.1	11.1	44.4
WEDNSDAY	4	7	19.4	19.4	63.9
THURSDAY	5	3	8.3	8.3	72.2
FRIDAY	6	6	16.7	16.7	88.9
SATURDAY	7	4	11.1	11.1	100.0
TOTAL		36	100.0	100.0	

VALID CASES   36   MISSING CASES   0

3.2
Visual Displays

While the numbers in the frequency table can be studied and compared, it is often useful to present results in a visually interpretable form. Figure 3.2a is a pie chart of the data displayed in Figure 3.1a. Each slice represents a day of the week. The size of the slice depends on the frequency of death for that day. Monday is represented by 10.0% of the pie chart since 10.0% of the deaths for which the day is known occurred on Monday.

Figure 3.2a   Frequency of death by day of the week
(Pie chart from SPSS Graphics)

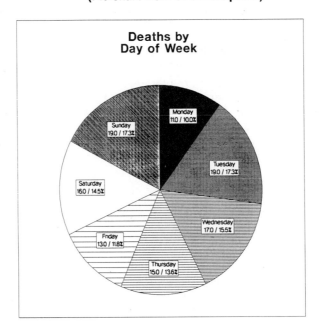

Another way to represent the data is with a bar chart, as shown in Figure 3.2b. There is a bar for each day, and the length of the bar is proportional to the number of deaths observed on that day. Inside each bar is the number of cases occurring on that day.

Figure 3.2b   Frequency of death by day of the week
(Bar chart from SPSS procedure FREQUENCIES)

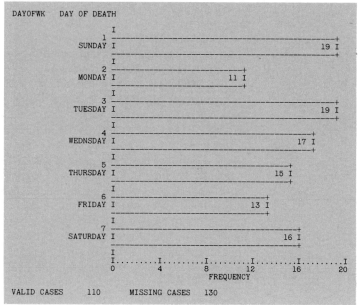

Only values that actually occur in the data are represented in the bar chart from procedure FREQUENCIES. For example, if no deaths took place on Thursday, no space would be left for Thursday and the bar for Wednesday would be followed by the one for Friday. If you chart the number of cars per family, the bar describing 6 cars may be next to the one for 25 cars if no family has 7 to 24 cars. Therefore, you should pay attention to where categories with no cases may occur.

Although the basic information presented by frequency tables, pie charts, and bar charts is the same, the visual displays enliven the data. Differences among the days of the week are apparent at a glance, eliminating the need to pore over columns of numbers.

3.3
What Day?

Although the number of sudden cardiac deaths is small in this study, the data in Figure 3.1b indicate that the number of deaths on Mondays is not particularly large. In fact, Sunday has the most deaths, slightly over 22%. A recent study of over a thousand sudden cardiac deaths in Rochester, Minnesota, also found a slightly increased incidence of death on weekends for men (Beard et al., 1982). The authors speculate that for men, this might mean "the home environment is more stressful than the work environment." But one should be wary of explanations that are not directly supported by data. It is only too easy to find a clever explanation for any statistical finding. (See Chapter 12 for further analysis of these data.)

3.4
Histograms

A frequency table or bar chart of all values for a variable is a convenient way of summarizing a variable that has a relatively small number of distinct values. Variables such as sex, country, and astrological sign are necessarily limited in the number of values they can have. For variables that can take on many different values, such as income to the penny or weight in ounces, a tally of the cases with each observed value may not be very informative. In the worst situation, when all cases have different values, a frequency table is little more than an ordered list of those values.

Variables that have many values can be summarized by grouping the values of the variables into intervals and counting the number of cases with values within each interval. For example, income can be grouped into $5,000 intervals such as 0–4999, 5000–9999, 10000–14999, and so forth, and the number of observations in each group can be tabulated. Such grouping should be done using SPSS-X during the actual analysis of the data. As indicated in Chapter 1, the values for variables should be entered into the data file in their original, ungrouped form.

A histogram is a convenient way to display the distribution of such grouped values. Consider Figure 3.4, which is a histogram for body weight in pounds of the sample of 240 men from the Western Electric Study. The first column indicates the number of cases with values within the interval, while the second column gives the midpoint, or middle value, for the interval. Each row of asterisks represents the number of cases with values in the interval. For example, the second row of the histogram has 10 asterisks, which represent 10 men who weighed between 130 and 140 pounds in 1958. The number of cases represented by each asterisk depends on the size of the sample and the maximum number of cases falling into an interval. For each histogram, the number of cases represented by an asterisk is printed on the top of the figure. Intervals that have no observations are included in the histogram but no asterisks are printed. This differs from a bar chart, which does not leave space for the empty categories.

A histogram can be used in any situation in which it is reasonable to group adjacent values. Histograms should not be used to display variables in which there is no underlying order to the values. For example, if 100 different religions are arbitrarily assigned codes of 1 to 100, grouping values into intervals is meaningless. Either a bar chart or a histogram in which each interval corresponds to a single value should be used to display such data.

Figure 3.4   A histogram of body weight

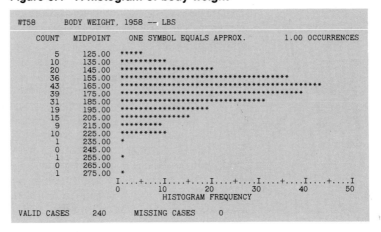

```
WT58        BODY WEIGHT, 1958 -- LBS

      COUNT    MIDPOINT     ONE SYMBOL EQUALS APPROX.          1.00 OCCURRENCES

          5     125.00    *****
         10     135.00    *********
         20     145.00    ********************
         36     155.00    ************************************
         43     165.00    *******************************************
         39     175.00    ***************************************
         31     185.00    *******************************
         19     195.00    *******************
         15     205.00    ***************
          9     215.00    *********
         10     225.00    **********
          1     235.00    *
          0     245.00
          1     255.00    *
          0     265.00
          1     275.00    *
                          I....+....I....+....I....+....I....+....I....+....I
                          0        10        20        30        40        50
                                          HISTOGRAM FREQUENCY

   VALID CASES    240      MISSING CASES      0
```

3.5
Screening Data

Frequency tables, bar charts, and histograms can serve purposes other than summarizing data. Unexpected codes in the tables may indicate errors in data entry or coding. Cases with death days coded as 0 or 8 are in error if the numbers 1 through 7 represent the days of the week and 9 stands for unknown. Since errors in the data should be eliminated as soon as possible, it is a good idea to run frequency tables as the first step in analyzing data.

Frequency tables and visual displays can also help you identify cases with values that are unusual but possibly correct. For example, a tally of the number of cars in families may show a family with 25 cars. Although such a value is possible, especially if the survey did not specify cars in working condition, it raises suspicion and should be examined to ensure that it is really correct.

Incorrect data values distort the results of statistical analyses, and correct but unusual values may require special treatment. In either case, early identification is valuable.

3.6
USING AN SPSS-X SYSTEM FILE

Once you have defined your data file in SPSS-X and saved it as an SPSS-X system file with the SAVE command, you do not need to repeat the data definition process. You can use the GET command to access the system file on subsequent SPSS-X jobs without respecifying variable locations, formats, missing values, or variable and value labels. The following example shows the first command of a job that reads a system file:

```
GET  FILE=CARDIAC
```

The only specification required on the GET command is the FILE subcommand, which identifies the system file that you want to use. Following the GET command, specify the commands for the statistical procedures that you want.

The dictionary of a system file is available at any time via the DISPLAY command. Specify the command DISPLAY, at least one blank, and the keyword DICTIONARY. For example,

```
GET  FILE=CARDIAC
DISPLAY  DICTIONARY
```

reads the system file CARDIAC and displays the list of variable names in the system file along with variable labels, sequential position of each variable in the file, print formats, missing values, and value labels. The DISPLAY command follows the GET command.

3.7
RUNNING PROCEDURE FREQUENCIES

Procedure FREQUENCIES produces frequency tables, histograms, and bar charts for numeric variables and frequency tables and bar charts for string variables. Subcommands are available for handling missing values, reformatting tables, and printing bar charts. SPSS-X also prints 14 optional statistics, including the measures of central tendency, dispersion, and shape described in Chapter 4. See Chapter 18 for a complete list of subcommands and associated keywords.

The following commands produce Figure 3.1a:

```
GET  FILE=CARDIAC
FREQUENCIES  VARIABLES=DAYOFWK
FINISH
```

• The GET command specifies the system file (CARDIAC) to be read.

• The FREQUENCIES command requests a table for one variable, DAYOFWK.

If you want more than one table, you can specify more than one variable, as in:

```
FREQUENCIES  VARIABLES=DAY AGE
```

You can use the keyword ALL to name all the variables on the file. However, if your file has a large number of cases, you may not want to print a frequencies table for variables that have a different value for each case. You can use the keyword TO to reference a set of consecutive variables. For example, the command

```
FREQUENCIES  VARIABLES=DAYOFWK TO CHD
```

produces a frequencies table for the variable DAYOFWK and all the variables that follow in the file up to variable CHD.

3.8
Bar Charts

The BARCHART subcommand requests a bar chart for each variable specified on the VARIABLES subcommand. To request the bar chart shown in Figure 3.2b, specify:

```
FREQUENCIES  VARIABLES=DAYOFWK /BARCHART
```

This command produces both a bar chart and frequencies table for variable DAYOFWK.

Several formatting specifications are available on the BARCHART subcommand. You can use the MIN and MAX keywords to specify minimum and maximum values to be plotted. Keywords are also available to control the scale of the horizontal axis, which can be specified in either frequencies or percentages. A complete list of these keywords and a discussion of their operation is in Chapter 18.

3.9
Histograms

The HISTOGRAM subcommand produces a histogram for each variable specified on the VARIABLES subcommand. You can use all the formatting options available with BARCHART on the HISTOGRAM subcommand (see Chapter 18). In addition, you can specify minimum and maximum values for the histogram and the interval width. For example, the following commands produce Figure 3.4:

```
FREQUENCIES  VARIABLES=WT58 /FORMAT=NOTABLE
  /HISTOGRAM MIN(120) MAX(280) INCREMENT(10)
```

• The FREQUENCIES command requests a histogram for variable WT58 and no frequencies table.
• For the histogram, the minimum value is set to 120 and the maximum value to 280.

3.10
Missing Values in Tables and Statistics

By default, cases with missing values are included in the frequency table and are labeled as missing. Cases with missing values are not included in bar charts, histograms, valid and cumulative percentages, and statistics. To include user-missing values as if they were not missing, use the MISSING subcommand with the INCLUDE keyword. For example,

```
FREQUENCIES  VARIABLES=DAYOFWK /BARCHART /MISSING=INCLUDE
```

produces a frequencies table and a bar chart that include all 240 cases. If variable DAYOFWK has any user-defined missing values (see Chapter 2), the MISSING subcommand and INCLUDE keyword override this specification for the FREQUENCIES procedure only. Including missing values in a statistical procedure such as FREQUENCIES does not affect the system file or subsequent procedures in the same job.

EXERCISES

Syntax

1. Given the following command, which of the statements below are true?

```
FREQUENCIES
  FORMAT=NO TABLE
  /VARIABLES=FIRSTCHD DAYOFWK
  /BARCHART
```

a. The slashes are misplaced.

b. Blanks must be inserted around the equals signs.

c. The keyword specifying no frequency table is misspelled.

d. The subcommands must begin on the same command line as the FREQUEN-
   CIES command.

e. Variables FIRSTCHD and DAYOFWK must be separated by a comma.

f. Variables FIRSTCHD and DAYOFWK are specified in the wrong order.

g. Two frequency tables are requested by this command.

h. Two bar charts are requested by this command.

2. Which command below created the following bar chart:

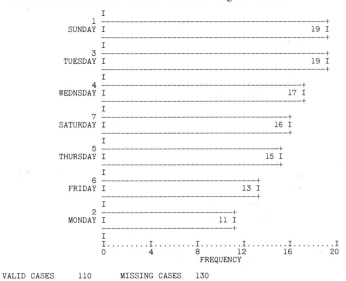

```
VALID CASES    110    MISSING CASES    130
```

a. FREQUENCIES VARIABLES=DAYOFWK/FORMAT=DFREQ/MISSING=INCLUDE

b. FREQUENCIES VARIABLES=DAYOFWK/FORMAT=DFREQ/BARCHART/
   MISSING=INCLUDE

c. FREQUENCIES VARIABLES=DAYOFWK/FORMAT=DFREQ/BARCHART

3. Consider the following section of SPSS-X output:

```
   2   0        GET FILE=CARDIAC

FILE CALLED CARDIAC :
  LABEL:
  CREATED 21 JAN 83 10:33:47      14 VARIABLES


   3   0        FREQUENCIES VARIABLES=WEEKDAY

>ERROR    701  LINE   3, COLUMN 25, TEXT: WEEKDAY
>Undefined variable name, or a scratch or system variable was specified in a
>variable list which accepts only standard variables.  Check spelling, verify
>the existence of this variable.
>THIS COMMAND NOT EXECUTED.
```

Which of the following problems could have caused the error message?
  a. The syntax of the FREQUENCIES command is in error and SPSS-X cannot recognize the variable named.
  b. The file specified on the GET command does not exist.
  c. The file found is not an SPSS-X system file.
  d. The variable named does not exist on the system file.

4. Correct the following commands:
  a. `FREQUENCIES BARCHART VARIABLES=DAYOFWK`
  b. `FREQUENCIES VARIABLES=DAYOFWK /FIRSTCHD /BARCHART`
  c. `FREQUENCIES VARIABLES=FIRSTCHD,DAYOFWK /NOTABLE /HISTOGRAM`
  d. `FREQUENCIES MISSING=INCLUDE /HISTOGRAM=FIRSTCHD`

5. Write a FREQUENCIES command that produces histograms for HT58 and WT58. Suppress the frequency tables.

6. Given variables NAME, AGE, and SEX from a random sample of the people who attended a film about Vietnam during its opening week:
  a. Can you test the hypothesis that men are more interested in films about Vietnam than are women?
  b. Can you test the hypothesis that most people interested in films about Vietnam are between the ages of 30 and 50?
  c. Can you represent the hypothesis in (b) with a bar chart?

Statistical Concepts

1. For each of the following variables, which is more appropriate: a histogram or a bar chart?
  a. Race.   e. Political party membership.
  b. Sex.   f. Yearly income.
  c. Age.   g. Number of children in family.
  d. Weight.

2. Which of these statements are true for frequency tables?
  a. Valid percentages must sum to 100.
  b. Percentages must sum to 100.
  c. Valid percentages are never greater than total percentages.
  d. The values for cumulative percentage can decrease.
  e. Cumulative percentages must sum to the total sample size.
  f. Missing values are excluded from the computation of valid percentages.

3. Below is a frequency table for a hypothetical variable. Fill in the missing frequencies and percentages.

VALUE LABEL	VALUE	FREQUENCY	PERCENT	VALID PERCENT	CUM PERCENT
	1	23	46	47.9	47.4
	2	12	24.0	25.0	72.9
	3	10	20.0	20.8	93.8
	4	3	6.0	6.3	
MISSING	9	2	4.0	MISSING	
	TOTAL	50	100.0	100.0	

4. Below are three histograms for diastolic blood pressure. Which do you think provides the best summary of the data and why?

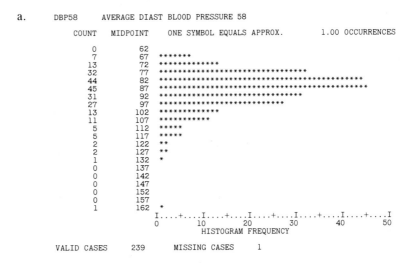

```
a.    DBP58     AVERAGE DIAST BLOOD PRESSURE 58

        COUNT   MIDPOINT   ONE SYMBOL EQUALS APPROX.        1.00 OCCURRENCES

           0       62
           7       67   *******
          13       72   *************
          32       77   ********************************
          44       82   ********************************************
          45       87   *********************************************
          31       92   *******************************
          27       97   ***************************
          13      102   *************
          11      107   ***********
           5      112   *****
           5      117   *****
           2      122   **
           2      127   **
           1      132   *
           0      137
           0      142
           0      147
           0      152
           0      157
           1      162   *
                        I....+....I....+....I....+....I....+....I....+....I
                        0        10       20       30       40       50
                                           HISTOGRAM FREQUENCY

        VALID CASES     239      MISSING CASES     1
```

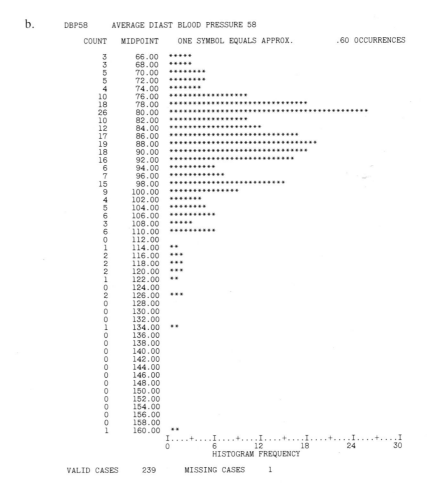

```
b.    DBP58     AVERAGE DIAST BLOOD PRESSURE 58

        COUNT   MIDPOINT   ONE SYMBOL EQUALS APPROX.        .60 OCCURRENCES

           3     66.00   *****
           3     68.00   *****
           5     70.00   ********
           5     72.00   ********
           4     74.00   *******
          10     76.00   ****************
          18     78.00   ******************************
          26     80.00   *******************************************
          10     82.00   ****************
          12     84.00   *********************
          17     86.00   ****************************
          19     88.00   *******************************
          18     90.00   ****************************
          16     92.00   **************************
           6     94.00   **********
           7     96.00   ************
          15     98.00   ************************
           9    100.00   **************
           4    102.00   *******
           5    104.00   ********
           6    106.00   **********
           3    108.00   *****
           6    110.00   *********
           0    112.00
           1    114.00   **
           2    116.00   ***
           2    118.00   ***
           2    120.00   ***
           1    122.00   **
           0    124.00
           2    126.00   ***
           0    128.00
           0    130.00
           0    132.00
           1    134.00   **
           0    136.00
           0    138.00
           0    140.00
           0    142.00
           0    144.00
           0    146.00
           0    148.00
           0    150.00
           0    152.00
           0    154.00
           0    156.00
           0    158.00
           1    160.00   **
                         I....+....I....+....I....+....I....+....I....+....I
                         0        6        12       18       24       30
                                           HISTOGRAM FREQUENCY

        VALID CASES     239      MISSING CASES     1
```

```
c.   DBP58     AVERAGE DIAST BLOOD PRESSURE 58

          COUNT  MIDPOINT   ONE SYMBOL EQUALS APPROX.      2.00 OCCURRENCES

            20     70.00   **********
            76     80.00   ****************************************
            76     90.00   ****************************************
            40    100.00   ********************
            16    110.00   ********
             7    120.00   ****
             3    130.00   **
             0    140.00
             0    150.00
             1    160.00   *
                          I....+....I....+....I....+....I....+....I....+....I
                          0        20       40       60       80       100
                                       HISTOGRAM FREQUENCY

       VALID CASES    239    MISSING CASES    1
```

5. Fill in the missing counts and midpoints in following histogram:

```
HT58      STATURE, 1958 -- TO NEAREST 0.1 INCH

     COUNT   MIDPOINT    ONE SYMBOL EQUALS APPROX.        1.00 OCCURRENCES

        0       59
                60
        1       61    *
        0
                63    ***
        8       64    ********
                65    ***********
                66    *************************
       32       67    *******************************
                68    ****************************************************
       29       69    **************************
                70    **************************
                71    ********************
                72    **************
        8       73    ********
                74    ******
        3       75    ***
        1       76    *
        1             *
        0       78
        0       79
                    I....+....I....+....I....+....I....+....I....+....I....+....I
                    0        10       20       30       40       50
                                 HISTOGRAM FREQUENCY

   VALID CASES    240    MISSING CASES    0
```

6. The following data represent the number of periodicals read by 25 college students: 1, 1, 1, 1, 1, 1, 2, 2, 2, 3, 3, 3, 3, 3, 3, 4, 4, 5, 5, 5, 5, 8, 9, 9, 10.

   a. Fill in the following frequency table:

VALUE LABEL	VALUE	FREQUENCY	PERCENT	VALID PERCENT	CUM PERCENT
	1.00	6			
	2.00	3			
	3.00	6			
	4.00	2			
	5.00	4			
	8.00	1			
	9.00	2			
	10.00	1			
	TOTAL	25	100.0	100.0	

b. Fill in the following histogram:

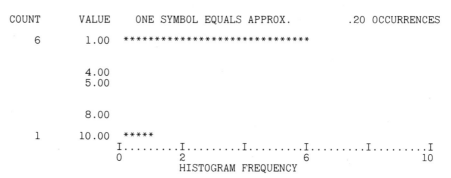

```
COUNT       VALUE    ONE SYMBOL EQUALS APPROX.              .20 OCCURRENCES
   6        1.00     *****************************

            4.00
            5.00

            8.00

   1       10.00     *****
                     I.........I.........I.........I.........I.........I
                     0         2         6                            10
                               HISTOGRAM FREQUENCY
```

c. Fill in the following bar chart:

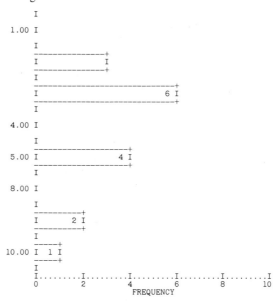

```
                        I
               1.00 I
                        I
                        ----------------+
                        I               I
                        ----------------+
                        I
                        ------------------------------+
                        I                        6 I
                        ------------------------------+
                        I
               4.00 I
                        I
                        --------------------+
               5.00 I              4 I
                        --------------------+
                        I
               8.00 I
                        I
                        ----------+
                        I     2 I
                        ----------+
                        I
                        -----+
              10.00 I  1 I
                        -----+
                        I
                        I.........I.........I.........I.........I.........I
                        0         2         4         6         8        10
                                        FREQUENCY
```

d. Which is more appropriate for summarizing the data: the histogram or the bar chart?

e. Run an SPSS-X job to produce the frequency table, histogram, and bar chart.

7. Which of the following statements about SPSS-X histograms and bar charts are correct?

a. For variables like AGE in years, a bar chart is preferable to a histogram since it has a bar for each value.

b. A bar chart includes bars for values that have not been observed in the data.

c. A histogram is useful for variables like place of birth, religious preference, and astrological sign since adjacent values (codes) may be grouped together.

d. A bar chart of weights may take up many pages of output.

8. A manufacturer of automobiles recorded the zip codes of people who bought cars during a particular sale. He asked a marketing-research specialist to analyze the information for him. The analyst returned with a histogram of zip codes. Explain to the manufacturer how these results should be interpreted.

9. For which of the following variables would cumulative percents be readily interpretable?
    a. Years of education completed
    b. Attitude toward federal spending
    c. Number of days of work missed in a year
    d. Favorite color
    e. Breed of dog owned

10. Describe five variables for which you would not construct a frequency table.

11. Describe five variables for which you would not make a histogram.

Data Analysis

1. Choose one of the files from Appendix B. For which variables on the file are frequency tables and bar charts appropriate?

2. a. For three variables of your choice, obtain bar charts and frequency tables. On the output, indicate how the entries of the frequency tables are calculated.
    b. For one of the variables selected in Question 2.a, obtain a histogram. Use the NOTABLE option to suppress printing of the frequency table. (Note that both histograms and bar charts cannot be obtained for the same variable on one FREQUENCIES command.) Describe the differences between the bar charts and histograms.
    c. Rerun one of the bar charts for a variable with missing values with the MISSING=INCLUDE subcommand. Compare the two bar charts and indicate under what circumstances you might want to include missing values in a bar chart.

3. Using the BANK system file, prepare frequency tables and bar charts for the distributions of the sex, race, education, and job category variables. Write a paragraph describing these characteristics of the sample.

4. Using the BANK system file, do the following:
    a. Obtain a histogram for the age variable.
    b. Explain why you would not want to obtain a bar chart for age.
    c. Rerun the histogram in (a) using specifications which will result in midpoints of 25, 35, 45, and so forth.

5. Using the Western Electric data file:
    a. Obtain a frequency table, bar chart, and histogram for the number of cigarettes smoked per day in 1958 (CGT58). Discuss the advantages and disadvantages of the different summaries.
    b. Obtain a frequency table for the type of first CHD event (FIRSTCHD). Discuss the meaning of the cumulative percent column for the table.
    c. Obtain histograms for the years of education (EDUYR) and the serum cholesterol (CHOL58) variables. Make sure to suppress the frequency tables for these two variables.

Chapter 4

Telling the Whole Truth and Nothing But: Descriptive Statistics

Survey data that rely on voluntary information are subject to many sources of error. People deliberately distort the truth, inadvertently fail to recall events correctly, or refuse to participate. Refusals influence survey results by failing to provide information about a particular type of person—one who refuses to answer surveys at all or avoids certain types of questions. For example, if college graduates tend to be unwilling to answer polls, results of surveys will be biased.

One possible way to examine the veracity of responses is to compare them to official records. Systematic differences between the two sources jeopardize the usefulness of the survey. Unfortunately, for many sensitive questions such as illicit drug use, abortion history, or even income, official records are usually unavailable.

Wyner (1980) examined the differences between the true and self-reported numbers of arrests obtained from 79 former heroin addicts enrolled in the Vera Institute of Justice Supported Employment Experiment. As part of their regular quarterly interviews, participants were asked about their arrest histories in New York City. The self-reported value was compared to arrest record data coded from New York City Police Department arrest sheets. The goal of the study was not only to quantify the extent of error but also to identify factors related to inaccurate responses.

4.1
EXAMINING THE DATA

Figure 4.1a shows histograms for the three variables—true number of arrests, reported arrests, and the discrepancy between the two. From a histogram it is possible to see the *shape* of the distribution, that is, how likely the different values are, how much spread or *variability* there is among the values, and where typical values are concentrated. Such characteristics are important because of the direct insight they provide into the data and because many statistical procedures are based on assumptions about the underlying distributions of variables.

The distributions of the reported and true number of arrests have a somewhat similar shape. Neither distribution has an obvious central value, although the self-reported values have the tallest peak at 4 to 5 arrests, while the actual number of arrests has its peak at 2 to 3 arrests. The distribution of self-reported arrests also has a peak at 20 to 21 arrests. The peaks corresponding to intervals which contain 5, 15, and 20 arrests arouse the suspicion that people may be more likely to report their arrest records as round numbers. Examination of the true number of arrests shows no corresponding peaks at multiples of five.

Figure 4.1a   Reported and true arrests
(Histograms from SPSS-X FREQUENCIES)

```
ACTUAL    ACTUAL NUMBER OF ARRESTS

   COUNT   MIDPOINT   ONE SYMBOL EQUALS APPROX.              .32 OCCURRENCES

       3     1.00   *********
      15     3.00   *****************************************************
       9     5.00   ****************************
       8     7.00   *************************
      10     9.00   *********************************
       9    11.00   *****************************
       7    13.00   **********************
       6    15.00   ********************
       3    17.00   *********
       3    19.00   *********
       3    21.00   *********
       1    23.00   ***
       0    25.00
       1    27.00   ***
       1    29.00   ***
                    I....+....I....+....I....+....I....+....I....+....I
                    0        4        8       12       16       20
                                            PERCENT

VALID CASES     79    MISSING CASES     0

 - - - - - - - - - - - - - - - - - - - - - - - - - - - - - - - - - -

SELF      SELF-REPORTED ARRESTS

   COUNT   MIDPOINT   ONE SYMBOL EQUALS APPROX.              .32 OCCURRENCES

       7     1.00   ***********************
       9     3.00   *****************************
      13     5.00   ******************************************
      11     7.00   ************************************
      11     9.00   ************************************
       6    11.00   *******************
       2    13.00   ******
       5    15.00   ****************
       2    17.00   ******
       1    19.00   ***
      10    21.00   *********************************
       1    23.00   ***
       1    25.00   ***
                    I....+....I....+....I....+....I....+....I....+....I
                    0        4        8       12       16       20
                                            PERCENT

VALID CASES     79    MISSING CASES     0

 - - - - - - - - - - - - - - - - - - - - - - - - - - - - - - - - - -

ERRORS    REPORTED ARRESTS MINUS ACTUAL ARRESTS

   COUNT   MIDPOINT   ONE SYMBOL EQUALS APPROX.              .39 OCCURRENCES

       2   -13.00   *****
       0   -11.00
       2    -9.00   *****
       5    -7.00   *************
       6    -5.00   ***************
       7    -3.00   ******************
      16    -1.00   ******************************************
      15     1.00   ***************************************
      12     3.00   *******************************
       7     5.00   ******************
       1     7.00   ***
       2     9.00   *****
       2    11.00   *****
       1    13.00   ***
       1    15.00   ***
                    I....+....I....+....I....+....I....+....I....+....I
                    0        5       10       15       20       25
                                            PERCENT

VALID CASES     79    MISSING CASES     0
```

The distribution of the differences between reported and true number of arrests is not as irregularly shaped as the two distributions from which it is derived. It has two adjacent peaks with midpoint values of −1 and +1. Most cases cluster around the peak values, and cases far from these values are infrequent. Figure 4.1b is a condensed frequency table for the response errors (the adjusted and cumulative percentages are rounded to the nearest integer). Almost 47% of the sample (37 cases) reported their arrest record to within two arrests of the true value. Only 22% (17 cases) misrepresented their records by more than 5 arrests. Underreporting is somewhat more likely than exaggeration, with 39% of the cases overestimating and 48% of the cases underestimating.

Figure 4.1b   Error in reported arrests
(Condensed frequency table from SPSS-X FREQUENCIES)

```
ERRORS     REPORTED ARRESTS MINUS ACTUAL ARRESTS


                      CUM                        CUM                        CUM
    VALUE  FREQ PCT PCT     VALUE  FREQ PCT PCT     VALUE  FREQ PCT PCT
      -14    2   3   3        -2     6   8  35         7     1   1  92
       -9    2   3   5        -1    10  13  48         8     1   1  94
       -8    3   4   9         0    10  13  61         9     1   1  95
       -7    2   3  11         1     5   6  67        10     1   1  96
       -6    1   1  13         2     6   8  75        11     1   1  97
       -5    5   6  19         3     6   8  82        12     1   1  99
       -4    3   4  23         4     4   5  87        15     1   1 100
       -3    4   5  28         5     3   4  91

VALID CASES     79        MISSING CASES      0
```

4.2
Percentile Values

Percentiles are values above and below which certain percentages of the cases fall. For example, 95% of the cases have values less than or equal to the 95th percentile. From the cumulative percentage column in the frequency table in Figure 4.1b, the value for the 95th percentile is 9.

Figure 4.2 contains some commonly used percentiles for the distributions in Figure 4.1a. The three percentiles (25%, 50%, and 75%) divide the observed distributions into approximately four equal parts. The actual and self-reported number of arrests have the same 25th percentile, the value 4. This means that about 75% of the values are greater than or equal to 4, and 25% less than 4.

Figure 4.2   Percentiles for reported and actual arrests and errors

```
ACTUAL     ACTUAL NUMBER OF ARRESTS

PERCENTILE    VALUE      PERCENTILE    VALUE      PERCENTILE    VALUE
  25.00       4.000        50.00       8.000        75.00      13.000

VALID CASES     79       MISSING CASES     0

- - - - - - - - - - - - - - - - - - - - - - - - - - - - - - - - - -

SELF       SELF-REPORTED ARRESTS

PERCENTILE    VALUE      PERCENTILE    VALUE      PERCENTILE    VALUE
  25.00       4.000        50.00       7.000        75.00      14.000

VALID CASES     79       MISSING CASES     0

- - - - - - - - - - - - - - - - - - - - - - - - - - - - - - - - - -

ERRORS     REPORTED ARRESTS MINUS ACTUAL ARRESTS

PERCENTILE    VALUE      PERCENTILE    VALUE      PERCENTILE    VALUE
  25.00      -3.000        50.00        .000        75.00       3.000

VALID CASES     79       MISSING CASES     0
```

4.3
SUMMARIZING THE DATA

Although frequency tables and bar charts are useful for summarizing and displaying data (see Chapter 3), further condensation and description is often desirable. A variety of summary measures that convey information about the data in single numbers can be computed. The choice of summary measure, or *statistic*, as it is often called, depends upon characteristics of the data as well as of the statistic. One important characteristic of the data that must be considered is the *level of measurement* of each variable being studied.

4.4
Levels of Measurement

Measurement is the assignment of numbers or codes to observations. Levels of measurement are distinguished by ordering and distance properties. A computer does not know what measurement underlies the values it is given. You must determine the level of measurement of your data and apply appropriate statistical techniques.

The traditional classification of levels of measurement into nominal, ordinal, interval, and ratio scales was developed by S. S. Stevens (1946). This remains the basic typology and is the one used throughout this manual. Variations exist, however, and issues concerning the statistical effect of ignoring levels of measurement have been debated (see, for example, Borgatta & Bohrnstedt, 1980).

4.5
Nominal Measurement

The nominal level of measurement is the "lowest" in the typology because no assumptions are made about relations between values. Each value defines a distinct category and serves merely as a label or name (hence, "nominal" level) for the category. For instance, the birthplace of an individual is a nominal variable. For most purposes, there is no inherent ordering among cities or towns. Although cities can be ordered according to size, density, or air pollution, a city thought of as "place of birth" is a concept that is normally not tied to any order. When numeric values are attached to nominal categories, they are merely identifiers. None of the properties of numbers such as relative size, addition, or multiplication, can be applied to these numerically coded categories. Therefore, statistics that assume ordering or meaningful numerical distances between the values do not ordinarily give useful information about nominal variables.

4.6
Ordinal Measurement

When it is possible to rank or order all categories according to some criterion, the ordinal level of measurement is achieved. For instance, classifying employees into clerical, supervisory, and managerial categories is an ordering according to responsibilities or skills. Each category has a position lower or higher than another category. Furthermore, knowing that supervisory is higher than clerical and that managerial is higher than supervisory automatically means that managerial is higher than clerical. However, nothing is known about how much higher; no distance is measured. Ordering is the sole mathematical property applicable to ordinal measurements, and the use of numeric values does not imply that any other property of numbers is applicable.

4.7
Interval Measurement

In addition to order, interval measurements have the property of meaningful distance between values. A thermometer, for example, measures temperature in degrees which are the same size at any point on the scale. The difference between 20°C and 21°C is the same as the difference between 5°C and 6°C. However, an interval scale does not have an inherently determined zero point. In the familiar Celsius and Fahrenheit systems, 0° is determined by an agreed-upon definition, not by the absence of heat. Consequently, interval-level measurement allows us to study differences between items but not their proportionate magnitudes. For example, it is incorrect to say that 80°F is twice as hot as 40°F.

4.8
Ratio Measurement

Ratio measurements have all the ordering and distance properties of an interval scale. In addition, a zero point can be meaningfully designated. In measuring physical distances between objects using feet or meters, a zero distance is naturally defined as the absence of any distance. The existence of a zero point means that ratio comparisons can be made. For example, it is quite meaningful to say that a 6-foot-tall adult is twice as tall as a 3-foot-tall child or that a 500-meter race is five times as long as a 100-meter race.

Because ratio measurements satisfy all the properties of the real number system, any mathematical manipulations appropriate for real numbers can be applied to ratio measures. However, the existence of a zero point is seldom critical for statistical analyses.

4.9
Summary Statistics

Figure 4.9 contains a variety of summary statistics that are useful in describing the distributions of reported arrests, true number of arrests, and the discrepancy. The statistics can be grouped into three categories according to what they quantify: central tendency, dispersion, and shape.

Figure 4.9   Statistics describing arrest data

```
ACTUAL    ACTUAL NUMBER OF ARRESTS


MEAN        9.253      STD ERR       .703     MEDIAN       8.000
MODE        3.000      STD DEV      6.248     VARIANCE    39.038
KURTOSIS     .597      S E KURT     1.977     SKEWNESS      .908
S E SKEW     .271      RANGE       28.000     MINIMUM      1.000
MAXIMUM    29.000      SUM        731.000


VALID CASES     79     MISSING CASES      0

- - - - - - - - - - - - - - - - - - - - - - - - - - - - - - - - -

SELF      SELF-REPORTED ARRESTS


MEAN        8.962      STD ERR       .727     MEDIAN       7.000
MODE        5.000      STD DEV      6.458     VARIANCE    41.704
KURTOSIS    -.485      S E KURT     1.977     SKEWNESS      .750
S E SKEW     .271      RANGE       25.000     MINIMUM       .000
MAXIMUM    25.000      SUM        708.000


VALID CASES     79     MISSING CASES      0

- - - - - - - - - - - - - - - - - - - - - - - - - - - - - - - - -

ERRORS    REPORTED ARRESTS MINUS ACTUAL ARRESTS


MEAN        -.291      STD ERR       .587     MEDIAN        .000
MODE       -1.000      STD DEV      5.216     VARIANCE    27.209
KURTOSIS    1.102      S E KURT     1.977     SKEWNESS      .125
S E SKEW     .271      RANGE       29.000     MINIMUM    -14.000
MAXIMUM    15.000      SUM        -23.000


VALID CASES     79     MISSING CASES      0
```

4.10
Measures of Central Tendency

The mean, median, and mode are frequently used to describe the location of a distribution. The *mode* is the most frequently occurring value (or values). For the true number of arrests, the mode is 3 (see Figure 4.9); for the self-reported values, it is 5. The distribution of the difference between the true and self-reported values is multimodal. That is, it has more than one mode since the values -1 and 0 occur with equal frequency. SPSS-X, however, prints only one mode, as shown in Figure 4.9. The mode can be used for data measured at any level. It is usually not the preferred measure for interval and ordinal data since it ignores much of the available information.

The *median* is the value above and below which one half of the observations fall. For example, if there are 79 observations the median is the 40th largest observation. When there is an even number of observations, no unique center value exists, so the mean of the two middle observations is usually taken as the median value. For the arrest data, the median is 0 for the differences, 8 for the true arrests, and 7 for reported arrests. For ordinal data the median is usually a good measure of central tendency since it uses the ranking information. The median should not be used for nominal data since ranking of the observations is not possible.

The *mean*, also called the arithmetic average, is the sum of the values of all observations divided by the number of observations. Thus

$$\bar{X} = \sum_{i=1}^{N} \frac{X_i}{N}$$

where N is the number of cases and X_i is the value of the variable for the *i*th case. Since the mean utilizes the distance between observations, the measurements should be interval or ratio. Mean race, religion, and auto color are meaningless. For dichotomous variables coded as 0 and 1, the mean has a special interpretation: it is the proportion of cases coded 1 in the data.

The three measures of central tendency need not be the same. For example, the mean number of true arrests is 9.25, the median is 8, and the mode is 3 (see Figure 4.9). The arithmetic mean is greatly influenced by outlying observations, while the median is not. Adding a single case with 400 arrests would increase the mean from 9.25 to 14.1, but it would not affect the median. Therefore, if there are values far removed from the rest of the observations, the median may be a better measure of central tendency than the mean.

For symmetric distributions, the observed mean, median, and mode are usually close in value. For example, the mean of the differences between reported and true arrest values is -0.291, the median is 0, and the modes are -1 and 0. All three measures give similar estimates of central tendency in this case.

4.11
Measures of Dispersion

Two distributions can have the same values for measures of central tendency and yet be very dissimilar in other respects. For example, if the true number of arrests for five cases in two methadone clinics is

CLINIC A: 0, 1, 10, 14, 20
CLINIC B: 8, 8, 9, 10, 10

the mean number of arrests (9) is the same in both. However, even a cursory examination of the data indicates that the two clinics are different. In the second clinic, all cases have fairly comparable arrest records while in the first the records are quite disparate. A quick and useful index of dissimilarity, or dispersion, is the *range*. It is the difference between the *maximum* and *minimum* observed values. For clinic B the range is 2, while for clinic A it is 20. Since the range is computed only from the minimum and maximum values, it is sensitive to extremes.

Although the range is a useful index of dispersion, especially for ordinal data, it does not take into account the distribution of observations between the maximum and minimum. A commonly used measure of variation that is based on all observations is the *variance*. For a sample, the variance is computed by summing the squared differences from the mean for all observations and then dividing by one less than the number of observations. In mathematical notation this is

$$S^2 = \sum_{i=1}^{N} \frac{(X_i - \bar{X})^2}{N - 1}$$

If all observations are identical—that is, if there is no variation—the variance is 0. The more spread out they are, the greater the variance. For the methadone clinic example above, the sample variance for Clinic A is 73, while for Clinic B it is 1.

The square root of the variance is termed the *standard deviation*. The standard deviation is expressed in the same units of measurement as the observations, while the variance is in units squared. This is an appealing property since it is much clearer to think of variability in terms of the number of arrests instead of the number of arrests squared.

4.12
The Normal Distribution

For many variables, most observations are concentrated near the middle of the distribution. As distance from the central concentration increases, the frequency of observation decreases. Such distributions are often described as "bell-shaped." An example is the *normal* distribution (see Figure 4.12a). A broad range of observed phenomena in nature and in society are approximately normally distributed. For example, the distributions of variables such as height, weight, and blood pressure are approximately normal. The normal distribution is by far the most important theoretical distribution in statistics and serves as a reference point for describing the form of many distributions of sample data.

Figure 4.12a   A normal curve

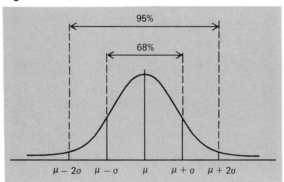

The normal distribution is symmetric: when it is folded in the center, the two sides are identical. Three measures of central tendency—the mean, median, and mode—coincide exactly (see Section 4.10). As shown in Figure 4.12a, 95% of all observations fall within two standard deviations (σ) of the mean (μ), and 68% within one standard deviation. The exact theoretical proportion of cases falling into various regions of the normal curve can be found in tables given in most introductory statistics textbooks.

In SPSS-X, you can superimpose a normal distribution on a histogram. Consider Figure 4.12b, which contains a histogram of the differences in arrest records. The colons and periods indicate what the distribution of cases would be if the variable had a normal distribution with the same mean and variance.

Figure 4.12b   Histogram of errors with the normal curve superimposed

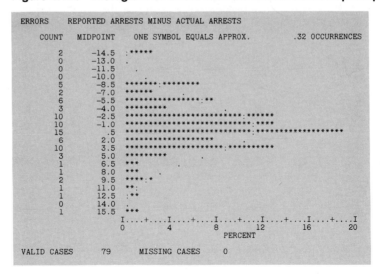

4.13
Measures of Shape

A distribution that is not symmetric but has more cases, or more of a "tail," toward one end of the distribution than the other is called *skewed*. If the tail is toward larger values, the distribution is positively skewed or skewed to the right. If the tail is toward smaller values, the distribution is negatively skewed or skewed to the left.

Another characteristic of the form of a distribution is called *kurtosis*, the extent to which, for a given standard deviation, observations cluster around a central point. If cases within a distribution cluster more than those in the normal distribution (that is, the distribution is more peaked), the distribution is called *leptokurtic*. A leptokurtic distribution also tends to have more observations straggling into the extreme tails than does a normal distribution. If cases cluster less than in the normal distribution (that is, it is flatter), the distribution is termed *platykurtic*.

Although examination of a histogram provides some indication of possible skewness and kurtosis, it is often desirable to compute formal indexes that measure these properties. Values for skewness and kurtosis are 0 if the observed distribution is exactly normal. Positive values for skewness indicate a positive skew, while positive values for kurtosis indicate a distribution that is more peaked than normal. For samples from a normal distribution, measures of skewness and kurtosis typically will not be exactly zero but will fluctuate about zero because of sampling variation.

4.14
Standard Scores

It is often desirable to describe the relative position of an observation within a distribution. Knowing that a person achieved a score of 80 in a competitive examination conveys little information about performance. Judgment of performance would depend on whether 80 is the lowest, the median, or the highest score.

One way of describing the location of a case in a distribution is to calculate its *standard score*. This score, sometimes called the Z score, indicates how many standard deviations above or below the mean an observation falls. It is calculated by finding the difference between the value of a particular observation X_i and the mean of the distribution, and then dividing this difference by the standard deviation:

$$Z_i = \frac{X_i - \overline{X}}{S}$$

The mean of Z scores is 0, and the standard deviation is 1.

For example, a participant with 5 actual arrests would have a Z score of $(5-9.25)/6.25$, or -0.68. Since the score is negative, the case had fewer arrests than the average for the individuals studied.

Standardization permits comparison of scores from different distributions. For example, an individual with Z scores of -0.68 for actual arrests and 1.01 for the difference between reported and actual arrests had fewer arrests than the average but exaggerated more than the average.

When the distribution of a variable is approximately normal and the mean and variance are known or are estimated from large samples, the Z score of an observation provides more specific information about its location. For example, if actual arrests and response error were normally distributed, 75% of cases would have more arrests than the example individual but only 16% would have exaggerated as much (75% of a standard normal curve lies above a Z score of -0.68, and 16% lies above a score of 1.01).

4.15
Who Lies?

The distribution of the difference between reported and actual arrests indicates that response error exists. Although observing a mean close to zero is comforting, misrepresentation is obvious. What then are the characteristics that influence willingness to be truthful?

Wyner identifies three factors that are related to inaccuracies: the number of arrests before 1960, the number of multiple-charge arrests, and the perceived desirability of being arrested. The first factor is related to a frequently encountered difficulty—the more distant an event in time, the less likely it is to be correctly recalled. The second factor, underreporting of multiple-charge arrests, is probably caused by the general social undesirability of serious arrests. Finally, persons who view arrest records as laudatory are likely to inflate their accomplishments.

4.16
STATISTICS AVAILABLE WITH PROCEDURE FREQUENCIES

In addition to frequency tables, bar charts, and histograms, procedure FREQUENCIES calculates univariate statistics for all variables named on the VARIABLES subcommand. To request statistics, use the STATISTICS subcommand followed by an equals sign and the keywords that correspond to the statistics you want. For example, the command

```
FREQUENCIES  VARIABLES=ACTUAL SELF ERRORS
         /STATISTICS=ALL
```

produces the output in Figure 4.9. See Chapter 18 for a complete list of the statistics available with FREQUENCIES.

4.17
Percentiles

You can use FREQUENCIES to request percentiles for all variables specified on the VARIABLES subcommand. Include the PERCENTILES subcommand followed by an equals sign and a list of percentiles between 0 and 100. For example, the command

```
FREQUENCIES  VARIABLES=ACTUAL SELF ERRORS
         /PERCENTILES=25 50 75
```

produces Figure 4.2.

In SPSS-X, percentiles are calculated by sorting the values from the smallest to the largest and finding the values below and above which the requisite number of cases fall. Therefore, it is possible for several percentiles to have the same value. For example, if the values are

0 1 1 1 1

all percentiles greater than the 20th are 1.

4.18
RUNNING PROCEDURE DESCRIPTIVES

Procedure DESCRIPTIVES produces all the statistics available with procedure FREQUENCIES, except the median and the mode, and prints a compact table of statistics for a number of variables. DESCRIPTIVES is particularly well-suited for continuous, interval-level, or ratio-level variables. It does not print tables or bar charts. You can request optional formats, methods for handling missing data, and Z-score transformations. See Chapter 18 for a more complete description of subcommands and keywords available with procedure DESCRIPTIVES.

The only required subcommand on DESCRIPTIVES is the VARIABLES subcommand, which specifies the variable list to be analyzed. The actual keyword VARIABLES can be omitted.

Figure 4.18 shows the default statistics produced by the DESCRIPTIVES command in the following SPSS-X command file:

```
TITLE   ARREST HISTORY
DATA LIST   FIXED  /1 ACTUAL 1-2 SELF 4-5
COMPUTE   ERRORS = SELF - ACTUAL
PRINT FORMATS   ERRORS (F2.0)
VARIABLE LABELS   ACTUAL, ACTUAL NUMBER OF ARRESTS/
                  SELF, SELF-REPORTED ARRESTS/
                  ERRORS, REPORTED ARRESTS MINUS ACTUAL ARRESTS/
DESCRIPTIVES VARIABLES=ACTUAL SELF ERRORS
BEGIN DATA
 1   1
 1   2
 4   0
data records
27  20
 5  10
12  10
END DATA
FINISH
```

• The DATA LIST command reads one record per case with two variables. The variable named ACTUAL is recorded in columns 1 and 2, and the variable named SELF is in columns 4 and 5.

• The COMPUTE command creates a new variable called ERRORS by subtracting the actual number of arrests of each participant from the number reported by the participant. See Chapter 18 for a discussion of this command.

• The PRINT FORMATS command assigns an integer format to variable ERRORS. By default, SPSS-X assigns a print format of F8.2 to computed variables.

• The VARIABLE LABELS command assigns labels to all three variables. Note that the command comes after the COMPUTE command because variable ERRORS cannot be given a label until it is created.

• The DESCRIPTIVES command requests descriptive statistics for the three variables. These statistics also appear in Figure 4.9, which shows the statistics available with the FREQUENCIES procedure.

Figure 4.18   Default statistics available with DESCRIPTIVES

```
NUMBER OF VALID OBSERVATIONS (LISTWISE) =        79.00
VARIABLE      MEAN      STD DEV    MINIMUM   MAXIMUM VALID N   LABEL

ACTUAL       9.253      6.248      1.000     29.000     79     ACTUAL NUMBER OF ARRESTS
SELF         8.962      6.458       .000     25.000     79     SELF-REPORTED ARRESTS
ERRORS       -.291      5.216    -14.000     15.000     79     REPORTED ARRESTS MINUS ACTUAL ARRESTS
```

4.19
Z Scores

The Z-score variable transformation standardizes variables with different observed scales to the same scale. When you specify the SAVE subcommand, DESCRIPTIVES generates new variables, each with a mean of 0 and a standard deviation of 1, and stores them on the active file. You can save these variables in a system file or use them in subsequent procedures in the same job. SAVE calculates one Z-score variable for each variable specified on the DESCRIPTIVES variable list. For example, the commands

```
DESCRIPTIVES VARIABLES=ACTUAL SELF ERRORS
    /SAVE
```

produce the table of old variables and new Z-score variables shown in Figure 4.19. DESCRIPTIVES automatically supplies variable names and labels for the new variables. The new variable name is created by prefixing the letter Z to the first seven characters of the variable name.

Figure 4.19 Z-score correspondence table

```
THE FOLLOWING Z-SCORE VARIABLES HAVE BEEN SAVED ON YOUR ACTIVE FILE:
FROM          TO                                                  WEIGHTED
VARIABLE      Z-SCORE    LABEL                                    VALID N
--------      -------    -----                                    --------

ACTUAL        ZACTUAL    ZSCORE:  ACTUAL NUMBER OF ARRESTS              79
SELF          ZSELF      ZSCORE:  SELF-REPORTED ARRESTS                 79
ERRORS        ZERRORS    ZSCORE:  REPORTED ARRESTS MINUS ACTUAL A       79
```

EXERCISES

Syntax

Read the section on the COMPUTE command in Chapter 18 before answering these questions.

1. Using the symbols + (addition), − (subtraction), * (multiplication), / (division), and ** (exponentiation) documented in Chapter 18, show the following COMPUTE commands:

    a. Compute new variable PCTINT as the percentage variable INTEREST is of variable INCOME. (Hint: the percentage is calculated by dividing interest by income and multiplying by 100.)

    b. Show two ways to create variable XSQ as the square of variable X.

    c. Compute the variable DIS from the following equation:

    $$DIS = \sqrt{a^2 + b^2} + 2$$

    d. Compute the variable SMALL as the minimum of variables A, B, and C.

2. In SPSS-X, multiplication and division are done before addition and subtraction and operations within parentheses are done first (see Chapter 18). If a case has variables VAR2=2, VAR3=3, and VAR4=4, what are the values of variables YA through YE for in each of the following?

    a. `COMPUTE YA = VAR2 + VAR3 * VAR4 - 1`

    b. `COMPUTE YB = (VAR2 + VAR3) * VAR4 -1`

    c. `COMPUTE YC = (VAR2 + VAR3) * (VAR4 -1)`

    d. `COMPUTE YD = VAR2 + VAR3 * (VAR4 - 1)`

    e. `COMPUTE YE = VAR2 + (VAR3 * VAR4) -1`

3. Given the functions SQRT (square root), SUM, and MEAN described in Chapter 18, if a case has variables VAR2=2, VAR3=3, and VAR4=4, what are the values for variables YF through YI for each of the following?

    a. `COMPUTE YF = SQRT(VAR4)`

    b. `COMPUTE YG = SUM(VAR2,VAR3,VAR4)`

    c. `COMPUTE YH = MEAN(VAR2,VAR3,VAR4)`

    d. `COMPUTE YI = SQRT(SUM(VAR2,VAR3,VAR4)+7)`

4. Five students boast scores of 90, 93, 87, 96, and 89 on a Statistics exam, when their actual scores are 79, 81, 77, 89, and 72. Write the complete SPSS-X job, including data definition, to compute descriptive statistics and a frequency table for the discrepancy between the two scores.

5. Modify your previous job to get descriptive statistics and a histogram, without the frequency table.

6. Modify the job again to get a compact table of descriptive statistics for the actual, boasted, and discrepancy scores.

Statistical Concepts

1. A sample consists of 21 patients with a mild case of a disease (coded 1), 10 patients with a moderately severe case (coded 2), and 12 patients with an extremely severe case (coded 3). Does it make sense to determine the following statistics? If so, compute them.
   a. Modal severity
   b. Median severity
   c. Mean severity

2. A sample consists of 11 blacks (coded 1), 10 Asians (coded 2), and 5 whites (coded 3). Does it make sense to determine the the following statistics? If so, compute them.
   a. Modal race
   b. Median race
   c. Mean race

3. Indicate the level of measurement for each of the following variables:
   a. Race
   b. Age
   c. The ranking of 100 judges by an independent lawyers' group.
   d. Diastolic blood pressure
   e. IQ score
   f. Eye color

4. If a sample has 155 observations ranked so that the first observation is the largest, the second is next largest, and so on, which observation is the median?

5. A certain variable is known to be normally distributed with a mean of 0.267 and a standard deviation of 0.112. Given this information, can you determine the following statistics? If so, what are they?
   a. The median
   b. The mode
   c. The variance
   d. The kurtosis

6. A researcher transformed data into standardized scores and obtained a mean standardized score of 1.438. Does this constitute grounds for rechecking the calculations? Why or why not?

7. The "average sex" for a sample where sex is coded as female=1 and male=0 is 0.72. What (if anything) does this average mean?

8. Which of the following statements are true?
   a. Unlike the variance, the range is not greatly affected by extreme values.
   b. Distributions with similar means, medians, and modes also tend to have similar variances.
   c. The variance measures how spread out observations are, with a larger variance indicating greater spread.

9. In a certain corporation, a very small group of employees has extremely high salaries, while the majority of employees receive much lower salaries. If you were the bargaining agent for the union, what statistic would you calculate to illustrate the low pay level and why? If you were the employer, what statistic would you use to demonstrate a higher pay level and why?

10. The numbers of cars owned by 10 families are as follows: 0, 1, 1, 1, 2, 2, 2, 2, 2, 4. Fill in the following table based on these values:

MEAN		MEDIAN		MODE	
STD DEV	1.059	VARIANCE		RANGE	
MINIMUM		MAXIMUM			

11. The following Z (standard) scores are printed from procedure DESCRIPTIVES: Calculate the original scores using the following descriptive statistics: mean=10; standard deviation=2.

Case   **Standard score**   **Original score**

Case	Standard score	Original score
1	1	
2	0	
3	−2	

12. The mean and standard deviation on a history test are mean=70, s=12. Calculate the Z (standard) scores for the following students:

Student   **Score**   **Standardized score**

Student	Score	Standardized score
1	70	
2	58	
3	94	

13. Compute the missing entries in the following table:

a.

VARIABLE	STD DEV	VARIANCE	VALID N
VARA	6.529		10

b.

VARIABLE	RANGE	MINIMUM	MAXIMUM	VALID N
VARB		.000	19.000	10

c.

VARIABLE	MEAN	SUM	VALID N
VARC		85.000	10

14. An absent-minded instructor calculated the following statistics for an examination: mean=50; range=50; N=99; minimum=20; and maximum=70. He then found an additional examination with a score of 50. Recalculate the statistics, including the additional exam score.

15. The numbers of pairs of shoes owned by seven college freshmen are 1, 2, 2, 3, 4, 4, and 5.
    a. Compute the mean, median, mode, range and standard deviation.
    b. An eighth student, the heir to a shoe empire, is added to the sample. This student owns 50 pairs of shoes. Recompute the statistics in (a).
    c. Which of the statistics are not much affected by the inclusion of an observation that is far removed from the rest?

Data Analysis

Use the BANK system file for Questions 1–3.

1. Variables of possible interest in describing the sample are ages of the employees, work experience, job seniority, beginning salary, and current salary. Calculate summary statistics for these variables. Summarize your findings.

2. a. Obtain separate histograms for beginning salaries for males and females using the SELECT command described in Chapter 18. Which, if any, look normal? What deviations from normality are evident?
   b. For the female and male beginning salaries, obtain all summary statistics concerned with the shape of the distribution. Examine the values of these statistics. Are they consistent with your observations in Question 2.a?
   c. For male and female beginning salaries, obtain the mean, median, mode, maximum, minimum, range, and standard deviation. How do these statistics differ for the two groups? In what ways would you expect them to differ if the bank discriminates against women?

3. Repeat Question 2 using nonwhite and white beginning salaries.

4. Choose one of the data sets in Appendix B.
   a. Determine the level of measurement for the variables on the data file.
   b. Choose four variables and obtain the appropriate summary statistics for them. Discuss the reasons for your selection.
   c. Obtain a frequency table, histogram, and percentiles for one variable. Indicate how you would calculate percentiles from the frequency table.
   d. Rerun the histogram, selecting your own interval widths and plotting percentages.

5. Write a brief description of the characteristics of the men included in the Western Electric study. Run whatever analysis you need to prepare your report.

6. Calculate the mean and median for the number of cigarettes smoked (CGT58). Explain why these two numbers are not the same. Based on a histogram of the variable, which of the measures of central tendency provides the best description of the smoking habits of the sample?

Chapter 5

Lost Letters in Cities and Towns: Crosstabulation and Measures of Association

Newspapers headline murders in subway stations, robberies on crowded main streets, suicides cheered by onlookers. All are indications of the social irresponsibility and apathy said to characterize city residents. Since overcrowding, decreased sense of community, and other urban problems are usually blamed, one might ask whether small town residents are more responsible and less apathetic than their urban counterparts.

Hansson and Slade (1977) used the "lost letter technique" to test the hypothesis that altruism is higher in small towns than in cities, unless the person needing assistance is a social deviant. In this technique, stamped and addressed letters are "lost," and the rate at which they are returned is examined. A total of 216 letters were lost in Hansson and Slade's experiment. Half were dropped within the city limits of Tulsa, Oklahoma, the others in 51 small towns within a 50-mile radius of Tulsa. The letters were addressed to three fictitious people at a post-office box in Tulsa: M. J. Davis; Dandee Davis, c/o Pink Panther Lounge; and M. J. Davis, c/o Friends of the Communist Party. The first person is considered a normal "control," the second a person whose occupation is questionable, and the third a subversive or political deviant.

5.1 CROSSTABULATION

To see whether the return rate is similar for the three addresses, the letters found and mailed and those not mailed must be tallied separately for each address. Figure 5.1 is a *crosstabulation* of address type and response. The number of cases (letters) for each combination of values of the two variables is displayed in a *cell* in the table, together with various percentages. These cell entries provide information about relationships between the variables.

In Figure 5.1, the address is called the *column* variable since each address is displayed in a column of the table. Similarly, the status of the letter, whether it was returned or not, is called the *row* variable. With three categories of the column variable and two of the row, there are six cells in the table.

49

Figure 5.1   Crosstabulation of status of letter by address

```
- - - - - - - - - - - - - - - -  C R O S S T A B U L A T I O N   O F  - - - - - - - - - - - - - - - -
   RETURNED  FOUND AND MAILED                           BY  ADDRESS   ADDRESS ON LETTER
- - - - - - - - - - - - - - - - - - - - - - - - - - - - - - - - - - - - - - - - - - - - -  PAGE  1 OF  1

                      ADDRESS
              COUNT  |
              ROW PCT|CONTROL  DANDEE   COMMUNIS   ROW
              COL PCT|                  T          TOTAL
              TOT PCT|      1|      2|      3|
         RETURNED    +-------+-------+-------+
                  1  |    35 |    32 |    10 |     77
         YES         |  45.5 |  41.6 |  13.0 |   35.6
                     |  48.6 |  44.4 |  13.9 |
                     |  16.2 |  14.8 |   4.6 |
                     +-------+-------+-------+
                  2  |    37 |    40 |    62 |    139
         NO          |  26.6 |  28.8 |  44.6 |   64.4
                     |  51.4 |  55.6 |  86.1 |
                     |  17.1 |  18.5 |  28.7 |
                     +-------+-------+-------+
              COLUMN       72      72      72      216
              TOTAL      33.3    33.3    33.3    100.0


 CHI-SQUARE     D.F.      SIGNIFICANCE        MIN E.F.      CELLS WITH E.F.| 5
 _____     ____      _____        _____      _____

  22.56265       2         0.0000            25.667           NONE

NUMBER OF MISSING OBSERVATIONS =        0
```

5.2
Cell Contents and
Marginals

The first entry in the table is the number of cases, or *frequency*, in that cell. It is labeled as COUNT in the key printed in the upper-left corner of the table. For example, 35 letters addressed to the control were returned, and 62 letters addressed to the Communist were not returned. The second entry in the table is the *row percentage* (ROW PCT). It is the percentage of all cases in a row that fall into a particular cell. Of the 77 letters returned, 45.5% were addressed to the control, 41.6% to Dandee, and 13.0% to the Communist.

The *column percentage* (COL PCT), the third item in each cell, is the percentage of all cases in a column that occur in a cell. For example, 48.6% of the letters addressed to the control were returned and 51.4% were not. The return rate for Dandee is similar (44.4%), while that for the Communist is markedly lower (13.9%).

The last entry in the table is the *table percentage* (TOT PCT). The number of cases in the cell is expressed as a percentage of the total number of cases in the table. For example, the 35 letters returned to the control represent 16.2% of the 216 letters in the experiment.

The numbers to the right and below the table are known as *marginals*. They are the counts and percentages for the row and column variables taken separately. In Figure 5.1, the row marginals show that 77 (35.6%) of the letters were returned, while 139 (64.4%) were not.

5.3
Choosing Percentages

Row, column, and table percentages convey different types of information, so it is important to choose carefully among them.

In this example, the row percentage indicates the distribution of address types for returned and "lost" letters. It conveys no direct information about the return rate. For example, if twice as many letters were addressed to the control, an identical return rate for all letters would give row percentages of 50%, 25%, and 25%. However, this does not indicate that the return rate is higher for the control. In addition, if each category had the same number of returned letters, the row percentages would have been 33.3%, 33.3%, and 33.3%, regardless of whether one or all letters were returned.

The column percentage is the percentage of letters returned and not returned for each address. By looking at column percentages across rows, one can compare return rates for the address types. Interpretation of this comparison would not be affected if unequal numbers of letters had been addressed to each category.

Since it is always possible to interchange the rows and columns of any table, general rules about when to use row and column percentages cannot be given. They depend on the nature of the two variables. If one of the two variables is under experimental control, it is termed an *independent variable*. This variable is hypothesized to affect the response, or *dependent variable*. If variables can be classified as dependent and independent, the following guideline may be helpful: If the independent variable is the row variable, select row percentages; if the independent variable is the column variable, select column percentages. In this example the dependent variable is the status of the letter, whether it was mailed or not. The type of address is the independent variable. Since the independent variable is the column variable in Figure 5.1, column percentages should be used for comparisons of return rates.

5.4
Adding a Control Variable

Since Figure 5.1 combines results from both the city and the towns, differences between the locations are obscured. Two separate tables, one for the city and one for the towns, are required. Figure 5.4 shows crosstabulations of response and address for each of the locations. SPSS-X produces a separate table for each value of the location (control) variable.

Figure 5.4   Crosstabulations of status of letter by address controlled for location

```
- - - - - - - - - - - - - - - - - - - -  C R O S S T A B U L A T I O N   O F  - - - - - - - - - - - - - - - - - - - -
     RETURNED  FOUND AND MAILED                                   BY  ADDRESS     ADDRESS ON LETTER
CONTROLLING FOR..
     LOCATION  LOCATION LOST                                      VALUE =          1.  CITY
- - - - - - - - - - - - - - - - - - - - - - - - - - - - - - - - - - - - - - - - - - - - - - - - - - - PAGE  1 OF  1
                       ADDRESS
               COUNT    |
               COL PCT  |CONTROL  DANDEE   COMMUNIS   ROW
                        |                  T          TOTAL
                        |      1|       2|       3|
     RETURNED  --------+--------+--------+--------+
                     1 |    16  |    14  |     9  |    39
       YES           |    44.4 |    38.9 |    25.0 |    36.1
                      +--------+--------+--------+
                     2 |    20  |    22  |    27  |    69
       NO            |    55.6 |    61.1 |    75.0 |    63.9
                      +--------+--------+--------+
               COLUMN     36       36       36      108
               TOTAL    33.3     33.3     33.3    100.0


CHI-SQUARE      D.F.      SIGNIFICANCE        MIN E.F.      CELLS WITH E.F.| 5
                                                           --------------
  3.13043        2          0.2090            13.000          NONE



- - - - - - - - - - - - - - - - - - - -  C R O S S T A B U L A T I O N   O F  - - - - - - - - - - - - - - - - - - - -
     RETURNED  FOUND AND MAILED                                   BY  ADDRESS     ADDRESS ON LETTER
CONTROLLING FOR..
     LOCATION  LOCATION LOST                                      VALUE =          2.  TOWN
- - - - - - - - - - - - - - - - - - - - - - - - - - - - - - - - - - - - - - - - - - - - - - - - - - - PAGE  1 OF  1
                       ADDRESS
               COUNT    |
               COL PCT  |CONTROL  DANDEE   COMMUNIS   ROW
                        |                  T          TOTAL
                        |      1|       2|       3|
     RETURNED  --------+--------+--------+--------+
                     1 |    19  |    18  |     1  |    38
       YES           |    52.8 |    50.0 |     2.8 |    35.2
                      +--------+--------+--------+
                     2 |    17  |    18  |    35  |    70
       NO            |    47.2 |    50.0 |    97.2 |    64.8
                      +--------+--------+--------+
               COLUMN     36       36       36      108
               TOTAL    33.3     33.3     33.3    100.0


CHI-SQUARE      D.F.      SIGNIFICANCE        MIN E.F.      CELLS WITH E.F.| 5
                                                           --------------
 24.92932        2          0.0000            12.667          NONE

NUMBER OF MISSING OBSERVATIONS =          0
```

These tables show interesting differences between cities and towns. Although the overall return rates are close, 36.1% for the city and 35.2% for the towns, there are striking differences between the addresses. Only 2.8% of the Communist letters were returned in towns, while 25.0% of them were returned in Tulsa. (At least two of the Communist letters were forwarded by small-town residents to the FBI for punitive action!) The return rates for both the control (52.8%) and Dandee (50.0%) are higher in towns.

The results support the hypothesis that, in small towns, suspected social deviance influences the response more than in big cities, although it is surprising that Dandee and the Pink Panther Lounge were deemed worthy of as much assistance as they received. If the Communist letter is excluded, inhabitants of small towns are somewhat more helpful than city residents, returning 51% of the other letters, in comparison to the city's 42%.

5.5 GRAPHICAL REPRESENTATION OF CROSSTABULATIONS

As with frequency tables, visual representation of a crosstabulation often simplifies the search for associations. Figure 5.5 is a bar chart of letters returned from the crosstabulations shown in Figure 5.4. In a bar chart, the length of each bar represents the frequencies or percentages for each category of a variable. In Figure 5.5, the percentages plotted are the column percentages shown in Figure 5.4 for the returned letters only. This chart clearly shows that the return rates for the control and Dandee are high compared to the return rate for the Communist. Also, it demonstrates more vividly than the crosstabulation that the town residents' return rates for the control and Dandee are higher than city residents' return rates but that the reverse is true for the Communist.

**Figure 5.5 Status of letter by address by location
(bar chart from SPSS Graphics)**

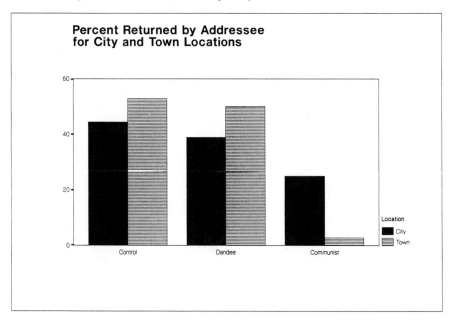

5.6
USING
CROSSTABULATION
FOR DATA
SCREENING

Errors and unusual values in data entry that cannot be spotted with FREQUEN-CIES can sometimes be identified using crosstabulation. For example, a case coded as a male with a history of three pregnancies would not be identified as suspicious in FREQUENCIES tables of sex and number of pregnancies. When considered separately, the code for male is acceptable for variable sex and the value 3 is acceptable for number of pregnancies. Jointly, however, the combination is unexpected.

Whenever possible, crosstabulations of related variables should be obtained so that anomalies can be identified and corrected before further statistical analysis of the data.

5.7
CROSSTABULATION
STATISTICS

Although examination of the various row and column percentages in a crosstabulation is a useful first step in studying the relationship between two variables, row and column percentages do not allow for quantification or testing of that relationship. For these purposes, it is useful to consider various indexes that measure the extent of association as well as statistical tests of the hypothesis that there is no association.

5.8
The Chi-Square Test of
Independence

The hypothesis that two variables of a crosstabulation are *independent* of each other is often of interest to researchers. Two variables are by definition independent if the probability that a case falls into a given cell is simply the product of the marginal probabilities of the two categories defining the cell.

For example, in Figure 5.1 if returns of the letter and address type are independent, the probability of a letter being returned to a Communist is the product of the probability of a letter being returned and the probability of a letter being addressed to a Communist. From the table, 35.6% of the letters were returned and 33.3% of the letters were addressed to a friend of the Communist party. Thus, if address type and status of the letter are independent, the probability of a letter being returned to the Communist is estimated to be

$$P(\text{return})\ P(\text{Communist})=0.356 \times 0.333 = 0.119$$

The *expected* number of cases in that cell is 25.7, which is 11.9% of the 216 cases in the sample. From the table, the *observed* number of letters returned to the Communist is 10 (4.6%), nearly 16 fewer than expected if the two variables are independent.

To construct a statistical test of the independence hypothesis, repeat the above calculations for each cell in the table. The probability under independence of an observation falling into cell (*ij*) is estimated by

$$P(\text{row} = i \text{ and column} = j) = \left(\frac{\text{count in row } i}{N}\right) \left(\frac{\text{count in column } j}{N}\right)$$

To obtain the expected number of observations in cell (*ij*), the probability is multiplied by the total sample size

$$E_{ij} = N\left(\frac{\text{count in row } i}{N}\right) \left(\frac{\text{count in column } j}{N}\right)$$
$$= \frac{(\text{count in row } i)\ (\text{count in column } j)}{N}$$

Figure 5.8 contains the observed and expected frequencies and the *residuals*, which are the observed minus the expected frequencies for the data in Figure 5.1.

Figure 5.8   Observed, expected, and residual values

```
- - - - - - - - - - - - - - - - - - CROSSTABULATION OF - - - - - - - - - - - - - - - - -
  RETURNED  FOUND AND MAILED                          BY  ADDRESS    ADDRESS ON LETTER
- - - - - - - - - - - - - - - - - - - - - - - - - - - - - - - - - - - - - - - PAGE  1 OF  1

                    ADDRESS
              COUNT
              EXP VAL │CONTROL  DANDEE  COMMUNIS  ROW
              RESIDUAL│                 T         TOTAL
                      │      1│      2│      3│
   RETURNED   --------+-------+-------+-------+
                  1   │    35 │    32 │    10 │    77
       YES          │  25.7 │  25.7 │  25.7 │  35.6%
                      │   9.3 │   6.3 │ -15.7 │
                      +-------+-------+-------+
                  2   │    37 │    40 │    62 │   139
        NO          │  46.3 │  46.3 │  46.3 │  64.4%
                      │  -9.3 │  -6.3 │  15.7 │
                      +-------+-------+-------+
              COLUMN       72      72      72     216
               TOTAL     33.3%   33.3%   33.3%  100.0%

NUMBER OF MISSING OBSERVATIONS =        0
```

A statistic often used to test the hypothesis that the row and column variables are independent is the *Pearson chi-square*. It is calculated by summing over all cells the squared residuals divided by the expected frequencies.

$$\chi^2 = \sum_i \sum_j \frac{(O_{ij} - E_{ij})^2}{E_{ij}}$$

The calculated chi-square is compared to the critical points of the theoretical chi-square distribution to produce an estimate of how likely (or unlikely) this calculated value is if the two variables are in fact independent. Since the value of the chi-square depends on the number of rows and columns in the table being examined, one must know the *degrees of freedom* for the table. The degrees of freedom can be viewed as the number of cells of a table that can be arbitrarily filled when the row and column totals (marginals) are fixed. For an $R \times C$ table, the degrees of freedom are $(R-1) \times (C-1)$, since once $(R-1)$ rows and $(C-1)$ columns are filled, frequencies in the remaining row and column cells must be chosen so that marginal totals are maintained.

In this example, there are two degrees of freedom (1×2), and the chi-square value is 22.56 (see Figure 5.1). If type of address and return rate are independent, the probability that a random sample would result in a chi-square value of at least that magnitude is less than 0.00005. On the SPSS-X output, the probability is rounded to four decimal places, which in this case is 0.0000. This probability is also known as the *observed significance level* of the test. If the probability is small enough (usually less than 0.05 or 0.01), the hypothesis that the two variables are independent is rejected.

Since the observed significance level in Figure 5.1 is very small (based on the combined city and town data), the hypothesis that address type and return rate are independent is rejected. When the chi-square test is calculated for the city and town data separately (Figure 5.4), different results are obtained. The observed significance level of the city data is 0.209, so the independence hypothesis is not rejected. For the towns, the observed significance level is less than 0.00005, and the hypothesis that address and return rate are independent is rejected. These results support the theory that city and town residents respond differently.

The chi-square test is a test of independence; it provides little information about the strength or form of the association between two variables. The magnitude of the observed chi-square depends not only on the goodness of fit of the independence model, but also on the sample size. If the sample size for a particular table increases *n*-fold, so does the chi-square value. Thus, large chi-square values can arise in applications where residuals are small relative to expected frequencies but where the sample size is large.

Certain conditions must be met for the chi-square distribution to be a good approximation of the distribution of the statistic in the equation given above. The data must be random samples from multinomial distributions and the expected values must not be too small. While it has been recommended that all expected frequencies be at least 5, recent studies indicate that this is probably too stringent and can be relaxed (Everitt, 1977). If there are cells with expected values less than 5, SPSS-X prints the number of such cells and the minimum expected value.

In hope of improving the approximation in the case of a 2×2 table, *Yates' correction for continuity* is sometimes applied. Yates' correction for continuity involves subtracting 0.5 from positive differences between observed and expected frequencies (the residuals) and adding 0.5 to negative differences before squaring. For a discussion of some of the controversy regarding the merits of this correction, see Conover (1974) and Mantel (1974).

An alternative test for the 2×2 table is based on the hypergeometric distribution. Exact probabilities of obtaining the observed results if the two variables are independent and the marginals fixed are calculated. This is called *Fisher's exact test*. It is most useful when the total sample size and the expected values are small. SPSS-X calculates Fisher's exact test when the sample size in a 2×2 table is 20 or less.

5.9
Measures of Association

In many research situations, the strength and nature of the dependence of variables is of central concern. Indexes that attempt to quantify the relationship between variables in a cross-classification are called *measures of association*. No single measure adequately summarizes all possible types of association. Measures vary in their interpretation and in the way they define perfect and intermediate association. These measures also differ in the way they are affected by various factors such as marginals. For example, many measures are "margin sensitive" in that they are influenced by the marginal distributions of the rows and columns. Such measures reflect information about the marginals along with information about association.

A particular measure may have a low value for a given table, not because the two variables are not related but because they are not related in the way to which the measure is sensitive. No single measure is best for all situations. The type of data, the hypothesis of interest, as well as the properties of the various measures must all be considered when selecting an index of association for a given table. It is not, however, reasonable to compute a large number of measures and then to report the most impressive as if it were the only one examined.

The measures of association available in SPSS-X CROSSTABS are computed only from bivariate tables (see Figure 5.4). For example, if three dichotomous variables are specified in the table, two sets of measures are computed, one for each subtable produced by the values of the controlling variable. In general, if relationships among more than two variables are to be studied, examination of bivariate tables is only a first step. For an extensive discussion of various more sophisticated multivariate procedures for the analysis of qualitative data, see Fienberg (1977), Everitt (1977), and Haberman (1978).

5.10
Nominal Measures

Consider measures that assume only that both variables in the table are nominally measured. As such, these measures can only provide some indication of the strength of association between variables; they cannot indicate direction or anything about the nature of the relationship. The measures provided are of two types: those based on the chi-square statistic and those that follow the logic of proportional reduction in error, denoted PRE.

5.11
Chi-Square-Based Measures

As explained above, the chi-square statistic itself is not a good measure of the degree of association between two variables. But its widespread use in tests of independence has encouraged the use of measures of association based upon it. Each of these measures based on the chi-square attempts to modify the chi-square statistic to minimize the influence of sample size and degrees of freedom as well as to restrict the range of values of the measure to those between 0 and 1. Without such adjustments, comparison of chi-square values from tables with varying dimensions and sample sizes is meaningless.

The *phi-coefficient* modifies the chi-square by dividing it by the sample size and taking the square root of the result:

$$\phi = \sqrt{\frac{\chi^2}{N}}$$

For tables in which one dimension is greater than 2, phi need not lie between 0 and 1 since the chi-square value can be greater than the sample size. To obtain a measure that must lie between 0 and 1, Pearson suggested the use of

$$C = \sqrt{\frac{\chi^2}{\chi^2 + N}}$$

which is called the *coefficient of contingency*. Although the value of this measure is always between 0 and 1, it cannot generally attain the upper limit of 1. The maximum value possible depends upon the number of rows and columns. For example, in a 4×4 table, the maximum value of C is 0.87.

Cramér introduced the following variant:

$$V = \sqrt{\frac{\chi^2}{N(k - 1)}}$$

where k is the smaller of the number of rows and columns. This statistic, known as *Cramér's V*, can attain the maximum of 1 for tables of any dimension. If one of the table dimensions is 2, V and phi are identical.

The chi-square-based measures are hard to interpret. Although when properly standardized they can be used to compare strength of association in several tables, the "strength of association" being compared is not easily related to an intuitive concept of association.

5.12
Proportional Reduction in Error

Common alternatives to chi-square-based measurements are those based on the idea of *proportional reduction in error* (PRE), introduced by Goodman and Kruskal (1954). With PRE measures, the meaning of association is clearer. These measures are all essentially ratios of a measure of error in predicting the values of one variable based on knowledge of that variable alone and the same measure of error applied to predictions based on knowledge of an additional variable.

For example, Figure 5.12 is a crosstabulation of depth of hypnosis and success in treatment of migraine headaches by suggestion (Cedercreutz, 1978). The best guess of the results of treatment when no other information is available is the outcome category with the largest proportion of observations (the modal category). In Figure 5.12, "no change" is the largest outcome category, with 45% of the subjects. The estimate of the probability of incorrect classification is 1 minus the probability of the modal category:

$P(1)=1-0.45=0.55$

Figure 5.12 Depth of hypnosis and success of treatment

```
- - - - - - - - - - - - - - - - -  C R O S S T A B U L A T I O N   O F  - - - - - - - - - - - - - - - -
    HYPNOSIS  DEPTH OF HYPNOSIS                           BY  MIGRAINE  OUTCOME
- - - - - - - - - - - - - - - - - - - - - - - - - - - - - - - - - - - - - - - - - - -  PAGE  1 OF  1

                        MIGRAINE
                COUNT
                TOT PCT   CURED    BETTER    NO        ROW
                                             CHANGE    TOTAL
                          1.00|    2.00|     3.00|
    HYPNOSIS    -------------+---------+----------+
                1.00    13       5                    18
    DEEP                13.0     5.0                  18.0
                    -------+---------+----------+
                2.00    10       26       17          53
    MEDIUM              10.0     26.0     17.0        53.0
                    -------+---------+----------+
                3.00             1        28          29
    LIGHT                        1.0      28.0        29.0
                    -------+---------+----------+
                COLUMN  23       32       45          100
                TOTAL   23.0     32.0     45.0        100.0


    CHI-SQUARE    D.F.      SIGNIFICANCE        MIN E.F.      CELLS WITH E.F.| 5
    ----------    ----      ------------        --------      -------------------

      65.52525     4          0.0000            4.140    1 OF     9 ( 11.1%)


                                                WITH HYPNOSIS    WITH MIGRAINE
            STATISTIC               SYMMETRIC   DEPENDENT        DEPENDENT
            ---------               ---------   -------------    -------------

    LAMBDA                          0.35294     0.29787          0.40000
    UNCERTAINTY COEFFICIENT         0.35514     0.36537          0.34547

            STATISTIC               VALUE       SIGNIFICANCE
            ---------               -----       ------------

    CRAMER'S V                      0.57239
    CONTINGENCY COEFFICIENT         0.62918

    NUMBER OF MISSING OBSERVATIONS =       0
```

Information about the depth of hypnosis can be used to improve the classification rule. For each hypnosis category, the outcome category that occurs most frequently for that hypnosis level is predicted. Thus, "no change" is predicted for participants achieving a "light" level of hypnosis, "better" for those achieving a "medium" level, and "cured" for those achieving a "deep" level. The probability of error when depth of hypnosis is used to predict outcome is the sum of the probabilities of all the cells that are not row modes:

$$P(2) = 0.05 + 0.10 + 0.17 + 0.01 = 0.33$$

Goodman and Kruskal's *lambda*, with outcome as the predicted (dependent) variable, is calculated as

$$\lambda_{\text{outcome}} = \frac{P(1) - P(2)}{P(1)} = \frac{0.55 - 0.33}{0.55} = 0.40$$

Thus, a 40% reduction in error is obtained when depth of hypnosis is used to predict outcome.

Lambda always ranges between 0 and 1. A value of 0 means the independent variable is of no help in predicting the dependent variable. A value of 1 means that the independent variable perfectly specifies the categories of the dependent variable (perfection can occur only when each row has at most one nonzero cell). When the two variables are independent, lambda is 0; but a lambda of 0 need not imply statistical independence. As with all measures of association, lambda is constructed to measure association in a very specific way. In particular, lambda reflects the reduction in error when values of one variable are used to predict values of the other. If this particular type of association is absent, lambda is 0. Other measures of association may find association of a different kind even when lambda is 0. A measure of association sensitive to every imaginable type of association does not exist.

For a particular table, two different lambdas can be computed, one using the row variable as the predictor and the other using the column variable. The two do not usually have identical values, so care should be taken to specify which is the dependent variable, that is, the variable whose prediction is of primary interest. In some applications, dependent and independent variables are not clearly distinguished. Then, a symmetric version of lambda, which predicts the row variable and column variable with equal frequency, can be computed. When the lambda statistic is requested, SPSS-X prints the symmetric lambda as well as the two asymmetric lambdas.

5.13
Ordinal Measures

Although relationships among ordinal variables can be examined using nominal measures, other measures reflect the additional information available from ranking. Consideration of the kind of relationships that may exist between two ordered variables leads to the notion of direction of relationship and to the concept of *correlation*. Variables are positively correlated if cases with low values for one variable also tend to have low values for the other and cases with high values on one also tend to be high on the other. Negatively correlated variables show the opposite relationship: the higher the first variable, the lower the second tends to be.

Several measures of association for a table of two ordered variables are based on the comparison of the values of both variables for all possible *pairs* of cases or observations. A pair of cases is *concordant* if the values of both variables for one case are higher (or both are lower) than the corresponding values for the other case. The pair is *discordant* if the value of one variable for a case is larger than the corresponding value for the other case, and the direction is reversed for the second variable. When the two cases have identical values on one or on both variables, they are *tied*.

Thus, for any given pair of cases with measurements on variables X and Y, the pair may be concordant or discordant, or tied in one of three ways: they may be tied on X but not on Y, they may be tied on Y but not on X, or they may be tied on both variables. When data are arranged in crosstabulated form, the number of concordant, discordant, and tied pairs can be easily calculated since all possible pairs can be conveniently determined.

If the preponderance of pairs is concordant, the association is said to be positive: as ranks of variable X increase (or decrease), so do ranks of variable Y. If the majority of pairs is discordant, the association is negative: as ranks of one variable increase, those of the other tend to decrease. If concordant and discordant pairs are equally likely, no association is said to exist.

The ordinal measures presented here all have the same numerator: the number of concordant pairs (P) minus the number of discordant pairs (Q) calculated for all distinct pairs of observations. They differ primarily in the way in which $P-Q$ is normalized. The simplest measure involves subtracting Q from P and dividing by the total number of pairs. If there are no pairs with ties, this measure (Kendall's tau-a) is in the range from -1 to $+1$. If there are ties, the range of possible values is narrower; the actual range depends on the number of ties. Since all observations within the same row are tied, so also are those in the same column, and the resulting tau-a measures are difficult to interpret.

A measure that attempts to normalize $P-Q$ by considering ties on each variable in a pair separately but not ties on both variables in a pair is tau-b:

$$\tau_b = \frac{P - Q}{\sqrt{(P + Q + T_x)(P + Q + T_y)}}$$

where T_X is the number of pairs tied on X but not on Y, and T_Y is the number of pairs tied on Y but not on X. If no marginal frequency is 0, tau-*b* can attain $+1$ or -1 only for a square table.

A measure that can attain, or nearly attain, $+1$ or -1 for any $R \times C$ table is tau-*c*.

$$\tau_c = \frac{2m(P - Q)}{N^2(m - 1)}$$

where m is the smaller of the number of rows and columns. The coefficients tau-*b* and tau-*c* do not differ much in value if each margin contains approximately equal frequencies.

Goodman and Kruskal's *gamma* is closely related to the tau statistics and is calculated as

$$G = \frac{P - Q}{P + Q}$$

Gamma can be thought of as the probability that a random pair of observations is concordant minus the probability that the pair is discordant, assuming the absence of ties. The absolute value of gamma is the proportional reduction in error between guessing concordant and discordant ranking of each pair depending on which occurs more often and guessing ranking according to the outcome of the toss of a fair coin. Gamma is 1 if all observations are concentrated in the upper-left to lower-right diagonal of the table. In the case of independence, gamma is 0. However, the converse (that a gamma of 0 necessarily implies independence) need not be true except in the 2×2 table.

In the computation of gamma, no distinction is made between the independent and dependent variable; the variables are treated symmetrically. Somers (1962) proposed an asymmetric extension of gamma that differs only in the inclusion of the number of pairs not tied on the independent variable (X) in the denominator. Somers' *d* is

$$d_Y = \frac{P - Q}{P + Q + T_Y}$$

The coefficient d_Y indicates the proportionate excess of concordant pairs over discordant pairs among pairs not tied on the independent variable. The symmetric variant of Somers' *d* uses for the denominator the average value of the denominators of the two asymmetric coefficients.

5.14
Measures Involving Interval Data

If the two variables in the table are measured on an interval scale, various coefficients that make use of this additional information can be calculated. A useful symmetric coefficient that measures the strength of the *linear* relationship is the Pearson correlation coefficient, or *r*. It can take on values from -1 to $+1$, indicating negative or positive linear correlation.

The *eta* coefficient is appropriate for data in which the dependent variable is measured on an interval scale and the independent variable on a nominal or ordinal scale. When squared, eta can be interpreted as the proportion of the total variability in the dependent variable that can be accounted for by knowing the values of the independent variable. The measure is asymmetric and does not assume a linear relationship between the variables.

5.15
RUNNING
PROCEDURE
CROSSTABS

Procedure CROSSTABS produces two-way to *n*-way crosstabulations and related statistical measures for variables that have a limited number of numeric or string values. In addition to cell counts, you can obtain cell percentages and expected values. You can also alter the handling of missing values, reorder the rows, request an index of tables, and write the cell frequencies to a file. SPSS-X prints 11 optional statistics including the chi-square and the measures of association described in Sections 5.7 through 5.14.

Specifications for procedure CROSSTABS depend on whether you want to use *general mode* or *integer mode*. You can use general mode for most applications because it permits string or noninteger variables. General mode requires only the TABLES subcommand. You can use integer mode if your variables have integer values and you want to make specifications that are not available with general mode. See Chapter 18 for the complete syntax of procedure CROSS-TABS.

The following commands run CROSSTABS in general mode and produce the crosstabulation shown in Figure 5.1:

```
CROSSTABS  TABLES=RETURNED BY ADDRESS
           /CELLS=ROW COLUMN TOTAL
```

The first variable, RETURNED, defines the rows of the table and the variable after the keyword BY, ADDRESS, defines the columns. The CELLS subcommand requests row, column, and total percentages in the cells. If you do not specify the CELLS subcommand, the cells include only the frequency counts.

If you have a control variable, enter a second BY keyword and the name of the variable. For example, the commands

```
CROSSTABS  TABLES=RETURNED BY ADDRESS BY LOCATION
           /CELLS=COLUMN
```

produce Figure 5.4. SPSS-X produces a bivariate table (or *subtable*) of the variables RETURNED by ADDRESS for each value of variable LOCATION. In general mode, you can specify up to eight control variables (that is, there can be up to nine BY keywords) and in integer mode you can specify up to six control variables (seven BY keywords). However, each new level further subdivides previous divisions, so you may create a large number of subtables with many empty cells unless you are working with a very large data file.

The complete SPSS-X command file used to produce the table and statistics shown in Figure 5.4 is

```
TITLE  LOST LETTER DATA
DATA LIST  FIXED/1 ADDRESS RETURNED LOCATION 1-3
VARIABLE LABELS   ADDRESS,ADDRESS ON LETTER
                  /RETURNED,FOUND AND MAILED
                  /LOCATION,LOCATION LOST
VALUE LABELS   ADDRESS 1 'CONTROL' 2 'DANDEE' 3 'COMMUNIST'/
               RETURNED 1 'YES' 2 'NO'/
               LOCATION 1 'CITY' 2 'TOWN'/
CROSSTABS  TABLES=RETURNED BY ADDRESS BY LOCATION
           /CELLS=COLUMN
           /STATISTICS=CHISQ
BEGIN DATA
  data records
END DATA
FINISH
```

- The DATA LIST command reads three single-column variables, ADDRESS, RETURNED, and LOCATION, in the first three columns of each data record. Note that SPSS-X allows you to specify a list of variables, and then a range of columns to be divided equally among those variables. (See Chapter 18 for more information on DATA LIST specifications.) Because no decimal places are recorded on the data or implied in the DATA LIST command, you could use CROSSTABS in integer mode.

- The variable and value labels appear on the output as they are specified on the VARIABLE LABELS and VALUE LABELS commands.

• The CROSSTABS command produces a subtable of the variables RETURNED by ADDRESS for each value of variable LOCATION.
• The CELLS subcommand requests column percentages in the cells.
• The STATISTICS subcommand calculates the chi-square statistic for each bivariate subtable.

Since the amount of print space is limited, CROSSTABS prints only the first 16 characters of the value labels. For the column variable, long value labels are split after the eighth character and printed on two lines. If you know this, you can make your value labels more readable, as shown in the following command file:

```
DATA LIST  FIXED/1 HYPNOSIS MIGRAINE 1-2
VARIABLE LABELS  HYPNOSIS DEPTH OF HYPNOSIS
                 /MIGRAINE OUTCOME
VALUE LABELS  HYPNOSIS 1 'DEEP' 2 'MEDIUM' 3 'LIGHT'
              /MIGRAINE 1 'CURED' 2 'BETTER' 3 'NO       CHANGE'
CROSSTABS  TABLES=HYPNOSIS BY MIGRAINE
           /CELLS=TOTAL
           /STATISTICS=CHISQ PHI CC LAMBDA UC
BEGIN DATA
  data records
END DATA
FINISH
```

These commands produce the output shown in Figure 5.12. The value labels for variable MIGRAINE are formatted so that the words are not broken across lines. Note that the label 'NO   CHANGE' has six blanks separating the words so that CHANGE is printed on one line.

5.16
Recoding Data

When your variables have many values, you may find that some cells in a CROSSTABS table have only a few cases. You can combine two or more values into a single category by placing the RECODE command before the procedure command, as in:

```
RECODE  MIGRAINE (2=1)
CROSSTABS  TABLES=HYPNOSIS BY MIGRAINE
           /CELLS=TOTAL
```

The RECODE command instructs SPSS-X to change all 2s found for variable MIGRAINE to 1s. Figure 5.16 shows the CROSSTABS table. The cases that were cured or became better as a result of hypnosis are now all in one column of the table. For a more complete description of the RECODE command, see Chapter 18.

Figure 5.16   Depth of hypnosis and success of treatment using recoded data

```
- - - - - - - - - - - - - - - -  C R O S S T A B U L A T I O N   O F  - - - - - - - - - - - - - - - - -
   HYPNOSIS  DEPTH OF HYPNOSIS                          BY  MIGRAINE  OUTCOME
- - - - - - - - - - - - - - - - - - - - - - - - - - - - - - - - - - - - - - - - - - -  PAGE  1 OF  1

                       MIGRAINE
              COUNT
              TOT PCT |CURED    NO      ROW
                      |         CHANGE  TOTAL
                      |   1.00|   3.00|
HYPNOSIS      --------+-------+-------+
                1.00  |   18  |       |   18
   DEEP              | 18.0  |       | 18.0
                      +-------+-------+
                2.00  |   36  |   17  |   53
   MEDIUM            | 36.0  | 17.0  | 53.0
                      +-------+-------+
                3.00  |    1  |   28  |   29
   LIGHT             |  1.0  | 28.0  | 29.0
                      +-------+-------+
              COLUMN     55      45      100
              TOTAL    55.0    45.0    100.0

NUMBER OF MISSING OBSERVATIONS =        0
```

5.17
Entering Crosstabulated Data

Frequently, you already have a crosstabulation that you want to present in a different way or for which you want to produce additional statistics. You can enter the crosstabulated data rather than the original observations into SPSS-X and proceed with your analysis. Each cell of the table is considered a case. For each case (cell of the table), enter the cell counts along with the values of the row, column, and control variables. Define this file as you would any other data file. Then use the WEIGHT command (see Chapter 18) to specify that each case should be counted as many times as specified by the cell frequency.

For example, to reproduce the table in Figure 5.1 from the crosstabulated data, use the following SPSS-X command file:

```
TITLE   ENTERING THE TABLE OF RETURNED BY ADDRESS
DATA LIST   FIXED/1 FREQ 1-5 RETURNED 7 ADDRESS 9
WEIGHT BY FREQ
VARIABLE LABELS
   RETURNED 'FOUND AND MAILED'/
   ADDRESS 'ADDRESS ON LETTER'/
VALUE LABELS
   RETURNED  1 'YES' 2 'NO'/
   ADDRESS  1 'CONTROL' 2 'DANDEE' 3 'COMMUNIST'/
CROSSTABS   TABLES=RETURNED BY ADDRESS
            /STATISTICS=CHISQ
BEGIN DATA
   35 1 1
   37 2 1
   32 1 2
   40 2 2
   10 1 3
   62 2 3
END DATA
FINISH
```

• The DATA LIST command defines the variables for the cells, which are treated like cases. The cell frequency is entered in columns 1 through 5 and is defined as variable FREQ. The value of RETURNED for each cell is entered in column 7 and the value of ADDRESS in column 9. So, the first line of data represents the first cell of the table, where RETURNED has value 1 and ADDRESS has value 1. The second line of data is the second cell in the first column of the table, and so forth.

• The WEIGHT command uses FREQ, the cell frequencies, as the weight variable. The value of this variable for each case is then used as a *replication factor:* SPSS-X reads the single case as though it were reading a number of separate cases equal to the replication factor. For example, the first case is counted as 35 cases in the table requested on the CROSSTABS command. The WEIGHT command allows you to represent the original data from the crosstabulated data.

• You can assign variable and value labels to crosstabulated data with the VARIABLE LABELS and VALUE LABELS commands.

• The CROSSTABS command specifies the desired crosstabulation.

You can also use the PRINT FORMATS command to specify the number of decimal positions that you want printed for the values. If you have included values in the crosstabulated data that you now want excluded from the table, use the MISSING VALUES command to specify the values to be excluded.

If you want to rearrange the variables in the crosstabulated input data or drop certain variables from the table, you can do so by specifying only the variables that you want and in the order that you want. For example, the command

```
CROSSTABS   TABLES=ADDRESS BY RETURNED
```

defines ADDRESS as the row variable and RETURNED as the column variable.

EXERCISES

Syntax

1. Given the following commands, which of the statements below are true?

   ```
   CROSSTABS  TABLES=ADDRESS BY LOCATION
              /CELLS=ROW
   ```

   a. Two subtables are produced.
   b. The variable ADDRESS is the row variable.
   c. The variable ADDRESS is the column variable.
   d. The CROSSTABS command will cause an error because the VARIABLES subcommand is missing.
   e. The TABLES subcommand is not necessary in this command.
   f. The cells include row percentages and total percentages.
   g. The cells include row percentages only.
   h. The output includes the chi-square statistic.

2. Which of the commands below produced the following crosstabulation?

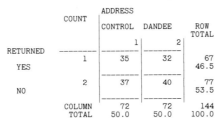

   a. CROSSTABS VARIABLES = RETURNED ADDRESS/
                 TABLES = RETURNED BY ADDRESS/
                 CELLS=TOTAL

   b. CROSSTABS VARIABLES = RETURNED (1,2) ADDRESS (1,2)/
                 TABLES = RETURNED BY ADDRESS

   c. CROSSTABS VARIABLES = RETURNED ADDRESS (1,2)
                 TABLES = ADDRESS BY RETURNED

   d. CROSSTABS TABLES = RETURNED (1,2) BY ADDRESS (1,2)

3. In a data set, you have coded the variable AGE, which has integer values ranging from 18 through 65 years. The following RECODE commands group the ages into categories. What ages fall into each category?

   a. RECODE AGE (LOWEST THRU 40=1) (41 THRU HIGHEST=2)

   b. RECODE AGE (18 THRU 29=1) (30 THRU 49=2) (50 THRU 65=3)

   c. RECODE AGE (18,19,20=1) (21 THRU 30=2) (41 THRU 50=3)
              (51 THRU 65=4)

   d. RECODE AGE (60 THRU 65=1) (ELSE=2)

   e. RECODE AGE (60 THRU 65=1) (ELSE=COPY)

4. Given the following job, fill in the cells of the CROSSTABS table below.

```
DATA LIST  FIXED/ VARA 1-2 VARB 4 VARC 6
WEIGHT BY VARA
CROSSTABS .TABLES = VARB BY VARC
BEGIN DATA
72 1 1
20 2 1
54 1 2
16 2 2
END DATA
FINISH
```

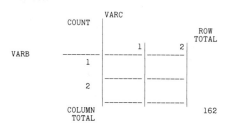

5. For variables SEX, JOBTITLE, and HAPPY, write the SPSS-X command to produce:
   a. A crosstabulation with HAPPY in rows and JOBTITLE in columns.
   b. A crosstabulation with JOBTITLE in rows and SEX in columns.
   c. A crosstabulation with JOBTITLE in rows and HAPPY in columns, controlling for SEX.
   d. The table in (a) with column, row, and total percents.
   e. The table in (b) with cell counts, column and row percents, and chi-square and lambda statistics.

6. Code values for variable AGE into three groups: those under 20, those 20 to 55, and those over 55. Then write the SPSS-X command that crosstabulates HAPPY by YRSEDUC, controlling for AGE.

Statistical Concepts

1. Which of the following statements are true?
   a. If one of the measures of association provided by CROSSTABS is very low, it is safe to assume that the other measures of association will also be low.
   b. PRE measures of association are easier to interpret than chi-square-based measures of association.
   c. Measures of association for nominal variables indicate the direction as well as the strength of the association.
   d. The eta coefficient measures the strength of the linear relationship between two variables.

2. For each of the following measures of association, indicate whether its value depends on which variable is specified as the row variable.
   a. Kendall's tau *a*.
   b. Goodman and Kruskal's gamma.
   c. Eta.
   d. Somers' *d*.
   e. Kruskal's lambda.

3. Which of the measures of association calculated by CROSSTABS are sensitive to all types of association?

4. What is the reason for normalizing measures of association, thereby forcing their values to range from -1 to $+1$ or from 0 to 1?

5. A researcher studying the association between two variables obtained all of the appropriate measures of association provided by CROSSTABS. Only one measure was large, so he included only this measure in his summary of results. Was this reasonable? Why or why not?

6. A study to determine the effect of grade-point average on performance on a test resulted in the following table:

```
                   PERFORM
         COUNT    |
                  | POOR     FAIR     GOOD    | ROW
                  |                           | TOTAL
                  |     1|      2|      3|
GPA      --------+------+------+------+
            1     |   56 |   54 |   12 |   122
BELOW AVERAGE     |      |      |      |   36.2
         --------+------+------+------+
            2     |   31 |  .65 |   43 |   139
AVERAGE           |      |      |      |   41.2
         --------+------+------+------+
            3     |   12 |   25 |   39 |    76
ABOVE AVERAGE     |      |      |      |   22.6
         --------+------+------+------+
         COLUMN        99    144     94     337
         TOTAL       29.4   42.7   27.9   100.0
```

a. What is the independent variable? What is the dependent variable?

b. Would you look at row percentages or column percentages to see whether the independent variable seems to affect the dependent variable?

7. a. Fill in the missing information in the following table:

```
                  DEPTH
         COUNT   |
         ROW PCT | SMALL   MEDIUM  LARGE   | ROW
         COL PCT |                         | TOTAL
                 |    1|      2|      3|
CURE     --------+------+------+------+
            1    |   29 |      |   30 |    69
NO               |      |      |      |
         --------+------+------+------+
            2    |   15 |   10 |   20 |
YES              |      |      |      |
         --------+------+------+------+
         COLUMN
         TOTAL
```

8. a. Fill in the missing information in the following table and calculate the chi-square test for independence.

```
                   VARB
         COUNT    |
         EXP VAL  |                       | ROW
         RESIDUAL |                       | TOTAL
                  |     1|      2|
VARA     --------+------+------+
            1     |   13 |   47 |    60
                  | 30.0 |      |   60.0%
                  |      | 17.0 |
         --------+------+------+
            2     |      |      |    40
                  | 20.0 |      |   40.0%
                  | 17.0 |      |
         --------+------+------+
         COLUMN       50     50     100
         TOTAL      50.0%  50.0%  100.0%
```

9. Suppose a random sample of size 100 resulted in Table 1 below, while another random sample of size 1,000 resulted in Table 2. If you know that the chi-square value for Table 1 is 9.09, can you find the chi-square value for Table 2 without doing any chi-square calculations involving the data in Table 2?

Table 1

COUNT	VARB COUGH 1	NO COUGH 2	ROW TOTAL
VARA 1 SMOKER	30	20	50 50.0
2 NONSMOKER	15	35	50 50.0
COLUMN TOTAL	45 45.0	55 55.0	100 100.0

Table 2

COUNT	VARB COUGH 1	NO COUGH 2	ROW TOTAL
VARA 1 SMOKER	300	200	500 50.0
2 NONSMOKER	150	350	500 50.0
COLUMN TOTAL	450 45.0	550 55.0	1000 100.0

10. Consider the following table:

COUNT	VARB SMOKER 1	NONSMOKER 2	ROW TOTAL
SEX 1 MALE	45	55	100 50.0
2 FEMALE	30	70	100 50.0
COLUMN TOTAL	75 37.5	125 62.5	200 100.0

  a. If sex and smoking status are independent, what frequencies would you expect in each cell?
  b. What are the degrees of freedom for this table?
  c. Calculate the chi-square test for independence.

Data Analysis

Use the BANK system file for Questions 1–4.

1. a. Prepare a table that shows the number of women and men in each of the first four job categories (use the SELECT IF command).
   b. Construct another table crosstabulating the first four job categories with the sex-race variable.
   c. What do you conclude and why? Justify your answer with a statistical analysis.

2. a. Collapse work experience into several categories and crosstabulate this collapsed variable with sex. Do sex and work experience appear to be related? Justify your answer with a statistical analysis. Can your choice of categories affect your answer? Why or why not?
   b. If sex and work experience appear to be related, obtain a measure of the strength of the association. What are the disadvantages of the measure you used?
   c. Repeat the analysis in Question 2.b using race instead of sex.

3. Collapse job seniority into several categories and examine the relationship between job seniority and sex and between job seniority and race, as in Question 2.

4. Collapse education into several categories. Are education and sex related at the bank? Are education and race related? Perform an analysis like the one in Question 2.

5. Choose one of the data files from Appendix B. Describe five possible relationships between variables that can be examined using crosstabulations. For example, the relationship between number of evenings spent at a bar and the sex of the respondent can be studied by tabulating SOCBAR against SEX on the GSS82 system file.

6. Run three of the tables described in Question 5, including at least one table that has a control variable. For example, tabulate husbands' and wives' responses to a particular product, controlling for whether the questionnaire included pictures or not.
   a. Write a brief paragraph summarizing your results. Indicate whether row or column percentages are appropriate for describing the relationships in the tables.
   b. Test the hypothesis that the two variables are independent.
   c. If some of the variables have many categories, the resulting tables may have many cells with few observations in each. Use the RECODE command to group some of the categories and rerun the tables.

7. Take a continuous variable like age or years of education and recode it into quartiles. In other words, assign a code of 1 to the lowest 25%, a code of 2 to the next 25%, and so forth. Obtain a crosstabulation of this variable with one of the other variables in the file. Describe the results.

8. Use the Western Electric data file for the following exercises:
   a. Write a short paragraph describing the relationship between incidence of coronary heart disease (CHD) and family history of CHD (FAMHXCVR).
   b. Describe the relationship between the type of first coronary event (FIRSTCHD) and family history of CHD (FAMHXCVR).
   c. Obtain a frequency table for the number of cigarettes smoked per day (CGT58). Based on the frequency table, recode the number of cigarettes per day into three categories. Make sure that one of the categories is no cigarettes smoked. Write a paragraph describing the relationship between incidence of coronary heart disease (CHD) and cigarette smoking.
   d. Repeat (c) for serum cholesterol (CHOL58) and diastolic blood pressure (DBP58). (Base your cut-points for these variables on a histogram.)

Chapter 6 Breaking Down Discrimination: Describing Subpopulation Differences

The 1964 Civil Rights Act prohibits discrimination in the workplace based on sex or race. Employers who violate the act by unfair hiring or advancement practices can be prosecuted. Numerous lawsuits have been filed on behalf of women, blacks, and other groups offered equal protection under the law.

The courts have ruled that statistics can be used as *prima facie* evidence of discrimination, and many lawsuits depend heavily on complex statistical analyses, which attempt to demonstrate that similarly qualified individuals are not treated equally. Identifying and measuring all variables that legitimately influence promotion and hiring is difficult, if not impossible, especially for nonroutine jobs. Years of schooling and prior work experience can be quantified, but what about the more intangible attributes such as enthusiasm and creativity? How are they to be objectively measured so as not to become convenient smoke screens for concealing discrimination?

6.1 SEARCHING FOR DISCRIMINATION

In this chapter, employee records for 474 individuals hired between 1969 and 1971 by a bank engaged in Equal Employment Opportunity (EEO) litigation are analyzed. Two types of unfair employment practices are of particular interest: shunting (placing some employees in lower job categories than others with similar qualifications) and salary and promotion inequities.

Although extensive and intricate statistical analyses are usually involved in studies of this kind (see, for example, Roberts, 1980), the discussion here is necessarily limited. The SPSS-X MEANS procedure is used to calculate average salaries for groups of employees based on race and sex. Additional grouping variables are introduced to help "explain" some of the observed variability in salary.

6.2 Who Does What?

Figure 6.2 is a crosstabulation of job category at the time of hiring with sex and race characteristics. The first three job classifications contain 64% of white males (adding column percents), 94% of both nonwhite males and white females, and 100% of nonwhite females. Among white males, 17% are in the college trainee program, compared to 4% of white females.

Figure 6.2   Crosstabulation of job category by sex-race

```
- - - - - - - - - - - - - - - - - - - - - - -  C R O S S T A B U L A T I O N   O F  - - - - - - - - - - - - - - - - - - -
    JOBCAT    EMPLOYMENT CATEGORY                                    BY  SEXRACE    SEX & RACE CLASSIFICATION
- - - - - - - - - - - - - - - - - - - - - - - - - - - - - - - - - - - - - - - - - - - - - - - - - - - - - - - - - - -  PAGE  1 OF  1
                         SEXRACE
                  COUNT I
                  COL PCT IWHITE    MINORITY WHITE    MINORITY   ROW
                  TOT PCT IMALES    MALES    FEMALES  FEMALES    TOTAL
                         I      1I        2I        3I        4I
  JOBCAT          --------+--------+--------+--------+--------+
                    1 I      75 I     35 I     85 I     32 I     227
  CLERICAL            I    38.7 I   54.7 I   48.3 I   80.0 I    47.9
                      I    15.8 I    7.4 I   17.9 I    6.8 I
                     +--------+--------+--------+--------+
                    2 I      35 I     12 I     81 I      8 I     136
  OFFICE TRAINEE      I    18.0 I   18.8 I   46.0 I   20.0 I    28.7
                      I     7.4 I    2.5 I   17.1 I    1.7 I
                     +--------+--------+--------+--------+
                    3 I      14 I     13 I        I        I      27
  SECURITY OFFICER I     7.2 I   20.3 I        I        I     5.7
                      I     3.0 I    2.7 I        I        I
                     +--------+--------+--------+--------+
                    4 I      33 I      1 I      7 I        I      41
  COLLEGE TRAINEE     I    17.0 I    1.6 I    4.0 I        I     8.6
                      I     7.0 I     .2 I    1.5 I        I
                     +--------+--------+--------+--------+
                    5 I      28 I      2 I      2 I        I      32
  EXEMPT EMPLOYEE     I    14.4 I    3.1 I    1.1 I        I     6.8
                      I     5.9 I     .4 I     .4 I        I
                     +--------+--------+--------+--------+
                    6 I       3 I      1 I      1 I        I       5
  MBA TRAINEE         I     1.5 I    1.6 I     .6 I        I     1.1
                      I      .6 I     .2 I     .2 I        I
                     +--------+--------+--------+--------+
                    7 I       6 I        I        I        I       6
  TECHNICAL           I     3.1 I        I        I        I     1.3
                      I     1.3 I        I        I        I
                     +--------+--------+--------+--------+
               COLUMN      194       64      176       40      474
               TOTAL      40.9     13.5     37.1      8.4    100.0

  NUMBER OF MISSING OBSERVATIONS =       0
```

Although these observations are interesting, they do not imply discriminatory placement into beginning job categories because the qualifications of the various groups are not necessarily similar. If women and nonwhites are more qualified than white males in the same beginning job categories, discrimination may be suspected.

6.3
Level of Education

One easily measured employment qualification is years of education. Figure 6.3a shows the average years of education for the entire sample (labeled FOR ENTIRE POPULATION) and then for each of the two sexes (labeled SEX and MALES or FEMALES) and then for each of the two race categories within each sex category (labeled MINORITY and WHITE or NONWHITE).

Figure 6.3a   Education broken down by race within sex

```
           D E S C R I P T I O N   O F   S U B P O P U L A T I O N S
   Criterion Variable    EDLEVEL    EDUCATIONAL LEVEL
      Broken Down by     SEX        SEX OF EMPLOYEE
                 by      MINORITY   MINORITY CLASSIFICATION


   Variable          Value  Label                   Mean      Std Dev    Cases

   For Entire Population                          13.4916     2.8848      474

   SEX                   0  MALES                 14.4302     2.9793      258
      MINORITY           0  WHITE                 14.9227     2.8484      194
      MINORITY           1  NONWHITE              12.9375     2.8888       64

   SEX                   1  FEMALES               12.3704     2.3192      216
      MINORITY           0  WHITE                 12.3409     2.4066      176
      MINORITY           1  NONWHITE              12.5000     1.9081       40

   Total Cases = 474
```

The entire sample has an average of 13.49 years of education. Males have more years of education than females—an average of 14.43 years compared to 12.37. White males have the highest level of education, almost 15 years, which is 2 years more than nonwhite males and approximately 2.5 years more than either group of females.

Figure 6.3b   Education by sex-race and job category

```
                           C R O S S - B R E A K D O W N

     Criterion Variable      EDLEVEL      EDUCATIONAL LEVEL
       Broken Down by        JOBCAT       EMPLOYMENT CATEGORY
                  by         SEXRACE      SEX & RACE CLASSIFICATION


                       SEXRACE
              Mean  I
              Count I   WHITE        MINORITY     WHITE        MINORITY
            Std Dev I   MALES        MALES        FEMALES      FEMALES      Row
                    I        1  I         2  I         3  I         4  I    Total
     JOBCAT         -------+--------+--------+--------+--------+
                  1 I    13.87 I   13.77 I   11.46 I   12.63 I    12.78
        CLERICAL     I       75 I      35 I      85 I      32 I      227
                   I     2.30 I    2.31 I    2.43 I    2.12 I     2.56
                    -------+--------+--------+--------+--------+
                  2 I    13.89 I   12.58 I   12.81 I   12.00 I    13.02
     OFFICE TRAINEE  I       35 I      12 I      81 I       8 I      136
                   I     1.41 I    2.61 I    1.93 I     .00 I     1.89
                    -------+--------+--------+--------+--------+
                  3 I    10.29 I   10.08 I          I          I    10.19
   SECURITY OFFICER  I       14 I      13 I          I          I       27
                   I     2.05 I    2.47 I          I          I     2.22
                    -------+--------+--------+--------+--------+
                  4 I    17.21 I   17.00 I   16.00 I          I    17.00
    COLLEGE TRAINEE  I       33 I       1 I       7 I          I       41
                   I     1.34 I       . I     .00 I          I     1.28
                    -------+--------+--------+--------+--------+
                  5 I    17.61 I   14.00 I   16.00 I          I    17.28
   EXEMPT EMPLOYEE   I       28 I       2 I       2 I          I       32
                   I     1.77 I    2.83 I     .00 I          I     1.97
                    -------+--------+--------+--------+--------+
                  6 I    18.33 I   19.00 I   16.00 I          I    18.00
     MBA TRAINEE     I        3 I       1 I       1 I          I        5
                   I     1.15 I       . I       . I          I     1.41
                    -------+--------+--------+--------+--------+
                  7 I    18.17 I          I          I          I    18.17
      TECHNICAL      I        6 I          I          I          I        6
                   I     1.47 I          I          I          I     1.47
                    -------+--------+--------+--------+--------+
         Column Total     14.92    12.94    12.34    12.50      13.49
                           194       64      176       40        474
                          2.85     2.89     2.41     1.91       2.88
```

In Figure 6.3b, the cases are further subdivided by their combined sex-race characteristics and by their initial job category. For each cell in the table, the average years of education, the standard deviation, and number of cases are printed. White males have the highest average years of education in all job categories except MBA trainees, where the single nonwhite male MBA trainee has nineteen years of education. From this table, it does not appear that females and nonwhites are overeducated when compared to white males in similar job categories. However, it is important to note that group means provide information about a particular class of employees. While discrimination may not exist for a class as a whole, some individuals within that class may be victims (or beneficiaries) of discrimination.

6.4
Beginning Salaries

The average beginning salary for the 474 persons hired between 1969 and 1971 is $6,806. The distribution by the four sex-race categories is shown in Figure 6.4a.

Figure 6.4a   Beginning salary by sex-race

```
        D E S C R I P T I O N   O F   S U B P O P U L A T I O N S

   Criterion Variable      SALBEG       BEGINNING SALARY
     Broken Down by         SEXRACE      SEX & RACE CLASSIFICATION


   Variable      Value  Label                    Mean      Std Dev    Cases

   For Entire Population                       6806.4346  3148.2553     474

   SEXRACE           1  WHITE MALES            8637.5258  3871.1017     194
   SEXRACE           2  MINORITY MALES         6553.5000  2228.1436      64
   SEXRACE           3  WHITE FEMALES          5340.4886  1225.9605     176
   SEXRACE           4  MINORITY FEMALES       4780.5000   771.4188      40

   Total Cases = 474
```

White males have the highest beginning salaries—an average of $8,638—followed by nonwhite males. Since males are in higher job categories than females, this difference is not surprising.

Figure 6.4b Beginning salary by sex-race and job category

```
                        C R O S S - B R E A K D O W N

Criterion Variable    SALBEG      BEGINNING SALARY
    Broken Down by    JOBCAT      EMPLOYMENT CATEGORY
              by      SEXRACE     SEX & RACE CLASSIFICATION


                  SEXRACE
           Mean  I
                 I    WHITE      MINORITY    WHITE      MINORITY
                 I    MALES      MALES       FEMALES    FEMALES      Row
                 I       1  I       2  I        3  I        4  I    Total
JOBCAT           ---------+----------+----------+----------+----------
            1    I  6553.44 I  6230.74 I  5147.32 I  4828.13 I   5733.95
  CLERICAL       I         I         I         I         I
                 ---------+----------+----------+----------+----------
            2    I  6262.29 I  5610.00 I  5208.89 I  4590.00 I   5478.97
OFFICE TRAINEE   I         I         I         I         I
                 ---------+----------+----------+----------+----------
            3    I  6102.86 I  5953.85 I          I          I   6031.11
SECURITY OFFICER I         I         I         I         I
                 ---------+----------+----------+----------+----------
            4    I 10467.64 I 11496.00 I  7326.86 I          I   9956.49
COLLEGE TRAINEE  I         I         I         I         I
                 ---------+----------+----------+----------+----------
            5    I 13255.29 I 15570.00 I 10998.00 I          I  13258.88
EXEMPT EMPLOYEE  I         I         I         I         I
                 ---------+----------+----------+----------+----------
            6    I 14332.00 I 13992.00 I  7200.00 I          I  12837.60
MBA TRAINEE      I         I         I         I         I
                 ---------+----------+----------+----------+----------
            7    I 19996.00 I         I          I          I  19996.00
TECHNICAL        I         I         I         I         I
                 ---------+----------+----------+----------+----------
   Column Total    8637.53    6553.50    5340.49    4780.50    6806.43
```

Figure 6.4b shows beginning salaries subdivided by race, sex, and job category. For most of the job categories, white males have higher beginning salaries than the other groups. There is a $1,400 salary difference between white males and white females in the clerical jobs and a $1,000 difference in the general office trainee classification. In the college trainee program, white males averaged over $3,000 more than white females. However, Figure 6.3b shows that white females in the college trainee program had only an undergraduate degree, while white males had an average of 17.2 years of schooling.

6.5
Introducing More Variables

The differences in mean beginning salaries between males and females are somewhat suspect. It is, however, unwise to conclude that salary discrimination exists since several important variables, such as years of prior experience, have not been considered. It is necessary to control (or to adjust statistically) for other relevant variables. Crossclassifying cases by the variables of interest and comparing salaries across the subgroups is one way of achieving control. However, as the number of variables increases, the number of cases in each cell rapidly diminishes, making statistically meaningful comparisons difficult. To circumvent these problems, regression methods, which achieve control by specifying certain statistical relations that may describe what is happening, are used. Regression methods are described in Chapter 13.

6.6
RUNNING PROCEDURE MEANS

Procedure MEANS prints sums, means, standard deviations, and variances of a variable within subgroups defined by other variables. For example, it provides income statistics broken down by sex, age group, level of education, and so forth. For most applications, you need to specify only the TABLES subcommand to name the variables. This is known as the *general mode* of MEANS. If your data are integer-valued and you want the special crosstabulation-like format, you can use the VARIABLES and CROSSBREAK subcommands. You can also request optional statistics and alter the handling of missing values. See Chapter 18 for the complete syntax of procedure MEANS.

To use MEANS in general mode, enter the MEANS command followed by the TABLES subcommand and specifications. Means, standard deviations, sums, variances, and numbers of cases are computed for the first variable for the categories defined by the variable list after the keyword BY. For example, to produce the table shown in Figure 6.4a, specify:

```
MEANS  TABLES=SALBEG BY SEXRACE
```

To display the alternative crosstabulation-like format shown in Figures 6.3b and 6.4b, use the VARIABLES subcommand to specify the variables and their ranges and the CROSSBREAK subcommand to specify the tables. The form of the CROSSBREAK subcommand is the same as for the TABLES subcommand. For example, to produce the output shown in Figure 6.3b, specify

```
MEANS  VARIABLES=EDLEVEL(LO,HI) SEXRACE(1,4) JOBCAT(1,7)
       /CROSSBREAK=EDLEVEL BY JOBCAT BY SEXRACE
```

The following SPSS-X command file produces Figures 6.3a and 6.4b:

```
GET FILE  BANK
COMPUTE   SEXRACE=1
IF      (MINORITY EQ 1 AND SEX EQ 0) SEXRACE=2
IF      (MINORITY EQ 0 AND SEX EQ 1) SEXRACE=3
IF      (MINORITY EQ 1 AND SEX EQ 1) SEXRACE=4
MEANS   TABLES=EDLEVEL BY SEX BY MINORITY
VALUE LABELS   SEXRACE 1 'WHITE    MALES' 2 'MINORITYMALES'
               3 'WHITE   FEMALES' 4 'MINORITYFEMALES'
MEANS   VARIABLES=SALBEG(LO,HI) SEXRACE(1,4) JOBCAT(1,7)
        /CROSSBREAK=SALBEG BY JOBCAT BY SEXRACE
        /CELLS=MEAN
```

- The COMPUTE command and the three IF commands create a single four-category variable that combines the sex and race variables already on the file. The COMPUTE command sets new variable SEXRACE to 1, which will be the white-male category. The IF commands change the value to 2 for nonwhite males, 3 for white females, and 4 for nonwhite females. Refer to Chapter 18 for an additional discussion of the COMPUTE and IF commands.

- The first MEANS command summarizes education for race within each sex category (see Figure 6.3a).

- A set of VALUE LABELS is assigned to new variable SEXRACE for the second MEANS command. These labels are specially formatted to print well in the CROSSBREAK tables in Figures 6.3b and 6.4b as described for CROSSTABS in Chapter 5.

- The second MEANS command uses integer mode and requests crosstabular format (see Figure 6.4b). Note that the keywords LO and HI specify the minimum and maximum values for variable SALBEG.

- The CELLS subcommand requests means in each cell. frequencies, sums, and standard deviations, respectively.

EXERCISES

Syntax

Read the section on the IF command in Chapter 18 before answering the following questions.

1. Write a MEANS command to request a summary of current salary (SALNOW) for job category (JOBCAT) within each sex category (SEX). Include cases with missing values on JOBCAT or SEX in the summary table.

2. The following MEANS command requesting a crosstabulation-like format has a syntax error. What is the error?

```
MEANS  CROSSBREAK=EDLEVEL BY SEX BY MINORITY
```

3. Which of the MEANS commands below produced the following table?

```
        D E S C R I P T I O N    O F   S U B P O P U L A T I O N S

   Criterion Variable    SALNOW      CURRENT SALARY
      Broken Down by      MINORITY    MINORITY CLASSIFICATION
                  by      SEX         SEX OF EMPLOYEE


   Variable         Value  Label                  Mean      Std Dev    Cases

   For Entire Population                        13767.8270   6830.2646    474

   MINORITY           0    WHITE                14409.3243   7217.6382    370
      SEX             0    MALES                17790.1649   8132.2646    194
      SEX             1    FEMALES              10682.7159   3204.7575    176

   MINORITY           1    NONWHITE             11485.5769   4568.6551    104
      SEX             0    MALES                12898.4375   5223.9525     64
      SEX             1    FEMALES               9225.0000   1588.9474     40

   Total Cases = 474
```

   a. MEANS TABLES=SALNOW BY SEX MINORITY

   b. MEANS TABLES=SALNOW BY MINORITY BY SEX

   c. MEANS TABLES=MINORITY BY SALNOW BY SEX

4. The following IF commands contain syntax errors. Circle the errors and write the correct form of the commands.

   a. IF (JOBCAT EQ 2,4, OR 6) TRAINEE=1

   b. IF EDLEVEL LE 12 AND SALNOW LE 10000 THEN LOW=1

   c. IF (AGE GE 20 OR LE 55) OLDYOUNG=1

5. The following set of data transformation commands create variables TRAINEE, ACHIEVER, and LOW. Fill in the values for these variables for the five cases listed in the table.

```
COMPUTE TRAINEE=0
COMPUTE LOW=0
IF ANY(JOBCAT,2,4,6) TRAINEE=1
IF (AGE LE 30 AND SALNOW GE 15000) ACHIEVER=1
IF (AGE LE 30 AND SALNOW LT 15000) ACHIEVER=0
IF (AGE GT 30 AND SALNOW GE 25000) ACHIEVER=1
IF (AGE GT 30 AND SALNOW LT 25000) ACHIEVER=0
IF RANGE(EDLEVEL,1,12) AND RANGE(SALNOW,1,10000) LOW=1
```

JOBCAT	AGE	SALNOW	EDLEVEL	TRAINEE	ACHIEVER	LOW
6	28.50	16080	16			
5	40.33	41400	16			
1	54.33	8880	12			
2	32.33	22000	17			
3	30.92	19020	19			

6. Write the command to calculate average ages (variable AGE) for people in various job categories (variable JOBTITLE).

7. Correct the following jobs:

   a. MEANS INCOME BY SEX /STATISTICS=MEAN STDDEV

   b. MEANS TABLES=INCOME, SEX /MISSING=TABLE /CELLS=TABLE

   c. MEANS TABLES=INCOME BY JOBTITLE BY SEX
       /VARIABLES=INCOME(LO,HI) BY JOBTITLE(1,4) BY SEX(1,2)

   d. MEANS TABLES=INCOME, AGE BY SEX
       CELLS=COLUMN ROW TOTAL

   e. MEANS TABLES=INCOME(LO,HI) BY SEX(1,2)/
       CELLS=COUNT COLUMN ROW

8. Assume data in file LIFE are defined and labeled. Use variables SEX (coded 1=female, 2=male) and LOOKS (coded 0=unattractive, 1=attractive) to create variable POPULAR and code it for attractive and unattractive women and men. Then write the SPSS-X command to display in crosstabulation-like format the average income (variable INCOME) of popular and unpopular (variable POPU-LAR) professionals (variable JOB, coded 1=counselor, 2=professor, 3=doctor, 4=lawyer, 5=politician).

Statistical Concepts

1. Indicate whether you would use procedure FREQUENCIES, CROSSTABS, or MEANS to find the following:
   a. The average years of education for members of different political parties.
   b. The number of men and women in each political party.
   c. The number of members in each political party.
   d. The average years of education for men and women in each political party.
   e. The number of men and women in each religious affiliation within each political party.

2. How are the values in the cells of MEANS tables different from those in CROSSTABS tables?

3. Suppose you are using MEANS to see whether women at a particular company are discriminated against in regard to salary. Indicate whether the following statements are true:
   a. If your MEANS analysis shows no discrimination as far as average salary is concerned, it is safe to assume that no individual women are discriminated against in regard to salary.
   b. If average salaries are the same for men and women, it is safe to assume that there appears to be no salary discrimination against women as a class at this company.

4. Below is a MEANS table of average diastolic blood pressure subdivided by family history of coronary heart disease and by status at 10 years.
   a. Fill in the missing information:

```
          D E S C R I P T I O N   O F   S U B P O P U L A T I O N S

   Criterion Variable    DBP58      AVERAGE DIAST BLOOD PRESSURE 58
       Broken Down by    FAMHXCVR   FAMILY HISTORY OF CHD
                 by      VITAL10    STATUS AT TEN YEARS


   Variable       Value  Label                   Mean      Std Dev    Cases

   For Entire Population                         88.7908   13.0499


   FAMHXCVR       Y      YES                                13.0039
      VITAL10        0   ALIVE                   90.4000    12.0593      45
      VITAL10        1   DEAD                    95.1176    15.0868      17

   FAMHXCVR       N      NO                      87.7740               177
      VITAL10        0                           86.6015    11.1137    133
      VITAL10        1   DEAD                                17.0304

   Total Cases =   240
   Missing Cases =    1 OR   0.4 PCT.
```

   b. Based on the table above can you determine mean diastolic blood pressure for all men without a history of heart disease?
   c. Can you determine mean diastolic blood pressure for all men still alive at 10 years?

5. A survey of new-car owners asks the question "What is the body style of your new car?" The following choices are offered: two-door with trunk; two-door with hatchback; convertible; four-door with trunk; four-door with hatchback; station

wagon. A research analyst assigns the code 1 through 6 to the above responses and uses procedure MEANS to find average styles controlling for sex and income level. How would you interpret the resulting table?

Data Analysis

Use the BANK system file for Questions 1–3.

1. Describe the distribution of age, educational level, work experience, and beginning salary for the sex-race groups. Summarize your findings.

2. Collapse education into several categories and describe the distribution of beginning salary for sex-race groupings, controlling for education. Do the results indicate that discrimination may be present? What are the weaknesses of this sort of analysis?

3. Collapse beginning salary into several categories and describe the distribution of current salary across the sex-race groups, controlling for beginning salary. Is there evidence of discrimination?

4. Choose one of the data files from Appendix B and formulate several hypotheses that can be examined using procedure MEANS. For example, the hypothesis that men and women of similar educational backgrounds watch comparable amounts of television can be studied by calculating average hours of television viewing for each sex for different education levels. Remember to group years of education into broader categories, such as high-school graduate, college graduate, and so forth. Otherwise, there will be only a few subjects at each education level.
   a. Obtain tables from procedure MEANS for three relationships. If there are only a few cases in any of the categories, RECODE the variables.
   b. Write a paragraph describing your results.

5. Use the Western Electric data file for the following questions:
   a. Calculate the average number of cigarettes smoked, serum cholesterol, diastolic blood pressure, age, and years of education for men who developed and those who did not develop coronary heart disease.
   b. Write a brief paragraph describing the results you found in (a). How do these compare to the results you obtained to Question 8.d. in the previous chapter?
   c. Determine whether there are differences in smoking, cholesterol, blood pressure, age, and years of education for the different types of CHD events (FIRSTCHD). Write a paragraph describing your results.
   d. Repeat (a) for men who have and do not have a family history of heart disease.

Chapter 7   Consumer Surveys: Testing Hypotheses about Differences in Means

Would you buy a disposable raincoat, vegetables in pop-top cans, or investment counseling via closed-circuit television? These products and 17 others were described in questionnaires administered to 100 married couples (Davis & Ragsdale, 1983). Respondents were asked to rate on a scale of 1 (definitely want to buy) to 7 (definitely do not want to buy) their likelihood of buying the product. Of the 100 couples, 50 received questionnaires with pictures of the products and 50 received questionnaires without pictures. (See Appendix B for details about the study.) In this chapter we will examine whether pictures affect consumer preferences and whether husbands' and wives' responses differ.

7.1
TESTING HYPOTHESES

The first part of the table in Figure 7.1 contains basic descriptive statistics for the buying scores of couples receiving questionnaires with and without pictures. A couple's buying score is simply the sum of all ratings assigned to products by the husband and wife individually. Low scores indicate buyers while high scores indicate reluctance to buy. The 50 couples who received questionnaires without pictures (Group 1) had a mean score of 168 while the 48 couples who received forms with pictures had an average score of 159. (Two couples did not complete the questionnaire and are not included in the analysis.) The standard deviations show that scores for the second group were somewhat more variable than those for the first.

Figure 7.1   Family buying scores by questionnaire type

```
- - - - - - - - - - - - - - - - - - - - - - - - - - - - - - - T - T E S T - - - - - - - - - - - - - - - - - - - - - - - - - - - - - - - -

GROUP 1 - VISUAL    EQ      0.
GROUP 2 - VISUAL    EQ      1.
                                                                     * POOLED VARIANCE ESTIMATE * SEPARATE VARIANCE ESTIMATE
                                                               *     *                           *
VARIABLE           NUMBER              STANDARD     STANDARD   *   F    2-TAIL  *   T    DEGREES OF 2-TAIL *   T    DEGREES OF 2-TAIL
                  OF CASES    MEAN     DEVIATION    ERROR      * VALUE  PROB.   * VALUE   FREEDOM   PROB.  * VALUE   FREEDOM   PROB.
FAMSCORE  FAMILY BUYING SCORE                                 *                 *                          *
       GROUP 1      50     168.0000    21.787       3.081     *                 *                          *
                                                              *  1.60  0.106    *  1.78     96     0.078   *  1.77    89.43    0.080
       GROUP 2      48     159.0833    27.564       3.979     *                 *                          *
                                                              *                 *                          *
```

If one is willing to restrict the conclusions to the 98 couples included in the study, it is safe to say that couples who received forms with pictures indicated a greater willingness to purchase the products than couples who received forms without pictures. However, this statement is not very satisfying. What is needed is some type of statement about the effect of the two questionnaire types for all couples—or at least some larger group of couples—not just those actually studied.

7.2
Samples and Populations

The totality of all cases about which conclusions are desired is called the *population*, while the observations actually included in the study are the *sample*. The couples in this experiment can be considered a sample from the population of couples in the United States.

The field of statistics helps us draw inferences about populations based on observations obtained from *random samples,* or samples in which the characteristics and relationships of interest are independent of the probabilities of being included in the sample. The necessity of a good research design cannot be overemphasized. Unless precautions are taken to ensure that the sample is from the population of interest and that the cases are chosen and observed without bias, the results obtained from statistical analyses may be misleading. For example, if a sample contains only affluent suburban couples, conclusions about all couples may be unwarranted.

If measurements are obtained from an entire population, the population can be characterized by the various measures of central tendency, dispersion, and shape described in Chapter 4. The results describe the population exactly. If, however, one obtains information from a random sample—the usual case—the results serve as *estimates* of the unknown population values. Special notation is used to identify population values, termed *parameters*, and to distinguish them from sample values, termed *statistics*. The mean of a population is denoted by μ, and the variance by σ^2. The symbols $\bar{X}$ and S^2 are reserved for the mean and variance of samples.

7.3
Sampling Distributions

The observations actually included in a study are just one of many random samples that could have been selected from a population. For example, if the population consists of married couples in the United States, the number of different samples that could be chosen for inclusion in a study is mind-boggling. The estimated value of a population parameter depends on the particular sample chosen. Different samples usually produce different estimates.

Figure 7.3 is a histogram of 400 means. Each mean is calculated from a random sample of 25 observations from a population which has a normal distribution with a mean value of zero and a standard deviation of 1. The estimated means are not all the same. Instead, they have a distribution. Most sample means are fairly close to zero, the population mean. The mean of the 400 means is 0.010 and the standard deviation of these means is 0.205. In fact, the distribution of the means appears approximately normal.

Although Figure 7.3 gives some idea of the appearance of the distribution of sample means of size 25 from a standard normal population, it is only an approximation since all possible samples of size 25 have not been taken. If the number of samples taken is increased to 1000, an even better picture of the distribution could be obtained. As the number of samples of a fixed size increases, the observed (or empirical) distribution of the means approaches the underlying or theoretical distribution.

The theoretical distribution of all possible values of a statistic obtained from a population is called the *sampling distribution* of the statistic. The mean of the sampling distribution is called the *expected value* of the statistic. The standard deviation is termed the *standard error*. The sampling distributions of most commonly used statistics calculated from random samples are tabulated and readily accessible. Knowing the sampling distribution of a statistic is very important for hypothesis testing, since from it one can calculate the probability of obtaining an observed sample value if a particular hypothesis is true. For example, from Figure 7.3, it appears quite unlikely that a sample mean based on a sample of size 25 from a standard normal distribution would be greater than 0.5 if the population mean were zero.

Figure 7.3   Means of 400 samples of size 25 from a normal distribution

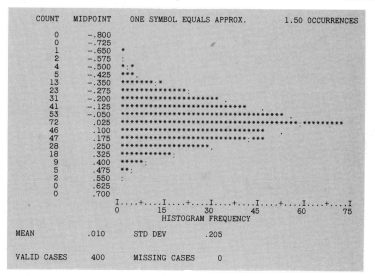

7.4
Sampling Distribution of the Mean

Since hypotheses about population means are often of interest, the sampling distribution of the mean is particularly important. If samples are taken from a normal population, the sampling distribution of the sample mean is also normal. As expected, the observed distribution of the 400 means in Figure 7.3 is approximately normal. The theoretical distribution of the sample mean, based on all possible samples of size 25, is exactly normal.

Even when samples are taken from a nonnormal population, the distribution of the sample means will be approximately normal for sufficiently large samples. This is one reason for the importance of the normal distribution in statistical inference. Consider Figure 7.4a, which shows a sample from a uniform distribution. In a uniform distribution all values of a variable are equally likely, and hence the proportion of cases in each bin of the histogram is roughly the same.

Figure 7.4a   Values from a uniform distribution

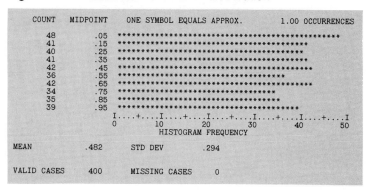

Figure 7.4b is a histogram of 400 means calculated from samples of size 25 from a uniform distribution. Note that the observed distribution is approximately normal even though the distribution from which the samples were taken is markedly nonnormal.

Figure 7.4b   Distribution of 400 means calculated from samples of size 25 from a uniform distribution

```
        COUNT    MIDPOINT     ONE SYMBOL EQUALS APPROX.          1.20 OCCURRENCES

           0      .30
           0      .32
           2      .34     :*
           1      .36     * .
           7      .38     *****:
          13      .40     **********:
          23      .42     *****************:.*
          41      .44     ****************************.*******
          53      .46     ****************************************.********
          44      .48     ************************************.**  .
          53      .50     *******************************************:
          35      .52     *****************************
          35      .54     *****************************       .
          36      .56     **************************:.***
          27      .58     *****************:.*****
          16      .60     **********:.**
           9      .62     *****:.**
           3      .64     **:
           2      .66     :*
           0      .68     .
           0      .70
                          I....+....I....+....I....+....I....+....I....+....I
                          0        12        24        36        48        60
                                          HISTOGRAM FREQUENCY

   MEAN             .500     STD DEV        .061


   VALID CASES      400      MISSING CASES     0
```

Both the size of a sample and the shape of the distribution from which samples are taken affect the shape of the sampling distribution of the mean. If samples are small and come from distributions that are far from normal, the distribution of the means will not be even approximately normal. As the size of the sample increases, the sampling distribution of the mean will approach normality.

The mean of the theoretical sampling distribution of the means of samples of size n is μ, the population mean. The standard error, which is another name for the standard deviation of the sampling distribution of the mean, is

$$\sigma_{\bar{X}} = \frac{\sigma}{\sqrt{N}}$$

where σ is the standard deviation of the population, and N is the sample size.

The standard deviation of the observed sampling distribution of means in Figure 7.3 is 0.205. This is close to the value of the standard error for the theoretical distribution which, from the previous formula, is 1/5, or 0.20.

Usually the value of the standard error is unknown and is estimated from a single sample using

$$S_{\bar{x}} = \frac{S}{\sqrt{N}}$$

where S is the *sample* standard deviation. The estimated standard error is printed in the FREQUENCIES procedure and is also part of the output shown in Figure 7.1. For example, for Group 1 the estimated standard error of the mean is

$$\frac{21.787}{\sqrt{50}} = 3.081$$

This value is printed in the column labeled STANDARD ERROR in Figure 7.1.

The standard error of the mean depends on both the sample standard deviation and the sample size. As the size of a sample increases, the standard error decreases. This is intuitively clear, since the more data are gathered, the more confident you can be that the sample mean is not too far from the population mean. Also, as the standard deviation of the observations decreases, the standard error decreases as well. Small standard deviations occur when observations are fairly homogeneous. In this case, means based on different samples should also not vary much.

7.5
THE TWO-SAMPLE
T TEST

Consider again whether there is evidence that the type of form administered influences couples' buying decisions. The question is not whether the two sample means are equal, but whether the two population means are equal.

To test the hypothesis that, in the population, buying scores for the two questionnaire types are the same, the following statistic can be calculated:

$$t = \frac{\overline{X}_1 - \overline{X}_2}{\sqrt{S_1^2/N_1 + S_2^2/N_2}}$$

$\overline{X}_1$ is the sample mean of Group 1, S_1^2 is the variance, and N_1 is the sample size.

Based on the sampling distribution of the above statistic, one can calculate the probability that a difference at least as large as the one observed would occur if the two population means (μ_1 and μ_2) are equal. This probability is called the *observed significance level*. If the observed significance level is small enough, usually less than 0.05, or 0.01, the hypothesis that the population means are equal is rejected.

The t value and its associated probability are given in Figure 7.1 in the section labeled SEPARATE VARIANCE ESTIMATE. The t value is

$$t = \frac{168.0 - 159.08}{\sqrt{\frac{21.787^2}{50} + \frac{27.564^2}{48}}} = 1.77$$

If $\mu_1 = \mu_2$, the probability of observing a difference at least as large as the one in the sample is estimated to be about 0.08. Since this probability is greater than 0.05, the hypothesis that mean buying scores in the population are equal for the two types of forms is not rejected. The entry under DEGREES OF FREEDOM in Figure 7.1 is a function of the sample size in the two groups and is used together with the t value in establishing the observed significance level.

Another statistic based on the t distribution can be used to test the equality of means hypothesis. This statistic, known as the *pooled-variance* t *test,* is based on the assumption that the population variances in the two groups are equal and is obtained using a pooled estimate of that common variance. The test statistic is identical to the equation for t given previously except that the individual group variances are replaced by a pooled estimate S_p^2. That is,

$$t = \frac{\overline{X}_1 - \overline{X}_2}{\sqrt{S_p^2/N_1 + S_p^2/N_2}}$$

where S_p^2, the pooled variance, is a weighted average of the individual variances and is calculated as

$$S_p^2 = \frac{(N_1 - 1)S_1^2 + (N_2 - 1)S_2^2}{N_1 + N_2 - 2}$$

From the output in Figure 7.1, the pooled t test value for the study is 1.78. The degrees of freedom for the pooled t test are 96, the sum of the sample sizes in both groups minus 2. If the pooled-variance t test is used when the population variances are not equal, the probability level associated with the statistic may be in error. The amount of error depends on the inequality of the sample sizes and of the variances. However, using the separate-variance t value when the population variances are equal will usually result in an observed significance level somewhat larger than it should be. For large samples, the discrepancy between the two methods is small. In general, it is a good idea to use the separate-variance t test whenever you suspect that the variances are unequal.

The statistic used to test the hypothesis that the two population variances are equal is the F value, which is the ratio of the larger sample variance to the smaller. In Figure 7.1, this value is $(27.6^2/21.8^2 = 1.6)$. If the observed significance level for the F test is small, the hypothesis that the population variances are equal is rejected, and the separate-variance t test for means should be used. In this example, the significance level for the F test is large, and thus the pooled-variance t test is appropriate.

7.6
Significance Levels

The commonsense interpretation of a small observed significance level is straightforward: it appears unlikely that the two population means are equal. Of course, there is a possibility that the means are equal and the observed difference is due to chance. The *observed significance level* is the probability that a difference at least as large as the one observed would have arisen if the means were really equal.

When the observed significance level is too large to reject the equality hypothesis, the two population means may indeed be equal, or the means may be unequal but the difference cannot be detected. Failure to detect can be due to a true difference that is very small. For example, if a new cancer drug prolongs survival time by only one day when compared to the standard treatment, it is unlikely that such a difference will be detected, especially if survival times vary substantially and the additional day represents a small increment.

There are other reasons why true differences may not be found. If the sample sizes in the two groups are small or the variability large, even substantial differences may not be detected. Significant t values are obtained when the numerator of the t statistic is large when compared to the denominator. The numerator is the difference between the sample means, and the denominator depends on the standard deviations and sample sizes of the two groups. For a given standard deviation, the larger the sample size, the smaller the denominator. Thus, a difference of a given magnitude may be significant if obtained with a sample size of 100, but not significant with a sample size of 25.

7.7
One-Tailed vs. Two-Tailed Tests

A two-tailed test is used to detect a difference in means between two populations regardless of the direction of the difference. For example, in the study of buying scores presented in this chapter, we are interested in whether buying scores without pictures are larger *or* smaller than buying scores with pictures. In applications where one is interested in detecting a difference in one direction—such as whether a new drug is better than the current treatment—a so-called one-tailed test can be performed. The procedure is the same as for the two-tailed test, but the resulting probability value is divided by 2, adjusting for the fact that the equality hypothesis is rejected only when the difference between the two means is sufficiently large and in the direction of interest. In a two-tailed test, the equality hypothesis is rejected for large positive or negative values of the statistic.

7.8
What's the Difference?

It appears that the questionnaire type has no significant effect on couples' willingness to purchase products. Overall buying scores for the two conditions are similar. Pictures of the products do not appear to enhance their perceived desirability. In fact, the pictures actually appear to make several products somewhat less desirable. However, since the purpose of the questionnaires is to ascertain buying intent, including a picture of the actual product may help gauge true product response. Although the concept of disposable raincoats may be attractive, if they make the owner look like a walking trash bag their appeal may diminish considerably.

7.9
USING PROCEDURE CROSSTABS TO TEST HYPOTHESES

The T-TEST procedure is used to test hypotheses about the equality of two means for variables measured on an interval or ratio scale. Procedure CROSSTABS and the chi-square statistic can be used to test hypotheses about a dichotomous variable, such as purchase of a particular product.

Figure 7.9 is a crosstabulation showing the number of husbands who would definitely want to buy (value 1) vegetables in pop-top cans when shown a picture and when not shown a picture of the product. The vegetables in pop-top cans were chosen by 6.0% of the husbands who were tempted with pictures and 16.0% of the husbands who were not shown pictures. The chi-square statistic provides a test of the hypothesis that the proportion of husbands selecting the vegetables in pop-top cans is the same for the picture and no-picture forms.

Figure 7.9   Husbands preference for vegetables in pop-top cans

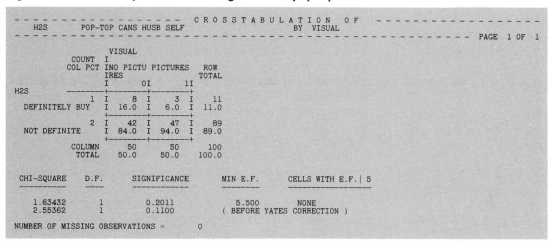

The probability of 0.2011 associated with the chi-square statistic in Figure 7.9 is the probability that a difference at least as large as the one observed would occur in the sample if in the population there were no difference in the selection of the product between the two formats. Since the probability is large, the hypothesis of no difference between the two formats is not rejected.

7.10
INDEPENDENT VS. PAIRED SAMPLES

Several factors contribute to the observed differences in response between two groups. Part of the observed difference in scores between the picture and no-picture formats may be attributable to form type. Another component is due to differences between individuals. Not all couples have the same buying desires, so even if the type of form does not affect buying, differences between the two groups will probably be observed due to differences between the couples within the two groups.

One method of minimizing the influence of individual variation is to choose the two groups so that the couples within them are comparable on characteristics that can influence buying behavior, such as income, education, family size, and so forth.

It is sometimes possible to obtain pairs of subjects, such as twins, and assign one member of each pair to each of the two treatments. Another frequently used experimental design is to expose the same individual to both types of conditions. (In this design, care must be taken to ensure that the sequential administration of treatments does not influence response by providing practice, decreasing attention span, or affecting the second treatment in other ways.) In both designs, subject-to-subject variability has substantially less effect. These designs are called *paired-samples designs,* since for each subject there is a corresponding pair in the other group. In the second design, a person is paired with himself or herself. In an *independent-samples design,* there is no pairing of cases; all observations are independent.

7.11
Analysis of Paired Data

Although the interpretation of the significance of results from paired experiments is the same as those from the two independent samples discussed previously, the actual computations are different. For each pair of cases, the difference in the responses is calculated. The statistic used to test the hypothesis that the mean difference in the population is zero is

$$t = \frac{\overline{D}}{S_D/\sqrt{N}}$$

where $\overline{D}$ is the observed difference between the two means and $S_{\overline{D}}$ is the standard deviation of the differences of the paired observations. The sampling distribution of t, if the differences are normally distributed with a mean of zero, is Student's t with $N-1$ degrees of freedom, where N is the number of pairs. If the pairing is effective, the standard error of the difference will be smaller than the standard error obtained if two independent samples with N subjects each were chosen. However, if the variables chosen for pairing do not affect the responses under study, pairing may result in a test that is less powerful since true differences can be detected less frequently.

For example, to test the hypothesis that there is no difference between husbands' and wives' buying scores, a paired t test should be calculated. A paired test is appropriate since husbands and wives constitute matched observations. Hopefully, including both members of a couple controls for some nuisance effects like socioeconomic status, age, and so forth. The observed differences are more likely to be attributable to differences in sex.

Figure 7.11 contains output from the paired t test. The entry under number of cases is the number of pairs of observations. The mean difference is the difference between the mean scores for males and females. The t value is the mean difference divided by the standard error of the difference (0.55/1.73=0.32). The two-tailed probability for this test is 0.75, so there is insufficient evidence to reject the null hypothesis that married males and females have similar mean buying scores.

Figure 7.11 Husbands' versus wives' buying scores

```
------------------------------------------ T - T E S T --------------------------------------------------

VARIABLE    NUMBER              STANDARD   STANDARD  *(DIFFERENCE) STANDARD   STANDARD   *    2-TAIL  *   T     DEGREES OF 2-TAIL
            OF CASES    MEAN    DEVIATION   ERROR    *   MEAN      DEVIATION   ERROR     * CORR. PROB. * VALUE    FREEDOM   PROB.

HSSCALE   HUSBANDS BUYING SCORE                      *                                  *             *
                      82.0918    14.352     1.450    *                                  *             *
                 98                                  *  0.5510      17.095     1.727     * 0.367 0.000 *  0.32      97      0.750
                      81.5408    15.942     1.610    *                                  *             *
WSSCALE   WIVES BUYING SCORE                         *                                  *             *
```

The correlation coefficient between husbands' and wives' scores is 0.367. A positive correlation indicates that pairing has been effective in decreasing the variability of the mean difference. The larger the correlation coefficient, the greater the benefit of pairing.

7.12
HYPOTHESIS
TESTING: A REVIEW

The purpose of hypothesis testing is to help draw conclusions about population parameters based on results observed in a random sample. The procedure remains virtually the same for tests of most hypotheses.

- A hypothesis of no difference (called a *null hypothesis*) and its alternative are formulated.
- A test statistic is chosen to evaluate the null hypothesis.
- For the sample, the test statistic is calculated.
- The probability, if the null hypothesis is true, of obtaining a test value at least as extreme as the one observed is determined.
- If the observed significance level is judged small enough, the null hypothesis is rejected.

7.13
The Importance of
Assumptions

In order to perform a statistical test of any hypothesis, it is necessary to make certain assumptions about the data. The particular assumptions depend on the statistical test being used. Some procedures require stricter assumptions than others. For *parametric tests,* some knowledge about the distribution from which samples are selected is required.

The assumptions are necessary to define the sampling distribution of the test statistic. Unless the distribution is defined, correct significance levels cannot be calculated. For the pooled t test, the assumption is that the observations are random samples from normal distributions with the same variance.

For many procedures, not all assumptions are equally important. Moderate violation of some assumptions may not always be serious. Therefore, it is important to know for each procedure not only what assumptions are needed but also how severely their violation may influence results. For example the F test for equality of variances is quite sensitive to departures from normality, while the t test for equality of means is less so.

The responsibility for detecting violations of assumptions rests with the researcher. Unfortunately, unlike the experimenter in chemistry, no explosions or disintegrating terminals threaten the investigator who does not comply with good statistical practice. However, from a research viewpoint, the consequences can be just as severe.

Wherever possible, tests of assumptions—often called diagnostic checks of the model—should be incorporated as part of the hypothesis-testing procedures. Throughout SPSS-X, attempts have been made to provide facilities for examining assumptions. For example, in the FREQUENCIES procedure, histograms and measures of skewness and kurtosis provide a convenient check for the normality assumption. Discussion of other such diagnostics is included with the individual procedures.

7.14
RUNNING
PROCEDURE T-TEST

Procedure T-TEST computes the Student's t statistic for testing the significance of a difference in means for independent or paired samples. For independent samples, procedure T-TEST provides both separate- and pooled-variance estimates. See Chapter 18 for a complete list of optional formats and methods of handling missing data.

For independent samples, use the GROUPS subcommand to name the variable and the criterion for dividing the sample into two independent groups and the VARIABLES subcommand to name the variable or variables to be tested. If your grouping variable is already coded with values 1 and 2, you need name only the variable. For example,

```
T-TEST GROUPS=VISUAL /VARIABLES=FAMSCORE
```

assigns cases with value 1 for variable VISUAL into one group and cases with value 2 into the second group. Alternatively, you can specify the values for the two groups, as in:

```
T-TEST GROUPS=VISUAL(0,1) /VARIABLES=FAMSCORE
```

In this case the data are coded 0 for one group and 1 for the other. This command produces the output in Figure 7.1. You can also divide the sample into two groups using the RECODE command. For example, to separate the sample into two income groups for an analysis based on income group rather than type of questionnaire, specify:

```
RECODE   INCOME (1 THRU 7=1) (8 THRU 15=2)
T-TEST   GROUPS=INCOME /VARIABLES=FAMSCORE
```

See Chapter 18 for a more complete discussion of the RECODE command.

To compute tests for paired samples, values for the two members of a pair must be separate variables on the same case. Use one PAIRS subcommand to name the pair or pairs of variables to be compared. For example, to generate the test shown in Figure 7.11, specify:

```
T-TEST  PAIRS=HSSCALE,WSSCALE
```

If you name three or more variables, T-TEST tests all possible pairs. You can use the keyword WITH to pair each variable to the left of the keyword with each variable to the right. For example,

```
T-TEST  PAIRS=TIME1,TIME2 WITH TIME3,TIME4
```

produces four tests: TIME1 with TIME3; TIME1 with TIME4; TIME2 with TIME3; and TIME2 with TIME4.

If you request both independent and paired sample tests on the same T-TEST command, you must specify the independent-samples test first. Thus, the GROUPS subcommand is first, followed by the VARIABLES subcommand and the PAIRS subcommand.

EXERCISES

Syntax

1. In the following T-TEST commands, who is in Group 1? Who is in Group 2?
   a. `T-TEST GROUPS=SHOESIZE(8)/VARIABLES=WEIGHT`
   b. `T-TEST GROUPS=SHOESIZE(1,9)/VARIABLES=WEIGHT`
   c. `T-TEST GROUPS=SHOESIZE/VARIABLES=WEIGHT`

2. Which of the following T-TEST commands contain errors?
   a. `T-TEST  GROUPS=SEX/VARIABLES=HEIGHT/PAIRS=TEST1 TEST2`
   b. `T-TEST  PAIRS=TEST1 TEST2/GROUPS=SEX/VARIABLES=WEIGHT`
   c. `T-TEST PAIRS=SCORE/`
   d. `T-TEST PAIRS=SCORE1 SCORE2 SCORE3/`
   e. `T-TEST GROUPS=SEX(1,2,3)/VARIABLES=WEIGHT`

3. Write the commands that produce the tables in Questions 8.a and 8.b below (Statistical Concepts).

4. You type the following command:

```
T-TEST  WORLD(2) /VARIABLES=NTCPUR
```

and get the following error message:

```
>Error # 11800 on line 7 in column 9.  Text: WORLD
>The T-TEST command includes an unrecognized subcommand.  The recognized
>subcommands are GROUPS, VARIABLES, PAIRS, MISSING, and FORMAT.
>This command not executed.
```

Fix the command.

5. You want to test the hypothesis that Republicans earn more money than Democrats. Write the T-TEST command to test the hypothesis that there is no difference in income between the two parties. Use variables PARTY and INCOME; code Republicans as 1 and Democrats as 2.

6. You want to test the hypothesis that people who meditate can reduce their heart rates and blood pressures. You have measures for the pulse and blood pressure of a group of meditation practitioners before and after they meditate. Test the hypothesis that meditation has no affect on pulse and blood pressure.

Statistical Concepts

1. Which of the following statements are true?
   a. The observed significance level for a *t* test is the probability that the population means are equal.
   b. If the observed significance level is large, you can be fairly sure that the means are exactly equal.
   c. The sample size influences, in part, whether a difference in means is detected.
   d. Small significance levels are associated with *t* values close to zero.
   e. The variance of the sample mean is the square of the standard error of the sample mean.
   f. The larger the sample, the larger the standard error of the sample mean.
   g. The paired *t* test is always more sensitive to true differences in means than is the independent-samples *t* test.
   h. A large positive correlation coefficient for paired variables indicates that pairing is a good strategy.

2. A researcher wants to determine whether a company is releasing, on the average, higher levels of sulfur into the air than are permitted by federal law.
   a. Should she use a one- or a two-tailed test?
   b. Suppose the company is notorious for violating pollution laws. Would it be in the company's interest for the researcher to use a one- or two-tailed test?
   c. If she uses a one-tailed test and the T-TEST output lists a 2-TAIL PROB of .082, what is the observed significance level?

3. If you use a paired *t* test to test the hypothesis that two means are equal and you obtain P=0.0002, is it possible that the two means are equal?

4. The *F* test for equality of variances requires that the two variables being compared be normally distributed.
   a. What SPSS-X procedure would you use to check this assumption?
   b. What output would you obtain from this procedure to check normality?

5. a. What is the null hypothesis for an independent-samples *t* test?
   b. What is the null hypothesis for a paired *t* test?

6. For the following experimental designs, indicate whether an independent-samples or paired *t* test is appropriate:

   a. Weight is obtained for each subject before and after Dr. Nogani's new treatment. The hypothesis to be tested is that the treatment has no effect on weight loss.

   b. The Jenkins Activity Survey is administered to 20 couples. The hypothesis to be tested is that husbands' and wives' scores do not differ.

   c. Elephants are randomly selected from a jungle and Trunkgro1 is administered to one group of elephants and Trunkgro2 to the other. The hypothesis to be tested is that both agents are equally effective in promoting trunk growth.

   d. Subjects are asked their height and then a measurement of height is obtained. The hypothesis to be tested is that self-reported and actual heights do not differ.

   e. Two sleeping pills (Drugs A and B) are given to a sample of insomniacs. The subjects take Drug A during the first week of the study and Drug B during the second week. The total amount of time before falling asleep is recorded for each subject for each week.

7. a. When is the separate-variance *t* test appropriate?

   b. When is the pooled-variance *t* test appropriate?

8. a. The following table is the output from an independent-samples *t* test. Fill in the missing information and interpret the results.

```
- - - - - - - - - - - - - - - - - - - - - - - - - - - - T - T E S T - - - - - - - - - - - - - - - - - - - - - - - - - - - - - - -

GROUP 1 - TYPE      EQ      1.
GROUP 2 - TYPE      EQ      2.
                                                               * POOLED VARIANCE ESTIMATE * SEPARATE VARIANCE ESTIMATE
                                                             *                            *
VARIABLE          NUMBER              STANDARD    STANDARD  *   F    2-TAIL  *    T   DEGREES OF 2-TAIL *    T   DEGREES OF 2-TAIL
                  OF CASES    MEAN    DEVIATION    ERROR    * VALUE   PROB.  *  VALUE   FREEDOM   PROB. *  VALUE   FREEDOM   PROB.
----------------------------------------------------------------------------------------------------------------------------------
RECALL    COMMERCIAL RECALL SCORE                          *                 *                          *
     GROUP 1     66    17.1087     2.804                   *                 *                          *
                                                           *          0.000  *   2.12          0.036    *   2.02   103.96   0.046
     GROUP 2     82    16.3093       .          0.193      *                 *                          *
                                                           *                 *                          *
----------------------------------------------------------------------------------------------------------------------------------
```

b. The following table is the output from a paired-sample test. Fill in the missing information and interpret the results.

```
- - - - - - - - - - - - - - - - - - - - - - - - - - - - T - T E S T - - - - - - - - - - - - - - - - - - - - - - - - - - - - - - -

VARIABLE      NUMBER             STANDARD   STANDARD  *(DIFFERENCE) STANDARD   STANDARD  *     2-TAIL  *    T    DEGREES OF 2-TAIL
              OF CASES    MEAN   DEVIATION   ERROR    *    MEAN     DEVIATION   ERROR    * CORR. PROB. *  VALUE    FREEDOM   PROB.
----------------------------------------------------------------------------------------------------------------------------------
SELF      SELF-REPORTED ARRESTS                       *                                  *             *
                          8.9620   6.458             *                                  *             *
               79                                    *               5.216             * 0.654 0.000 *                     0.621
                          9.2532   6.248             *                                  *             *
ACTUAL    ACTUAL ARRESTS                             *                                  *             *
----------------------------------------------------------------------------------------------------------------------------------
```

Data Analysis

Use the BANK system file for Questions 2–6.

1. Seven patients each underwent three different methods of kidney dialysis (Daugirdas, 1982). The following values were obtained for weight change in kilograms between dialysis sessions:

Patient	Treatment 1	Treatment 2	Treatment 3
1	2.90	2.97	2.67
2	2.56	2.45	2.62
3	2.88	2.76	1.87
4	2.73	2.20	2.33
5	2.50	2.16	1.27
6	3.18	2.89	2.39
7	2.83	2.87	2.39

   a. Using SPSS-X, test the null hypothesis that there is no difference in mean weight change between Treatments 1 and 3 and between Treatments 2 and 3.

   b. Compute a new variable which is the difference in weight gain between Treatments 1 and 3. Using procedure FREQUENCIES, calculate the mean, standard deviation, and standard error for the new variable.

   c. Compare the values obtained in 1.a to those obtained in 1.b.

2. a. Evaluate the overall difference between men and women in beginning salary. Repeat this evaluation for each of the first two job categories (use the SELECT IF command). Is there evidence suggesting that women and men are not equally compensated? Which of these tests is the better comparison?

   b. Repeat the analysis above for the race variable.

   c. What statistical assumptions are you making?

3. For the analysis in Question 2.a, what are some arguments in favor of a one-tailed test? What arguments can you state for a two-tailed test? Which test would you use?

4. Repeat the analysis in Question 2.a, using current salary instead of beginning salary.

5. a. Do the educational backgrounds of women and men appear to be the same? Justify your answer with a statistical analysis.

   b. Obtain histograms of female and male educational levels. How appropriate does a *t* test seem, given the appearance of these histograms? What does the large sample size have to do with the appropriateness of the *t* test?

6. Repeat the analysis in Question 5, comparing the educational backgrounds of nonwhites and whites instead of women and men.

7. Choose one of the data sets from Appendix B and formulate several hypotheses that can be tested using paired- or independent-samples *t* tests. For example, using the Western Electric data, you can test the hypothesis that men who develop coronary heart disease have higher diastolic blood pressure or smoke more than those who do not.

   a. Obtain a separate histogram for the variables to be tested for each of the two groups. In each of the groups, do the data appear to be approximately normally distributed?

   b. Perform the appropriate *t* tests. Indicate whether you would use pooled- or separate-variance *t*-test results and why. Write a paragraph summarizing your findings. Be sure to include a statement about the observed significance level and its interpretation.

   c. Use the chi-square test to test the hypothesis that two proportions are equal. Summarize your findings.

8. Test the null hypothesis that the average number of cigarettes smoked does not differ for men who develop heart disease and those who do not.

9. Repeat Question 8 for the following variables: age at entry, average diastolic blood pressure, years of education, serum cholesterol, and body weight.

10. Write a paragraph describing differences between men who develop coronary heart disease and those who do not.

11. Perform the analyses necessary to determine whether there are differences in the previously described variables for men who have a family history of heart disease and those who do not.

Chapter 8   Lost Inches: Plotting Data

Today the quest for the Fountain of Youth has been replaced by the Search for Slimness. It's almost acceptable to grow old, as long as one remains trim and fit. Programs for weight loss are assuming ever increasing attention, and behavioral psychologists are studying the effectiveness of many different weight-loss strategies. Black and Sherba (1983) studied the effects of two different types of behavior programs on weight loss. One group of subjects was taught behavioral weight-loss techniques, while the second was taught weight-loss techniques and problem-solving behavior. Their data set is examined in this chapter.

8.1
DESCRIBING WEIGHT LOSS

As discussed in Chapter 3, a histogram is a convenient method for displaying the distribution of a variable that can have many values. Figure 8.1a is the percent of excess weight actually lost during the treatment for each of the twelve cases in the study. From this figure we can see that about one third of the participants lost 20% or more of the required weight during treatment. To see if weight loss is maintained, consider Figure 8.1b which is the percent of weight loss one year after treatment. It appears that subjects did not gain back the weight but maintained weight loss.

Figure 8.1a   Histogram of weight loss during treatment

```
TREATRED  REDUCTION QUOTIENT AT TREATMENT

     COUNT    MIDPOINT      ONE SYMBOL EQUALS APPROXIMATELY     .10 OCCURRENCES

         0     -27.50
         4     -22.50    ******************************************
         1     -17.50    **********
         4     -12.50    ******************************************
         1      -7.50    **********
         1      -2.50    **********
         1       2.50    **********
         0       7.50
                         I....+....I....+....I....+....I....+....I....+....I
                         0         1         2         3         4         5
                                        HISTOGRAM FREQUENCY

     VALID CASES       12      MISSING CASES        0
```

Figure 8.1b   Histogram of weight loss after one year

```
TWELVRED  REDUCTION QUOTIENT AT TWELVE MONTHS

     COUNT    MIDPOINT      ONE SYMBOL EQUALS APPROXIMATELY     .10 OCCURRENCES

         3     -45.00    ******************************
         1     -35.00    **********
         1     -25.00    **********
         3     -15.00    ******************************
         2      -5.00    ********************
         2       5.00    ********************
                         I....+....I....+....I....+....I....+....I....+....I
                         0         1         2         3         4         5
                                        HISTOGRAM FREQUENCY

     VALID CASES       12      MISSING CASES        0
```

Although the histograms provide information about the weight loss during treatment and weight loss after twelve months, they reveal nothing about the relationship between the two variables since they each describe single variables. To determine whether lost weight during treatment is maintained or replaced at twelve months, the two variables must be studied together.

Figure 8.1c is a scatterplot of the percent of weight loss during treatment and at one year for the twelve cases. Each symbol 1 on the plot represents one case, showing the values for that case on two variables—loss during treatment and loss at one year. For example, the circled point represents a case with a treatment loss of 25% and a twelve month value of −18%.

Figure 8.1c   Scatterplot for weight loss during treatment and after one year

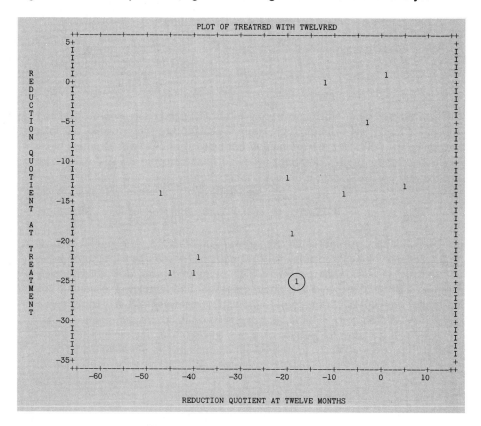

Since plots generated for terminals and printers have a limited number of positions in which to display points, it may not be possible to distinguish cases with similar values for the two variables. When two or more cases with similar values fall on the same point on the scatterplot, a number is displayed indicating how many cases overlap at that point. The scale of the plot depends on the minimum and maximum values for the two variables plotted. If the values for a few cases are far removed from the others, the majority of cases may appear bunched together in order to permit the outlying cases to appear on the same plot.

Figure 8.1d contains the symbols used to represent multiple cases at each point. For example, the symbol D is used when there are 13 coincident points.

Figure 8.1d   Scatterplot symbols for multiple cases

```
Frequencies and symbols used (not applicable for control or overlay plots)
          1 - 1      11 - B      21 - L      31 - V
          2 - 2      12 - C      22 - M      32 - W
          3 - 3      13 - D      23 - N      33 - X
          4 - 4      14 - E      24 - O      34 - Y
          5 - 5      15 - F      25 - P      35 - Z
          6 - 6      16 - G      26 - Q      36 - *
          7 - 7      17 - H      27 - R
          8 - 8      18 - I      28 - S
          9 - 9      19 - J      29 - T
         10 - A      20 - K      30 - U
```

8.2
Controlled Scatterplots

Often it is informative to identify each point on a scatterplot by its value on a third variable. For example, cases may be designated as males or females, or as originating from the West, Midwest, or East. Figure 8.2 is the same plot as Figure 8.1c except each case is identified as being a participant in the behavior program (the value 1) or the problem-solving program (the value 2). A dollar sign is displayed if cases from different groups coincide.

Figure 8.2   Scatterplot identifying the two programs

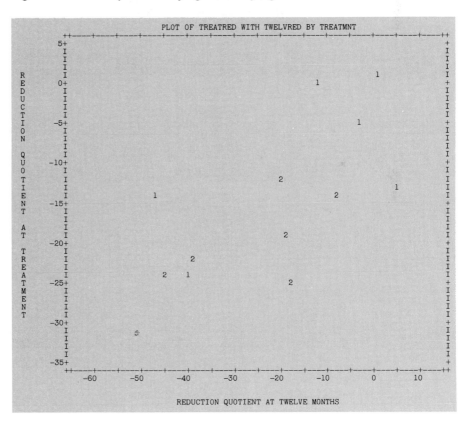

By examining Figure 8.2 one can see if the weight-loss-maintenance relationships are similar for the two groups.

8.3
Plotting Multiple Variables

Weight-loss maintenance may be associated with many variables, including age. Figure 8.3a is a plot of age with weight loss during treatment while Figure 8.3b is a plot of weight loss at twelve months with age. There appears to be a somewhat negative relationship between age and weight loss. Older people appear to have lost a greater percentage of weight than younger ones.

Figure 8.3a   Scatterplot of age with weight loss during treatment

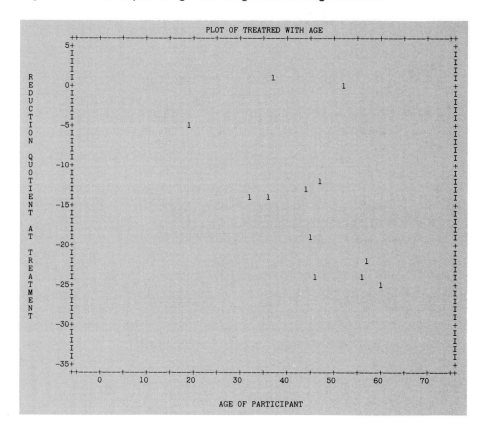

Figures 8.3a and 8.3b can be combined into a single plot as shown in Figure 8.3c Each case appears twice on Figure 8.3c, once with treatment weight loss (denoted as 1) and once with twelve month loss (denoted as 2). When there are several cases with similar ages one cannot tell which are the matching points. For example, at age 36, there are four points since there are two cases with similar ages (one is 36, one is 35). The $ which is displayed represents multiple occurrences at a given location. However, we cannot tell if these are the two values for the same case, or one value from one case, and one from another.

Figure 8.3b   Scatterplot of age with weight loss at twelve months

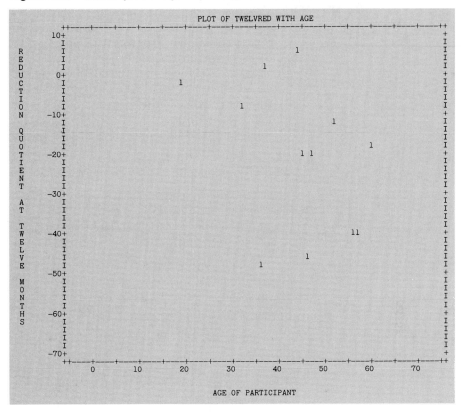

Figure 8.3c   Overlay plot of weight loss during treatment and at twelve months

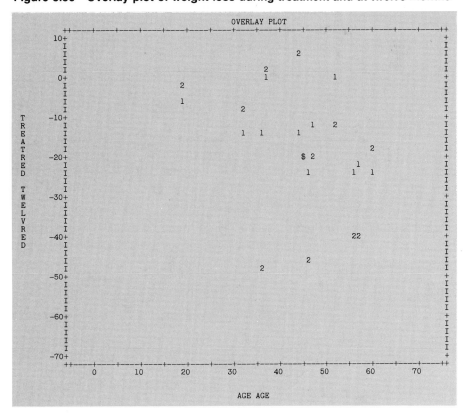

8.4
RUNNING
PROCEDURE PLOT

You can use the PLOT procedure to obtain bivariate scatterplots or regression plots (with or without control variables), contour plots, overlay plots, and some regression statistics. (For complete regression analysis, use procedure REGRESSION, described in Chapter 13.) Formatting options enable you to control axis size and scale, the plotting symbols used, and the frequency they represent. You can also label the plot and axes, request reference lines, and plot standardized variables. The following sections provide a brief overview of these available options. See Chapter 18 for more detail. Also see Chapter 18 for information on assigning plot titles and handling missing values in procedure PLOT.

8.5
Specifying the Variables

Use the PLOT subcommand to specify the variables to be plotted. Variables to be plotted on the vertical (Y) axis are specified first, followed by the WITH keyword, followed by the variables to be plotted on the horizontal (X) axis.

By default, PLOT produces bivariate scatterplots. For example, the following command produces the output in Figure 8.1c:

```
PLOT PLOT=TREATRED WITH TWELVRED
```

You can produce multiple plots with one PLOT subcommand. For example, the command

```
PLOT PLOT=IQ GRE WITH GPA SAT
```

produces four plots: IQ with GPA, IQ with SAT, GRE with GPA, and GRE with SAT.

You can also specify plots of individual pairs of variables on one PLOT subcommand by using the PAIR keyword. For example, the command

```
PLOT PLOT=IQ GRE WITH GPA SAT (PAIR)
```

produces two plots: IQ with GPA and GRE with SAT.

A control variable or contour variable (see Section 8.6) can be specified on the PLOT subcommand by naming it after the BY keyword following the list of horizontal-axis variables. For example, the command

```
PLOT PLOT=TREATRED WITH TWELVRED BY TREATMNT
```

was used to obtain the plot in Figure 8.2. Only one control or contour variable can be specified on a plot list. PLOT uses the first character of a control variable's value label as a plotting symbol. For example, if SEX is the control variable, with value labels FEMALE and MALE, the observations for females are represented by F and those for males by M. If a variable has no value labels, the first character of the actual value is used as the plotting symbol. When cases with different values for the control variable fall in the same position on the plot, they are represented by a single $.

8.6
Choosing the Type of Plot

Use the FORMAT subcommand to specify the type of plot you want to produce. Four types of plots are available: scatterplots, regression plots, contour plots, and overlay plots. If FORMAT is not used, or is used without further specification, scatterplots are displayed. To specify plot type, use the following keywords on the FORMAT subcommand.

DEFAULT   *Bivariate scatterplot.* When there are no control variables each symbol represents the case count at that plot position. When a control variable is specified, each symbol represents the first character of the value label of the control variable.

REGRESSION   *Scatterplot plus regression statistics.* The vertical-axis variable is regressed on the horizontal-axis variable, and the regression line intercepts on each axis are indicated with the letter R. In a control plot, regression statistics are pooled over all categories.

CONTOUR(n)   *Contour plot with* n *levels.* Contour plots use a continuous variable as the control variable. The control variable is specified after BY on the PLOT subcommand. The contour variable is recoded into *n* intervals of equal width. Up to 35 contour levels can be specified. If *n* is omitted, the default is 10 levels.

OVERLAY   *Overlay plots.* All plots specified on the next PLOT subcommand are displayed in one plot frame. A unique plotting symbol is used for each overlaid plot. An additional symbol indicates multiple plot points at the same position. Control plots cannot be overlaid.

For more information on these keywords, refer to Chapter 18.

Specify the FORMAT subcommand before the PLOT subcommand to which it refers. One FORMAT subcommand can be specified before each PLOT subcommand.

For example, the command

```
PLOT FORMAT=OVERLAY
 /PLOT=TREATRED TWELVRED WITH AGE
```

produces the overlay plot in Figure 8.3c.

Overlay plots are useful when several variables represent the same type of measurement or when the same variable is measured at different times. For example, the command

```
PLOT SYMBOLS='MD'
 /VSIZE=30 /HSIZE=70
 /FORMAT=OVERLAY
 /TITLE 'MARRIAGE AND DIVORCE RATES  1900-1981'
 /VERTICAL='RATES PER 1000 POPULATION'
 /HORIZONTAL='YEAR' REFERENCE (1918,1945) MIN (1900) MAX (1983)
 /PLOT=MARRATE DIVRATE WITH YEAR
```

produces the overlay plot of marriage and divorce rates over time shown in Figure 8.6a (data taken from the *Information Please Almanac*, 1983).

Figure 8.6a An overlay plot

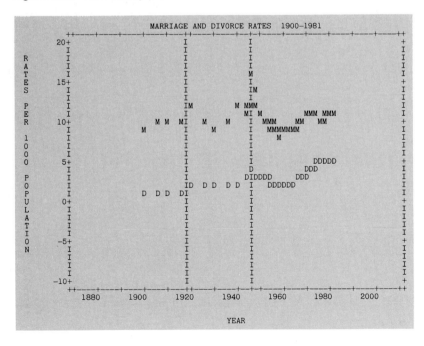

Contour plots evaluate the effect of a continuous variable as a control variable. If you use symbols with different degrees of density, you can produce a visual representation of the density of your contour variable. For example, the command

```
PLOT FORMAT=CONTOUR (10)
 /HSIZE=100/VSIZE=60
 /SYMBOLS='.-=*+OXOXM','          -OW'
 /TITLE='SOLUBILITY OF AMMONIA IN WATER'
 /HORIZONTAL='ATMOSPHERIC PRESSURE'
 /VERTICAL='TEMPERATURE'
 /PLOT=TEMP WITH PRESSURE BY CONCENT
```

produces the output in Figure 8.6b, representing the concentration of ammonia in water under varying conditions of temperature and atmospheric pressure.

Figure 8.6b   A contour plot

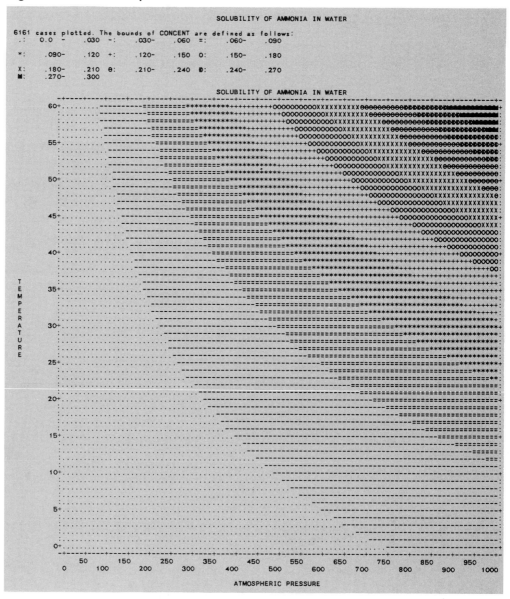

Plots with regression statistics are described and shown in Chapter 9.

8.7
Setting Plot Symbols

A wide range of alphabetical, numeric, and overprint characters are available as plot symbols. Use the CUTPOINT and SYMBOLS subcommands to control the display of plot symbols.

The CUTPOINT subcommand specifies the number of cases represented by plotting symbols. By default, the symbol 1 represents one case at a position, the symbol 2 represents two cases at a position, and the symbol 3 represents three or more cases at a position. You can modify the number of cases the symbols 1, 2, and 3 represent by specifying keyword EVERY (to define frequency intervals for each symbol) or a value list (to define specific cutpoints). For example, if the command

```
PLOT CUTPOINT=EVERY(4)
 /PLOT=SCORE WITH ANXIETY
```

is used, one to four cases in the same position are represented by a 1, five to eight cases by a 2, and so on. If the command

```
PLOT CUTPOINT=(5,10,25)
 /PLOT=SCORE WITH ANXIETY
```

is used, one to five cases in the same position are represented by a 1, six to ten cases by a 2, 11 to 25 cases by a 3, and more than 25 cases by a 4.

CUTPOINT can be used only once on a PLOT command and applies to all plots requested. The CUTPOINT subcommand cannot be used for control plots, overlay, or contour plots.

The SYMBOLS subcommand allows you to choose other plotting symbols to represent a plot position. For scatterplots and regression plots, each symbol represents the number of cases at a plot position. For overlay plots, each symbol represents one of the overlaid plots. For contour plots, each symbol represents one level of the contour variable.

On SYMBOLS you specify keyword ALPHANUMERIC (for alphanumeric plotting symbols), NUMERIC (for numeric plotting symbols), or a list of plotting symbols. If you use the SYMBOLS subcommand, a table of symbols and their equivalents like the one shown in Figure 8.1d is displayed. If you omit the SYMBOLS subcommand, the default alphanumeric symbol set is used.

For example, the command

```
PLOT CUTPOINTS=(1,2,3,4)
 /SYMBOLS='.:x*X'
 /PLOT=INCOME WITH ASTRSIGN
```

requests a scatterplot with a period (.) representing one case at a position, a colon (:) representing two cases, x representing three cases, an asterisk (*) representing four cases, and X representing five or more cases.

The SYMBOLS subcommand can be used only once on a PLOT command and applies to all plots requested. SYMBOLS cannot be used with control plots.

8.8
Scaling and Labeling Plot Axes

The VERTICAL and HORIZONTAL subcommands allow you to control the scaling and labeling of the vertical and horizontal axes, obtain reference lines at specified positions, specify minimum and maximum values, and obtain plots of standardized variables. Resetting minimum or maximum values is especially useful when you want to focus on a subset of a larger plot. Standardized plots are appropriate when you want to overlay plots of variables with very different scales.

The VERTICAL and HORIZONTAL subcommands can be used once before each PLOT subcommand and apply to all plots specified in the following PLOT subcommand. See Chapter 18 for the keywords available with these subcommands.

8.9
Setting the Plot Size

The VSIZE and HSIZE subcommands control the height and width, respectively, of the plot. The default size of the PLOT depends on the current page size (see Chapter 18 for defaults). These subcommands override the page size set on the SET command. For example, the command

```
PLOT VSIZE=30/HSIZE=45
 /PLOT=SALES WITH REP DISTRICT
```

requests a height of 30 lines and a width of 45 positions for the plots of SALES with REP and SALES with DISTRICT.

The VSIZE and HSIZE subcommands can be used only once: all plots requested are then drawn to the specified size.

EXERCISES

Syntax

1. Write the appropriate command to obtain a plot of INCOME and AGE. Put values of INCOME on the vertical axis.

2. How would you change the command in Question 1 so that INCOME is on the horizontal axis?

3. Write the command to identify each of the points on the INCOME and AGE plot as males or females (variable SEX).

4. Correct the errors in the following PLOT commands:
   a. PLOT SBP BY AGE
   b. PLOT SPB WITH AGE
   c. PLOT PLOT SBP WITH AGE BY SEX(1,2)
   d. PLOT PLOT AGE BY SEX WITH SBP

5. You run the PLOT procedure and obtain the following error messages. Explain the error messages and indicate how you would correct the mistake.

```
>ERROR   14104 LINE   4, COLUMN  6, TEXT: EDUC
>An illegal subcommand has been specified.  The valid subcommands are: MISSING,
>HSIZE, VSIZE, CUTPOINT, SYMBOL, TITLE, HORIZONTAL, VERTICAL, FORMAT and PLOT.
>THIS COMMAND NOT EXECUTED.


>ERROR   14102
>'PLOT' must be the last subcommand.
```

Statistical Concepts

1. Indicate whether you would use the CROSSTABS procedure, the MEANS procedure, or the PLOT procedure to display the relationship between the following pairs of variables:
   a. Job satisfaction and income measured in dollars.
   b. Race and marital status.
   c. Systolic blood pressure and age.
   d. Husband's highest degree and wife's highest degree.
   e. Hours studied for an examination and letter grade on the exam.
   f. Miles per gallon that a car gets and its weight in pounds.

2. Describe the relationships between the variables in the following plots:

a.

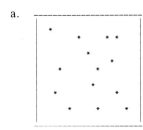

c.

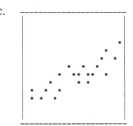

b.

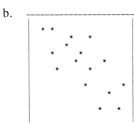

d.

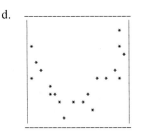

3. The following table contains age at first marriage, years of education, and sex for five people. Plot these values, identifying whether each is for a male or female.

AGEWED	EDUC	SEX
18	12	Male
22	13	Female
30	16	Male
16	10	Male
25	18	Female

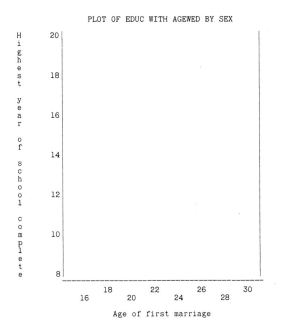

Data Analysis

1. Use the BANK data file for the following questions:

   a. Obtain a plot of current salary and educational level. Describe the relationship if any.

   b. Obtain separate plots of current salary and educational level for males and females. Does the relationship appear to be similar?

   c. Select several pairs of variables whose relationship you might examine using the PLOT procedure. Analyze the variables you have selected and write a brief paragraph summarizing your results.

2. Use the Western Electric data file for the following questions:

   a. Obtain a plot of serum cholesterol and weight. Write a brief paragraph describing any relationship you might see.

   b. Repeat question (a) obtaining separate plots for men who developed CHD and those who did not. Do the relationships, if any, appear similar?

   c. Select several pairs of variables and examine their relationship using the plot procedure. Write a paragraph summarizing your results.

Chapter 9 Making Sales Click: Measuring Linear Association

Youthful lemonade-stand entrepreneurs as well as balding executives of billion-dollar corporations share a common concern—increasing sales. Hand-lettered signs affixed to neighborhood trees, television campaigns, siblings and friends canvassing local playgrounds, and international sales forces are known to be effective tactics. However, the impact of various intertwined factors on sales can be difficult to isolate, and much effort in the business world is expended on determining exactly what makes a product sell.

Churchill (1979) describes a study undertaken by the manufacturer of Click ball-point pens on the effectiveness of the firm's marketing efforts. A random sample of forty sales territories is selected, and sales, amount of advertising, and number of sales representatives are recorded. This chapter looks at the relationship between sales and these variables.

9.1 EXAMINING RELATIONSHIPS

Figure 9.1a is a scatterplot of the amount of sales and the number of television spots in each of forty territories. A scatterplot can reveal various types of associations between two variables. Figure 9.1b contains some commonly encountered patterns. In the first panel there appears to be no discernible relationship between the two variables. The variables are related exponentially in the second panel. That is, Y increases very rapidly for increasing values of X. In the third panel, the relationship between the two variables is U-shaped. Small and large values of the X variable are associated with large values of the Y variable.

From Figure 9.1a there appears to be a positive association between sales and advertising. That is, as the amount of advertising increases, so does the number of sales. The relationship between sales and advertising may also be termed *linear,* since the observed points cluster more or less around a straight line.

Figure 9.1a   Scatterplot showing a linear relationship

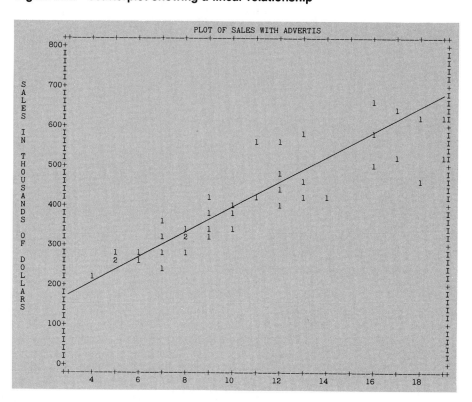

Figure 9.1b   Some common relationships

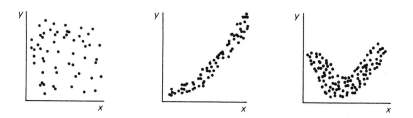

9.2
THE CORRELATION
COEFFICIENT

Although a scatterplot is an essential first step in studying the association between two variables, it is often useful to quantify the strength of the association by calculating a summary index. One commonly used measure is the Pearson correlation coefficient, denoted by r. It is defined as

$$r = \frac{\sum_{i=1}^{N} (X_i - \bar{X})(Y_i - \bar{Y})}{(N-1)S_X S_Y}$$

where N is the number of cases and S_x and S_y are the standard deviations of the two variables. The absolute value of r indicates the strength of the linear relationship. The largest possible absolute value is 1, which occurs when all points fall exactly on the line. When the line has a positive slope, the value of *r* is positive, and when the slope of the line is negative, the value of *r* is negative (see Figure 9.2a).

Figure 9.2a   Scatterplots with correlation coefficients of +1 and −1

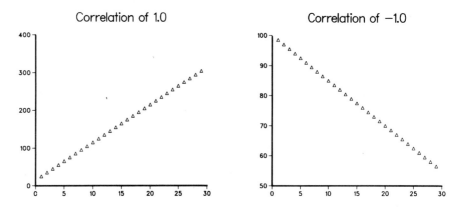

A value of 0 indicates no *linear* relationship. Two variables can have a strong association but a small correlation coefficient if the relationship is not linear. Figure 9.2b shows two plots with zero correlation.

Figure 9.2b   Scatterplots with correlation coefficients of zero

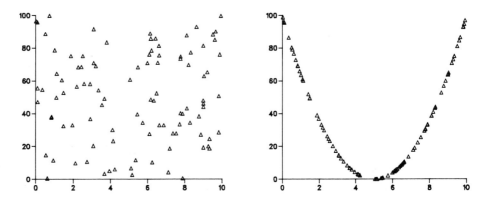

It is important to examine correlation coefficients together with scatterplots since the same coefficient can result from very different underlying relationships. The variables plotted in Figure 9.2c have a correlation coefficient greater than 0.8, as do the variables plotted in Figure 9.1a. But note how different the relationships are between the two sets of variables. In Figure 9.2c there is a strong positive linear association only for part of the graph. The relationship between the two variables is basically nonlinear. The scatterplot in Figure 9.1a is very different. The points cluster more or less around a line. Thus, the correlation coefficient should be used only to summarize the strength of linear association.

Figure 9.2c   Scatterplot of percentage no facial hair with year

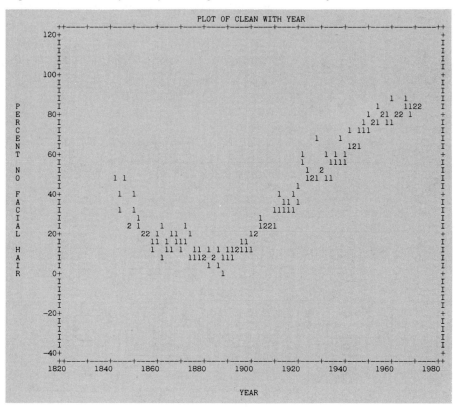

9.3
Some Properties of the Correlation Coefficient

A common mistake in interpreting the correlation coefficient is to assume that correlation implies causation. No such conclusion is automatic. While sales are highly correlated with advertising, they are also highly correlated with other variables, such as the number of sales representatives in a territory. Advertising alone does not necessarily result in increased sales. For example, territories with high sales may simply have more money to spend on TV spots, regardless of whether the spots are effective.

The correlation coefficient is a symmetric measure since interchanging the two variables X and Y in the formula does not change the results. The correlation coefficient is not expressed in any units of measure, and it is not affected by linear transformations such as adding or subtracting constants or multiplying or dividing all values of a variable by a constant.

9.4
Calculating Correlation Coefficients

Figure 9.4 is a table of correlation coefficients for the number of television spots, number of sales representatives, and amount of sales. The entry in each cell is the correlation coefficient. For example, the correlation coefficient between advertising and sales is .8802. This value indicates that there is a fairly strong linear association between the two variables, as shown in Figure 9.1a. The table is symmetric since the correlation between X and Y is the same as the correlation between Y and X. The values on the diagonal are all 1 since a variable is perfectly related to itself. The sample size and significance levels are displayed after the table. In this example, 40 cases were used in all computations since all territories had values for the three variables.

Figure 9.4   Correlation coefficients

```
              ADVERTIS    REPS       SALES

ADVERTIS      1.0000      .7763      .8802
              (    40)    (    40)   (    40)
              P= .        P= .000    P= .000

REPS           .7763     1.0000      .8818
              (    40)    (    40)   (    40)
              P= .000     P= .       P= .000

SALES          .8802      .8818     1.0000
              (    40)    (    40)   (    40)
              P= .000     P= .000    P= .

(COEFFICIENT / (CASES) / 1-TAILED SIG)          " . " IS PRINTED IF A COEFFICIENT CANNOT BE COMPUTED
```

9.5
Hypothesis Tests about the Correlation Coefficient

Although the correlation coefficient is sometimes used only as a summary index to describe the observed strength of the association, in some situations description and summary are but a first step. The primary goal may be to test hypotheses about the unknown population correlation coefficient—denoted as ρ—based on its estimate, the sample correlation coefficient r. In order to test such hypotheses, certain assumptions must be made about the underlying joint distribution of the two variables. A common assumption is that independent random samples are taken from a distribution in which the two variables are together distributed normally. If this condition is satisfied, the test that the population coefficient is 0 can be based on the statistic

$$t = r\sqrt{\frac{N-2}{1-r^2}}$$

which, if $\rho=0$, has a Student's t distribution with $N-2$ degrees of freedom. Either one- or two-tailed tests can be calculated. If nothing is known in advance, a two-tailed test is appropriate. That is, the hypothesis that the coefficient is zero is rejected for both extreme positive and extreme negative values of t. If the direction of the association can be specified in advance, the hypothesis is rejected only for t values that are of sufficient magnitude and in the direction specified.

From Figure 9.4, the probability that a correlation coefficient of at least 0.88 is obtained when there is no linear association in the population between sales and advertising is less than 0.001. Care should be exercised when examining the significance levels for large tables. Even if there is no association between the variables, if many coefficients are computed some would be expected to be statistically significant by chance alone.

Special procedures must be employed to test more general hypotheses of the form $\rho=\rho_0$ where ρ_0 is a constant. If the assumptions of bivariate normality appear unreasonable, a variety of *nonparametric* measures, which make limited assumptions about the underlying distributions of the variables, can be calculated. See Chapter 12 for further discussion.

9.6
Correlation Matrices and Missing Data

For a variety of reasons, data files frequently contain incomplete observations. Respondents in surveys scrawl illegible responses or refuse to answer certain questions. Laboratory animals die before experiments are completed. Patients fail to keep scheduled clinic appointments.

Analysis of data with missing values is troublesome. Before even considering possible strategies, you should determine whether there is evidence that the missing-value pattern is not random. That is, are there reasons to believe that missing values for a variable are related to the values of that variable or other variables? For example, people with low incomes may be less willing to report their financial status than more affluent people. This may be even more pronounced for people who are poor but highly educated.

One simple method of exploring such possibilities is to subdivide the data into two groups—those observations with missing data on a variable and those with complete data—and examine the distributions of the other variables in the file across these two groups. The SPSS-X procedures CROSSTABS and T-TEST are particularly useful for this. For a discussion of more sophisticated methods for detecting nonrandomness, see Frane (1976).

If it appears that the data are not missing randomly, use great caution in attempting to analyze the data. It may be that no satisfactory analysis is possible, especially if there are only a few cases.

If you are satisfied that the missing data are random, several strategies are available. First, if the same few variables are missing for most cases, exclude those variables from the analysis. Since this luxury is not usually available, you can alternatively keep all variables but eliminate the cases with missing values on any of them. This is termed *listwise* missing-value treatment since a case is eliminated if it has a missing value on any variable in the list.

If many cases have missing data for some variables, listwise missing-value treatment could eliminate too many cases and leave you with a very small sample. One common technique is to calculate the correlation coefficient between a pair of variables based on all cases with complete information for the two variables regardless of whether the cases have missing data on any other variable. For example, if a case has values only for variables 1, 3, and 5, it is used only in computations involving variable pairs 1 and 3, 1 and 5, and 3 and 5. This is *pairwise* missing-value treatment.

9.7
Choosing Pairwise Missing-Value Treatment

Several problems can arise with pairwise matrices, one of which is inconsistency. There are some relationships between coefficients that are impossible but may occur when different cases are used to estimate different coefficients. For example, if age and weight and age and height have a high positive correlation, it is impossible in the same sample for height and weight to have a high negative correlation. However, if the same cases are not used to estimate all three coefficients, such an anomaly can occur.

There is no single sample size that can be associated with a pairwise matrix since each coefficient can be based on a different number of cases. Significance levels obtained from analyses based on pairwise matrices must be viewed with caution since little is known about hypothesis testing in such situations.

It should be emphasized that missing-value problems should not be treated lightly. You should base your decision on careful examination of the data and not leave the choices up to system defaults.

9.8
THE REGRESSION LINE

If there is a linear relationship between two variables, a straight line can be used to summarize the data. When the correlation coefficient is +1 or −1, little thought is needed to determine the line that best describes the data: the line passes through all of the observations. When the observations are less highly correlated, many different lines can be drawn to represent the data.

One of the most commonly used procedures for fitting a line to the observations is the method of *least squares*. This method results in a line that minimizes the sum of squared vertical distances from the data points to the line.

The equation for the straight line that relates predicted sales to advertising is

PREDICTED SALES = a + b(ADVERTISING)

The intercept, *a*, is the predicted sales when there is no advertising. The slope, *b*, is the change in predicted sales for a unit change in advertising. That is, it is the amount of change in sales per television spot.

The actual values of *a* and *b* calculated with the method of least squares are printed as part of the SPSS-X PLOT output (see Figure 9.8). The least-squares equation for the line is

PREDICTED SALES = 135.4 + 25.31(ADVERTISING)

Figure 9.1a shows this regression line.

Figure 9.8   Intercept and slope from PLOT

```
     40 cases plotted. Regression statistics of SALES on ADVERTIS:
Correlation  .88016 R Squared  .77467  S.E. of Est  59.56023  2-tailed Sig.  .0000
Intercept(S.E.)  135.43360( 25.90649)  Slope(S.E.)  25.30770(  2.21415)
```

For each pair of variables, two different regression lines can be calculated, since the values of the slope and intercept depend on which variable is dependent (the one being predicted) and which is independent (the one used for prediction). In the SPSS-X PLOT output, the variable plotted on the vertical axis is considered the dependent variable in the calculation of statistics.

9.9
Prediction

Based on the regression equation, it is possible to predict sales from advertising. For example, a territory with 10 television spots per month is expected to have sales of about $388,400 (135.4 + 25.3(10)). Considerable caution is needed when predictions are made for values of the independent variable which are much larger or much smaller than those used to derive the equation. A relationship which is linear for the observed range of values may not be linear everywhere. For example, estimating *Y* values for the beginning of Figure 9.2c based on a regression line for the latter part of the plot would result in a very poor fit.

The difference between observed sales and sales predicted by the model is called a *residual*. The residual for a territory with 10 television spots and observed sales of 403.6 is 15.2:

RESIDUAL = OBSERVED − PREDICTED
= 403.6 − 388.4 = 15.2

Residuals can be calculated for each of the sales territories. Figure 9.9 contains the observed value (SALES), the predicted value (*PRED), and the residual for the first 10 territories (*RESID). The residuals provide an idea of how well the calculated regression line actually fits the data.

Figure 9.9   Residuals from the regression line

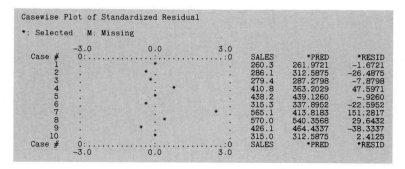

```
Casewise Plot of Standardized Residual

*: Selected   M: Missing

        -3.0          0.0          3.0
Case #   0:...................:...................:0    SALES      *PRED      *RESID
   1     .              *                        .     260.3    261.9721    -1.6721
   2     .                    *                  .     286.1    312.5875   -26.4875
   3     .                   *                   .     279.4    287.2798    -7.8798
   4     .                        *              .     410.8    363.2029    47.5971
   5     .                    *                  .     438.2    439.1260     -.9260
   6     .                  *                    .     315.3    337.8952   -22.5952
   7     .                              *        .     565.1    413.8183   151.2817
   8     .                      *                .     570.0    540.3568    29.6432
   9     .                *                      .     426.1    464.4337   -38.3337
  10     .                   *                   .     315.0    312.5875     2.4125
Case #   0:...................:...................:0    SALES      *PRED      *RESID
        -3.0          0.0          3.0
```

9.10
Goodness of Fit

Although the regression line is a useful summary of the relationship between two variables, the values of the slope and intercept alone do little to indicate how well the line actually fits the data. A goodness-of-fit index is needed.

The observed variation in the dependent variable can be subdivided into two components: the variation "explained" by the regression and the residual from the regression, or

TOTAL SS = REGRESSION SS + RESIDUAL SS

The *total sum of squares* is a measure of overall variation and is given by

$$\text{TOTAL SUM OF SQUARES} = \sum_{i=1}^{N} (Y_i - \overline{Y})^2$$

The total sum of squares for sales is 598,253. (It is N-1 times the variance.)

The *regression sum of squares*, or the sum of squares due to regression, is

$$\text{REGRESSION SUM OF SQUARES} = \sum_{i=1}^{N} (\hat{Y}_i - \overline{Y})^2$$

where $\hat{Y}_i$ is the predicted value for the ith case. The regression sum of squares is a measure of how much variability in the dependent variable is attributable to the linear relationship between the two variables. For this example, the regression sum of squares is 463,451.

The *residual sum of squares*, sometimes called the error sum of squares, is obtained by squaring each of the residuals and then summing them.

$$\text{RESIDUAL SUM OF SQUARES} = \sum_{i=1}^{N} (Y_i - \hat{Y}_i)^2$$

The residual sum of squares for sales is 134,802. The standard deviation of the residuals, called the standard error of the estimate, is

$$\text{SEE} = \sqrt{\frac{\text{RESIDUAL SUM OF SQUARES}}{N - 2}} = \sqrt{\frac{134,802}{38}} = 59.56$$

The standard error is displayed in Figure 9.8.

The proportion of the variation in the dependent variable that is *explained* by the linear regression is computed by comparing the total sum of squares and the regression sum of squares:

$$r^2 = \frac{\text{REGRESSION SUM OF SQUARES}}{\text{TOTAL SUM OF SQUARES}} = \frac{463,451}{598,253} = 0.775$$

If there is no linear association in the sample, the value of r^2 is 0 since the predicted values are just the mean of the dependent variable and the regression sum of squares is 0. If Y and X are perfectly linearly related, the residual sum of squares is 0 and r^2 is 1. The square root of r^2 is r, the Pearson correlation coefficient between the two variables.

9.11
Further Topics in Regression

In this chapter, only the most basic concepts in regression analysis are discussed. Chapter 13 contains detailed descriptions of simple two-variable regression as well as multiple regression analysis.

9.12
RUNNING
PROCEDURE
CORRELATION

The CORRELATION (alias PEARSON CORR) procedure calculates Pearson product-moment correlations for pairs of variables. The display includes the coefficient (r), an indication of significance level, and the number of cases upon which the coefficients are computed. Means, standard deviations, crossproduct deviations, and covariances are available. The following paragraphs provide a brief overview of CORRELATION's available options. See Chapter 18 for more detail. Also see Chapter 18 for information on the optional formats and methods of handling missing values available in procedure CORRELATION.

The VARIABLES subcommand lists all variables to be included in the correlation matrix. For example, to produce the correlation matrix shown in Figure 9.4, specify

```
CORRELATION VARIABLES=ADVERTIS REPS SALES
```

The actual keyword VARIABLES can be omitted.

The order in which you name the variables is the order in which they are displayed. Use the keyword WITH to obtain the correlations of one set of variables with another set. For example, the command

```
CORRELATION VARIABLES=ADVERTIS WITH REPS SALES
```

produces two correlations, ADVERTIS with REPS and ADVERTIS with SALES. You can specify several analysis lists by separating them with slashes.

Only numeric variables can be named on the VARIABLES subcommand. Long or short string variables on an analysis list will prevent execution of CORRELATION.

By default, CORRELATIONS prints Pearson correlation coefficients based on a one-tailed test. The PRINT subcommand switches to a two-tailed test and/or suppresses the display of the number of cases and the significance level. For example

```
CORRELATION VARIABLES=ADVERTIS REPS SALES
 /PRINT=TWOTAIL
```

prints Pearson correlation coefficients based on a two-tailed test.

The correlation coefficient, number of cases, and significance level are automatically printed for every combination of variable pairs in the variable list. The STATISTICS subcommand obtains additional statistics. Keyword DESCRIP-TIVES obtains the mean, standard deviation, and number of nonmissing cases for each variable, and keyword XPROD obtains cross-product deviations and covariance for each pair of variables. Figure 9.12 shows the mean, standard deviation, and number of nonmissing cases for each variable. The following command produces the statistics shown in Figure 9.12:

```
CORRELATIONS VARIABLES=ADVERTIS REP SALES
 /STATISTICS=DESCRIPTIVES
```

Figure 9.12 Univariate statistics

VARIABLE	CASES	MEAN	STD DEV
ADVERTIS	40	10.9000	4.3074
REPS	40	5.0000	1.6486
SALES	40	411.2875	123.8540

EXERCISES

Syntax

1. Write the SPSS-X command to obtain correlation coefficients and two-tailed significance levels for all pairs of the following variables: MONEY, INVEST, SALARY, and WEALTH.

2. Correct the errors in the following commands:
   a. `CORRELATIONS  VARIABLES= A B C D /PRINT=SERIAL`
   b. `CORRELATIONS ONE TWO THREE MANY /XPROD`
   c. `CORRELATIONS VAR=AGE`
   d. `CORRELATIONS ONE TWO MANY / SIG = 2`

3. Correct the errors in the following commands:
   a. `PLOT PLOT DEP WITH INDEP / FORMAT REGRESSION`
   b. `PLOT FOR=REG / DEP WITH INDEP`
   c. `PLOT PLOT FORMAT REG / FATIGUE BY HOMEWORK`
   d. `PLOT  PLOT FORMAT=NOREG / PLOT= GRADE WITH EFFORT`

4. Write the SPSS-X commands to obtain a plot of AGEDEATH and EDUCATION. Obtain the regression statistics, with age at death being the dependent variable and years of education the independent variable.

5. Repeat the previous analysis with education as the dependent variable and age at death as the independent variable.

Statistical Concepts

1. For the following pairs of variables, would you expect the correlation coefficient to be positive, negative, or zero?
   a. A person's total family income and his neighbor's total family income.
   b. Number of registered voters in a district and the number voting on election day.
   c. Number of cigarettes smoked and lung function.
   d. Calories consumed and weight.
   e. Altitude and mean temperature.
   f. Gross national product and infant mortality rate.
   g. Age at first marriage and years of education.
   h. Number of cars in a household and total family income.

2. A medical researcher studying the relationship between two variables finds a correlation coefficient of 0.02. She concludes that there is no relationship between the two variables. Do you agree or disagree with her conclusion? Why?

3. A mail-order house is interested in studying the relationship between income and type of product purchased. They take a random sample of orders, and then they call people to determine family income. They then calculate the correlation

coefficient between income and product code. The value is 0.76, and the two-tailed observed significance level is 0.03. Based on this study, what can you conclude about the relationship between income and type of product purchased? Explain.

4. A dental association is studying the relationship between ounces of orange juice consumed per week and yearly family dental bill. They find a large positive coefficient, with an observed significance level of less than .01. What do you think of their conclusion that orange juice causes tooth decay? Discuss other possible explanations for their findings.

5. A friend of yours is analyzing the relationships among large numbers of variables. He's decided that the best strategy is to compute correlation coefficients among all of them and see which relationships appear to be significant. Advise him on issues he must consider when using the correlation coefficient to describe the relationships between variables.

6. The correlation coefficient between variables A and B is 0.62. For variables C and D, it is −.62. Which of the pairs of variables is more strongly related?

7. An educator wishes to study the relationship between father's and son's educational attainment. Five hundred randomly selected fathers of sons are interviewed and the years of education are recorded for both fathers and sons. Since a fairly high proportion of "Unknown" responses was obtained, the educator divides the education variables into two groups and obtains the following table:

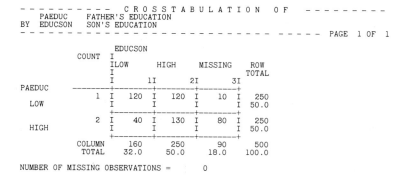

```
- - - - - - - - - - -   C R O S S T A B U L A T I O N   O F   - - - - - - - - -
      PAEDUC     FATHER'S EDUCATION
BY  EDUCSON    SON'S EDUCATION
- - - - - - - - - - - - - - - - - - - - - - - - -  - - - - -  PAGE  1 OF  1
                         EDUCSON
                 COUNT I
                       ILOW       HIGH      MISSING    ROW
                       I                               TOTAL
                       I          1I        2I     3I
      PAEDUC    -------+---------+---------+---------+
                   1 I   120  I   120  I    10  I    250
        LOW        I        I        I        I    50.0
                   +---------+---------+---------+
                   2 I    40  I   130  I    80  I    250
        HIGH       I        I        I        I    50.0
                   +---------+---------+---------+
                COLUMN     160       250        90      500
                 TOTAL    32.0      50.0      18.0    100.0

NUMBER OF MISSING OBSERVATIONS =        0
```

a. Is there reason to suspect that there is a relationship between father's education and nonresponse to son's education level? What may be going on?
b. Is there a satisfactory way to deal with the missing values when estimating the correlation coefficient between father's and son's education?

8. Plot the following two points and write the equation of the straight line that passes through them:
    Point 1   age = 20   income = 20,000
    Point 2   age = 30   income = 25,000

9. In the previous question, what is the value for the intercept? For the slope? If the line you've calculated predicts income exactly, what would be the income for a 40-year-old?

10. Consider the following plot:

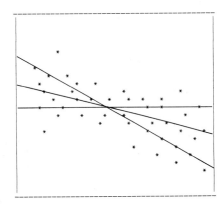

   a. Of the three lines drawn on the plot, which one is most likely to be the regression line?

   b. Is the correlation between the two variables positive, negative, or can you not tell from the plot? Why?

11. Consider the following plot and statistics obtained from procedure PLOT:

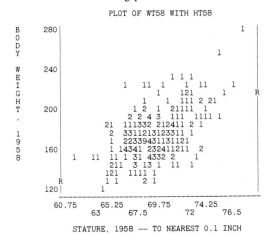

```
                  PLOT OF WT58 WITH HT58
  B    280 |                                        1
  O        |
  D        |
  Y        |                                   1
           |
  W    240 |
  E        |                       1 1 1
  I        |              1    11  1    1  11     1
  G        |                     1   121       1        R
  H        |                1   1  111 2  21
  T    200 |                1 2  1 21111  1
  ,        |                  2 2 4 3  111  1111 1
           |            21  111332 212411 2 1
  1        |             2  3311213123311 1
  9        |             1  22339431131121
  5    160 |             1 14341 232411211   2
  8        |          1  11  11 1 31 4332 2     1
           |            211  3 13 1  11  1
           |            121  1111 1
         R |            1 1      2 1
     120 |              1
           ---------------------------------------------
          60.75      65.25     69.75     74.25
               63        67.5       72       76.5

              STATURE, 1958 -- TO NEAREST 0.1 INCH
```

240 cases plotted. Regression statistics of WT58 on HT58:
Correlation .53553 R Squared .28679 S.E. of Est   20.92697 Sig.   .0000
Intercept(S.E.) -166.51879(34.77567) Slope(S.E.)   4.96169(.50719)

   a. Write the equation predicting WT58 from HT58 and draw the line on the plot.

   b. For a case with an observed value of 68 for HT58 and 200 for WT58, calculate the predicted value for WT58 and the residual.

   c. Draw a line that represents the residual on the plot.

12. Here are the equations for two regression lines:

   Predicted weight $= 100 + 5 \times$ Adjusted height

   Predicted weight $= 105 + 50 \times$ Ring size

   Is the correlation coefficient larger for weight and adjusted height, or for weight and ring size? How can you tell?

Data Analysis

1. Use the BANK data file for the following questions:
    a. Obtain correlation coefficients for the variables you analyzed in the previous chapter. Describe the strength of the observed relationships on the basis of the correlation coefficients.
    b. Calculate the regression lines for the variables you examined in (a). For each pair of variables, write the regression equation.
    c. Obtain a regression equation describing the relationship, if any, between years of work experience and current salary. If necessary, try to transform the data to obtain a linear relationship between the variables.

2. Use the Western Electric data for the following questions:
    a. Obtain a correlation matrix for serum cholesterol, weight, age, and number of cigarettes smoked. Write a brief paragraph describing the relationships you see.
    b. Repeat (a) separately for men who experienced an episode of CHD and those who did not. Do the relationships appear to be similar?
    c. Compute a regression equation to try to predict cholesterol levels from weight. Describe how successful your analysis was.

Chapter 10 What's Your Proof? One-Way Analysis of Variance

Rotund Italians washing down carbohydrate-laden feasts with jugs of chianti, somber Jews ritualistically sipping Sabbath wine, melancholy Irish submerging grief and frustration in a bottle—all are common ethnic stereotypes. Is there any evidence to support these notions? In *Ethnic Drinking Subcultures,* Greeley et al. (1980) examine drinking habits in a sample of five ethnic populations within four major American cities.

A total of 1,107 families completed questionnaires detailing their drinking behavior and ancestral origins. Irish, Italian, Jewish, Swedish, and English families were included. The authors investigate possible differences in drinking habits and a variety of cultural and psychological explanations for them. In this chapter, only differences in total alcohol consumption are considered.

10.1 DESCRIPTIVE STATISTICS AND CONFIDENCE INTERVALS

Figure 10.2 contains basic descriptive statistics for total yearly alcohol consumption in pints for the adult males in the study. The Italians and Irish are the biggest consumers, drinking an average of 24 pints a year. The Jewish males drink the least, an average of slightly more than 9 pints a year.

The sample mean for a group provides the single best guess for the unknown population value μ_i. It is unlikely that the value of the sample mean is exactly equal to the population parameter. Instead, it is probably not too different. Based on the sample mean, it is possible to calculate a range of values that, with a designated likelihood, include the population value. Such a range is called a *confidence interval*. For example, as shown in Figure 10.2, the 95% confidence interval for μ_{Irish} is the range 19.61 to 28.89 pints. This means that if repeated samples are selected from a population under the same conditions and 95% confidence intervals are calculated, 95% of the intervals will contain the unknown parameter μ_{Irish}. Since the parameter value is unknown, it is not possible to determine whether a particular interval contains it.

10.2 ANALYSIS OF VARIANCE

Looking at the sample means in Figure 10.2, you might wonder whether the observed differences can be reasonably attributed to chance or whether there is reason to suspect true differences between the five groups. One of the statistical procedures commonly used to test the hypothesis that several population means are equal is *analysis of variance* or ANOVA.

Figure 10.2   Total yearly alcohol consumption for adult males (in pints)

GROUP	COUNT	MEAN	STANDARD DEVIATION	STANDARD ERROR	MINIMUM	MAXIMUM	95 PCT CONF INT FOR MEAN		
IRISH	119	24.2500	25.5620	2.3433	0.0	145.0	19.6097	TO	28.8903
ITALIAN	84	24.3120	24.1880	2.6391	0.0	128.0	19.0629	TO	29.5611
JEWISH	41	9.2500	21.6250	3.3773	0.0	87.0	2.4243	TO	16.0757
SWEDISH	74	16.5630	26.7500	3.1096	0.0	112.0	10.3655	TO	22.7605
ENGLISH	90	21.8750	21.5630	2.2729	0.0	117.0	17.3587	TO	26.3913
TOTAL	408	20.8373	24.6519	1.2204	0.0	145.0	18.4381	TO	23.2365

Certain assumptions are required for correct application of the ANOVA test. Independent samples from normally distributed populations with the same variance must be selected. In subsequent discussion, it is assumed that the populations sampled constitute the entire set of populations about which conclusions are desired. For example, the five ethnic groups are considered to be the only ones of interest. They are not viewed as a sample from all possible ethnic groups. This is called a *fixed-effects model*.

10.3
Partitioning Variation

In analysis of variance, the observed variability in the sample is subdivided into two components—variability of the observations within a group about the group mean and variability of the group means. If the amount of alcohol consumed doesn't vary much for individuals within the same ethnic group—for example, all the Swedes seem to drink about the same—but the group means differ substantially, there is evidence to suspect that the population means are not all equal.

The *within-groups sum of squares* is a measure of the variability within groups. It is calculated as

$$SSW = \sum_{i=1}^{k} (N_i - 1) S_i^2$$

where S_i^2 is the variance of group i about its mean, and N_i is the number of cases in group i. For the data shown in Figure 10.2, the within-groups sum of squares is

$$SSW = 25.56^2(118) + 24.19^2(83) + 21.63^2(40) + 26.75^2(73) + 21.56^2(89)$$
$$= 237,986.20$$

Variability of the group means is measured by the *between-groups sum of squares*, which is

$$SSB = \sum_{i=1}^{k} N_i (\overline{X}_i - \overline{X})^2$$

The mean of the ith group is denoted $\overline{X}_i$, and the mean of the entire sample is $\overline{X}$. For the drinking study, the between-groups sum of squares is

$$SSB = (24.25-20.84)^2(119) + (24.31-20.84)^2(84) + (9.25-20.84)^2(41)$$
$$+ (16.56-20.84)^2(74) + (21.88-20.84)^2(90)$$
$$= 9,353.89$$

The sums of squares, and other related statistics, are usually displayed in an analysis of variance table, as shown in Figure 10.3.

The mean squares in Figure 10.3 are obtained by dividing the sums of squares by their degrees of freedom. The between-groups degrees of freedom are $k-1$, where k is the number of groups. The within-groups degrees of freedom are $N-k$, where N is the number of cases in the entire sample.

Figure 10.3   Analysis of variance table

```
- - - - - - - - - - - - - - - - - - - - - - - - O N E W A Y - - - - - - - - - - - - - - - - - - - - - - - - - -
      VARIABLE   AMOUNT      AMOUNT OF ALCOHOL CONSUMED IN PINTS
    BY VARIABLE   ETHNIC     ETHNIC BACKGROUND

                                         ANALYSIS OF VARIANCE

                   SOURCE          D.F.      SUM OF SQUARES      MEAN SQUARES       F RATIO    F PROB.

          BETWEEN GROUPS             4          9353.8877         2338.4717          3.960     0.0036

          WITHIN GROUPS            403        237986.2031          590.5364

          TOTAL                    407        247340.0625
```

10.4
Testing the Hypothesis

To test the hypothesis that the five ethnic groups under study consume the same average amount of alcohol—that is, that

$$\mu_{Irish} = \mu_{Italian} = \mu_{Jewish} = \mu_{Swedish} = \mu_{English}$$

the following statistic is calculated (see Figure 10.3):

$$F = \frac{\text{BETWEEN GROUPS MEAN SQUARE}}{\text{WITHIN GROUPS MEAN SQUARE}} = \frac{2338.47}{590.54} = 3.96$$

When the assumptions described in Section 10.2 are met, the observed significance level is obtained by comparing the calculated F to values of the F distribution with $k-1$ and $N-k$ degrees of freedom. The observed significance level is the probability of obtaining an F statistic at least as large as the one calculated when all population means are equal. If this probability is small enough, the hypothesis that all population means are equal is rejected. In this example, the observed significance level is approximately 0.0036 (Figure 10.3). Thus, it appears unlikely that men in the five ethnic populations consume the same mean amount of alcohol.

10.5
MULTIPLE COMPARISON PROCEDURES

A significant F statistic indicates only that the population means are probably unequal. It does not pinpoint where the differences are. A variety of special techniques, termed *multiple comparison* procedures, are available for determining which population means are different from each other.

You may question the need for special techniques—why not just calculate the t test described in Chapter 7 for all possible pairs of means? The problem is that when many comparisons are made, some will appear to be significant even when all population means are equal. With five groups, for example, there are ten possible comparisons between pairs of means. When all population means are equal, the probability that at least one of the ten observed significance levels will be less than 0.05 is about 0.29 (Snedecor, 1967).

Multiple comparison procedures protect against calling too many differences significant. These procedures set up more stringent criteria for declaring differences significant than does the usual t test. That is, the difference between two sample means must be larger to be identified as a true difference.

10.6
The Scheffé Test

Many multiple comparison procedures are available, and they all provide protection in slightly different ways (for further discussion, see Winer, 1971). Figure 10.6a is output from the *Scheffé* multiple comparison procedure for the ethnic drinking data. The Scheffé method is conservative for pairwise comparisons of means. It requires larger differences between means for significance than most of the other methods.

Figure 10.6a The Scheffé multiple comparison procedure

```
        VARIABLE   AMOUNT       AMOUNT OF ALCOHOL CONSUMED IN PINTS
     BY VARIABLE   ETHNIC       ETHNIC BACKGROUND


MULTIPLE RANGE TEST


SCHEFFE PROCEDURE
RANGES FOR THE 0.050 LEVEL -

        4.38   4.38   4.38   4.38


THE RANGES ABOVE ARE TABLE RANGES.  THE VALUE ACTUALLY COMPARED WITH MEAN(J)-MEAN(I) IS..
      17.1834 * RANGE * SQRT(1/N(I) + 1/N(J))


  (*) DENOTES PAIRS OF GROUPS SIGNIFICANTLY DIFFERENT AT THE 0.050 LEVEL


                             J S E I I
                             E W N R T
                             W E G I A
                             I D L S L
                             S I I H I
                             H S S   A
                             H H     N
        MEAN      GROUP

        9.2500    JEWISH
       16.5630    SWEDISH
       21.8750    ENGLISH
       24.2500    IRISH     *
       24.3120    ITALIAN   *
```

The means are ordered and printed from smallest to largest, as shown in Figure 10.6a. Pairs of means that are significantly different at the 0.05 level in this case are indicated with an asterisk in the lower half of the matrix at the bottom of the output. In this example, the asterisks under the vertical column labeled "Jewish" mean that Jews are significantly different from the Irish and the Italians. No other pair is found to be significantly different. If no pairs are significantly different, a message is printed and the matrix is suppressed.

The formula above the matrix indicates how large an observed difference must be to attain significance using the particular multiple comparison procedure. The table ranges are the values for the range variable in the formula.

If the sample sizes in all groups are equal, or an average sample size is used in the computations, a somewhat modified table is also printed (Figure 10.6b). Instead of indicating which groups are significantly different, means that are not different are grouped. Subset 1 shows that Jews, Swedes, and English are not different. Subset 2 groups Swedes, English, Irish, and Italians. Jews do not appear in the same subset as Irish and Italians since they are significantly different from these two.

Figure 10.6b Homogeneous subsets

```
        VARIABLE   AMOUNT       AMOUNT OF ALCOHOL CONSUMED IN PINTS
     BY VARIABLE   ETHNIC       ETHNIC BACKGROUND


MULTIPLE RANGE TEST


SUBSET  1

GROUP      JEWISH       SWEDISH       ENGLISH
MEAN       9.2500       16.5630       21.8750
- - - - - - - - - - - - - - - - - - - - - -

SUBSET  2

GROUP      SWEDISH      ENGLISH       IRISH        ITALIAN
MEAN       16.5630      21.8750       24.2500      24.3120
```

10.7
EXPLANATIONS

Both cultural and psychological explanations for differences in drinking habits among ethnic groups have been suggested (Greeley, 1981). In Jewish culture, the religious symbolism associated with drinking, as well as strong cultural norms against drunkenness, seem to discourage alcohol consumption. For the Irish, alcohol is a vehicle for promotion of fun and pleasure, as well as a potent tranquilizer for dissipating grief and tension. Such high expectations of alcohol make it a convenient escape and foster dependency. Italians have accepted drinking as a natural part of daily life. Alcohol is treated almost as a food and not singled out for its special pleasures.

10.8
Tests for Equality of Variance

As previously discussed, one of the assumptions needed for applying analysis of variance properly is that of equality of variances. That is, all of the populations from which random samples are taken must not only be normal but must also have the same variance σ^2. Several procedures are available for testing this assumption of *homogeneity of variance*. Unfortunately, many of them are not very useful since they are influenced by characteristics of the data other than the variance.

Figure 10.8   Tests for homogeneity of variance

```
TESTS FOR HOMOGENEITY OF VARIANCES

    COCHRANS C = MAX. VARIANCE/SUM(VARIANCES) = 0.2479, P = 0.248 (APPROX.)
    BARTLETT-BOX F =                            1.349, P = 0.249
    MAXIMUM VARIANCE / MINIMUM VARIANCE =       1.539
```

Figure 10.8 contains the three tests for homogeneity of variance available in SPSS-X. If the significance levels are not small, there is no reason to worry. Also, even if the variances appear different but the sample sizes in all groups are similar, there is no cause for alarm since the ANOVA test is not particularly sensitive to violations of equality of variance under such conditions. However, if the sample sizes are quite dissimilar and the variances are unequal, you should consider transforming the data or using a statistical procedure that requires less stringent assumptions (Chapter 12).

10.9
RUNNING PROCEDURE ONEWAY

Procedure ONEWAY produces a one-way analysis of variance. Output includes sums of squares, degrees of freedom, mean squares, and the *F* ratio and its significance.

The only required specifications for procedure ONEWAY are the name of at least one dependent variable, the keyword BY, and the name of the independent variable followed by the minimum and maximum values separated by a comma and enclosed in parentheses. For example, to produce the analysis shown in Figure 10.3, specify:

```
ONEWAY  AMOUNT BY ETHNIC(1,5)
```

Use the RANGES subcommand to request one of the seven multiple comparison procedures: least significant difference, Duncan's multiple range test, Student-Newman-Keuls test, Tukey's alternate procedure, honestly significant difference, modified least significant difference, and Scheffé's test. For example, to produce the Scheffé multiple comparison shown in Figure 10.6a, specify:

```
ONEWAY  AMOUNT BY ETHNIC(1,5) /RANGES=SCHEFFE
```

Use the MISSING, FORMAT, MATRIX, and HARMONIC subcommands to specify missing-value treatment and formatting options. For example, to label the output using the first eight characters of the value labels, specify:

```
ONEWAY  AMOUNT BY ETHNIC(1,5) /RANGES=SCHEFFE
        /FORMAT=LABELS
```

Use the HARMONIC subcommand to request the harmonic mean for range tests. Use the STATISTICS subcommand to request group means, standard deviations, standard errors, minimum, maximum, and 95% confidence intervals for the means; fixed- and random-effects measures; and homogeneity-of-variance statistics. Figure 10.2 shows DESCRIPTIVE statistics produced by procedure ONE-WAY; Figure 10.8 shows HOMOGENEITY statistics.

The complete syntax for ONEWAY appears in Chapter 18.

10.10
ONEWAY and Other SPSS-X Commands

The SPSS-X command file used to produce the output in this chapter is

```
TITLE DRINKING STUDY
DATA LIST /1 ETHNIC 1 AMOUNT 2-6 (2)
VARIABLE LABELS
  AMOUNT 'AMOUNT OF ALCOHOL CONSUMED IN PINTS'
 /ETHNIC 'ETHNIC BACKGROUND'
VALUE LABELS
  ETHNIC  1 'IRISH' 2 'ITALIAN' 3 'JEWISH' 4 'SWEDISH' 5 'ENGLISH'
ONEWAY AMOUNT BY ETHNIC(1,5)/RANGES=SCHEFFE
       /FORMAT=LABELS
       /STATISTICS=DESCRIPTIVES HOMOGENEITY
BEGIN DATA
[data records]
END DATA
FINISH
```

The commands do the following:

• The TITLE command puts the text, DRINKING STUDY, at the top of each page of output.

• The DATA LIST, VARIABLE LABELS, and VALUE LABELS commands define the variables used in this analysis. To define the variable AMOUNT with two decimal places, specify the number 2 enclosed in parentheses following the column specification, as shown in the DATA LIST command.

• The ONEWAY command requests a one-way analysis of variance of variable AMOUNT for five ethnic groups (variable ETHNIC). The RANGES subcommand requests Scheffé tests for comparing group means.

• The FORMAT subcommand instructs SPSS-X to use the first eight characters of the value labels to label output.

• The STATISTICS subcommand requests the group means, standard deviations, standard errors, minimum, maximum, 95% confidence intervals, and homogeneity-of-variance statistics.

EXERCISES

Syntax

1. The following commands contain syntax errors. Write the correct syntax.

   a. `ONEWAY INCOME EDUCATION(1,6)/ RANGES=LSD SCHEFFE/`

   b. `ONEWAY INCOME BY EDUCATION(6)/`

   c. `INCOME BY EDUCATION(1,6) SEX(1,2)/ RANGES SCHEFFE/`

2. Write the command that produces the following table:

```
- - - - - - - - - - - - - - - - - - - - - - - - O N E W A Y - - - - - - - - - - - - - - - - - - - - - - - - - - -
    VARIABLE   WELL      SENSE OF WELL-BEING SCALE
 BY VARIABLE   EDUC6     EDUCATION IN 6 CATEGORIES

                                    ANALYSIS OF VARIANCE

              SOURCE         D.F.    SUM OF SQUARES   MEAN SQUARES      F RATIO   F PROB.

       BETWEEN GROUPS          5         361.3217        72.2643        11.526   0.0000

       WITHIN GROUPS         494        3097.3463         6.2699

       TOTAL                 499        3458.6680
```

3. You type the following command:

   `ONEWAY  WELL BY EDUC6 (1,6) HAPPY(1,3) /MISSING=INCLUDE`

   and get the following warning:

   ```
   >Warning # 11415 on line 24.  Command name: ONEWAY
   >The slash is missing following the parenthesized range values on the ONEWAY
   >command.
   ```

   Fix the command.

4. Given data for the sex, age, weight, daily fiber consumption (variable FIBER), and blood iron levels (variable IRON) of a random selection of office workers, write the SPSS-X transformation commands and ONEWAY analysis for each of the following:

   a. Test the hypothesis that there is no difference in average iron levels between people in three age categories: people under 25, people from 25–45, and people over 45. Perform separate analyses for men and women.

   b. Test the hypothesis that there is no difference in average iron levels between women in four weight categories: women under 80 pounds, women 80–120 pounds, women 120–150 pounds, and women over 150 pounds. Calculate descriptive statistics for the analysis.

   c. Test the hypothesis that there is no difference in average iron levels for people whose daily fiber consumption is: under 2 grams, 2–4 grams, 4–6 grams, 6–8 grams, and over 8 grams. Perform both TUKEY's and DUNCAN's range tests. Perform separate analyses for men and women, and include only men who weigh 100–150 pounds and women who weigh 80–130 pounds.

Statistical Concepts

1. Indicate whether the following statements are true or false.

   a. If you calculate a 95% confidence interval for a population mean and obtain the range 4.89 to 13.23, there is a 95% chance that the population mean is between 4.89 and 13.23.

   b. If group sample sizes are equal, inequality of variances does not cause major problems in the analysis of variance.

2. In an experiment comparing four drugs, each drug was randomly assigned to ten subjects, yielding a total of 40 observations. An analysis of variance produces a pooled estimate of variance of 21.69 and the (incomplete) analysis of variance table below. Fill in the missing entries in this table.

```
                            ANALYSIS OF VARIANCE

     SOURCE              D.F.   SUM OF SQUARES   MEAN SQUARES   F RATIO

     BETWEEN GROUPS

     WITHIN GROUPS

     TOTAL                           964.84
```

3. Are the entries in the analysis of variance table shown below correct?

```
     SOURCE              D.F.   SUM OF SQUARES   MEAN SQUARES   F-RATIO

     BETWEEN GROUPS        3          258            43.00       2.6331

     WITHIN GROUPS         6           49            16.33

     TOTAL                 9          304
```

4. Using the Scheffé output shown below, determine which means are significantly different and which are not.

```
HOMOGENEOUS SUBSETS     (SUBSETS OF GROUPS, WHOSE HIGHEST AND LOWEST MEANS DO NOT DIFFER BY MORE THAN THE SHORTEST
                         SIGNIFICANT RANGE FOR A SUBSET OF THAT SIZE)

SUBSET  1

GROUP        GROUP1       GROUP2
MEAN         9.2500       16.5630
- - - - - - - - - - - - - - -

SUBSET  2

GROUP        GROUP2       GROUP3       GROUP4       GROUP5
MEAN         16.5630      21.8750      24.2500      24.3120
- - - - - - - - - - - - - - - - - - - - - - - - - - - - -
```

5. Using the Scheffé output shown below, determine which pairs of means have differences that are significantly different from zero.

```
                               1 2 3 4 5 6
            MEAN    GROUP

            102.22    1
            118.31    2
            143.62    3      *
            165.89    4      * *
            177.64    5      * *
            201.45    6      * *  *
```

6. What is wrong with the following Scheffé output?

```
                    1 2 3
         MEAN  GROUP

         0.11    1    *
         0.34    2    *
         0.39    3    *
```

7. Suppose you perform an analysis of variance and then make six comparisons between means by using six *t* tests. Someone else then uses multiple comparison procedures to make the same comparisons using the same significance level. Is it possible that you will find fewer significant differences than the person using multiple comparisons? Why or why not?

Data Analysis

Use the BANK system file for Exercises 1–4.

1. For job category 1, test the hypothesis that the four race-sex groups are initially equally compensated.

2. a. Although you would not expect people in different job categories to have the same beginning salaries, you might be interested in examining to what degree average salaries differ for the various job categories and how much variation there is in individuals' salaries within job categories. Perform the appropriate analysis of variance for investigating these questions using only the first four job categories.

   b. What assumptions are you making? Obtain histograms of beginning salary for each of the first four job categories? Are these histograms consistent with your assumptions?

   c. Do salaries appear to be more variable between the first four job categories than within these categories? (Hint: Look at the mean squares.)

   d. What comparisons between means might be of interest? Carry out these comparisons using one of the multiple comparison procedures.

3. Collapse education into fewer categories and examine the effect of collapsed education on beginning salary using a one-way analysis of variance. What do your results indicate? Obtain the appropriate histograms for checking your assumptions.

4. Collapse beginning salary into several categories and perform a one-way analysis of variance to investigate the effect of collapsed beginning salary on current salary. Interpret your results. Obtain the histograms appropriate for checking your assumptions.

5. a. Choose three hypotheses that can be tested using a one-way analysis of variance. If necessary, use the COMPUTE command to create new variables, such as a combined minority and sex variable, which can be used to define the groups. State and check your assumptions.

   b. Obtain a separate histogram for each of the groups. Do the observations appear to be normally distributed with constant variance?

   c. Obtain the analysis of variance table for your hypotheses. Summarize your results.

   d. If there are statistically significant differences between the groups, run one of the multiple comparison procedures and interpret the output.

6. Enter the lost-letter data from Chapter 5. Test the hypothesis that overall return rates are the same in cities and towns.

7. Use the Western Electric data for the following exercises:

   a. Test the null hypothesis that the average number of cigarettes smoked does not differ for men who did not develop CHD, those who died of sudden death, those who had nonfatal MIs and those who had other CHD. (FIRSTCHD) If necessary, perform a multiple comparison procedure to determine where the differences are. Write a paragraph describing your results.

   b. Recode the number of years of education into 3 categories: 8 years or fewer, 9–12, and more than 12. Test the null hypothesis that the average number of cigarettes smoked is the same in the three groups. Write a paragraph describing your results.

   c. Repeat (a) and (b) for average diastolic pressures, averages weights, and average cholesterols.

Chapter 11 Beauty and the Writer: Analysis of Variance

Despite constitutional guarantees, any mirror will testify that all citizens are not created equal. The consequences of this inequity are pervasive. Physically attractive persons are perceived as more desirable social partners, more persuasive communicators, and generally more likeable and competent. Even cute children and attractive burglars are disciplined more leniently than their homely counterparts (Sigall & Ostrove, 1975).

Much research on physical attractiveness focuses on its impact on heterosexual relationships and evaluations. Its effect on same-sex evaluations has received less attention. Anderson and Nida (1978) examined the influence of attractiveness on the evaluation of writings by college students. In the study, 144 male and 144 female students were asked to appraise essays purportedly written by college freshmen. A slide of the "author" was projected during the rating as part of "supplemental information." Half of the slides were of authors of the same sex as the rater; the other half were of authors of the opposite sex. The slides had previously been determined to be of high, medium, and low attractiveness. Each participant evaluated one essay for creativity, ideas, and style. The three scales were combined to form a composite measure of performance.

11.1 DESCRIPTIVE STATISTICS

Figure 11.1 contains average composite scores for the essays, subdivided by the three categories of physical attractiveness and the two categories of sex similarity. The table is similar to the summary table shown for the one-way analysis of variance in Chapter 10. The difference here is that there are two independent (or grouping) variables, attractiveness and sex similarity. The first mean printed (25.11) is for the entire sample. The number of cases (288) is shown in parentheses. Then for each of the independent variables, mean scores are displayed for each of the categories. The attractiveness categories are ordered from low (coded 1) to high (coded 3). Evaluations in which the rater and author are of the same sex are coded as 1, while opposite-sex evaluations are coded as 2. Finally, a table of means is printed for cases classified by both grouping variables. Attractiveness is the row variable, and sex is the column variable. Each mean is based on the responses of 48 subjects.

The overall average score is 25.11. Highly attractive individuals received the highest average score (26.59), while those rated low in physical appeal had the lowest score (22.98). There doesn't appear to be much difference between the average scores assigned to same (25.52) and opposite-sex (24.71) individuals. Highly attractive persons received an average rating of 25.13 when evaluated by individuals of the same sex and 28.04 when evaluated by students of the opposite sex.

Figure 11.1 Table of group means

```
* * * * * * * * * * * *   C E L L   M E A N S   * * * * * * * * * * * * * *
                SCORE
             BY ATTRACT
                SEX
* * * * * * * * * * * * * * * * * * * * * * * * * * * * * * * * * * * * * *
TOTAL POPULATION

     25.11
   (  288)


ATTRACT
         1           2           3

     22.98       25.78       26.59
   (   96)  (    96)  (    96)


SEX
         1           2

     25.52       24.71
   (  144)  (   144)


           SEX
                     1           2
ATTRACT
         1        22.79       23.17
               (   48)  (    48)

         2        28.63       22.92
               (   48)  (    48)

         3        25.13       28.04
               (   48)  (    48)
```

11.2
ANALYSIS OF
VARIANCE

Three hypotheses are of interest in the study: Does attractiveness relate to the composite scores? Does sex similarity relate to the scores? And is there an interaction between the effects of attractiveness and sex? The statistical technique used to evaluate these hypotheses is an extension of the one-way analysis of variance outlined in Chapter 10. The same assumptions as before are needed for correct application: the observations should be independently selected from normal populations with equal variances. Again, discussion here is limited to the situation in which both grouping variables are considered fixed. That is, they constitute the populations of interest.

The total observed variation in the scores is subdivided into four components: the sums of squares due to attractiveness, sex, their interaction, and the residual. This can be expressed as

TOTAL SS = ATTRACTIVENESS SS + SEX SS + INTERACTION SS + RESIDUAL SS

Figure 11.2 is the analysis of variance table for this study. The first column lists the sources of variation. The sums of squares attributable to each of the components are given in the second column. The sums of squares for each independent variable alone are sometimes termed the "main effect" sums of squares. The "explained" sum of squares is the total sum of squares for the main effect and interaction terms in the model.

The degrees of freedom for sex and attractiveness, listed in the third column, are one fewer than the number of categories. For example, since there are three levels of attractiveness, there are two degrees of freedom. Similarly, sex has one degree of freedom. Two degrees of freedom are associated with the interaction term (the product of the degrees of freedom of each of the individual variables). The degrees of freedom for the residual are $N-1-k$, where k equals the degrees of freedom for the explained sum of squares.

Figure 11.2 Analysis of variance table

```
* * * * * * * * * A N A L Y S I S   O F   V A R I A N C E * * * * * * * * * *
                 SCORE
            BY ATTRACT
               SEX
* * * * * * * * * * * * * * * * * * * * * * * * * * * * * * * * * * * * * * *
                               SUM OF                    MEAN              SIGNIF
SOURCE OF VARIATION            SQUARES    DF            SQUARE      F       OF F

MAIN EFFECTS                   733.700     3           244.567    3.276    0.022
    ATTRACT                    686.850     2           343.425    4.600    0.011
    SEX                         46.850     1            46.850    0.628    0.429

2-WAY INTERACTIONS             942.350     2           471.175    6.311    0.002
    ATTRACT   SEX              942.350     2           471.175    6.311    0.002

EXPLAINED                     1676.050     5           335.210    4.490    0.000

RESIDUAL                     21053.140   282            74.656

TOTAL                        22729.190   287            79.196
```

The mean squares shown in Figure 11.2 are obtained by dividing each sum of squares by its degrees of freedom. Hypothesis tests are based on the ratios of the mean squares of each source of variation to the mean square for the residual. When the assumptions are met and the true means are in fact equal, the distribution of the ratio is an F with the degrees of freedom for the numerator and denominator terms.

11.3
Testing for Interaction

The F value associated with the attractiveness and sex interaction is 6.311. The observed significance level is approximately 0.002. Therefore, it appears that there is an interaction between the two variables. What does this mean?

Figure 11.3a Cell means (Plot from SPSS Graphics)

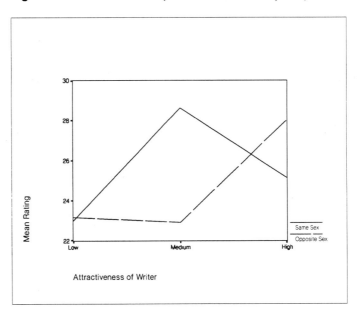

Consider Figure 11.3a, which is a plot of the cell means in Figure 11.1. Notice how the mean scores relate not only to the attractiveness of the individual and to the sex of the rater, but also to the particular combination of the values of the variables. Opposite-sex raters assign the highest scores to highly attractive individuals. Same-sex raters assign the highest scores to individuals of medium attractiveness. Thus, the ratings for each level of attractiveness depend on the sex variable. If there were no interaction between the two variables, a plot like that shown in Figure 11.3b might result, where the difference between the two types of raters is the same for the three levels of attractiveness.

Figure 11.3b   Cell means with no interaction (Plot from SPSS Graphics)

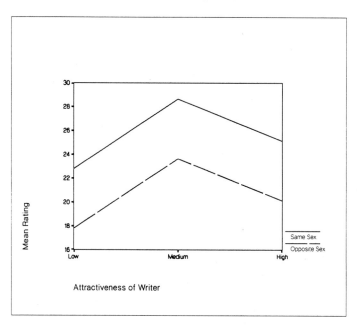

11.4
Tests for Sex and Attractiveness

Once the presence of interaction has been established, it is not particularly useful to continue hypothesis testing since the two variables *jointly* affect the dependent variable. If there is no significant interaction, the grouping variables can be tested individually. The F value associated with attractiveness would provide a test of the hypothesis that attractiveness does not affect the rating. Similarly, the F value associated with sex would test the hypothesis that sex has no main effect on evaluation.

Note that the small F value associated with sex does not indicate that response is unaffected by sex, since sex *is* included in the significant interaction term. Instead, it shows that when response is averaged over attractiveness levels, the two sex category means are not significantly different.

11.5
EXPLANATIONS

Several explanations are consistent with the results of this study. Since most people consider themselves moderately attractive, the highest degree of identification should be with same-sex individuals of moderate attractiveness. The higher empathy may result in the higher scores. An alternative theory is that moderately attractive individuals are generally perceived as more desirable same-sex friends: they have more favorable personality profiles and don't encourage unfavorable comparisons. Their writing scores may benefit from their perceived popularity.

Although we don't want friends who outshine us, handsome (and beautiful) dates provide a favorable reflection and enhance our status. Physical beauty is advantageous for heterosexual relationships, but not same-sex friendships. This prejudice may affect all evaluations of highly attractive members of the opposite sex. Regardless of the explanation, certain practical conclusions are apparent. Students, choose your instructors carefully! Authors, think twice before including your photo on the book jacket!

11.6
EXTENSIONS

Analysis of variance techniques can be used with any number of grouping variables. For example, the data in Table 11.1 originated from a more complicated experiment than described here. There were four factors—essay quality, physical attractiveness, sex of writer, and sex of subject. The original data were analyzed with a $3 \times 3 \times 2 \times 2$ ANOVA table. (The numbers indicate how many categories each grouping variable has.) The conclusions from our simplified analysis are the same as those from the more elaborate analysis.

Each of the cells in our experiment had the same number of subjects. This greatly simplifies the analysis and its interpretation. When unequal sample sizes occur in the cells, the total sum of squares cannot be partitioned into nice components that sum to the total. A variety of techniques are available for calculating sums of squares in such "non-orthogonal" designs. The methods differ in the way they adjust the sums of squares to account for other effects in the model. Each method results in different sums of squares and tests different hypotheses. However, when all cell frequencies are equal, the methods yield the same results. For discussion of various procedures for analyzing designs with unequal cell frequencies, see Kleinbaum and Kupper (1978) and Overall and Klett (1972).

11.7
RUNNING
PROCEDURE ANOVA

Procedure ANOVA produces an *n*-way analysis of variance. Up to five factors or independent variables can be used in one design, and several dependent variables can be analyzed in one ANOVA procedure. In addition to the analysis of variance table, ANOVA also prints cell means and sample sizes.

The only required subcommand for procedure ANOVA is the VARIABLES subcommand, and the actual keyword VARIABLES may be omitted. VARIABLES specifies the name of at least one dependent variable, the keyword BY, and one to five independent variables followed by their minimum and maximum values separated by a comma and enclosed in parentheses. To produce the analysis of variance table in Figure 11.2, specify:

```
ANOVA VARIABLES=SCORE BY ATTRACT(1,3) SEX (1,2)
```

Since the independent variables are simply categories, the numbers you use to represent the categories are arbitrary from a statistical point of view. However, they are not arbitrary from a computational point of view since these values define the dimensions of the table of means and variances from which the analysis of variance is computed. If your categorical variables do not have consecutive values, recode them using the RECODE command (Section 11.8 and Chapter 18) before running ANOVA. Otherwise, you may find that SPSS-X does not have enough computer resources to complete your job.

Use the STATISTICS subcommand to request optional statistics such as a table of means and counts. For example, to produce the table of group means shown in Figure 11.1, specify:

```
ANOVA  VARIABLES=SCORE BY ATTRACT(1,3) SEX (1,2)
       /STATISTICS=MEAN
```

ANOVA has other subcommands for selecting missing-data treatment, specifying format options, and deleting interaction terms from the analysis. The complete syntax for procedure ANOVA appears in Chapter 18.

11.8
ANOVA and Other SPSS-X Commands

The SPSS-X command file used to produce the results in Figures 11.1 and 11.2 is

```
TITLE   ANALYSIS OF VARIANCE
DATA LIST   /1 ATTRACT 1-2 SEX 3 SCORE 4-5
RECODE   ATTRACT (1=1) (5=2) (10=3)
VARIABLE LABELS
   ATTRACT 'ATTRACTIVENESS LEVEL'
   SEX 'SEX SIMILARITY'
   SCORE 'COMPOSITE SCORE'
VALUE LABELS
   ATTRACT  1 'LOW' 2 'MEDIUM' 3 'HIGH'
  /SEX   1 'SAME' 2 'OPPOSITE'
ANOVA   VARIABLES=SCORE BY ATTRACT (1,3) SEX (1,2)
        /STATISTICS=MEAN
BEGIN DATA
data records
END DATA
FINISH
```

This SPSS-X job assumes that the variable ATTRACT is originally coded 1=low, 5=medium, and 10=high.

- The TITLE command prints the title ANALYSIS OF VARIANCE at the top of each page of output.
- The DATA LIST command defines the variables.
- The RECODE command changes the values of ATTRACT to consecutive values of 1, 2, and 3 so that the ANOVA procedure will be more efficient. The recode specification (1=1), although unnecessary, is included to give a complete description of the values of ATTRACT. All values not mentioned on the RECODE command remain unchanged. See Chapter 18 for a discussion of the RECODE command.
- The VARIABLE LABELS and VALUE LABELS commands assign variable and and value labels.
- The ANOVA command requests an analysis of variance of variable SCORE by SEX and three categories of attractiveness (variable ATTRACT).
- The STATISTICS command requests the means and counts table.

EXERCISES

Syntax

1. Write the command to perform a two-way analysis of variance where DIAS is the dependent variable and RACE (coded 1 through 4) and CHD (coded 0 and 1) are the independent variables.

2. The following commands contain errors. Write the correct commands.
   a. `ANOVA SCORE BY REGION (1,4) SEX`
   b. `ANOVA SCORE BY REGION BY SEX`
   c. `ANOVA SCORE(1,100) BY RACE(1,3) SEX(1,2)`
   d. `ANOVA SCORE1 SCORE2 BY RACE(1,3) SEX`
   e. `ANOVA SCORE1 BY RACE(1,3), SCORE2 BY SEX(1,2)`

3. If variable REGION has four categories coded 1 through 4 and ATTRACT has three categories coded 1 through 3, how many cells result from the following specifications?
   a. `ANOVA SCORE BY REGION(1,4) ATTRACT(1,3)`
   b. `ANOVA SCORE BY REGION(2,4) ATTRACT(1,3)`
   c. `ANOVA SCORE BY REGION(2,4) ATTRACT(2,3)`

4. You type the following command:

```
ANOVA VARIABLES=PRESTIGE BY SEX
```

and get the following error message:

```
>Error # 10713 on line 4 in column 72.  Text: (End of Command)
>You omitted the parenthesized value range after a list of independent
>variables in an ANOVA command model specification.
>This command not executed.
```

Fix the command.

5. Given data for the sex, age, weight, daily fiber consumption (variable FIBER), and blood iron levels (variable IRON) of a random selection of office workers, write the SPSS-X transformation commands and ANOVA analysis for each of the following:

   a. Perform a two-way analysis of variance to determine whether there is an interaction between the effects of age and sex on an individual's blood iron level. Use the following age categories: people under 25, people 25–45, and people over 45.

   b. Perform a two-way analysis of variance to determine whether there is an interaction between the effects of age and weight on an individual's blood iron level. Use the same age categories as in (a). Use the following weight categories: under 100 pounds, 100–130 pounds, 130–160 pounds, 160–190 pounds, and over 190 pounds.

   c. Perform a two-way analysis of variance to determine whether weight and daily fiber intake affect an individual's blood iron level. Perform separate analyses for men and women. For women, use weight categories from 80 to 160 pounds, in increments of 20 pounds, and account for women under 80 pounds and for women over 160 pounds. For men, use weight categories from 100 to 250 pounds, in increments of 30 pounds, and account for men under 100 pounds and for men over 250 pounds. For both men and women, use the following fiber categories: under 2 grams, 2–4 grams, 4–6 grams, 6–8 grams, and over 8 grams.

Statistical Concepts

1. Are the following statements true or false?

   a. If an interaction effect is evident, it is important to perform individual F tests for the variables in the interaction.

   b. If an interaction term has a significant F value, it is not possible to obtain a nonsignificant F value for one of the variables in the interaction.

2. Complete the following two-way analysis of variance table.

```
          * * *   A N A L Y S I S   O F   V A R I A N C E   * * *

          VAR A
    BY    FACTOR1
          FACTOR2
```

SOURCE OF VARIATION	SUM OF SQUARES	DF	MEAN SQUARE	F
MAIN EFFECTS	524.61	5		
FACTOR1	310.11	3		
FACTOR2	214.50	2		
2-WAY INTERACTIONS	104.17	6		
FACTOR1 FACTOR2	104.17	6		
EXPLAINED	628.78	11		
RESIDUAL	4988.02	49		
TOTAL	5616.80	60		

3. Based on the plot of cell means given below, do you think there is an interaction between treatment and smoking status?

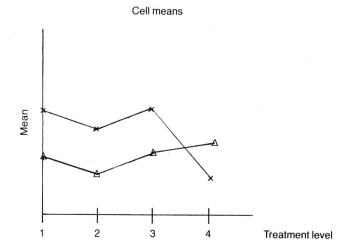

Cell means

Data Analysis

Use the BANK system file for Questions 1–4.

1. Examine the effects of the first two job categories and the sex-race variable on beginning salary using a two-way analysis of variance. Is there an interaction effect? What do your results suggest?

2. Repeat the analysis in Question 1 looking at current salary instead of beginning salary.

3. Use a two-way analysis of variance to examine the effects of collapsed educational level (up to 16 years) and the first two job categories on beginning salary. What assumptions are you making? Summarize your results.

4. Using a two-way analysis of variance, investigate the effects of collapsed educational level (up to 16 years) and collapsed job seniority on current salary. Summarize your results.

5. Choose one of the data sets from Appendix B.

   a. Formulate four hypotheses that can be tested using two-way analysis of variance techniques. For example, with the Western Electric data file you can use a two-way analysis of variance to test the hypothesis that family history of heart disease and cigarette smoking are related to diastolic blood pressure. Make sure to indicate which variables are the factors and how many levels there are for each factor.

   b. For two of the hypotheses in Question 5.a, use the ANOVA procedure to determine whether there are significant main effects and a significant interaction. Summarize your findings.

   c. Using the cell means obtained from procedure ANOVA, draw a plot like the one in Figure 11.3b.

6. Use the Western Electric data for the following exercises.

   a. Use analysis of variance to examine the relationship between family history of coronary heart disease, incidence of coronary heart disease, and diastolic blood pressure. Write a paragraph describing your results.

b. Use analysis of variance to examine the relationship between education (8 years or fewer, 9–12, and more than 12), incidence of coronary heart disease, and number of cigarettes smoked. Is there a difference in the average number of cigarettes smoked for men who developed heart disease and those who did not? Is there a difference in the average number of cigarettes smoked for the three categories of education? Is there an interaction between incidence of coronary heart disease and education?

c. If there is an interaction in (b) does it make sense to look at the main effects? Why or why not?

Chapter 12   Fats and Rats: Distribution-Free or Nonparametric Tests

Coffee and carrots have recently joined saccharin, tobacco, Laetrile, and interferon on the ever-expanding list of rumored causes of and cures for cancer. This list is necessarily tentative and complicated. The two major sources of evidence—experiments on animals and examination of the histories of afflicted persons—are fraught with problems. It is difficult to predict, based on large doses of suspect substances given to small animals, the consequences of small amounts consumed by humans over a long time span.

In studies of people, lifestyle components are difficult to isolate, and it is challenging—if not impossible—to unravel the contribution of a single factor. For example, what is the role of caffeine based on a sample of overweight, sedentary, coffee- and alcohol-drinking, cigarette-smoking, urban dwellers?

Nutrition is also thought to be an important component in cancer development and progression. For example, the per capita consumption of dietary fats is positively correlated with the incidence of mammary and colon cancer in humans (Wynder, 1976). In a recent study, King et al. (1979) examined the relationship between diet and tumor development in rats. Three groups of animals of the same age, species, and physical condition were injected with tumor cells. The rats were divided into three groups and fed diets of either low, saturated, or unsaturated fat.

One hypothesis of interest is whether the length of time until a tumor develops in rats fed saturated diets differs from the length of time in rats fed unsaturated diets. If it is tenable to assume that tumor-free time is normally distributed, the two-sample t test described in Chapter 7 can be used to test the hypothesis that the population means are equal. However, if the distribution of times does not appear to be normal, and especially if the sample sizes are small, statistical procedures that do not require assumptions about the shapes of the underlying distributions should be considered.

12.1 THE MANN-WHITNEY TEST

The *Mann-Whitney test*, also known as the Wilcoxon test, does not require assumptions about the shape of the underlying distributions. It tests the hypothesis that two independent samples come from populations having the same distribution. The form of the distribution need not be specified. The test does not require that the variable be measured on an interval scale; an ordinal scale is sufficient.

12.2
Ranking the Data

To compute the test, the observations from both samples are first combined and ranked from smallest to largest. Consider Table 12.2, which shows a sample of the King data reported by Lee (1979). Case 4 has the shortest elapsed time to development of a tumor, 68 days. It is assigned a rank of 1. The next shortest time is for Case 3, so it is assigned a rank of 2. Cases 5 and 6 both exhibited tumors on the same day. They are both assigned a rank of 3.5, the average of the ranks (3 and 4) for which they are tied. Case 2, the next largest, is given a rank of 5, and Case 1 is given a rank of 6.

Table 12.2   Ranking the data

Saturated			Unsaturated		
Case	Time	Rank	Case	Time	Rank
1	199	6	4	68	1
2	126	5	5	112	3.5
3	81	2	6	112	3.5

12.3
Calculating the Test

The statistic for testing the hypothesis that the two distributions are equal is the sum of the ranks for each of the two groups. If the groups have the same distribution, their sample distributions of ranks should be similar. If one of the groups has more than its share of small or large ranks, there is reason to suspect that the two underlying distributions are different.

Figure 12.3 shows the output from the Mann-Whitney test for the complete King data. For each group, the mean rank and number of cases is given. (The mean rank is the sum of the ranks divided by the number of cases.) Note that the unsaturated-diet group has only 29 cases since one rat died of causes unrelated to the experiment. The entry printed under W is the sum of the ranks for the group with the smaller number of observations. If both groups have the same number of observations, W is the rank sum for the group named first in the NPAR TESTS command (see Section 12.12). For this example, W is 963, the sum of the ranks for the saturated-diet group.

Figure 12.3   Mann-Whitney output

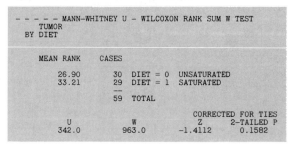

The number identified on the output as U is the number of times a value in the unsaturated-diet group precedes a value in the saturated-diet group. To understand what this means, consider the data in Table 12.2 again. All three cases in the unsaturated-diet group have smaller ranks than the first case in the saturated-diet group, so they all precede Case 1 in the rankings. Similarly, all three cases in the unsaturated-diet group precede Case 2. Only one unsaturated-diet case (Case 4) is smaller in value than Case 3. Thus, the number of times the value for an unsaturated-diet case precedes the value for a saturated-diet case is

3+3+1=7. The number of times the value of a saturated-diet case precedes the value of an unsaturated-diet case is 2, since Case 3 has a smaller rank than both Cases 5 and 6. The smaller of these two numbers is printed on the output as U. If the two distributions are equal, values from one group should not consistently precede values in the other.

The significance levels associated with U and W are the same. They can be obtained by transforming the score to a standard normal deviate (Z). If the total sample size is less than 30, an exact probability level based on the distribution of the score is also printed. From Figure 12.3, the observed significance level for this example is 0.158. Since the significance level is large, the hypothesis that tumor-free time has the same distribution for the two diet groups is not rejected.

12.4
Which Diet?

You should not conclude from these findings that it doesn't matter—as far as tumors are concerned—what kind of fat you (or rats) eat. King et al. found that rats fed the unsaturated diet had a total of 96 tumors at the end of the experiment, while rats fed the saturated diet had only 55 tumors. They also found that large tumors were more common in the unsaturated-diet group than in the saturated-diet group. Thus, unsaturated fats may be more hazardous than saturated fats.

12.5
Assumptions

The Mann-Whitney test requires only that the observations be a random sample and that values can be ordered. These assumptions, especially randomness, are not to be made lightly, but they are less restrictive than those for the two-sample t test for means. The t test further requires that the observations be selected from normally distributed populations with equal variances. (An approximate test for the case of unequal variances is presented in Chapter 7).

Since the Mann-Whitney test can always be calculated instead of the t test, what determines which should be used? If the assumptions needed for the t test are met, the t test is more powerful than the Mann-Whitney test. That is, the t test will detect true differences between the two populations more often than will the Mann-Whitney test since the t test uses more information from the data. Substitution of ranks for the actual values loses potentially useful information. On the other hand, using the t test when its assumptions are substantially violated may result in an erroneous observed significance level.

In general, if the assumptions of the t test appear reasonable, it should be used. When the data are ordinal—or interval but from a markedly nonnormal distribution—the Mann-Whitney test is the procedure of choice.

12.6
NONPARAMETRIC TESTS

Many statistical procedures, like the Mann-Whitney test, require limited distributional assumptions about the data. Collectively these procedures are termed *distribution-free* or *nonparametric tests*. Like the Mann-Whitney test, distribution-free tests are generally less powerful than their parametric counterparts. They are most useful in situations where parametric procedures are not appropriate: when the data are nominal or ordinal, or when interval data are from markedly nonnormal distributions. Significance levels for certain nonparametric tests can be determined regardless of the shape of the population distribution since they are based on ranks.

In the following sections, various nonparametric tests will be used to reanalyze some of the data described in previous chapters. Since the data were chosen to illustrate the parametric procedures, they satisfy assumptions that are more restrictive than those for nonparametric procedures. However, they provide an opportunity for learning new procedures with familiar data and for comparing results from different types of analyses.

12.7
The Sign Test

In Chapter 7, the paired *t*-test for means is used to test the hypothesis that the mean buying scores for husbands and wives are equal. Remember that the assumption that the differences are normally distributed is required for this test.

The *sign test* is a nonparametric procedure used with two related samples to test the hypothesis that the distributions of two variables are the same. This test makes no assumptions about the shape of these distributions.

To compute the sign test, the difference between the buying scores of husbands and wives is calculated for each case. Next, the numbers of positive and negative differences are obtained. If the distributions of the two variables are the same, the numbers of positive and negative differences should be similar.

Figure 12.7 Sign test output

```
- - - - - SIGN TEST
    HSSCALE    HUSBAND SELF SCALE
WITH WSSCALE   WIFE SELF SCALE


     CASES

       56   - DIFFS (WSSCALE LT HSSCALE)          Z =      1.6416
       39   + DIFFS (WSSCALE GT HSSCALE)
        3     TIES                        2-TAILED P =      .1007
     ----
       98     TOTAL
```

The output in Figure 12.7 shows that the number of negative differences is 56, while the number of positive differences is 39. The total number of cases is 98, including 3 with 0 differences. The observed significance level is 0.1007. Since this value is large, the hypothesis that the distributions are the same is not rejected.

12.8
The Wilcoxon Signed-Ranks Test

The sign test uses only the direction of the differences between the pairs and ignores the magnitude. A discrepancy of 15 between husbands' and wives' buying scores is treated in the same way as a discrepancy of 1. The *Wilcoxon signed-ranks test* incorporates information about the magnitude of the differences and is therefore more powerful than the sign test.

To compute the Wilcoxon signed-ranks test, the differences are ranked ignoring the signs. In the case of ties, average ranks are assigned. The sums of the ranks for positive and negative differences are then calculated.

Figure 12.8 Wilcoxon signed-ranks test output

```
- - - - - WILCOXON MATCHED-PAIRS SIGNED-RANKS TEST
    HSSCALE    HUSBAND SELF SCALE
WITH WSSCALE   WIFE SELF SCALE


  MEAN RANK     CASES

     45.25        56    - RANKS (WSSCALE LT HSSCALE)
     51.95        39    + RANKS (WSSCALE GT HSSCALE)
                   3      TIES
                 ----
                  98      TOTAL

      Z =     -.9428           2-TAILED P =   .3458
```

From Figure 12.8, the average rank of the 56 negative differences is 45.25. The average positive rank is 51.95. There are 3 cases with the same value for both variables. This is the entry under TIES in Figure 12.8. The observed significance level associated with the test is large (0.3458), and again the hypothesis of no difference is not rejected.

12.9
The Kruskal-Wallis Test

The experiment described in the first sections of this chapter investigates the effects of three diets on tumor development. The Mann-Whitney test was calculated to examine possible differences between saturated and unsaturated diets. To test for differences between all three diets, an extension of the Mann-Whitney test can be used. This test is known as the *Kruskal-Wallis one-way analysis of variance*.

The procedure for computing the Kruskal-Wallis test is similar to that used in the Mann-Whitney test. All cases from the groups are combined and ranked. Average ranks are assigned in the case of ties. For each group, the ranks are summed, and the Kruskal-Wallis *H* statistic is computed from these sums. The *H* statistic has approximately a chi-square distribution under the hypothesis that the three groups have the same distribution.

Figure 12.9   Kruskal-Wallis one-way analysis of variance output

```
- - - - - KRUSKAL-WALLIS 1-WAY ANOVA
     TUMOR
  BY DIET


     MEAN RANK     CASES

        34.12         30    DIET = 0    UNSATURATED
        43.50         29    DIET = 1    SATURATED
        56.24         29    DIET = 2    LOW-FAT
                      --
                      88    TOTAL

                                                      CORRECTED FOR TIES
         CASES    CHI-SQUARE  SIGNIFICANCE   CHI-SQUARE   SIGNIFICANCE
            88       11.1257        0.0038      11.2608         0.0036
```

The output in Figure 12.9 shows that the third group, the low-fat-diet group, has the largest average rank. The value of the Kruskal-Wallis statistic (labeled CHI-SQUARE) is 11.1257. When the statistic is adjusted for the presence of ties, the value changes to 11.2608 (labeled CORRECTED CHI-SQUARE). The small observed significance level suggests that the time until development of a tumor is not the same for all three groups.

12.10
The One-Sample Chi-Square Test

In Chapter 3, frequencies of deaths for the days of the week are examined. The FREQUENCIES output suggests that the days of the week are equally hazardous in regard to death. To test this conclusion, the *one-sample chi-square test* can be used. This nonparametric test requires only that the data be a random sample.

To calculate the one-sample chi-square statistic, the data are first classified into mutually exclusive categories of interest—days of the week in this example—and then expected frequencies for these categories are computed. Expected frequencies are the frequencies that would be expected if a given hypothesis is true. For the death data, the hypothesis to be tested is that the probability of death is the same for each day of the week. The day of death is known for 110 subjects. The hypothesis implies that the expected frequency of deaths for each weekday is 110 divided by 7, or 15.71. Once the expected frequencies are obtained, the chi-square statistic is computed as

$$\chi^2 = \sum_{i=1}^{k} (O_i - E_i)^2 / E_i$$

where O_i is the observed frequency for the ith category, E_i is the expected frequency for the ith category, and k is the number of categories.

Figure 12.10 One-sample chi-square output

```
 - - - - - CHI-SQUARE TEST
    DAYOFWK    DAY OF DEATH

                                              CASES
                            CATEGORY        OBSERVED     EXPECTED    RESIDUAL

            SUNDAY               1              19         15.71         3.29
            MONDAY               2              11         15.71        -4.71
            TUESDAY              3              19         15.71         3.29
            WEDNSDAY             4              17         15.71         1.29
            THURSDAY             5              15         15.71         -.71
            FRIDAY               6              13         15.71        -2.71
            SATURDAY             7              16         15.71          .29
                                             ----
                            TOTAL            110

              CHI-SQUARE                   D.F.              SIGNIFICANCE
                3.400                       6                   0.757
```

If the hypothesis is true, the chi-square statistic has approximately a chi-square distribution with $k-1$ degrees of freedom. This statistic will be large if the observed and expected frequencies are substantially different. Figure 12.10 is the output from the one-sample chi-square test for the death data. The codes associated with the days of the week are listed in the column labeled CATEGORY. The observed frequencies are in the next column, labeled CASES OBSERVED. The observed significance level is 0.757, so it appears that the day of the week does not affect the chance of death.

12.11
The Rank Correlation Coefficient

The Pearson product-moment correlation discussed in Chapter 9 is appropriate only for data that attain at least an interval level of measurement, such as the sales and advertising data used as examples in that chapter. Normality is also assumed when testing hypotheses about this correlation coefficient. For ordinal data or interval data that do not satisfy the normality assumption, another measure of the linear relationship between two variables, *Spearman's rank correlation coefficient*, is available.

The rank correlation coefficient is the Pearson correlation coefficient based on the ranks of the data if there are no ties (adjustments are made if some of the data are tied). If the original data for each variable have no ties, the data for each variable are first ranked and then the Pearson correlation coefficient between the ranks for the two variables is computed. Like the Pearson correlation coefficient, the rank correlation ranges between -1 and 1, where -1 and 1 indicate a perfect linear relationship between the ranks of the two variables. The interpretation is therefore the same except that the relationship between *ranks* and not values is examined.

Figure 12.11 shows the matrix of rank correlation coefficients for the sales and advertising data. As expected, these coefficients are similar in sign and magnitude to the Pearson coefficients obtained in Chapter 9.

Figure 12.11 The rank correlation coefficient

```
- - - - - - - - - - -  S P E A R M A N   C O R R E L A T I O N   C O E F F I C I E N T S  - - - - - - - - - - -


     EFFIC           .0253
                 N(    40)
                 SIG .438


     REPS            .7733        -.1741
                 N(    40)     N(    40)
                 SIG .000      SIG .141


     SALES           .8242         .0866          .7260
                 N(    40)     N(    40)      N(    40)
                 SIG .000      SIG .298       SIG .000


                 ADVERTIS       EFFIC          REPS

     " . " IS PRINTED IF A COEFFICIENT CANNOT BE COMPUTED.
```

12.12
RUNNING
PROCEDURE NPAR
TESTS

All of the nonparametric tests described in Sections 12.1 through 12.10, and several more, are available in the NPAR TESTS procedure. In addition to the test statistics, you can specify optional statistics, methods of handling missing data, and random sampling of cases. See Chapter 18 for a complete list of the nonparametric tests, options, and statistics available in the NPAR TESTS procedure.

Use the M-W subcommand to specify the Mann-Whitney test or the K-W subcommand for the Kruskal-Wallis test. The subcommand specification for either is the name of the variable to be analyzed, followed by the keyword BY, the name of the grouping variable, and the value range defining the groups in parentheses. The grouping variable indicates to which group each case belongs. For example, to produce the output in Figure 12.3, specify

```
NPAR TESTS  M-W=TUMOR BY DIET(0,1)
```

where TUMOR is the time until development of a tumor and DIET indicates either an unsaturated (value 0) or saturated (value 1) diet. The Kruskal-Wallis test in Figure 12.9 is obtained with the following:

```
NPAR TESTS  K-W=TUMOR BY DIET(0,2)
```

Use the SIGN subcommand for the sign test and the WILCOXON subcommand for the Wilcoxon test. For either test, you specify one variable name, the keyword WITH, and the other variable name. For example, to produce the output shown in Figure 12.8, specify

```
NPAR TESTS  WILCOXON=HSSCALE WITH WSSCALE
```

where variable HSSCALE is the buying score for husbands and WSSCALE is the buying score for wives. The sign-test output in Figure 12.7 is produced by:

```
NPAR TESTS  SIGN=HSSCALE WITH WSSCALE
```

12.13
The One-Sample
Chi-Square Test and
Freefield Input

For the one-sample chi-square test, use the CHI-SQUARE subcommand followed by the variable name. The following SPSS-X job will produce the output in Figure 12.10:

```
DATA LIST FREE/ DAY DAYFREQ
VARIABLE LABELS  DAYFREQ 'FREQ OF CARDIAC DEATH BY DAYS OF WEEK'
VALUE LABELS DAY 1'SUNDAY' 2'MONDAY' 3'TUESDAY' 4'WEDNSDAY'
 5'THURSDAY' 6'FRIDAY' 7'SATURDAY'/
WEIGHT BY DAYFREQ
NPAR TESTS  CHI-SQUARE=DAY
BEGIN DATA
1 19   2 11   3 19   4 17
 5 15   6 13   7 16
END DATA
FINISH
```

In this job, the data are entered as aggregated data in freefield format. Each day of the week represents one case in the aggregated file—a total of seven cases. Variable DAY is entered with the same coding scheme used in Chapter 2, and the total number of deaths, variable DAYFREQ, is entered for each day. The first case in the aggregated data represents Sunday, with value 1 for DAY and 19, the frequency of deaths on that day, for DAYFREQ. Likewise, for the second case (Monday), value 2 is recorded for DAY and 11 for DAYFREQ, and so forth for each day of the week. Then variable DAYFREQ is used on the WEIGHT command to replicate cases for the analysis (see Chapter 5).

The data are entered in freefield format with multiple cases on the same line and each value separated by a comma or one or more blanks. The values must be entered in the same sequence for each case but not necessarily in the same columns. A value cannot be continued onto another line. However, you can leave extra blanks at the end of a line. The keyword FREE is specified on the DATA

LIST command, along with the names of the variables in the order that they are entered in the data. See Chapter 18 for further discussion of freefield-format data.

12.14
RUNNING
PROCEDURE
NONPAR CORR

The NONPAR CORR procedure produces Spearman rank correlations for pairs of variables. Output includes the coefficient, the test of significance, and the number of cases on which the coefficient is based. You can specify optional formats, methods of handling missing data, and random sampling of cases. See Chapter 18 for a complete list of the options and statistics available for procedure NONPAR CORR.

To produce the output shown in Figure 12.11, specify:

```
NONPAR CORR   ADVERTIS EFFIC REPS SALES
```

The order in which you name the variables is the order in which NONPAR CORR displays them. You can use the keyword WITH to specify rank correlations for specific pairs of variables. For example, the command

```
NONPAR CORR   ADVERTIS WITH REPS SALES
```

requests rank correlations for ADVERTIS with REPS, and ADVERTIS with SALES.

EXERCISES

Syntax

1. The following commands contain syntax errors. Write the correct syntax.

   a. NPAR TESTS CHI-SQUARE=DAY/EXPECTED=10 9 8 7 0 9 10/

   b. NPAR TESTS K-W TUMOR BY DIET/

   c. NPAR TESTS M-W TUMOR DIET(0,1)/

2. Write the NPAR TESTS command that produces the following output:

```
- - - - - MANN-WHITNEY U - WILCOXON RANK SUM W TEST
    TUMOR
  BY DIET


    MEAN RANK    CASES

       26.90       30  DIET = 0  UNSATURATED
       33.21       29  DIET = 1  SATURATED
                   --
                   59  TOTAL

                                    CORRECTED FOR TIES
         U            W             Z       2-TAILED P
      342.0        963.0        -1.4112       0.1582
```

3. Use the DATA LIST command and the data in the job to fill in the values for each case in the table below.

```
DATA LIST  FREE / VARA VARB VARC
BEGIN DATA
14 3 267 18 9 122 1
7 537 19 -3 711 13 0
5
END DATA
LIST  VARIABLES=VARA TO VARC
```

VARA VARB VARC

4. You want to test the hypothesis that vitamin C helps cure the common cold. Variable MEDS (coded 1=200mg vitamin C/day, 2=placebo, and 3=no meds) indicates whether an individual took vitamin C, and variable RECOVER indicates for each individual the time it took cold symptoms to subside.
   a. What SPSS-X command(s) perform a Mann-Whitney test that compares the recovery times of people who took vitamin C with the recovery times of people who did not take medications?
   b. What SPSS-X command(s) perform a Kruskal-Wallis one-way analysis of variance on the recovery times of all three groups of people?

5. You want to determine whether secondary school experience fosters an interest in sports. You randomly ask 100 students from each of three categories (variable EDUC, coded 1=public school education, 2=private school education, 3= attended both) whether they love sports. You discover that 79 students from public schools, 74 students from private schools, and 68 students who have attended both public and private schools express a love for sports.
   a. Write an SPSS-X job to test the hypothesis that secondary school experience has no influence on an individual's love of sports.
   b. How would you modify the job in (a) to determine whether secondary school experience fosters a dissatisfaction with sports?

Statistical Concepts

1. For each of the nonparametric procedures below, indicate the lowest level of measurement for which the procedure is appropriate:
   a. Mann-Whitney test.
   b. Sign test.
   c. Kruskal-Wallis test.
   d. One-sample chi-square test.
   e. Rank correlation coefficient.

2. Identify the nonparametric analogs of each of the following parametric statistics or procedures.
   a. Pearson correlation coefficient.
   b. Independent-samples t test.
   c. Analysis of variance.
   d. Paired-samples t test.

3. State the null hypothesis tested by the following nonparametric procedures:
   a. Mann-Whitney test.
   b. Kruskal-Wallis test.
   c. Sign test.
   d. One-sample chi-square test.

4. If your data satisfy the assumptions for a one-way analysis of variance, is it reasonable to perform a Kruskal-Wallis test instead of a (parametric) one-way analysis of variance? Why or why not?

Data Analysis

Use the BANK system file for Questions 1–3.

1. a. Using the Mann-Whitney procedure, test the hypothesis that work experience has the same distribution for women and men. What do your results indicate?
   b. Repeat the above analysis, comparing nonwhites and whites rather than women and men.

2. a. Use the Kruskal-Wallis procedure to test the hypothesis that the four sex-race groups have the same age distribution. Summarize your results.

   b. What assumptions are you making? Are they satisfied for these data?

3. Compute the Spearman rank correlation coefficients for the education, sex, work experience, race, and age variables. Compute Pearson correlations for the same variables and compare the coefficients from the two procedures.

4. Data for cardiac arrests are given below. Use the WEIGHT command to enter these data and obtain a one-sample chi-square test of the hypothesis that the days of the week are equally hazardous for people with a history of heart disease. Repeat the analysis, this time examining people with *no* history of heart disease. What do the results indicate?

DAY	NO	YES
MONDAY	22	16
TUESDAY	7	10
WEDNESDAY	6	10
THURSDAY	13	16
FRIDAY	5	10
SATURDAY	4	13
SUNDAY	6	14

5. a. Redo some of your analyses from previous chapters using the appropriate nonparametric tests described in this chapter. Identify a situation in which each test is useful.

   b. Compare the results obtained from the nonparametric procedures to those obtained from the parametric tests. Do you obtain similar results?

6. Use the Western Electric data for the following exercises.

   a. Use an appropriate nonparametric procedure to test the hypothesis that smokers and nonsmokers have the same distribution of serum cholesterol.

   b. Calculate a nonparametric correlation coefficient between serum cholesterol and diastolic blood pressure. Compare this value to that obtained from the correlations procedure. Why are the values different?

   c. For the three education groups, use a nonparametric procedure to examine the relationship between educational level and number of cigarettes smoked.

Chapter 13   Statistical Models for Salary: Multiple Linear Regression Analysis

In Chapter 6, procedure MEANS was used to describe beginning salary levels for groups of bank employees based on race and sex. In this chapter, we will examine both beginning salary and salary progression for bank employees hired between 1969 and 1971. To do this, we will formulate a mathematical model that relates beginning salary to various employee characteristics such as seniority, education, and previous work experience. One important objective is to determine whether the sex and race variables are important predictors of salary.

The technique used to develop the model is linear regression analysis, one of the most versatile procedures for data analysis. Regression can be used to summarize data as well as to quantify relationships among variables. Another frequent application of regression analysis is predicting values of new observations based on a previously derived model.

13.1
INTRODUCTION TO REGRESSION STATISTICS

Before examining a model that relates beginning salary to several other variables, consider the relationship between beginning salary and "current" (March 1977) salary. For employees hired during a similar time period, beginning salary should serve as a reasonably good predictor of salary at a later date. Although superstars and underachievers might progress differently from the group as a whole, salary progression should be similar for the others. The scatterplot of beginning salary and current salary in Figure 13.1 supports this hypothesis.

A scatterplot may suggest what type of mathematical functions may be appropriate for summarizing the data. A variety of functions are useful in fitting models to data. Parabolas, hyperbolas, polynomials, trigonometric functions, and many more are potential candidates. For the scatterplot in Figure 13.1, current salaries tend to increase linearly with increases in beginning salary. If the plot indicates that a straight line is not a good summary measure of the relationship, you should consider other possibilities, including attempts to transform the data to achieve linearity (see Section 13.25).

Figure 13.1   Scatterplot of beginning and current salaries

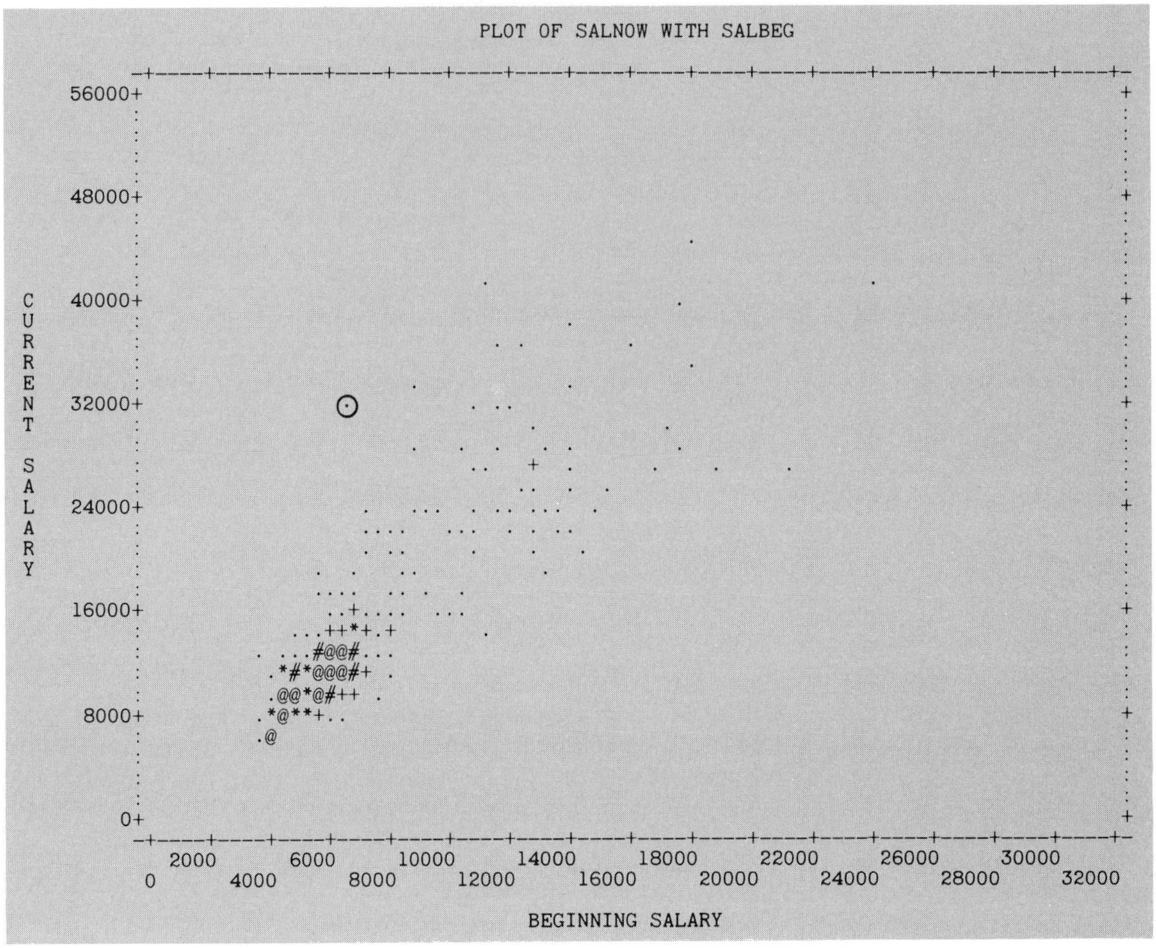

PLOT OF SALNOW WITH SALBEG

13.2
Outliers

A plot may also indicate the presence of points suspiciously different from the others. Examine carefully such observations, termed *outliers*, to see if they came from errors in gathering, coding, or entering data. The circled point in Figure 13.1 appears to be an outlier. Though neither the value of beginning salary ($6,300) nor the value of current salary ($32,000) is unique, jointly they are unusual.

The treatment of outliers can be difficult. If the point is really incorrect, due to coding or entry problems, you should correct it and rerun the analysis. If there is no apparent explanation for the outlier, consider interactions with other variables as a possible explanation. For example, the outlier may represent an employee who was hired as a low-paid clerical worker while pursuing an MBA degree. After graduation, a rapid rise in position was possible, making education the variable that explains the unusual salary characteristics of the employee.

13.3
Choosing a Regression Line

Since current salary tends to increase linearly with beginning salary, a straight line can be used to summarize the relationship. The equation for the line is

predicted current salary $= B_0 + B_1$(beginning salary)

The *slope* (B_1) is the dollar change in the fitted current salary for a dollar change in the beginning salary. The *intercept* (B_0) is the theoretical estimate of current salary if there were a beginning salary of 0.

However, the observed data points do not all fall on a straight line but cluster about it. Many lines can be drawn through the data points; the problem is to select among them. The method of *least squares* results in a line that minimizes the sum of squared vertical distances from the observed data points to the line. Any other line has a larger sum. Figure 13.3a shows the least-squares line superimposed on the salary scatterplot. Several vertical distances from points to the line are also shown.

Figure 13.3a   Regression line for beginning and current salaries

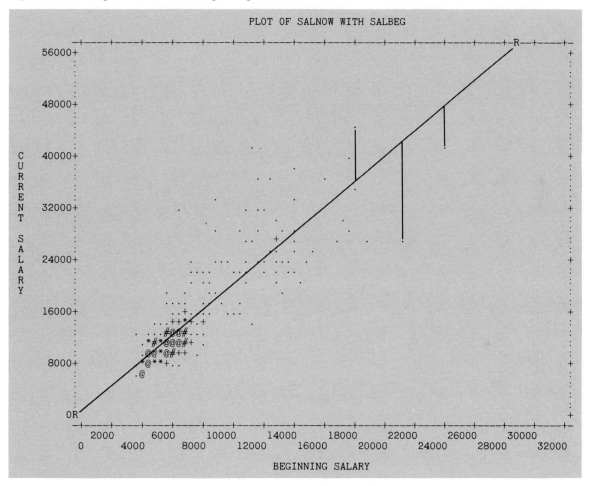

You can use the SPSS-X REGRESSION procedure to calculate the least-squares line. For the data in Figure 13.1, that line is

predicted current salary = 771.28 + 1.91(beginning salary)

The slope and intercept values are shown in the column labeled B in the output shown in Figure 13.3b.

Figure 13.3b   Statistics for variables in the equation

```
------------------ VARIABLES IN THE EQUATION ------------------

VARIABLE              B           SE B        BETA         T  SIG T

SALBEG           1.90945       0.04741     0.88012    40.276 0.0000
(CONSTANT)     771.28230     355.47194                 2.170 0.0305
```

13.4
The Standardized Regression Coefficient

The *standardized regression coefficient*, labeled BETA in Figure 13.3b, is defined as

$$BETA = B_1 \frac{S_X}{S_Y}$$

Multiplication of the regression coefficient (B_1) by the ratio of the standard deviation of the independent variable (S_X) to the standard deviation of the dependent variable (S_Y) results in a dimensionless coefficient. In fact, the BETA coefficient is the slope of the least-squares line when both X and Y are expressed as Z scores. The BETA coefficient is further discussed in Section 13.35.

13.5
From Samples to Populations

Generally, more is sought in regression analysis than a description of observed data. One usually wishes to draw inferences about the relationship of the variables in the population from which the sample was taken. How are beginning and current salaries related for all employees, not just those included in the sample? To draw inferences about population values based on sample results, the following assumptions are needed:

Normality and Equality of Variance. For any fixed value of the independent variable X, the distribution of the dependent variable Y is normal, with mean $\mu_{Y/X}$ (the mean of Y for a given X) and a constant variance of σ^2. Figure 13.5 illustrates this assumption. This assumption specifies that not all employees with the same beginning salary have the same current salary. Instead, there is a normal distribution of current salaries for each beginning salary. Though the distributions have different means, they have the same variance σ^2.

Figure 13.5   Regression assumptions

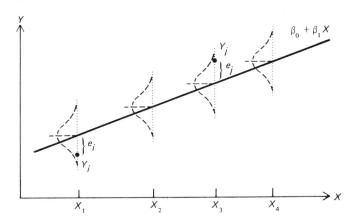

Independence. The Y's are statistically independent of each other. That is, observations are in no way influenced by other observations. For example, observations are *not* independent if they are based on repeated measurements from the same experimental unit. If three observations are taken from each of four families, the twelve observations are not independent.

Linearity. The mean values $\mu_{Y/X}$ all lie on a straight line, which is the population regression line. This line is drawn in Figure 13.5. An alternative way of stating this assumption is that the linear model is correct.

When there is a single independent variable, the model can be summarized by

$$Y_i = \beta_0 + \beta_1 X_i + e_i$$

The population values (parameters) for the slope and intercept are denoted by β_1 and β_0. The term e_i, often called an error or disturbance, is the difference between the observed value of Y_i and the subpopulation mean at the point X_i. The e_i are assumed to be normally distributed, independent, random variables with a mean of 0 and variance of σ^2 (see Figure 13.5).

13.6
Estimating Population Parameters

Since β_0 and β_1 are unknown population parameters, they must be estimated from the sample. The least-squares coefficients B_0 and B_1, discussed in Section 13.3, are used to estimate the population parameters.

However, the slope and intercept estimated from a single sample typically differ from the population values and vary from sample to sample. To use these estimates for inference about the population values, the sampling distributions of the two statistics are needed. (See Chapter 7 for further discussion of sampling distributions and hypothesis testing.) When the assumptions of linear regression are met, the sampling distributions of B_0 and B_1 are normal with means of β_0 and β_1.

The standard error of B_0 is

$$\sigma_{B_0} = \sigma \sqrt{\frac{1}{N} + \frac{\overline{X}^2}{(N-1)S_X{}^2}}$$

where $S_X{}^2$ is the sample variance of the independent variable. The standard error of B_1 is

$$\sigma_{B_1} = \frac{\sigma}{\sqrt{(N-1)S_X{}^2}}$$

Since the population variance of the errors, σ^2, is not known, it must also be estimated. The usual estimate of σ^2 is

$$S^2 = \frac{\sum_{i=1}^{N}(Y_i - B_0 - B_1X_i)^2}{N-2}$$

The positive square root of σ^2 is termed the *standard error of the estimate,* or the standard deviation of the residuals. (The reason for this name is discussed in Section 13.15.) The estimated standard errors of the slope and intercept are printed in the third column (labeled SE B) in Figure 13.3b.

13.7
Testing Hypotheses

A frequently tested hypothesis is that there is no linear relationship between X and Y—that the slope of the population regression line is 0. The statistic used to test this hypothesis is

$$t = \frac{B_1}{S_{B_1}}$$

The distribution of the statistic, when the assumptions are met and the hypothesis of no linear relationship is true, is the Student's t distribution with $N-2$ degrees of freedom. The statistic for testing the hypothesis that the intercept is 0 is

$$t = \frac{B_0}{S_{B_0}}$$

Its distribution is also the Student's t with $N-2$ degrees of freedom.

These t statistics and their two-tailed observed significance levels are printed in the last two columns of Figure 13.3b. The small observed significance level (less than 0.00005) associated with the slope for the salary data supports the hypothesis that beginning and current salary are linearly related.

13.8
Confidence Intervals

A statistic calculated from a sample provides a point estimate of the unknown parameter. A point estimate can be thought of as the single best guess for the population value. The estimated value from the sample is typically different from the value of the unknown population parameter. Hopefully, it isn't too far away. Based on the sample estimate, it is possible to calculate a range of values that, with a designated likelihood, includes the population value. Such a range is called a *confidence interval*. For example, as shown in Figure 13.8, the 95% confidence interval for β_1, the population slope, is 1.816 to 2.003.

Figure 13.8 Confidence intervals

```
VARIABLE       95% CONFDNCE INTRVL B

SALBEG            1.81629      2.00261
(CONSTANT)       72.77921   1469.78540
```

Ninety-five percent confidence means that, if repeated samples are drawn from a population under the same conditions and 95% confidence intervals are calculated, 95% of the intervals will contain the unknown parameter β_1. Since the parameter value is unknown, it is not possible to determine whether or not a particular interval contains it.

13.9
Goodness of Fit

An important part of any statistical procedure that builds models from data is establishing how well the model actually fits. This topic encompasses the detection of possible violations of the required assumptions in the data being analyzed. Sections 13.10 through 13.16 are limited to the question of how close to the fitted line the observed points fall. Subsequent sections discuss other assumptions and tests for their violation.

13.10
The R^2 Coefficient

A commonly used measure of the goodness of fit of a linear model is R^2, sometimes called the *coefficient of determination*. It can be thought of in a variety of ways. Besides being the square of the correlation coefficient between variables X and Y, it is the square of the correlation coefficient between Y, the observed value of the dependent variable, and $\hat{Y}$, the predicted value of Y from the fitted line. If for each employee one computes (based on the coefficients in the output in Figure 13.3b) the predicted salary

predicted current salary $= 771.28 + 1.91(\text{beginning salary})$

and then calculates the square of the Pearson correlation coefficient between predicted current salary and observed current salary, R^2 is obtained. If all the observations fall on the regression line, R^2 is 1. If there is no linear relationship between the dependent and independent variables, R^2 is 0.

Note that R^2 is a measure of the goodness of fit of a particular model and that an R^2 of 0 does not necessarily mean that there is no association between the variables. Instead, it indicates that there is no *linear relationship*.

Figure 13.10 Summary statistics for the equation

```
MULTIPLE R            0.88012
R SQUARE              0.77461
ADJUSTED R SQUARE     0.77413
STANDARD ERROR     3246.14226
```

In the output shown in Figure 13.10, R^2 is labeled R-SQUARE; its square root is called MULTIPLE R. The sample R^2 tends to be an optimistic estimate of how well the model fits the population. The model usually does not fit the population as well as it fits the sample from which it is derived. The statistic *adjusted* R^2 attempts to correct R^2 to more closely reflect the goodness of fit of the model in the population. Adjusted R^2 is given by

$$R_a{}^2 = R^2 - \frac{p(1 - R^2)}{N - p - 1}$$

where p is the number of independent variables in the equation (1 in the salary example).

13.11
Analysis of Variance

To test the hypothesis of no linear relationship between X and Y, several equivalent statistics can be computed. When there is a single independent variable, the hypothesis that the population R^2 is 0 is identical to the hypothesis that the population slope is 0. The test for $R^2_{pop}=0$ is usually obtained from the *analysis of variance* (ANOVA) table (see Figure 13.11a).

Figure 13.11a   Analysis of variance table

```
ANALYSIS OF VARIANCE
                 DF        SUM OF SQUARES        MEAN SQUARE
REGRESSION        1    17092967800.01931    17092967800.0193
RESIDUAL        472     4973671469.79483       10537439.55465

F =     1622.11776       SIGNIF F =    .0000
```

The total observed variability in the dependent variable is subdivided into two components—that which is attributable to the regression (REGRESSION) and that which is not (RESIDUAL). Consider Figure 13.11b. For a particular point, the distance from Y_i to $\bar{Y}$ (the mean of the Y's) can be subdivided into two parts.

$$Y_i - \bar{Y} = (Y_i - \hat{Y}_i) + (\hat{Y}_i - \bar{Y})$$

Figure 13.11b   Components of variability

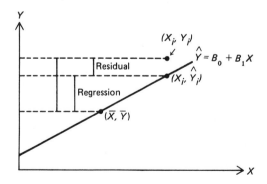

The distance from Y_i, the observed value, to $\hat{Y}_i$, the value predicted by the regression line, or $Y_i - \hat{Y}_i$, is 0 if the regression line passes through the point. It is called the *residual from the regression*. The second component $(\hat{Y}_i - \bar{Y})$ is the distance from the regression line to the mean of the Y's. This distance is "explained" by the regression in that it represents the improvement in the estimate of the dependent variable achieved by the regression. Without the regression, the mean of the dependent variable $(\bar{Y})$ is used as the estimate. It can be shown that

$$\sum_{i=1}^{N} (Y_i - \overline{Y})^2 = \sum_{i=1}^{N} (Y_i - \hat{Y}_i)^2 + \sum_{i=1}^{N} (\hat{Y}_i - \overline{Y})^2$$

The first quantity following the equals sign is called the *residual sum of squares* and the second quantity is the *regression sum of squares*. The sum of these is called the *total sum of squares*.

The ANOVA table displays these two sums of squares under the heading SUM OF SQUARES (Figure 13.11a). The MEAN SQUARE for each entry is the SUM OF SQUARES divided by the degrees of freedom. If the regression assumptions are met, the ratio of the mean square regression to the mean square residual is distributed as an F statistic with p and $N-p-1$ degrees of freedom. F serves to test how well the regression model fits the data. If the probability associated with the F statistic is small, the hypothesis that $R^2_{pop}=0$ is rejected. For the present example, the F statistic is

$$F = \frac{\text{MEAN SQUARE REGRESSION}}{\text{MEAN SQUARE RESIDUAL}} = 1622$$

The observed significance level (SIGNIF F) is less than 0.00005.

The square root of the F value, 40.28, is the value of the t statistic for the slope in Figure 13.3b. The square of a t value with k degrees of freedom is an F value with 1 and k degrees of freedom. Therefore, either t or F values can be computed to test that $\beta_i=0$.

Another useful summary statistic is the standard error of the estimate (Section 13.15), S, which can also be calculated as the square root of the residual mean square.

13.12
Another Interpretation of R^2

Partitioning the sum of squares of the dependent variable allows another interpretation of R^2. It is the proportion of the variation in the dependent variable "explained" by the model.

$$R^2 = 1 - \frac{\text{RESIDUAL SUM OF SQUARES}}{\text{TOTAL SUM OF SQUARES}} = 0.775$$

Similarly, adjusted R^2 is

$$R^2_a = 1 - \frac{\text{RESIDUAL SUM OF SQUARES}/(N - p - 1)}{\text{TOTAL SUM OF SQUARES}/(N - 1)}$$

where p is the number of independent variables in the equation (1 in the salary example).

13.13
Predicted Values and Their Standard Errors

By comparing the observed values of the dependent variable to the values predicted by the regression equation, you can learn a good deal about how well a model and the various assumptions fit the data (see the discussion of residuals beginning with Section 13.17). Predicted values are also of interest when the results are used to predict new data. You may wish to predict the mean Y for all cases with a given value of X, denoted X_0, or to predict the value of Y for a single case. For example, you can predict either the mean salary for all employees with a beginning salary of $10,000 or the salary for a particular employee with a beginning salary of $10,000. In both situations, the predicted value

$$\hat{Y}_0 = B_0 + B_1 X_0 = 771 + 1.91 \times 10,000 = 19,871$$

is the same. What differs is the standard error.

13.14
Predicting Mean Response   The estimated standard error for the predicted mean Y at X_0 is

$$S_{\hat{Y}} = S \sqrt{\frac{1}{N} + \frac{(X_0 - \overline{X})^2}{(N-1)S_X^2}}$$

The formula for the standard error shows that the smallest value occurs when X_0 is equal to $\overline{X}$, the mean of X. The larger the distance from the mean, the greater the standard error. Thus, the mean of Y for a given X is better estimated for central values of the observed X's than for outlying values. Figure 13.14a is a plot of the standard errors of predicted mean salaries for different values of beginning salary.

Figure 13.14a   Standard errors for predicted mean responses

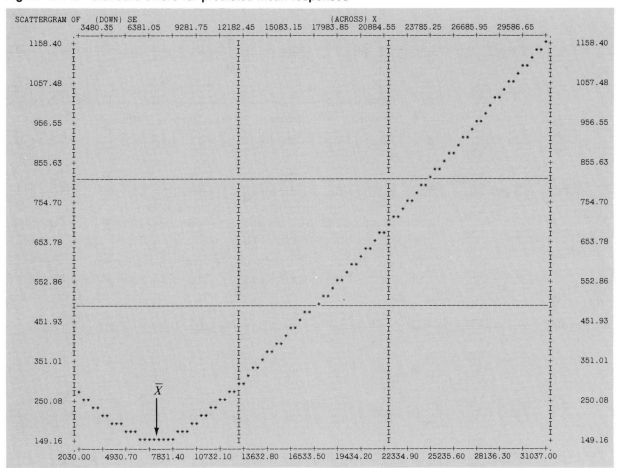

Prediction intervals for the mean predicted salary are calculated in the standard way. The 95% confidence interval at X_0 is

$$\hat{Y} \pm t_{\left(1 - \frac{\alpha}{2}, N-2\right)} S_{\hat{Y}}$$

Figure 13.14b shows a typical 95% confidence band for predicted mean responses. It is narrowest at the mean of X and increases as the distance from the mean $(X_0 - \overline{X})$ increases.

Figure 13.14b   95% confidence band for mean prediction

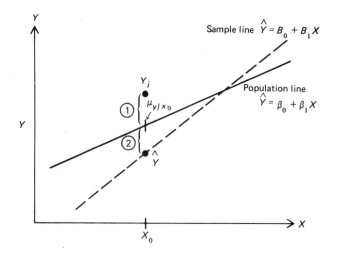

13.15
Predicting a New Value   Although the predicted value for a single new observation at X_0 is the same as the predicted value for the mean at X_0, the standard error is not. The two sources of error when predicting an individual observation are illustrated in Figure 13.15. They are

• The individual value may differ from the population mean of Y for X_0.

• The estimate of the population mean at X_0 may differ from the population mean.

Figure 13.15   Sources of error in predicting individual observations

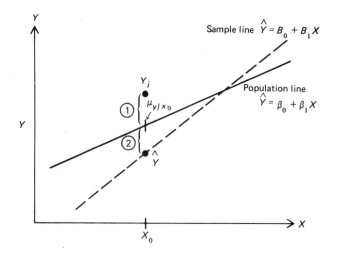

When estimating the mean response, only the second error component is considered. The variance of the individual prediction is the variance of the mean prediction plus the variance of Y_i for a given X. This can be written as

$$S^2_{ind\hat{Y}} = S^2_{\hat{Y}} + S^2 = S^2\left(1 + \frac{1}{N} + \frac{(X_0 - \bar{X})^2}{(N-1)S_X^2}\right)$$

Prediction intervals for the new observation are obtained by substituting S_{indY} for S_Y in the equation for the confidence intervals for the mean given in Section 13.14. If the sample size is large, the terms $1/N$ and

$$\frac{(X_0 - \bar{X})^2}{(N-1)S_X^2}$$

are negligible. In that case, the standard error is simply S, which explains the name *standard error of the estimate* for S (see Section 13.6).

13.16
Reading the Casewise Plot

Figure 13.16 shows the output from the beginning and end of a plot of the salary data. The sequence number of the case and an optional labeling variable (SEXRACE) are listed first; then, the plot of standardized residuals; then, the observed (SALNOW), predicted (PRED), and residual (RESID) values; and finally, the standard error of the mean prediction (SEPRED). The variance of an individual prediction can be obtained by adding S^2 to the square of each of the standard error values. You can generate and save predicted values and the standard errors of the mean responses in the REGRESSION procedure, and you can print both of these values for all cases or for a subset of cases along with a casewise plot.

Figure 13.16   Casewise plot with predicted values and standard errors

```
CASEWISE PLOT OF STANDARDIZED RESIDUAL
                      -3.0           0.0           3.0
       SEQNUM   SEXRACE   0:.............:.............:0     SALNOW       *PRED      *RESID     *SEPRED
            1    1.0000   .              *.           .    16080.0000   16810.6600   -730.6600   167.1489
            2    1.0000   .       *      .            .    41400.0000   46598.0758  -5198.0758   828.6655
            3    1.0000   .              .  *         .    21960.0000   20247.6695   1712.3305   219.3531
            4    1.0000   .              .   *        .    19200.0000   17383.4949   1816.5051   174.0406
            5    1.0000   .       *      .            .    28350.0000   33995.7076  -5645.7076   523.9021
            6    1.0000   .              . *          .    27250.0000   25586.4910   1663.5090   329.1520
            7    1.0000   .              .  *         .    16080.0000   13946.4854   2133.5146   149.1662
            8    1.0000   .              .    *       .    14100.0000   11082.3108   3017.6892   163.3307
            9    1.0000   .              . *          .    12420.0000   10394.9089   2025.0911   171.0096
           10    1.0000   .              *.           .    12300.0000   12800.8156   -500.8156   151.0211
           11    1.0000   .              .  *         .    15720.0000   12800.8156   2919.1844   151.0211
           12    1.0000   .       *      .            .     8880.0000   12227.9807  -3347.9807   153.9241
          ...
          ...
          ...
          470    4.0000   .              *            .     9420.0000    9592.9401   -172.9401   181.5927
          471    4.0000   .              .*           .     9780.0000    9134.6721    645.3279   188.3196
          472    4.0000   .             *.            .     7680.0000    9249.2391  -1569.2391   186.5956
          473    4.0000   .             * .           .     7380.0000    8561.8372  -1181.8372   197.3294
          474    4.0000   .          *   .            .     8340.0000   10738.6099  -2398.6099   166.9964
       SEQNUM   SEXRACE   0:.............:.............:0     SALNOW       *PRED      *RESID     *SEPRED
                          -3.0           0.0           3.0
```

13.17
Searching for Violations of Assumptions

You usually don't know in advance the appropriateness of a model such as linear regression. Therefore, a search focused on residuals is conducted to look for evidence that the necessary assumptions are violated.

13.18
Residuals

In model building, a *residual* is what is left after the model is fit. It is the difference between an observed value and the value predicted by the model.

$$E_i = Y_i - B_0 - B_1X_i = Y_i - \hat{Y}_i$$

In regression analysis, the true errors e_i are assumed to be independent normal values with a mean of 0 and a constant variance of σ^2. If the model is appropriate for the data, the observed residuals E_i, which are estimates of the true errors e_i, should have similar characteristics.

If the intercept term is included in the equation, the mean of the residuals is always 0, so it provides no information about the true mean of the errors. Since the sum of the residuals is constrained to be 0, they are *not* strictly independent. However, if the number of residuals is large when compared to the number of independent variables, the dependency among the residuals can be ignored for practical purposes.

The relative magnitudes of residuals are easier to judge when they are divided by estimates of their standard deviations. The resulting standardized residuals are expressed in standard deviation units above or below the mean. For example, the fact that a particular residual is -5198.1 provides little information. If you know that its standardized form is -3.1, you know not only that the observed value is less than the predicted value but also that the residual is larger than most in absolute value.

Residuals are sometimes adjusted in one of two ways. The *standardized residual* for case i is the residual divided by the sample standard deviation of the residuals. Standardized residuals have a mean of 0 and a standard deviation of 1. The *Studentized residual* is the residual divided by an estimate of its standard deviation that varies from point to point, depending on the distance of X_i from the mean of X. Usually standardized and Studentized residuals are close in value, but not always. The Studentized residual reflects more precisely differences in the true error variances from point to point.

13.19
Linearity

For the bivariate situation, a scatterplot is a good means for judging how well a straight line fits the data. Another convenient way is to plot the residuals against the predicted values. If the assumptions of linearity and homogeneity of variance are met, there should be no relationship between the predicted and residual values. You should be suspicious of any observable pattern.

For example, fitting a least-squares line to the data in the two left-hand plots in Figure 13.19a yields the residual plots shown on the right. The two residual plots show patterns since straight lines do not fit the data well. Systematic patterns between the predicted values and the residuals suggest possible violations of the linearity assumption. If the assumption were met, the residuals would be randomly distributed in a band about the horizontal straight line through 0 as shown in Figure 13.19b.

Residuals can also be plotted against individual independent variables. Again, if the assumptions are met, you should see a horizontal band of residuals. Consider plotting the residuals against independent variables not in the equation as well. If the residuals are not randomly distributed, you may want to include the variable in the equation for a multiple regression model (see Sections 13.30 through 13.50).

Figure 13.19a   Standardized residuals scatterplots

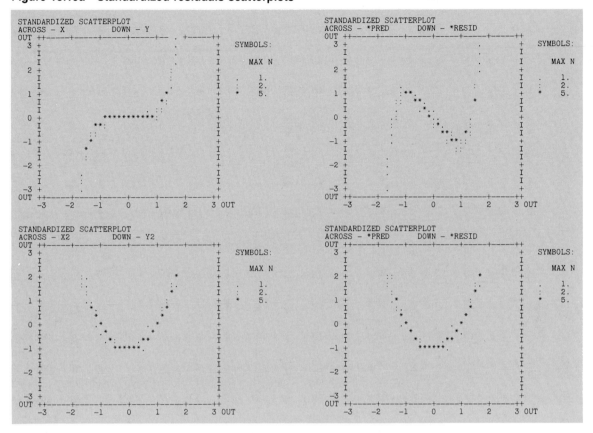

Figure 13.19b   Randomly distributed residuals

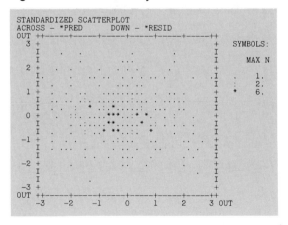

13.20
Equality of Variance

You can also use the previously described plots to check for violations of the equality of variance assumption. If the spread of the residuals increases or decreases with values of the independent variables or with predicted values, you should question the assumption of constant variance of Y for all values of X.

Figure 13.20 Unequal variance

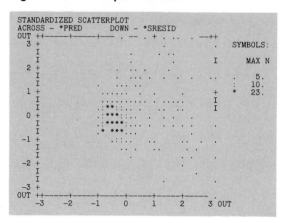

```
STANDARDIZED SCATTERPLOT
ACROSS - *PRED      DOWN - *SRESID
OUT ++-----+-----+--- . --- . + . .. . ---++
  3 +                .        .         .    SYMBOLS:
    I                    .    .
    I                    .    .         I     MAX N
  2 +               .  ...    .
    I               . ...   .                 .    5.
    I               ... .                 ..  :   10.
  1 +              ......  .    .          +  *   23.
    I             .:::::.  . .      .       I
    I            :.**:::. ...   ...         I
  0 +            :.***.:  ...
    I            .:****.:...  .
    I            .* ***...
 -1 +            .:::..  ..
    I             .. .. .  .
    I                .   .
 -2 +
    I
    I
 -3 +
OUT ++-----+-----+-----+-----+-----+-----.
    -3   -2   -1    0    1    2    3 OUT
```

Figure 13.20 is a plot of the Studentized residuals against the predicted values for the salary data. The spread of the residuals increases with the magnitude of the predicted values, suggesting that the variability of current salaries increases with salary level. Thus, the equality of variance assumption appears to be violated.

13.21
Independence of Error

Whenever the data are collected and recorded sequentially, you should plot residuals against the sequence variable. Even if time is not considered a variable in the model, it could influence the residuals. For example, suppose you are studying survival time after surgery as a function of complexity of surgery, amount of blood transfused, dosage of medication, and so forth. In addition to these variables, it is also possible that the surgeon's skill increased with each operation and that a patient's survival time is influenced by the number of prior patients treated. The plot of residuals corresponding to the order in which patients received surgery shows a shorter survival time for earlier patients than for later patients (see Figure 13.21). If sequence and the residual are independent, you should not see a discernible pattern.

Figure 13.21 Casewise serial plot

```
CASEWISE PLOT OF STUDENTIZED RESIDUAL
              -3.0      0.0      3.0      LIFE    *PRED   *RESID  *SRESID
   SEQNUM  TIME  0:........:........:0
        1  78012      . *      .        .    15.0000  19.5624  -4.5624  -2.2598
        2  78055      . *      .        .    13.5000  17.8974  -4.3974  -2.1856
        3  78122      .  *     .        .     9.9000  13.8390  -3.9390  -1.9871
        4  78134      .    *   .        .    15.5000  18.5218  -3.0218  -1.4997
        5  78233      .     *  .        .    35.0000  38.2933  -3.2933  -1.7466
        6  78298      .      * .        .    14.7000  16.6487  -1.9487   -.9720
        7  78344      .       *.        .    34.8000  36.0040  -1.2040   -.6258
        8  79002      .       .*        .    20.8000  20.8111   -.0111   -.0055
        9  79008      .       . *       .    15.9000  14.8796   1.0204    .5123
       10  79039      .       .  *      .    22.0000  21.6436    .3564    .1762
       11  79101      .       .   *     .    13.7000  11.7578   1.9422    .9910
       12  79129      .       .    *    .    14.2000  11.4456   2.7544   1.4082
       13  79178      .       .    *    .    33.2000  30.3847   2.8153   1.4144
       14  79188      .       .     *   .    26.2000  22.4761   3.7239   1.8401
       15  79189      .       .      *  .    37.4000  33.2984   4.1016   2.0920
      ...
```

The *Durbin-Watson* statistic, a test for sequential correlation of adjacent error terms, is defined as

$$D = \frac{\sum_{t=2}^{N} (E_t - E_{t-1})^2}{\sum_{t=1}^{N} E_t^2}$$

The differences between successive residuals tend to be small when error terms are positively correlated and large when error terms are negatively correlated. Thus, small values of D indicate positive correlation and large values of D indicate negative correlation. Consult tables of the D statistic for bounds upon which significance tests can be based (Neter & Wasserman, 1974).

13.22
Normality

The distribution of residuals may not appear to be normal for reasons other than actual nonnormality: misspecification of the model, nonconstant variance, a small number of residuals actually available for analysis, etc. Therefore, you should pursue several lines of investigation. One of the simplest is to construct a histogram of the residuals such as the one shown in Figure 13.22a for the salary data.

Figure 13.22a   Histogram of Studentized residuals

```
HISTOGRAM
STUDENTIZED RESIDUAL
   N   EXP N      ( * = 2 CASES,    . : = NORMAL CURVE)
   7    0.37    OUT ****
   2    0.73   3.00 *
   4    1.85   2.66 :*
   2    4.23   2.33 *.
   6    8.65   2.00 ***.
  12   15.85   1.66 ******  .
   7   26.01   1.33 ****           .
  18   38.23   1.00 ********           .
  35   50.34   0.66 ****************       .
  63   59.38   0.33 *******************************.**
  87   62.74   0.00 *******************************:.*************
 114   59.38  -0.33 *******************************:******************************
  64   50.34  -0.66 ************************:*******
  32   38.23  -1.00 ****************   .
   9   26.01  -1.33 *****          .
   6   15.85  -1.66 ***      .
   1    8.65  -2.00 *   .
   1    4.23  -2.33 *.
   2    1.85  -2.66 :
   0    0.73  -3.00 .
   2    0.37    OUT *
```

The REGRESSION histogram contains a tally of the observed number of residuals (labeled N) in each interval and the number expected in a normal distribution with the same mean and variance as the residuals (EXP N). The first and last intervals (OUT) contain residuals more than 3.16 standard deviations from the mean. Such residuals deserve examination. A histogram of expected N's is superimposed on that of the observed N's. Expected frequencies are indicated by a period. When observed and expected frequencies overlap, a colon is printed. However, it is unreasonable to expect the observed residuals to be exactly normal—some deviation is expected because of sampling variation. Even if the errors are normally distributed in the population, sample residuals are only approximately normal.

In the histogram in Figure 13.22a, the distribution does not seem normal since there is an exaggerated clustering of residuals toward the center and a straggling tail toward large positive values. Thus, the normality assumption may be violated.

Another way to compare the observed distribution of residuals to that expected under the assumption of normality is to plot the two cumulative distributions against each other for a series of points. If the two distributions are identical, a straight line results. By observing how points scatter about the expected straight line, you can compare the two distributions.

Figure 13.22b   A normal probability (P-P) plot

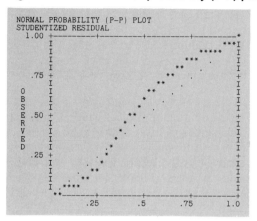

Figure 13.22b is a cumulative probability plot of the salary residuals. Initially, the observed residuals are below the straight line since there is a smaller number of large negative residuals than expected. However, once the greatest concentration of residuals is reached, the observed points are above the line since the observed cumulative proportion exceeds the expected.

13.23
Locating Outliers

You can spot outliers readily on residual plots since they are cases with very large positive or negative residuals. In the histogram, cases with values greater than 3.16 or less than −3.16 appear in the OUT interval. In the scatterplots, they appear on the borders of the plot, labeled OUT. Since you usually want more information about outliers, use the casewise plotting facility to print identification numbers and a variety of other statistics for cases having residuals beyond a specified cutoff point.

Figure 13.23   Casewise plot of residuals outliers

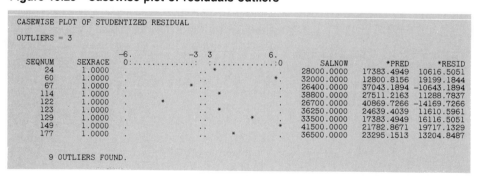

Figure 13.23 lists information for the nine cases with Studentized residuals greater than 3 in absolute value. Only two of these nine employees have current salaries less than those predicted by the model (cases 67 and 122), while the others

have larger salaries. The second column contains identifier information that indicates that all outliers are white males (SEXRACE=1). They all have large salaries, an average of $33,294, while the average for the sample is only $13,767. Thus, there is some evidence to suspect that the model may not fit well for the highly paid cases.

13.24
When Assumptions
Appear To Be Violated

When evidence of violation of assumptions appears, you can pursue one of two strategies. You can either formulate an alternative model, such as weighted least squares, or you can transform the variables so that the current model will be more adequate. For example, taking logs, square roots, or reciprocals can stabilize the variance, achieve normality, or linearize a relationship.

13.25
Coaxing a Nonlinear
Relationship to Linearity

To try to achieve linearity, you can transform either the dependent or independent variables or both. If you alter the scale of independent variables, linearity can be achieved without any effect on the distribution of the dependent variable. Thus, if the dependent variable is normally distributed with constant variance for each value of X, it remains so.

When you transform the dependent variable, its distribution is changed. This new distribution must then satisfy the assumptions of the analysis. For example, if logs of the values of the dependent variable are taken, log Y—not the original Y—must be normally distributed with constant variance.

The choice of transformations depends on several considerations. If the form of the true model governing the relationship is known, it should dictate the choice. For instance, if it is known that $\hat{Y}=AC^X$ is an adequate model, taking logs of both sides of the equation results in

$$\log \hat{Y}_i = \underset{[B_0]}{(\log A)} + \underset{[B_1]}{(\log C)} X_i$$

Thus log Y is linearly related to X.

Figure 13.25   A transformed relationship

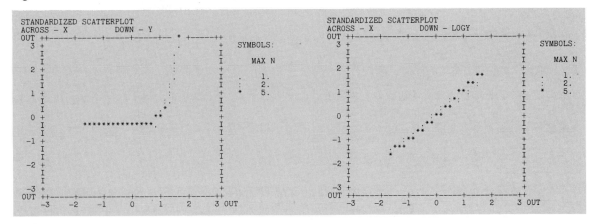

If the true model is not known, you should choose the transformation by examining the plotted data. Frequently, a relationship appears nearly linear for part of the data but is curved for the rest. The first plot in Figure 13.25 is an example. Taking the log of the dependent variable results in the second plot—an improved linear fit.

Other transformations that may diminish curvature are the square root of Y and $-1/Y$. The choice depends, to a certain extent, on the severity of the problem.

13.26
Coping with Skewness

When the distribution of residuals is positively skewed, the log transformation of the dependent variable is often helpful. For negatively skewed distributions, the square transformation is common. It should be noted that the F tests used in regression hypothesis testing are usually quite insensitive to moderate departures from normality.

13.27
Stabilizing the Variance

If the variance of the residuals is not constant, you can try a variety of remedial measures:

- When the variance is proportional to the mean of Y for a given X, use the square root of Y if all Y_i are positive.
- When the standard deviation is proportional to the mean, try the logarithmic transformation.
- When the standard deviation is proportional to the square of the mean, use the reciprocal of Y.
- When Y is a proportion or rate, the arcsin transformation may stabilize the variance.

13.28
Transforming the Salary Data

The assumptions of constant variance and normality appear to be violated with the salary data (see Figures 13.20 and 13.22a). A regression equation using logs of beginning and current salary was developed to obtain a better fit to the assumptions. Figure 13.28a is a scatterplot of Studentized residuals against predicted values when logs of both variables are used in the regression equation.

Figure 13.28a   Scatterplot of transformed salary data

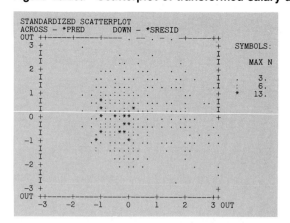

Compare Figures 13.20 and 13.28a and note the improvement in the behavior of the residuals. The spread no longer increases with increasing salary level. Also compare Figures 13.22a and 13.28b and note that the distribution in Figure 13.28b is nearly normal.

For the transformed data, the multiple R increases slightly to 0.8864, and the outlier plot contains only 4 cases (compare with Figures 13.10 and 13.23). Thus, the transformation appears to have resulted in a better model.

Figure 13.28b   Histogram of transformed salary data

```
HISTOGRAM
STUDENTIZED RESIDUAL
   N  EXP N     (  * = 2 CASES,     . : = NORMAL CURVE)
   3   0.37  OUT  **
   1   0.73  3.00  *
   3   1.85  2.66  :*
   4   4.23  2.33  *:
  10   8.65  2.00  ***.*
  14  15.85  1.66  *******.
  21  26.01  1.33  **********
  31  38.23  1.00  ***************
  48  50.34  0.66  ***********************.
  55  59.38  0.33  ****************************  .
  63  62.74  0.00  ***************************:*
  64  59.38 -0.33  **************************:**
  62  50.34 -0.66  ***********************:******
  44  38.23 -1.00  *****************:***
  28  26.01 -1.33  *************:*
  14  15.85 -1.66  *******.
   7   8.65 -2.00  ***:
   1   4.23 -2.33  *.
   1   1.85 -2.66  :
   0   0.73 -3.00
   0   0.37  OUT
```

13.29
A Final Comment on Assumptions

Rarely are assumptions not violated in one way or another in regression analysis as well as in many other statistical procedures. However, this is not a justification for ignoring the assumptions. Cranking out regressions with little thought to possible departures from the necessary assumptions can lead to problems in interpreting and applying results. Significance levels, confidence intervals, and other results are sensitive to certain types of violations and cannot be interpreted in the usual fashion if serious departures exist.

By carefully examining residuals and, if need be, using transformations or other methods of analysis, you are in a much better position to pursue analyses that solve the problems you are investigating. Even if everything isn't perfect, you can at least knowledgeably gauge the possible extent of difficulties.

13.30
MULTIPLE REGRESSION MODELS

Beginning salary seems to be a good predictor of current salary, given the evidence shown above. Nearly 80% ($R^2 = 0.77$ from Figure 13.10) of the observed variability in current salaries can be explained by beginning salary levels. Given the importance of beginning salary, how do variables such as education level, years of experience, race, and sex contribute to the prediction of the salary level at which one enters the company?

13.31
Predictors of Beginning Salary

Multiple linear regression extends bivariate regression by incorporating multiple independent variables. The model can be expressed as

$$Y_i = \beta_0 + \beta_1 X_{1i} + \beta_2 X_{2i} + \ldots + \beta_p X_{pi} + e_i$$

The notation X_{ki} indicates the value of the kth independent variable for case i. Again, the β_k terms are unknown parameters and the e_i terms are independent random variables that are normally distributed with mean 0 and constant variance σ^2. The model assumes that there is a normal distribution of the dependent variable for every combination of the values of the independent variables in the model. For example, if child's height is the dependent variable and age and maternal height are the independent variables, it is assumed that for every combination of age and maternal height there is a normal distribution of children's heights and that, though the means of these distributions may differ, all have the same variance.

13.32
The Correlation Matrix

One of the first steps in calculating an equation with several independent variables is to calculate a correlation matrix for all variables, as shown in Figure 13.32. The variables are the log of beginning salary, years of education, sex, years of work experience, race, and age in years. Variables sex and race are represented by *indicator variables*, that is, variables coded as 0 or 1. SEX is coded 1 for female and 0 for male, and MINORITY is coded 1 for nonwhite and 0 for white.

Figure 13.32   The correlation matrix

	LOGBEG	EDLEVEL	SEX	WORK	MINORITY	AGE
LOGBEG	1.000	0.686	-0.548	0.040	-0.173	-0.048
EDLEVEL	0.686	1.000	-0.356	-0.252	-0.133	-0.281
SEX	-0.548	-0.356	1.000	-0.165	-0.076	0.052
WORK	0.040	-0.252	-0.165	1.000	0.145	0.804
MINORITY	-0.173	-0.133	-0.076	0.145	1.000	0.111
AGE	-0.048	-0.281	0.052	0.804	0.111	1.000

The matrix shows the correlations between the dependent variable (LOGBEG) and each independent variable, as well as the correlations between the independent variables. Particularly note any large intercorrelations between the independent variables, since such correlations can substantially affect the results of multiple regression analysis.

13.33
Partial Regression Coefficients

The summary output for the multiple regression equation when all independent variables are included is given in Figure 13.33a. The *F* test associated with the analysis of variance table is a test of the hypothesis that

$$\beta_1 = \beta_2 = \beta_3 = \beta_4 = \beta_5 = 0$$

In other words, it is a test of whether there is a linear relationship between the dependent variable and the entire set of independent variables.

Figure 13.33a   Statistics for the equation and analysis of variance table

```
MULTIPLE R         0.78420      ANALYSIS OF VARIANCE
R SQUARE           0.61497                      DF      SUM OF SQUARES     MEAN SQUARE
ADJUSTED R SQUARE  0.61086      REGRESSION        5             6.83036         1.36607
STANDARD ERROR     0.09559      RESIDUAL        468             4.27641         0.00914

                                F =      149.49952      SIGNIF F = 0.0000
```

The statistics for the independent variables in Figure 13.33b parallel those obtained in regression with a single independent variable (see Figure 13.3b). The coefficients labeled B are called *partial regression coefficients* since the coefficient for a particular variable is adjusted for other independent variables in the equation. The equation that relates the predicted log of beginning salary to the independent variables is

LOGBEG=3.3853+0.00102(AGE)−0.10358(SEX)−0.05237(MINORITY)
        +0.03144(EDLEVEL)+0.00161(WORK)

Figure 13.33b   Statistics for variables in the equation

```
------------------- VARIABLES IN THE EQUATION -------------------

VARIABLE           B          SE B         BETA         T  SIG T

AGE           0.00102    0.6613D-03      0.07811     1.535 0.1254
SEX          -0.10358       0.01032     -0.33699   -10.038 0.0000
MINORITY     -0.05237       0.01084     -0.14157    -4.832 0.0000
EDLEVEL       0.03144       0.00175      0.59195    17.988 0.0000
WORK          0.00161    0.9241D-03      0.09143     1.740 0.0826
(CONSTANT)    3.38530       0.03323                101.866 0.0000
```

Since the dependent variable is in log units, the coefficients can be approximately interpreted in percentage terms. For example, the coefficient of -0.104 for the SEX variable when females are coded as 1 indicates that female salaries are estimated to be about 10% less than male salaries, after statistical adjustment for age, education, work history, and minority status.

13.34
Determining Important Variables

In multiple regression, one sometimes wants to assign relative importance to each independent variable. For example, you might want to know whether education is more important in predicting beginning salary than previous work experience. There are two possible answers, depending on which of the following questions is asked:

- How important are education and work experience when each one is used alone to predict beginning salary?
- How important are education and work experience when they are used to predict beginning salary along with other independent variables in the regression equation?

The first question is answered by looking at the correlation coefficients between salary and the independent variables. The larger the absolute value of the correlation coefficient, the stronger the linear association. Figure 13.32 shows that education correlates more highly with the log of salary than does previous work experience (0.686 and 0.040, respectively). Thus, you would assign more importance to education as a predictor of salary.

The answer to the second question is considerably more complicated. When the independent variables are correlated among themselves, the unique contribution of each is difficult to assess. Any statement about an independent variable is contingent upon the other variables in the equation. For example, note that the regression coefficient *(B)* for work experience is 0.0007 when it is the sole independent variable in the equation, compared to 0.00161 when the other four independent variables are also in the equation. The second coefficient is more than twice the size of the first.

13.35
BETA Coefficients

It is inappropriate to interpret the *B*'s as indicators of the relative importance of variables. The actual magnitude of the coefficients depends on the units in which the variables are measured. Only if all independent variables are measured in the same units—years, for example—are their coefficients directly comparable. When variables differ substantially in units of measurement, the sheer magnitude of their coefficients does not reveal anything about relative importance.

One way to make regression coefficients somewhat more comparable is to calculate *BETA* weights, which are the coefficients of the independent variables when all variables are expressed in standardized (*Z*-score) form. The BETA coefficients can be calculated directly from the regression coefficients using

$$BETA_k \ = \ B_k\left(\frac{S_k}{S_Y}\right)$$

where S_k is the standard deviation of the *k*th independent variable.

The values of the BETA coefficients, like the *B*'s, are contingent on the other independent variables in the equation. They are also affected by the correlations of the independent variables and do not in any absolute sense reflect the importance of the various independent variables.

13.36
Part and Partial Coefficients

Another way of assessing the relative importance of independent variables is to consider the increase in R^2 when a variable is entered into an equation that already contains the other independent variables. This increase is

$$R^2_{change} = R^2 - R^2_{(i)}$$

where $R^2_{(i)}$ is the square of the multiple correlation coefficient when all independent variables except the ith are in the equation. A large change in R^2 indicates that a variable provides unique information about the dependent variable that is not available from the other independent variables in the equation. The signed square root of the increase is called the *part correlation coefficient*. It is the correlation between Y and X_i when the linear effects of the other independent variables have been removed from X_i. If all independent variables are uncorrelated, the change in R^2 as a variable is entered into the equation is simply the square of the correlation coefficient between that variable and the dependent variable.

Figure 13.36   Zero-order, part, and partial correlation coefficients

```
VARIABLE(S) ENTERED ON STEP NUMBER  5..    EDLEVEL      EDUCATIONAL LEVEL

MULTIPLE R             0.78420
R SQUARE              0.61498       R SQUARE CHANGE   0.26619
ADJUSTED R SQUARE     0.61086       F CHANGE        323.55430
STANDARD ERROR        0.09559       SIGNIF F CHANGE   0.0000

------------- VARIABLES IN THE EQUATION -------------

VARIABLE     CORREL PART COR  PARTIAL        F   SIG F

AGE         -0.04780  0.04404  0.07080     2.357 0.1254
SEX         -0.54802 -0.28792 -0.42090   100.761 0.0000
MINORITY    -0.17284 -0.13860 -0.21799    23.349 0.0000
WORK         0.03994  0.04990  0.08015     3.026 0.0826
EDLEVEL      0.68572  0.51593  0.63934   323.554 0.0000
(CONSTANT)                            10376.612 0.0000
```

The output in Figure 13.36 shows that the addition of years of education to an equation that contains the other four independent variables results in a change in R^2 of 0.266 (0.51593^2). The square of the part coefficient tells only how much R^2 increases when a variable is added to the regression equation. It does not indicate what proportion of the unexplained variation this increase constitutes. If most of the variation had been explained by the other variables, a small part correlation is all that is possible for the remaining variable. It may therefore be difficult to compare part coefficients.

A coefficient that measures the proportional reduction in variation is

$$Pr^2_i = \frac{R^2 - R^2_{(i)}}{1 - R^2_{(i)}}$$

The numerator is the square of the part coefficient; the denominator is the proportion of unexplained variation when all but the ith variable are in the equation. The signed square root is the *partial correlation coefficient*. It can be interpreted as the correlation between the ith independent variable and the dependent variable when the linear effects of the other independent variables have been removed from both X_i and Y. Since the denominator of Pr^2_i is always less than or equal to 1, the part correlation coefficient is never larger in absolute value than the partial correlation coefficient.

13.37
Building a Model

Our selection of the five variables to predict beginning salary has been arbitrary to some extent. It is unlikely that all relevant variables have been identified and measured. Instead, some relevant variables have no doubt been excluded, while others that were included may not be very important determinants of salary level. This is not unusual; one frequently must try to build a model from available data, as voluminous or scanty as the data may be. Before considering several formal procedures for model building, we will examine some of the consequences of adding and deleting variables from regression equations. The SPSS-X statistics for variables not in the equation are also described.

13.38
Adding and Deleting
Variables

The first step in Figure 13.38 shows the equation and summary statistics when years of education is the sole independent variable and log of beginning salary is the dependent variable. Consider the second step in the same figure, when another variable, sex, is added. The value printed as R SQUARE CHANGE in the second step is the change in R^2 when sex is added. R^2 for education alone is 0.47021, so R^2_{change} is $0.57598-0.47021$, or 0.10577.

Figure 13.38   Adding a variable to the equation

```
VARIABLE(S) ENTERED ON STEP NUMBER
    1..   EDLEVEL        EDUCATIONAL LEVEL

MULTIPLE R           0.68572
R SQUARE             0.47021        R SQUARE CHANGE    0.47021
ADJUSTED R SQUARE    0.46909        F CHANGE         418.92032
STANDARD ERROR       0.11165        SIGNIF F CHANGE    0.0000

------------------ VARIABLES IN THE EQUATION ------------------

VARIABLE            B          SE B        BETA         T   SIG T

EDLEVEL          0.03642     0.00178      0.68572    20.468 0.0000
(CONSTANT)       3.31001     0.02455                134.821 0.0000


BEGINNING BLOCK NUMBER  2.  METHOD:  ENTER     SEX

VARIABLE(S) ENTERED ON STEP NUMBER
    2..   SEX          SEX OF EMPLOYEE

MULTIPLE R           0.75893
R SQUARE             0.57598        R SQUARE CHANGE    0.10577
ADJUSTED R SQUARE    0.57418        F CHANGE         117.48557
STANDARD ERROR       0.09999        SIGNIF F CHANGE    0.0000

------------------ VARIABLES IN THE EQUATION ------------------

VARIABLE            B          SE B        BETA         T   SIG T

EDLEVEL          0.02984     0.00171      0.56183    17.498 0.0000
SEX             -0.10697     0.00987     -0.34802   -10.839 0.0000
(CONSTANT)       3.44754     0.02539                135.806 0.0000
```

The null hypothesis that the true population value for the change in R^2 is 0 can be tested using

$$F_{change} = \frac{R^2_{change}(N - p - 1)}{q(1 - R^2)} = \frac{(0.1058)(474-2-1)}{1(1-0.5760)} = 117.48$$

where N is the number of cases in the equation, p is the total number of independent variables in the equation, and q is the number of variables entered at this step. Sometimes, this is referred to as a *partial F test*. Under the hypothesis that the true change is 0, the significance of the value labeled F CHANGE can be obtained from the F distribution with q and $N-p-1$ degrees of freedom.

The hypothesis that the real change in R^2 is 0 can also be formulated in terms of the β parameters. When only the ith variable is added in a step, the hypothesis that the change in R^2 is 0 is equivalent to the hypothesis that β_i is 0. The F value printed for the change in R^2 is the square of the t value printed for the test of the coefficient, as shown in Figure 13.38. For example, the value for SEX from Figure 13.38 is -10.839. This value squared is 117.48, the value printed for F CHANGE.

When q independent variables are entered in a single step, the test that R^2 is 0 is equivalent to the simultaneous test that the coefficients of all q variables are 0. For example, if sex and age were added in the same step to the regression equation that contains education, the F test for R^2 change would be the same as the F test which tests the hypothesis that $\beta_{sex}=\beta_{age}=0$.

Entering sex into the equation with education has effects in addition to changing R^2. For example, note the decrease in magnitude of the regression coefficient from step 1 to step 2 (from 0.03642 to 0.02984) in Figure 13.38. This is attributable to the correlation between sex and level of education.

When highly intercorrelated independent variables are included in a regression equation, results may appear anomalous. The overall regression may be significant while none of the individual coefficients are significant. The signs of the regression coefficients may be counterintuitive. High correlations between independent variables inflate the variances of the estimates, making individual coefficients quite unreliable without adding much to the overall fit of the model. The problem of linear relationships between independent variables is discussed further in Sections 13.48 through 13.50.

13.39
Statistics for Variables Not in the Equation

When you have independent variables that have not been entered into the equation, you can examine what would happen if they were entered at the next step. Statistics describing these variables are shown in Figure 13.39. The column labeled BETA IN is the standardized regression coefficient that would result if the variable were entered into the equation at the next step. The F test and level of significance are for the hypothesis that the coefficient is 0. (Remember that the partial F test and the t test for the hypothesis that a coefficient is zero are equivalent.) The partial correlation coefficient with the dependent variable adjusts for the variables already in the equation.

Figure 13.39   Coefficients for variables not in the equation

```
--------------- VARIABLES NOT IN THE EQUATION ---------------

VARIABLE       BETA IN   PARTIAL  MIN TOLER         F  SIG F

WORK           0.14425   0.20567   0.77382    20.759 0.0000
MINORITY      -0.12902  -0.19464   0.84758    18.507 0.0000
AGE            0.13942   0.20519   0.80425    20.659 0.0000
```

From statistics calculated for variables not in the equation, you can decide what variable should be entered next. This process is detailed in Section 13.41.

13.40
The "Optimal" Number of Independent Variables

Having witnessed what happens when sex is added to the equation containing education (Figure 13.38), consider now what happens when the remaining three independent variables are entered one at a time in no particular order. Summary output is shown in Figure 13.40. Step 5 shows the statistics for the equation with all independent variables entered. Step 3 describes the model with education, sex, and work experience as the independent variables.

Figure 13.40   All independent variables in the equation

```
STEP   MULTR    RSQ  ADJRSQ   F(EQU)  SIGF  RSQCH     FCH SIGCH      VARIABLE BETAIN  CORREL  LABEL
  1   0.6857  0.4702  0.4691  418.920 0.000 0.4702  418.920 0.000  IN: EDLEVEL  0.6857  0.6857  EDUCATIONAL LEVEL
  2   0.7589  0.5760  0.5742  319.896 0.000 0.1058  117.486 0.000  IN: SEX     -0.3480 -0.5480  SEX OF EMPLOYEE
  3   0.7707  0.5939  0.5913  229.130 0.000 0.0179   20.759 0.000  IN: WORK     0.1442  0.0399  WORK EXPERIENCE
  4   0.7719  0.5958  0.5923  172.805 0.000 0.0019    2.149 0.143  IN: AGE      0.0763 -0.0478  AGE OF EMPLOYEE
  5   0.7842  0.6150  0.6109  149.501 0.000 0.0192   23.349 0.000  IN: MINORITY -0.1416 -0.1728  MINORITY CLASSIFICATION
```

Examination of Figure 13.40 shows that R^2 never decreases as independent variables are added. This is always true in regression analysis. However, this does not necessarily mean that the equation with more variables better fits the population. As the number of parameters estimated from the sample increases, so does the goodness of fit to the sample as measured by R^2. For example, if a sample contains six cases, a regression equation with six parameters fits the sample exactly, even though there may be no true statistical relationship at all between the dependent variable and the independent variables.

As indicated in Section 13.10, the sample R^2 in general tends to overestimate the population value of R^2. Adjusted R^2 attempts to correct the optimistic bias of the sample R^2. Adjusted R^2 does not necessarily increase as additional variables are added to an equation and is the preferred measure of goodness of fit because it is not subject to the inflationary bias of unadjusted R^2. This statistic is shown in the column labeled ADJRSQ in the output.

Although adding independent variables increases R^2, it does not necessarily decrease the standard error of the estimate. Each time a variable is added to the equation, a degree of freedom is lost from the residual sum of squares and one is gained for the regression sum of squares. The standard error may increase when the decrease in the residual sum of squares is very slight and not sufficient to make up for the loss of a degree of freedom for the residual sum of squares. The F value for the test of the overall regression decreases when the regression sum of squares does not increase as fast as the degrees of freedom for the regression.

Including a large number of independent variables in a regression model is never a good strategy, unless there are strong, previous reasons to suggest that all should be included. The observed increase in R^2 does not necessarily reflect a better fit of the model in the population. Including irrelevant variables increases the standard errors of all estimates without improving prediction. A model with many variables is often difficult to interpret.

On the other hand, it is important not to exclude potentially relevant independent variables. The following sections describe various procedures for selecting variables to be included in a regression model. The goal is to build a concise model that makes good prediction possible.

13.41
Procedures for Selecting Variables

You can construct a variety of regression models from the same set of variables. For instance, you can build seven different equations from three independent variables: three with only one independent variable, three with two independent variables, and one with all three. As the number of variables increases, so does the number of potential models (ten independent variables yield 1,023 models).

Although there are procedures for computing all possible regression equations, several other methods do not require as much computation and are more frequently used. Among these procedures are forward selection, backward elimination, and stepwise regression. None of these variable selection procedures is "best" in any absolute sense; they merely identify subsets of variables that, for the sample, are good predictors of the dependent variable.

13.42
Forward Selection

In *forward selection*, the first variable considered for entry into the equation is the one with the largest positive or negative correlation with the dependent variable. The F test for the hypothesis that the coefficient of the entered variable is 0 is then calculated. To determine whether this variable (and each succeeding variable) is entered, the F value is compared to an established criterion. You can specify one of two criteria in SPSS-X. One criterion is the minimum value of the F statistic that a variable must achieve in order to enter, called *F-to-enter* (keyword FIN), with a default value of 3.84. The other criterion you can specify is the probability associated with the F statistic, called *probability of F-to-enter* (keyword PIN), with a default of 0.05. In this case, a variable enters into the equation only if the probability associated with the F test is less than or equal to the default 0.05 or the value you specify. By default, the probability of F-to-enter is the criterion used.

These two criteria are not necessarily equivalent. As variables are added to the equation, the degrees of freedom associated with the residual sum of squares decrease while the regression degrees of freedom increase. Thus, a fixed F value has different significance levels depending on the number of variables currently in the equation. For large samples, the differences are negligible.

The actual significance level associated with the *F*-to-enter statistic is not the one usually obtained from the *F* distribution, since many variables are being examined and the largest *F* value is selected. The problems encountered are similar to the multiple comparison problems described for procedures ONEWAY and CORRELATIONS. Unfortunately, the true significance level is difficult to compute since it depends not only on the number of cases and variables but also on the correlations between independent variables.

If the first variable selected for entry meets the criterion for inclusion, forward selection continues. Otherwise, the procedure terminates with no variables in the equation. Once one variable is entered, the statistics for variables not in the equation are used to select the next one. The partial correlations between the dependent variable and each of the independent variables not in the equation, adjusted for the independent variables in the equation, are examined. The variable with the largest partial correlation is the next candidate. Choosing the variable with the largest partial correlation in absolute value is equivalent to selecting the variable with the largest *F* value.

If the criterion is met, the variable is entered into the equation and the procedure is repeated. The procedure stops when there are no other variables that meet the entry criterion.

To include a specific number of independent variables in the equation, you can specify the number of steps and SPSS-X selects only the first *n* variables that meet entry requirements. Another criterion that is always checked before a variable is entered is the tolerance, which is discussed in Section 13.50.

Figure 13.42a   Summary statistics for forward selection

STEP	MULTR	RSQ	ADJRSQ	F(EQU)	SIGF	RSQCH	FCH	SIGCH		VARIABLE	BETAIN	CORREL
1	0.6857	0.4702	0.4691	418.920	0.000	0.4702	418.920	0.000	IN:	EDLEVEL	0.6857	0.6857
2	0.7589	0.5760	0.5742	319.896	0.000	0.1058	117.486	0.000	IN:	SEX	-0.3480	-0.5480
3	0.7707	0.5939	0.5913	229.130	0.000	0.0179	20.759	0.000	IN:	WORK	0.1442	0.0399
4	0.7830	0.6130	0.6097	185.750	0.000	0.0191	23.176	0.000	IN:	MINORITY	-0.1412	-0.1728

Figure 13.42a shows output generated from a forward-selection procedure using the salary data. The default entry criterion is PIN=0.05. In the first step, education is entered since it has the highest correlation with beginning salary. The significance level associated with education is less than 0.0005, so it certainly meets the criterion for entry.

Figure 13.42b   Status of the variables at the first step

---------- VARIABLES IN THE EQUATION ----------						---------- VARIABLES NOT IN THE EQUATION ----------					
VARIABLE	B	SE B	BETA	F	SIG F	VARIABLE	BETA IN	PARTIAL	MIN TOLER	F	SIG F
EDLEVEL	0.03642	0.00178	0.68572	418.920	0.0000	SEX	-0.34802	-0.44681	0.87327	117.486	0.0000
(CONSTANT)	3.31001	0.02455		18176.766	0.0000	WORK	0.22747	0.30241	0.93632	47.408	0.0000
						MINORITY	-0.08318	-0.11327	0.98234	6.121	0.0137
						AGE	0.15718	0.20726	0.92113	21.140	0.0000

To see how the next variable, sex, was selected, look at the statistics shown in Figure 13.42b for variables not in the equation (when only education is in the equation). The variable with the largest partial correlation is SEX. If entered at the next step, it would have an *F* value of approximately 117 for the test that its coefficient is 0. Since the probability associated with the *F* is less than 0.05, variable SEX is entered in the second step.

Figure 13.42c   The last step

----------- VARIABLES NOT IN THE EQUATION -----------				
VARIABLE	BETA IN	PARTIAL	MIN TOLER	F SIG F
AGE	*0.07811	0.07080	0.29784	2.357 0.1254

Once variable SEX enters at step 2, the statistics for variables not in the equation must be examined (see Figure 13.39). The variable with the largest absolute value for the partial correlation coefficient is now years of work experience. Its F value is 20.759 with a probability less than 0.05, so variable WORK is entered in the next step. The same process takes place with variable MINORITY and it is entered, leaving AGE as the only variable out of the equation. However, as shown in Figure 13.42c, the significance level associated with the age coefficient F value is 0.1254, which is too large for entry. Thus, forward selection yields the summary table for the four steps shown in Figure 13.42a.

13.43
Backward Elimination

While forward selection starts with no independent variables in the equation and sequentially enters them, *backward elimination* starts with all variables in the equation and sequentially removes them. Instead of entry criteria, removal criteria are specified.

Two removal criteria are available in SPSS-X. The first is the minimum F value (FOUT) that a variable must have in order to remain in the equation. Variables with F values less than this *F-to-remove* are eligible for removal. The second criterion available is the maximum probability of F (keyword POUT) a variable can have. The default FOUT value is 2.71 and the default POUT value is 0.10. The default criterion is POUT.

Figure 13.43a   Backward elimination at the first step

VARIABLE	B	SE B	BETA	CORREL	PART COR	PARTIAL	F	SIG F
AGE	0.00102	0.6613D-03	0.07811	-0.04780	0.04404	0.07080	2.357	0.1254
SEX	-0.10358	0.01032	-0.33699	-0.54802	-0.28792	-0.42090	100.761	0.0000
MINORITY	-0.05237	0.01084	-0.14157	-0.17284	-0.13860	-0.21799	23.349	0.0000
EDLEVEL	0.03144	0.00175	0.59195	0.68572	0.51593	0.63934	323.554	0.0000
WORK	0.00161	0.9241D-03	0.09143	0.03994	0.04990	0.08015	3.026	0.0826
(CONSTANT)	3.38530	0.03323					10376.612	0.0000

Look at the salary example again, this time constructing the model with backward elimination. The output in Figure 13.43a is from the first step, in which all variables are entered into the equation. The variable with the smallest partial correlation coefficient, AGE, is examined first. Since the probability of its F is 0.1254, which is greater than the default POUT criterion value of 0.10, variable AGE is removed.

Figure 13.43b   Backward elimination at the last step

VARIABLE	B	SE B	BETA	CORREL	PART COR	PARTIAL	F	SIG F
SEX	-0.09904	0.00990	-0.32223	-0.54802	-0.28733	-0.41933	100.063	0.0000
MINORITY	-0.05225	0.01085	-0.14125	-0.17284	-0.13828	-0.21700	23.176	0.0000
EDLEVEL	0.03143	0.00175	0.59176	0.68572	0.51577	0.63827	322.412	0.0000
WORK	0.00275	0.5458D-03	0.15659	0.03994	0.14489	0.22685	25.444	0.0000
(CONSTANT)	3.41195	0.02838					14454.042	0.0000

The equation is then recalculated without AGE, producing the statistics shown in Figure 13.43b. The variable with the smallest partial correlation is MINORITY. However, its significance is less than the 0.10 criterion, so backward elimination stops. The equation resulting from backward elimination is the same as the one from forward selection. This is not always the case, however. Forward- and backward-selection procedures can give different results, even with comparable entry and removal criteria.

13.44
Stepwise Selection

Stepwise selection of independent variables is probably the most commonly used procedure in regression. It is really a combination of backward and forward procedures. The first variable is selected in the same manner as in forward selection. If the variable fails to meet entry requirements (either FIN or PIN), the procedure terminates with no independent variables in the equation. If it passes the criterion, the second variable is selected based on the highest partial correlation. If it passes entry criteria, it also enters the equation.

From this point, stepwise selection differs from forward selection: the first variable is examined to see whether it should be removed according to the removal criterion (FOUT or POUT) as in backward elimination. In the next step, variables not in the equation are examined for entry. After each step, variables already in the equation are examined for removal. Variables are removed until none remain that meet the removal criterion. To prevent the same variable from being repeatedly entered and removed, PIN must be less than POUT (or FIN greater than FOUT). Variable selection terminates when no more variables meet entry and removal criteria.

In the salary example, stepwise selection with the default criteria results in the same equation produced by both forward selection and backward elimination. In general, the three procedures need not result in the same equation, though you should be encouraged when they do. The model selected by any of the methods should be carefully studied for violations of the assumptions. It is often a good idea to develop several acceptable models and then choose among them based on interpretability, ease of variable acquisition, parsimony, and so forth.

13.45
Checking for Violation of Assumptions

The procedures discussed in Section 13.17 for checking for violations of assumptions in bivariate regression apply in the multivariate case as well. Residuals should be plotted against predicted values as well as against each of the independent variables. The distribution of residuals should be examined for normality.

13.46
Interpreting the Equation

The multiple regression equation estimated above suggests several findings. Education appears to be the best predictor of beginning salary, at least among the variables included in this study (Figure 13.43a). The sex of the employee also appears to be important. Women are paid less than men since the sign of the regression coefficient is negative (men are coded 0 and women are coded 1). Years of prior work experience and race are also related to salary, but when education and sex are included in the equation, the effect of experience and race is less striking.

Do these results indicate that there is sex discrimination at the bank? Not necessarily. It is well recognized that all education is not equally profitable. Master's degrees in business administration and political science are treated quite differently in the marketplace. Thus, a possible explanation of the observed results is that women enter areas that are just not very well paid. Although this may suggest inequities in societal evaluation of skills, it does not necessarily imply discrimination at the bank. Further, many other potential job-related skills or qualifications are not included in the model. Also, some of the existing variables, such as age, may make nonlinear as well as linear contributions to the fit. Such contributions can often be approximated by including new variables that are simple functions of the existing one. For example, the age values squared may improve the fit.

13.47
Statistics for Unselected Cases

As previously noted, a model usually fits the sample from which it is derived better than it fits the population. A sometimes useful strategy for obtaining an estimate of how well the model fits the population is to split the sample randomly into two parts. One part is then used to estimate the model, while the remaining cases are reserved for testing the goodness of fit.

Figure 13.47   Histograms for males (selected) and females (unselected)

```
HISTOGRAM                    - SELECTED CASES
STUDENTIZED RESIDUAL
  N  EXP N     ( * = 1 CASES.     . : = NORMAL CURVE)
  3   0.20   OUT ***
  3   0.40  3.00 ***
  0   1.01  2.66 .
  1   2.30  2.33 *.
  2   4.71  2.00 ** .
  7   8.63  1.66 ****** .
 10  14.16  1.33 *********
 18  20.81  1.00 ****************
 28  27.40  0.66 ***************************.*
 33  32.32  0.33 ********************************.*
 31  34.15  0.00 ********************************
 30  32.32 -0.33 ******************************
 42  27.40 -0.66 *************************.***************
 30  20.81 -1.00 ********************.*********
 11  14.16 -1.33 ***********
  5   8.63 -1.66 ***** .
  3   4.71 -2.00 *** .
  0   2.30 -2.33 .
  1   1.01 -2.66 :
  0   0.40 -3.00
  0   0.20  OUT


HISTOGRAM                    - UNSELECTED CASES
STUDENTIZED RESIDUAL
  N  EXP N     ( X = 1 CASES.     . : = NORMAL CURVE)
  0   0.17   OUT
  0   0.33  3.00
  0   0.84  2.66 .
  0   1.93  2.33 .
  0   3.94  2.00 .
  1   7.22  1.66 X   .
  1  11.85  1.33 X      .
  2  17.42  1.00 XX          .
  5  22.94  0.66 XXXXX
 10  27.06  0.33 XXXXXXXXX
 14  28.59  0.00 XXXXXXXXXXXXX
 32  27.06 -0.33 XXXXXXXXXXXXXXXXXXXXXXXX :XXXXX
 35  22.94 -0.66 XXXXXXXXXXXXXXXXXXXXXX:XXXXXXXXXX
 49  17.42 -1.00 XXXXXXXXXXXXXX:XXXXXXXXXXXXXXXXXXXXXXXXXXXXXXXX
 22  11.85 -1.33 XXXXXXXXXX:XXXXXXXXX
 13   7.22 -1.66 XXXXX:XXXXX
 13   3.94 -2.00 XXX:XXXXXXXX
  7   1.93 -2.33 X:XXXXX
  7   0.84 -2.66 :XXXXX
  1   0.33 -3.00 X
  4   0.17  OUT XXXX
```

It is also sometimes interesting to split the data on some characteristics of the sample. For example, you can develop the salary equation for males alone and then apply it to females to see how well it fits. For example, Figure 13.47 shows histograms of residuals for males (denoted as selected cases) and females (unselected cases). Note that the females' salaries are too large when predicted from the male equation since most of the residuals are negative. The multiple R for the females is 0.45596, which is smaller than the 0.73882 for males (stepwise selection was used).

13.48
Problems of Multicollinearity

Preceding sections deal with the consequences of correlated independent variables in regression analysis. The estimates of the β and the sum of squares attributable to each variable are dependent on the other variables in the equation. Variances of the estimators also increase when independent variables are interrelated. This may result in a regression equation with a significant R^2, although virtually none of the coefficients is significantly different from 0. If any independent variable is a perfect linear combination of other independent variables, the correlation matrix is *singular* and a unique, unbiased least-squares solution does not exist.

Although situations involving singularities do occur, they are not as common as those involving near-singularities—variables that are almost linear combinations of other independent variables. These variables are often called *multicollinear*.

13.49
Methods of Detection

Multicollinearities can be detected in several ways. Large coefficients in the correlation matrix always signal the presence of multicollinearity. However, multicollinearity can exist without any of the correlation coefficients being very large.

One of the most frequently used indicators of interdependency between variables is the tolerance (see Section 13.50). If the variable has a large R^2—or equivalently a small tolerance—when it is predicted from the other independent variables, a potentially troublesome situation exists. Not only are the variances of the estimators inflated, but computational problems can occur.

13.50
SPSS-X and Multicollinearity

In the SPSS-X REGRESSION procedure, various steps are taken to warn you of multicollinearity. Before an independent variable is entered into the equation, its tolerance with other independent variables already in the equation is calculated. The tolerance is the proportion of variability in an independent variable not explained by the other independent variables. It is calculated as $1-R_i^2$, where R_i^2 is the squared multiple correlation when the ith independent variable is considered the dependent variable and the regression equation between it and the other independent variables is calculated. SPSS-X prints the tolerances as shown in Figure 13.50.

Figure 13.50   Tolerances

```
VARIABLE    TOLERANCE

AGE          0.31792
SEX          0.72998
MINORITY     0.95839
EDLEVEL      0.75966
WORK         0.29784
```

It is possible for a variable not in the equation to have an acceptable tolerance level but when entered to cause the tolerance of other variables already in the equation to become unacceptably small (Berk, 1977; Frane, 1977). Thus, the tolerances of all the variables in the equation are recomputed at each step. If either the tolerance of the variable or the tolerance of any variable already in the equation is less than 0.0001, a warning is issued and the variable is not entered unless the default TOLERANCE criterion has been altered (see Section 13.55).

In SPSS-X, you can print both the tolerance of a variable and the minimum tolerance of all independent variables in the equation if the variable were entered.

13.51
RUNNING PROCEDURE REGRESSION

The REGRESSION procedure provides five equation-building methods: forward selection, backward elimination, stepwise selection, forced entry, and forced removal. The subcommands for residuals analysis help detect influential data points, outliers, and violations of the regression model assumptions. See Chapter 18 for a more complete description of the REGRESSION procedure.

13.52
Building the Equation

To build a simple regression model, specify three subcommands: a VARIABLES subcommand to name the variables to be analyzed; a DEPENDENT subcommand to indicate which variable is dependent; and a subcommand that names the method to be used. For example, to build the simple bivariate model of beginning salary and current salary shown in Figures 13.3b, 13.10, and 13.11a, specify:

```
REGRESSION VARIABLES=SALBEG,SALNOW
  /DEPENDENT=SALNOW
  /ENTER SALBEG
```

The beginning (SALBEG) and current (SALNOW) salaries are named, with the latter specified as the dependent variable. Then the ENTER subcommand is used to enter beginning salary into the equation. You may omit the VARIABLES subcommand, and REGRESSION will use all the variables named on the DEPENDENT and method subcommands.

To build the multivariate model shown in Figures 13.33a and 13.33b, specify:

```
REGRESSION VARIABLES=LOGBEG,EDLEVEL,SEX,WORK,MINORITY,AGE
           /DEPENDENT=LOGBEG
           /ENTER EDLEVEL TO AGE
```

The TO keyword in the ENTER subcommand refers to the order in which the variables are named on the previous VARIABLES subcommand.

The method used in developing the regression equation is specified by one (or more) of the method subcommand keywords, optionally followed by a list of variables. For example, to request the backward-elimination method discussed in Section 13.43, specify:

```
REGRESSION VARIABLES=LOGBEG,EDLEVEL,SEX,WORK,MINORITY,AGE
  /DEPENDENT=LOGBEG
  /BACKWARD
```

13.53
Requesting Statistics

Two subcommands, DESCRIPTIVES and STATISTICS, request statistics. The DESCRIPTIVES subcommand requests a number of statistics based on your variable list, and the STATISTICS subcommand requests statistics for the equation. By default, REGRESSION prints four sets of statistics: R, R^2, adjusted R^2, and standard error for the equation; the analysis of variance table; statistics for variables in the equation; and statistics for variables not in the equation. The first three sets of statistics are shown in Figures 13.3b, 13.10, and 13.11a for the bivariate equation and in Figures 13.33a and 13.33b for the multivariate equation. The statistics for variables not in the equation are shown in Figure 13.39.

You can specify exactly which statistics you want for the equation by using combinations of the keywords for the STATISTICS subcommand. For example, to produce the output for the equation including the change in R^2 between steps, and the statistics for the variables in the equation shown in Figure 13.38 for the multivariate example, specify:

```
REGRESSION VARIABLES=LOGBEG,EDLEVEL,SEX,WORK,MINORITY,AGE
  /STATISTICS=R,CHANGE,COEFF
  /DEPENDENT=LOGBEG
  /ENTER EDLEVEL /ENTER SEX
```

Or to produce the confidence intervals shown in Figure 13.8, specify:

```
REGRESSION VARIABLES=SALBEG,SALNOW
  /STATISTICS=CI
  /DEPENDENT=SALNOW
  /ENTER SALBEG
```

You can also request the zero-order, part, and partial correlation coefficients (Figure 13.36), the F value for B and significance of F instead of t (Figures 13.42b, 13.42c, 13.43a, and 13.43b), the tolerance (Figure 13.50), and step history (Figures 13.40 and 13.42a).

You can use the DESCRIPTIVES subcommand to request variable means, standard deviations, and variances, and a correlation matrix and covariance matrix for the variable list. For example, to produce the correlation matrix shown in Figure 13.32, specify:

```
REGRESSION WIDTH=90
  /DESCRIPTIVES=CORR
  /VARIABLES=LOGBEG,EDLEVEL,SEX,WORK,MINORITY,AGE
  /DEPENDENT=LOGBEG
  /ENTER EDLEVEL TO AGE
```

13.54
Residuals Analysis

Residuals analysis is specified with three subcommands: RESIDUALS, CASE-WISE, and SCATTERPLOT. Once you have built an equation, REGRESSION can calculate temporary variables containing several types of residuals, predicted values, and related measures for detecting outliers and influential data points and for examining regression assumptions (see Sections 13.13 through 13.23).

The following temporary variables are discussed in this chapter and can be specified with the RESIDUALS, CASEWISE, or SCATTERPLOT subcommands:

PRED *Unstandardized predicted values.* (See Section 13.13.)

ZPRED *Standardized predicted values.* (See Section 13.13.)

SEPRED *Standard errors of the predicted values.* (See Section 13.14.)

RESID *Unstandardized residuals.* (See Section 13.18.)

ZRESID *Standardized residuals.* (See Section 13.18.)

SRESID *Studentized residuals.* (See Section 13.18.)

The RESIDUALS subcommand requests histograms, normal probability plots, outliers, and the Durbin-Watson test (Section 13.21). For example, to produce the small histogram and normal probability plots shown in Figures 13.22a and 13.22b, specify:

```
REGRESSION VARIABLES=SALBEG,SALNOW
  /DEPENDENT=SALNOW
  /ENTER SALBEG
  /RESIDUALS=SIZE(SMALL) HISTOGRAM(SRESID) NORMPROB(SRESID)
```

Use the CASEWISE subcommand to display a casewise plot of one of the temporary variables accompanied by a listing of the values of the dependent and the temporary variables. The plot can be requested for all cases or limited to outliers. For example, to produce the casewise plot based on standardized residuals for all cases labeled with the values of the SEXRACE variable shown in Figure 13.16, specify:

```
REGRESSION VARIABLES=SALBEG,SALNOW
  /DEPENDENT=SALNOW
  /ENTER SALBEG
  /RESIDUALS=SIZE(SMALL) ID(SEXRACE)
  /CASEWISE=ALL DEPENDENT PRED RESID SEPRED
```

To obtain a plot of outliers whose absolute values are equal to or greater than 3 based on Studentized residuals (SRESID) and a list of values of the dependent variable, PRED, and RESID, as shown in Figure 13.23, specify:

```
REGRESSION VARIABLES=SALBEG,SALNOW
  /DEPENDENT=SALNOW
  /ENTER SALBEG
  /RESIDUALS=SIZE(SMALL) ID(SEXRACE)
  /CASEWISE=PLOT(SRESID)
```

Use the SCATTERPLOT subcommand to generate scatterplots of the temporary variables and any of the variables in the regression equation. Whenever you name a temporary variable in a SCATTERPLOT subcommand, preface the keyword with an asterisk to identify it as a temporary variable. For example, to generate the scatterplot shown in Figure 13.20, specify:

```
REGRESSION VARIABLES=SALBEG,SALNOW
  /DEPENDENT=SALNOW
  /ENTER SALBEG
  /SCATTERPLOT=(*SRESID,*PRED)
```

The first variable named inside the parentheses is the vertical-axis (Y) variable and the second is the horizontal-axis (X) variable.

All scatterplots are standardized in REGRESSION. For example, the specification SCATTERPLOT=(Y,X) generates a scatterplot of the standardized values of variables X and Y (see Figure 13.25).

To produce the scatterplot of SRESID and PRED based on the logarithmic transformation of both the dependent and independent variables (see Figure 13.28a), you must use transformation commands, as in:

```
COMPUTE LOGBEG=LG10(SALBEG)
COMPUTE LOGNOW=LG10(SALNOW)
REGRESSION VARIABLES=LOGBEG,LOGNOW
  /DEPENDENT=LOGNOW
  /ENTER LOGBEG
  /SCATTERPLOT=(*SRESID,*PRED)
```

13.55
Additional Subcommands for the Equation

In addition to the subcommands described in Sections 13.51 through 13.54, you can control your output with the WIDTH subcommand, select cases within the REGRESSION procedure with the SELECT subcommand, control missing-value treatment with the MISSING subcommand, and control the criteria for variable selection with the CRITERIA subcommand.

For example, to make certain that the equation statistics shown in Figure 13.10 are displayed separately from the ANOVA statistics shown in Figure 13.11a rather than side-by-side, specify a smaller page width, as in:

```
REGRESSION WIDTH=90
  /VARIABLES=SALBEG,SALNOW
  /DEPENDENT=SALNOW
  /ENTER SALBEG
```

Within REGRESSION, you can select a subset of your data for constructing the equation. Then, you can observe residuals and predicted values both for cases used in computing the coefficients and for cases not used. For example, to generate the separate residuals histograms for males and females shown in Figure 13.47 based on the equation developed for males alone (SEX=0), specify:

```
REGRESSION WIDTH=90
  /SELECT SEX EQ 0
  /VARIABLES=LOGBEG,EDLEVEL,SEX,WORK,MINORITY,AGE
  /DEPENDENT=LOGBEG
  /STEPWISE
  /RESIDUALS=HISTOGRAM
```

By default, REGRESSION deletes cases from the analysis if they have a missing value for any variable in the VARIABLES subcommand. Use the MISSING subcommand to request pairwise deletion, mean substitution of missing values, or inclusion of cases with missing values.

Use the CRITERIA subcommand to control the statistical criteria by which REGRESSION chooses variables for entry into or removal from an equation.

13.56
REGRESSION and Other SPSS-X Commands

The complete SPSS-X command file used to run the stepwise example shown in Figure 13.56 is

```
GET FILE=BANK
COMPUTE LOGBEG=LG10(SALBEG)
REGRESSION VARIABLES=LOGBEG,EDLEVEL,SEX,WORK,MINORITY,AGE
  /STATISTICS=R,COEFF,OUTS,F
  /DEPENDENT=LOGBEG
  /STEPWISE
```

Figure 13.56   Stepwise output

```
                        * * * *   M U L T I P L E   R E G R E S S I O N   * * * *
VARIABLE LIST NUMBER  1.  LISTWISE DELETION OF MISSING DATA.
EQUATION NUMBER  1.

DEPENDENT VARIABLE..  LOGBEG

BEGINNING BLOCK NUMBER  1.  METHOD: STEPWISE

VARIABLE(S) ENTERED ON STEP NUMBER  1..   EDLEVEL      EDUCATIONAL LEVEL

MULTIPLE R          0.68572
R SQUARE            0.47021
ADJUSTED R SQUARE   0.46909
STANDARD ERROR      0.11165


----------------- VARIABLES IN THE EQUATION -----------------       ------------- VARIABLES NOT IN THE EQUATION -------------

VARIABLE          B          SE B       BETA       F  SIG F          VARIABLE    BETA IN   PARTIAL   MIN TOLER      F  SIG F

EDLEVEL        0.03642     0.00178    0.68572    418.920 0.0000       SEX        -0.34802  -0.44681   0.87327   117.486 0.0000
(CONSTANT)     3.31001     0.02455             18176.766 0.0000       WORK        0.22747   0.30241   0.93632    47.408 0.0000
                                                                     MINORITY   -0.08318  -0.11327   0.98234     6.121 0.0137
                                                                     AGE         0.15718   0.20726   0.92113    21.140 0.0000


              * * * * * * * * * * * * * * * * * * * * * * * * * * * *


VARIABLE(S) ENTERED ON STEP NUMBER  2..   SEX        SEX OF EMPLOYEE

MULTIPLE R          0.75893
R SQUARE            0.57598
ADJUSTED R SQUARE   0.57418
STANDARD ERROR      0.09999


----------------- VARIABLES IN THE EQUATION -----------------       ------------- VARIABLES NOT IN THE EQUATION -------------

VARIABLE          B          SE B       BETA       F  SIG F          VARIABLE    BETA IN   PARTIAL   MIN TOLER      F  SIG F

EDLEVEL        0.02984     0.00171    0.56183    306.192 0.0000       WORK        0.14425   0.20567   0.77382    20.759 0.0000
SEX           -0.10697     0.00987   -0.34802    117.486 0.0000       MINORITY   -0.12902  -0.19464   0.84758    18.507 0.0000
(CONSTANT)     3.44754     0.02539             18443.279 0.0000       AGE         0.13942   0.20519   0.80425    20.659 0.0000


              * * * * * * * * * * * * * * * * * * * * * * * * * * * *


VARIABLE(S) ENTERED ON STEP NUMBER  3..   WORK       WORK EXPERIENCE

MULTIPLE R          0.77066
R SQUARE            0.59391
ADJUSTED R SQUARE   0.59132
STANDARD ERROR      0.09796


----------------- VARIABLES IN THE EQUATION -----------------       ------------- VARIABLES NOT IN THE EQUATION -------------

VARIABLE          B          SE B       BETA       F  SIG F          VARIABLE    BETA IN   PARTIAL   MIN TOLER      F  SIG F

EDLEVEL        0.03257     0.00177    0.61321    336.772 0.0000       MINORITY   -0.14125  -0.21700   0.75967    23.176 0.0000
SEX           -0.09403     0.01008   -0.30594     87.099 0.0000       AGE         0.07633   0.06754   0.29839     2.149 0.1433
WORK           0.00254  0.5566D-03    0.14425     20.759 0.0000
(CONSTANT)     3.38457     0.02845             14150.641 0.0000


              * * * * * * * * * * * * * * * * * * * * * * * * * * * *


VARIABLE(S) ENTERED ON STEP NUMBER  4..   MINORITY   MINORITY CLASSIFICATION

MULTIPLE R          0.78297
R SQUARE            0.61304
ADJUSTED R SQUARE   0.60974
STANDARD ERROR      0.09573


----------------- VARIABLES IN THE EQUATION -----------------       ------------- VARIABLES NOT IN THE EQUATION -------------

VARIABLE          B          SE B       BETA       F  SIG F          VARIABLE    BETA IN   PARTIAL   MIN TOLER      F  SIG F

EDLEVEL        0.03143     0.00175    0.59176    322.412 0.0000       AGE         0.07811   0.07080   0.29784     2.357 0.1254
SEX           -0.09904     0.00990   -0.32223    100.063 0.0000
WORK           0.00275  0.5458D-03    0.15659     25.444 0.0000
MINORITY      -0.05225     0.01085   -0.14125     23.176 0.0000
(CONSTANT)     3.41195     0.02838             14454.042 0.0000

FOR BLOCK NUMBER  1   PIN = 0.050 LIMITS REACHED.
```

- The GET command defines the BANK system file to SPSS-X.
- The COMPUTE command creates a logarithmic transformation of the beginning salary variable as discussed in Section 13.28 and used in this chapter.
- The REGRESSION command requests a stepwise-selection analysis, with LOGBEG as the dependent variable and EDLEVEL, SEX, WORK, MINORITY, and AGE as the independent variables. The requested statistics are equation statistics, statistics for variables in the equation, statistics for variables not in the equation, and the F value rather than the t value.

EXERCISES

Syntax

1. The following REGRESSION commands contain errors. Write the correct commands.
   a. `REGRESSION VARIABLES=IQ TO ACHIEVE/`
      `   STEP/DEPENDENT=ACHIEVE`
   b. `REGRESSION VARIABLES=IQ TO ACHIEVE/ DESCRIPTIVES=`
      `   MEAN STDDEV/DEPENDENT=ACHIEVE/ENTER`
   c. `REGRESSION VARS=IQ TO ACHIEVE/ENTER`
   d. `REGRESSION VARS=IQ TO ACHIEVE/DEP=ACHIEVE/`
      `   SCATTER(*RES, *PRE)/STEP`

2. Write an SPSS-X command that requests a multiple regression equation, stepwise variable selection, and means and standard deviations. Y is the dependent variable and X1 and X2 are the independent variables.

3. What are the dependent and independent variables in each analysis in the following specification:
   ```
   REGRESSION VARS=X Y A B C/
     DEP=X/ENT/
     DEP=Y/ENT/
     DEP=X,Y/ENT/
   ```

4. Is there any reason to prefer one of the following setups to the other? Why or why not?
   a. `REGRESSION VARIABLES=X Y Z A B C/DEPENDENT=X/FORWARD=A B C/`
      `   VARIABLES=X Y Z A B C/DEPENDENT=C/FORWARD=X Y Z`
   b. `REGRESSION VARIABLES=X Y Z A B C/DEPENDENT=X/FORWARD=A B C/`
      `   DEPENDENT=C/FORWARD=X Y Z`

5. What is wrong with the following command?
   ```
   REGRESSION VARIABLES=Y X1 TO X10/DEP=Y/STEPWISE/REMOVE
   ```

6. What is wrong with the following command?
   ```
   REGRESSION VARIABLES SAVINGS TO GROWTH/
     DEPENDENT SAVINGS/ENTER/
     SCAT (RESID, PRED)/
   ```

7. Write the REGRESSION subcommands to obtain the following analyses:
   a. A scatterplot of the residual and variable X1.
   b. A histogram of the residuals.
   c. A listing of the cases with the 10 largest residuals labeled with the variable ID.
   d. A listing for all cases of the predicted and observed values of the dependent variable Y.

Statistical Concepts

1. Why is the hypothesis $\beta_1 = \beta_2 = \ldots = \beta_k = 0$ of interest?

2. What assumptions are you checking when you examine a casewise serial plot (a plot of residuals in time sequence)?

3. What null hypothesis is tested by the following statistics:

    a. $F = \dfrac{\text{MEAN SQUARE REGRESSION}}{\text{MEAN SQUARE RESIDUAL}}$

    b. $F_{change} = \dfrac{R^2_{change}(N - p - 1)}{q(1 - R^2)}$

4. Is the following regression output possible if a variable is added at each step and none are dropped from the equation?

STEP	MULTR	RSQ
1	0.5821	0.3388
2	0.6164	0.3799
3	0.6025	0.3630
4	0.6399	0.4095

5. A researcher writes his own regression analysis program. The program produces the following regression line and confidence band. Do you think the new computer program is working properly?

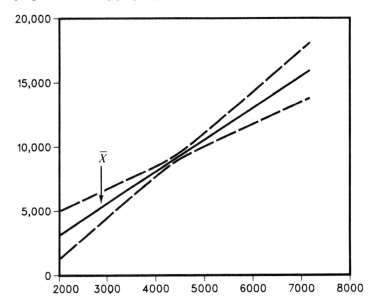

6. For what values of X can you make the best (least variable) predictions of the mean of Y at X? For what values of X can you make the best predictions of new values of Y?

7. What violations of assumptions, if any, are suggested by the following plots:

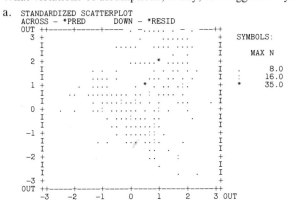

b. STANDARDIZED SCATTERPLOT

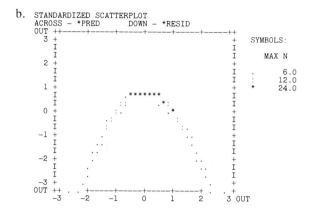

```
   ACROSS - *PRED     DOWN - *RESID
OUT ++-----+-----+-----+-----+-----+-----++
  3 +                                      +     SYMBOLS:
    I                                      I
    I                                      I       MAX N
  2 +                                      +
    I                                      I     .        6.0
    I                                      I     :       12.0
  1 +                                      +     *       24.0
    I           . *******                  I
    I          :.        . *.              I
  0 +          :.          . *             +
    I          :.            .             I
    I         .:              .            I
 -1 +         .                . .         +
    I         . .              ..          I
    I         ..                .          I
 -2 +         .                  ..        I
    I         .                  .         I
    I         .                   .        I
 -3 +                              .       +
OUT ++ . . +-----+-----+-----+-----+ . . +
    -3   -2   -1    0    1    2    3 OUT
```

c. CASEWISE PLOT OF STANDARDIZED RESIDUAL

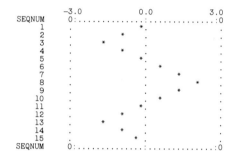

```
            -3.0           0.0            3.0
SEQNUM     0:.................:.................:0
      1     .              .    *           .
      2     .              . *              .
      3     .      *       .                .
      4     .         *    .                .
      5     .              . *              .
      6     .              .    *           .
      7     .              .       *        .
      8     .              .         *      .
      9     .              .       *        .
     10     .              .    *           .
     11     .              . *              .
     12     .         *    .                .
     13     .      *       .                .
     14     .          *   .                .
     15     .              *                .
SEQNUM     0:.................:.................:0
```

d. HISTOGRAM - STANDARDIZED RESIDUAL

```
   N EXP N          (* = 1 CASES.     . : = NORMAL CURVE)
   0   .33   OUT
   0   .17  3.00
   0   .24  2.88
   0   .34  2.75
   0   .48  2.63
   0   .66  2.50 .
   0   .89  2.38 .
   0  1.19  2.25 .
   0  1.57  2.13  .
   0  2.03  2.00  .
   0  2.58  1.88   .
   0  3.24  1.75    .
   2  4.00  1.63 ** .
  16  4.86  1.50 ****:***********
  18  5.82  1.38 *****.*************
   9  6.85  1.25 ******:**
  12  7.95  1.13 *******:****
  12  9.07  1.00 ********:***
   8 10.20   .88 ********  .
  16 11.29   .75 **********:*****
  21 12.30   .63 **********:*.********
   6 13.20   .50 ******        .
   6 13.94   .38 ******          .
   8 14.49   .25 ********         .
   6 14.83   .13 ******            .
  17 14.95   .00 ***************.**
   9 14.83  -.13 *********         .
  15 14.49  -.25 ***************:*
  10 13.94  -.38 **********      .
  11 13.20  -.50 ***********   .
   7 12.30  -.63 *******     .
   8 11.29  -.75 *******   .
  13 10.20  -.88 ********:.***
  10  9.07 -1.00 ********:.*
   8  7.95 -1.13 *******:
  11  6.85 -1.25 ******:****
  15  5.82 -1.38 *****.*********
  10  4.86 -1.50 ****:*****
  12  4.00 -1.63 ***:********
   4  3.24 -1.75 **:.*
   0  2.58 -1.88   .
   0  2.03 -2.00  .
   0  1.57 -2.13  .
   0  1.19 -2.25 .
   0   .89 -2.38 .
   0   .66 -2.50 .
   0   .48 -2.63
   0   .34 -2.75
   0   .24 -2.88
   0   .17 -3.00
   0   .33   OUT
```

e.

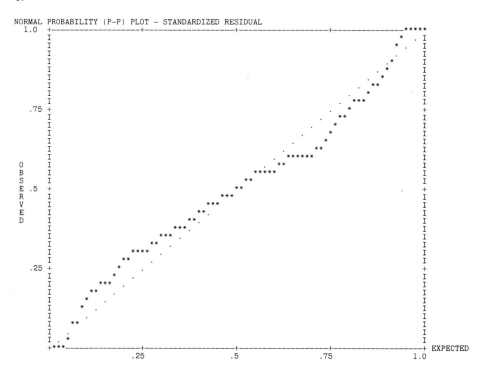

```
NORMAL PROBABILITY (P-P) PLOT - STANDARDIZED RESIDUAL
```

8. From the following statistics for variables not in the equation, which variable is entered next if forward variable selection with *F*-to-enter of 3.84 is used?

```
-------------- VARIABLES NOT IN THE EQUATION --------------

VARIABLE     BETA IN   PARTIAL   MIN TOLER        F   SIG F

AGE           .18107    .22453    .92113     25.005   .0000
SEX          -.26483   -.31974    .87327     53.637   .0000
MINORITY     -.07477   -.09575    .98234      4.358   .0374
WORK          .21888    .27364    .93632     38.122   .0000
```

9. From the following statistics for variables in the equation, which variable is removed next if backward elimination with FOUT of 3 is used?

```
----------- IN -----------

VARIABLE        F   SIG F

WORK         1.217   .2705
MINORITY    13.822   .0002
SEX         45.159   .0000
EDLEVEL    238.736   .0000
AGE          4.696   .0307
(CONSTANT)   7.935   .0051
```

10. Suppose you obtain the following correlation matrix:

```
- - - - - - - - - - - P E A R S O N   C O R R E L A T I O N   C O E F F I C I E N T S - - - - - - - - - - - -

           X1          X2          X3          X5          X4          Y

X1       1.0000      -0.0003      0.0206      -0.1384      0.9999      0.3595
        (     0)     (   300)    (   300)     (   300)    (   300)    (   300)
         P=*****     P=0.498     P=0.361      P=0.008     P=0.000     P=0.000

X2      -0.0003       1.0000     -0.0262      -0.0741     -0.0003     -0.0025
        (   300)     (     0)    (   300)     (   300)    (   300)    (   300)
         P=0.498     P=*****     P=0.325      P=0.100     P=0.498     P=0.483

X3       0.0206      -0.0262      1.0000       0.0364      0.0206      0.0322
        (   300)     (   300)    (     0)     (   300)    (   300)    (   300)
         P=0.361     P=0.325     P=*****      P=0.265     P=0.361     P=0.289

X5      -0.1384      -0.0741      0.0364       1.0000     -0.1384     -0.0083
        (   300)     (   300)    (   300)     (     0)    (   300)    (   300)
         P=0.008     P=0.100     P=0.265      P=*****     P=0.008     P=0.443

X4       0.9999      -0.0003      0.0206      -0.1384      1.0000      0.3595
        (   300)     (   300)    (   300)     (   300)    (     0)    (   300)
         P=0.000     P=0.498     P=0.361      P=0.008     P=*****     P=0.000

Y        0.3595      -0.0025      0.0322      -0.0083      0.3595      1.0000
        (   300)     (   300)    (   300)     (   300)    (   300)    (     0)
         P=0.000     P=0.483     P=0.289      P=0.443     P=0.000     P=*****
```

(COEFFICIENT / (CASES) / SIGNIFICANCE)   (A VALUE OF 99.0000 IS PRINTED IF A COEFFICIENT CANNOT BE COMPUTED)

When running procedure REGRESSION, you try to enter variable X4 into an equation that already contains variables X1 to X3. The following message is obtained:

```
FOR BLOCK NUMBER  2   TOLERANCE = 0.0001 LIMITS REACHED.
NO VARIABLES ENTERED FOR THIS BLOCK.
```

What does this message mean? Why does it occur?

11. Fill in the missing information in the following table and calculate R^2:

```
ANALYSIS OF VARIANCE
                      DF       SUM OF SQUARES        MEAN SQUARE
     REGRESSION        1                             28.90000
     RESIDUAL                      20.30000           6.76667

     F =                      SIGNIF F =   .1307
```

12. Below are regression statistics and values of the independent and dependent variables for five cases. Fill in the missing information in the casewise plot.

```
------------------- VARIABLES IN THE EQUATION -------------------

VARIABLE              B           SE B         BETA        T    SIG T

X                 1.70000       .82260       .76642     2.067   .1307
(CONSTANT)        4.30000      2.72825                  1.576   .2131
```

```
CASEWISE PLOT OF STANDARDIZED RESIDUAL

*: SELECTED   M: MISSING

              -3.0            0.0           3.0
   CASE # X    0:.............:.............:0     Y      *PRED      *RESID
     1  1      .                 . *         .     7     6.0000     1.0000
     2  2      .                   . *       .     9
     3  3      .          *         .        .     6
     4  4      .                 * .         .          11.1000    -1.1000
     5  5      .                   .  *      .    15                 2.2000
   CASE # X    0:.............:.............:0     Y      *PRED      *RESID
              -3.0            0.0           3.0
```

13. Fill in the missing information in the following table:

```
------------------- VARIABLES IN THE EQUATION -------------------

VARIABLE              B          SE B            T   SIG T

WORK            23.77950     21.55603                 .2705
MINORITY      -939.85580                    -3.718    .0002
SEX          -1617.52918    240.70102       -6.720    .0000
EDLEVEL                      40.77734       15.451    .0000
AGE             33.43079     15.42695                 .0307
(CONSTANT)   -2183.78652                    -2.817    .0051
```

Data Analysis

Use the BANK system file for Question 1–2.

1. a. For one of the job categories (or sex-race groups), develop a regression equation relating beginning salary to some of the other variables. Check your assumptions.

    b. Prepare a brief report summarizing your findings.

2. Repeat the analysis in Question 1 looking at current salary instead of beginning salary.

3. Formulate a multiple regression model using one of the data files in Appendix B. (Do not use the PRODUCTS system file.)

    a. Use procedure REGRESSION to obtain least squares estimates of the parameters and summary statistics. What proportion of the variability in the dependent variable is explained by the regression model? Is this a statistically significant fit?

    b. Use the diagnostic plots available in REGRESSION to look for possible violations of the assumptions. Do you have reason to suspect that assumptions have been violated?

    c. Use one of the variable selection methods in REGRESSION to develop a model using the same variables as above. Do any of the coefficients change markedly? Why can this occur?

4. Use the Western Electric data for the following exercises.

    a. Use multiple linear regression analysis to study the relationship between cholesterol level (dependent variable) and age, weight, and number of cigarettes smoked as the independent variables.

    b. Does there appear to be a relationship between the independent variables and the dependent variables? Write a paragraph explaining your results.

    c. Develop a linear regression model between diastolic blood pressure (dependent variable) and whatever independent variables you may think would be related to it. Write a short paper describing your results.

Chapter 14   To Grant or Not to Grant: Discriminant Analysis

The ability to correctly predict outcomes is a skill valued in many professions. A good stockbrocker can predict the future value of a stock; a good marketing professional, the type of people who will purchase a particular product; a good surgeon, which patients will benefit from a surgical intervention. If you ask any of these professionals how they arrive at a prediction, they will most likely mention experience. They've seen a lot of stocks decrease and increase in value. They know what distinguishes a profitable corporation from a nonprofitable one. They compare companies, products, and treatments and determine which ones are successes and which ones are failures. How the different pieces of information are used to arrive at a prediction cannot be easily described. It's a process that varies from person to person and from problem to problem.

There is a class of statistical techniques that attempts to quantify the prediction process. It is based on the same principles as human decision making. Information is obtained for a set of cases for which the outcome is known. This is the equivalent of experience. The subjective "synthesis" of the information is replaced by equations that are derived from the data and used to classify the cases into groups. Unlike human decision making, the process is objective and reproducible.

14.1 DISCRIMINANT ANALYSIS

In this chapter, we will consider one of these techniques: discriminant analysis. The goal of discriminant analysis, as outlined above, is to classify cases into one of several mutually exclusive groups on the basis of a set of observed characteristics. (Mutually exclusive means that a case can belong to only one group. For example, a patient may be either a good surgical risk, a poor surgical risk, or an uncertain surgical risk. The same patient can fall into only one of the categories. You can't be both a good risk and a bad risk.)

The actual characteristics (independent variables) used to establish the decision rule depend on the problem. You must select independent variables that you think are potentially good predictors of the outcome. For example, if you're trying to predict surgical success, you might want to include characteristics such as the severity and duration of the disease and the age of the patient. If you're trying to predict corporate success, you would include variables such as profits, sales, and expenditures. During the course of the analysis, you can determine whether all of the variables you've selected help in distinguishing among the groups, or whether some of them provide little information. If you fail to include variables that are good predictors, you will arrive at a prediction rule that does not work well. For a more detailed discussion of discriminant analysis, see Kleinbaum & Kupper (1978), Tasuoka (1971), and Lachenbruch (1975).

14.2
Basic Discriminant Analysis

To illustrate the basics of discriminant analysis, let's consider a credit-worthiness example described by Churchill (1979). (Determining who should be granted credit was one of the early applications of discriminant analysis to business.) The Consumer Finance Company, which screens credit applicants, wants to be able to classify cases into one of two groups: good credit risks and poor or equivocal risks. It has available for analysis 30 cases for which the credit rating is known. That is, these cases have been observed for a certain period of time, and the company knows whether each of the cases has turned out to be a good risk or a poor risk. The characteristics available to be used for arriving at a prediction are the annual income (in thousands of dollars), the number of credit cards, the number of children, and the age of the head of the household. On the basis of this sample, we will try to determine the relationship between the independent variables and the group to which a case belongs. Once we know what the relationship is, we can use this information to predict to whom credit should be granted, based on income, credit cards, children and age of the head of the household.

14.3
Necessary Assumptions

You can use discriminant analysis whenever you want to predict group membership. However, you have no guarantee that the results you obtain will be the best you can do. In order for linear discriminant analysis to be optimal, that is, result in the smallest number of cases being incorrectly classified, certain conditions must be met. Each of your groups must be a sample from a multivariate normal population, and all of the populations must have the same covariance matrix.

In discriminant analysis, your grouping variable can be any measured on any type of scale. For example, it can be nominal, such as religion, or ordinal, such as satisfaction with a product. The independent variables, however, cannot be nominal. If you have nominal independent variables, they must be coded into a set of dummy variables. For example, if one of your variables is the color of a car, you must create a set of dichotomous variables to represent it. That is, you have one two-category variable that tells you whether a car is yellow or not, another two-category variable which tells you whether a car is blue or not, and so on.

14.4
Describing the Sample

The first step of any analysis should be to examine the data. This will give you some idea of how much or how little the groups differ on individual characteristics. Figure 14.4 contains means and standard deviations for each of the variables for the two groups. From this you can see that the average income for people in the second group (good credit risks) is $19,660, while for poor or equivocal risks it is $11,865. The average income for both of the groups combined is $14,463. There also appear to be differences in the number of credit cards and the age of the household for the two groups. The number of children, however, appears to be fairly similar in both.

Figure 14.4 Group means and standard deviations

```
GROUP MEANS

    GROUP          INCOME          CREDIT          AGEHEAD          CHILDREN

         1        11.86500         3.40000         32.20000          2.45000
         2        19.66000         6.40000         43.60000          2.40000

    TOTAL         14.46333         4.40000         36.00000          2.43333


GROUP STANDARD DEVIATIONS

    GROUP          INCOME          CREDIT          AGEHEAD          CHILDREN

         1         2.47371         2.08756          4.58372          1.50350
         2         4.26854         2.98887          4.32563          1.50555

    TOTAL          4.86128         2.77427          7.03195          1.47819
```

Descriptive statistics provide basic information about the distributions of the variables in the groups and help identify differences among the groups. In discriminant analysis and other multivariate statistical techniques, however, the emphasis is on analyzing the variables together, not one at a time. This allows you to incorporate information about the relationships of variables into the analysis.

In discriminant analysis, like multiple linear regression analysis, a linear combination of the independent variables is formed. This linear combination is used to assign cases to the groups. For example, consider the following equation:

Score= .21 × Income + .08 × Credit +.13 × Age of the head + .07 × Children

For each case, we can compute a score based on the values of the independent variables. Based on this score, we can determine to which group a case belongs. Cases with scores above a certain cutoff are assigned to the good risk group, cases with scores below the cutoff are assigned to the poor risk group.

**14.5
Estimating the Coefficients**

Where do the coefficients for the equation come from? In regression analysis, we compute the coefficients so that the sum of the squared differences between the observed and predicted values is as small as possible. In discriminant analysis, we select the coefficients so that the scores are similar within a group but differ as much as possible among the groups. Specifically, for our example, we want all of the good risks to have large scores, while the poor risks have small scores. Unless the scores differ across groups, we won't be able to distinguish among them. The actual computation of the coefficients is complicated, so we'll leave their calculation to the computer. Figure 14.5a contains the discriminant function coefficients for this example. (In the output, the letter E followed by a number indicates that the result is expressed in scientific notation. The number after the E, if it is positive, tells you how many places to move the decimal point to the right. If the number after the E is negative, it tells you how many places to move the decimal point to the left.)

Figure 14.5a   Discriminant function coefficients

```
                 FUNC  1

INCOME        0.2126181
CREDIT        0.8034637E-01
AGEHEAD       0.1326113
CHILDREN      0.7396355E-01
(CONSTANT)   -8.382677
```

Using these coefficients, we can calculate the score for a 42-year-old head of household with an income of $20,000, 10 credit cards, and 2 children as

Score= −8.38 + .21 × 20 + .08 × 10 + .07 × 2 +.13 × 42 = 2.2

Figure 14.5b   Average scores

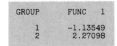

```
GROUP     FUNC  1

   1      -1.13549
   2       2.27098
```

Figure 14.5b shows the average scores for cases in the two groups. Poor credit risks have an average score of −1.13, while good credit risks have an average score of 2.27. Since the coefficients for all of the variables are positive, this means that higher incomes, numbers of credit cards, ages of head of households, and children are associated with good credit card risks. Not an unexpected finding, is it? Figure 14.5c shows the distributions of the discriminant score for cases in each of the two groups. The number 1 represents the poor credit risks; the number 2, good credit risks. Since there is little or no overlap in the two sets of discriminant scores, we will be able to classify the cases well. If there is a lot of overlap in the discriminant scores for the two groups, we can't accurately predict group membership.

Figure 14.5c   Distribution of discriminant scores

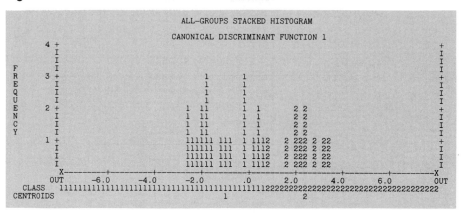

14.6
Testing for Equality of the Discriminant Function Means

Since we want to use the discriminant scores to classify the cases into one of two groups, it is of interest to know whether the average scores in the two groups differ significantly. That is, we want to test the null hypothesis that, in the population, there is no difference in the means of the discriminant scores for the two groups. The *Wilks' lambda statistic* is often used for this. Wilks' lambda, together with its observed significance level, is shown in Figure 14.6. The observed significance level is very small, less than 0.0005, so we can reject the null hypothesis that the two groups have the same mean. If we could not reject the null hypothesis that the groups have the same means, there would be little point in trying to classify cases into groups based on their discriminant scores. On the other hand, just because two groups have significantly different means, it doesn't mean that we will be able to separate the cases well. There may be so much overlap in their distributions that good classification is not possible, even though the means are significantly different.

Figure 14.6   Lambda and the significance level

```
                                   CANONICAL DISCRIMINANT FUNCTIONS

                         PERCENT OF   CUMULATIVE    CANONICAL  :  AFTER
     FUNCTION EIGENVALUE  VARIANCE     PERCENT     CORRELATION : FUNCTION  WILKS' LAMBDA  CHI-SQUARED  D.F.  SIGNIFICANCE
                                                               :    0       0.2657550      34.455       4      0.0000
        1*     2.76286    100.00      100.00       0.8568810   :

        * MARKS THE   1 CANONICAL DISCRIMINANT FUNCTIONS REMAINING IN THE ANALYSIS.
```

14.7
Assigning Cases to Groups

Although it's possible to classify the cases into groups based on the actual discriminant scores, it's convenient to convert the discriminant scores into probabilities and then to use these probabilities for assigning the cases to groups. What we must calculate is the probability that a case with a score D is a member of a particular group. For example, we need to know the probability that someone with a score of $-.2$ is a good credit risk and the probability that someone with that score is a poor credit risk. (Since we only have two groups in this example, these two probabilities must sum to one. That is, a case is either a good risk, or a poor risk.) A case is assigned to that group for which, based on the available information, it has the largest probability of membership. If the case has a probability of 0.3 of being a good credit risk, and a probability of 0.7 of being a poor credit risk, we would assign it to the poor risk group. Again we can use SPSS-X to calculate these probabilities for us.

Figure 14.7 contains discriminant scores and probabilities of group membership for a subset of cases used in our analysis. The group to which a case actually belongs is listed in the column labeled "Actual Group." The group to which a case is assigned based on the discriminant analysis is shown in the column labeled "Highest Group." If the actual group to which a case belongs and the group to which a case is assigned based on the discriminant analysis are not the same, asterisks are printed after the the actual group number.

Figure 14.7   Discriminant scores and probabilities

CASE SEQNUM	MIS VAL	SEL	ACTUAL GROUP	HIGHEST PROBABILITY GROUP P(D/G) P(G/D)	2ND HIGHEST GROUP P(G/D)	DISCRIMINANT SCORES...
16			1	1 0.1005 0.5516	2 0.4484	0.5069
17			1	1 0.1053 0.5705	2 0.4295	0.4844
18			1	1 0.8744 0.9948	2 0.0052	-0.9774
19			1	1 0.3190 0.9174	2 0.0826	-0.1390
20			1	1 0.7942 0.9927	2 0.0073	-0.8746
21			2	2 0.7301 0.9903	1 0.0097	1.9260
22			2	2 0.8961 0.9981	1 0.0019	2.4015
23			2	2 0.9872 0.9968	1 0.0032	2.2549
24			2	2 0.9310 0.9978	1 0.0022	2.3575
25			2	2 0.5496 0.9773	1 0.0227	1.6727
26			2	2 0.7276 0.9902	1 0.0098	1.9227
27			2	2 0.1484 0.7067	1 0.2933	0.8259
28			2	2 0.3103 0.9999	1 0.0001	3.2856
29			2	2 0.6243 0.9994	1 0.0006	2.7607
30			2	2 0.3024 0.9999	1 0.0001	3.3024

The probabilities involved in the the classification of cases into groups are displayed in the next set of columns. The number of interest here is the probability that a case is a member of a particular group based on its discriminant score. This probability is labeled "P(G/D)." (Those of you familiar with probability will recognize this notation as symbolizing the probability of group membership given a particular score. The entry P(D/G) is the probability of a particular score given membership in a group. Bayes' rule is used to arrive at the posterior probability, P(G/D), from the conditional probability P(D/G) and the prior probability.) For a particular case we can calculate the probability that it is a member of each of the groups.

Let's consider the values shown for case 27 in Figure 14.7. The column labeled "Highest Probability Group" contains the number of the group to which the case is assigned based on the discriminant score. This is the group with the highest probability, P(G/D). The probability that case 27 is a member of group 2 is estimated to be 0.7067, so case 27 is assigned to group 2. (The probability that the case is a member of group 1 is shown in the column entitled "2nd Highest." For case 27 the probability that it is a member of group 1 is 0.2933. Since a case must be a member of one or the other group, these two probabilities must sum to 1.) The actual group number for case 27 is also 2, so the case is correctly classified on the basis of the discriminant analysis. If the case was incorrectly classified, the output would contains asterisks after the actual group number. The values of the discriminant scores from which the probabilities are estimated are shown in the column labeled "Discriminant Scores...."

14.8
How Well Are the Cases Classified?

Although we can figure out the number of cases correctly and incorrectly classified by comparing the actual groups and predicted groups from Figure 14.7, it is easier to just look at Figure 14.8, which is a summary of the classification results. From the table you can see how cases in each of the groups are classified by the discriminant analysis. Each row and column corresponds to one of the groups. The numbers on the diagonal are cases that are correctly classified. That is, they have the same actual and predicted group numbers. For example, there are 20 cases in the poor risk group. All of these are correctly predicted to be members of the poor risk group by the discriminant analysis. That's why there's a 20 in the cell labeled "Actual Group 1" and "Predicted Group 1." There are no poor risk cases who were predicted to be members of group 2, the good risk group. That's why there's a 0 in that cell of the table. The percentages shown in the cells of Figure 14.8 tell you what percent of the members of each group falls into each of the predicted groups. Since all poor risks are correctly predicted to be poor risks, 100% of poor risks fall into the first cell of the table, and 0% of poor risks fall into predicted group 2 , the good risks. At the bottom of the table, you see the percent of cases in all groups that is correctly classified by the discriminant analysis. In this example, all cases are correctly classified. Such perfect classification is unusual and should not be expected for analyses of this nature.

Figure 14.8   Summary of classification results

ACTUAL GROUP	NO. OF CASES	PREDICTED GROUP MEMBERSHIP 1	2
GROUP 1 poor risk	20	20 100.0%	0 0.0%
GROUP 2 good risk	10	0 0.0%	10 100.0%

PERCENT OF "GROUPED" CASES CORRECTLY CLASSIFIED: 100.00%

14.9
From a Sample to the Population

A model usually fits the sample from which it is derived better than it will fit another sample from the same population. For example, in regression analysis, the sample R^2 is an overly optimistic estimate of how the model would fit another set of data. The percentage of cases classified correctly by the discriminant function is also an inflated estimate of how well the rule would work when applied to other cases. There are several ways to obtain a better estimate of the true misclassification rate. If the sample is large enough to be randomly split into two parts, you can use one part to estimate the coefficients and the other part to see how well they work. If you do this you're not using the same cases to both build a model and to see how well it works. Another technique for obtaining misclassification rates is called the "jackknifing" or "leaving-one-out" method. In this method, each case is left out in turn from the estimation of the function. The function is then used to classify the "left out" case.

14.10
Comparing the Results to Chance

The percentage of cases classified correctly is often taken as an index of the effectiveness of the discriminant model. When evaluating this measure, it is important to compare the observed misclassification rate to that expected by chance alone. For example, if you have two groups of equal size, assigning cases to groups based on the whether a coin comes up heads or tails results in an expected misclassification rate of 50%. In this situation, a discriminant analysis that results in an observed misclassification rate of 50% is no better than chance. As the number of equal-sized groups increases, the percentage of cases that can be classified correctly by chance alone decreases. If there are 10 groups, you would expect only 10% of the cases to be correctly classified by chance.

14.11
More about Discriminant Analysis

The credit risk example involves only two groups. Discriminant analysis, however, is not restricted to the two-group situation. You can use it to predict group membership for any number of groups. When you have more than two groups, the number of discriminant functions computed is one less than the number of groups. For each case, scores are obtained for each discriminant function, and all of these scores are used in assigning the cases to groups.

14.12
Selecting Variables for Inclusion in the Model

In the example, we had four variables we could use for classifying the cases, and we built a model that included all of them. We made no attempt to determine whether all of the variables contributed to our ability to classify the cases. It's possible that some of the variables did not contribute any new information to the problem. Eliminating such variables from the model may be desirable. As in linear regression analysis, stepwise variable selection procedures may be used in discriminant analysis to identify variables that appear to be important in distinguishing the groups.

14.13
Relationship to Multiple Regression Analysis

In the two-group situation only, there is a close relationship between regression analysis and discriminant analysis. If you code the two groups as 0 and 1, for example, and use this as the dependent variable in a regression analysis, the regression coefficients you obtain for the independent variables will be proportional to the discriminant coefficients for the same variables. (*Proportional* means that you can multiply all of the discriminant coefficients by the same number and arrive at the regression coefficients.) When you have a dependent variable with only two categories, however, you are obviously violating the regression assumption that there is a normal distribution of the values of the dependent variable for all combinations of the independent variables, and the usual hypothesis tests for regression analysis are not appropriate.

14.14
RUNNING PROCEDURE DISCRIMINANT

To run the DISCRIMINANT procedure you need only two subcommands. The GROUPS subcommand specifies the variable to be used in establishing the groups. The VARIABLES subcommand indicates which variables are to be used in predicting group membership. See Chapter 18 for a complete list of the subcommands available with procedure DISCRIMINANT.

14.15
Specifying the Groups

Use the GROUPS subcommand to specify the variable used to establish the group and its range of values. You can have only one GROUPS subcommand.

For example, the subcommand,

```
GROUPS = RISK(1,2)
```

indicates that RISK is the variable that identifies the group, and it can have integer values of 1 and 2. The subcommand

```
GROUPS = PATHOLGY(1,4)
```

indicates the variable PATHOLGY is to be used for forming groups, and it can have the four integer values between 1 and 4.

Cases with values outside the range are not used in obtaining the discriminant functions. However, such cases are classified into one of the existing groups if classification is requested.

14.16
Specifying the Variables

List all variables to be used in predicting group membership on the VARIABLES subcommand. You can specify only numeric variables, and you can have only one VARIABLES subcommand. For example,

```
DISCRIMINANT GROUPS = RISK (1,2)
  /VARIABLES = INCOME CREDIT AGEHEAD CHILDREN
```

requests a two-group discriminant analysis based on the values of the variable RISK. The variables named INCOME, CREDIT, AGEHEAD, and CHILDREN are to be used as predictors.

14.17
Selecting Variables

By default, DISCRIMINANT enters all variables specified on the variable list. This method is termed the *direct-entry method*. Optionally, you can specify any one of five different stepwise methods on the METHOD subcommand. These methods enter and remove variables one at time, selecting them on the basis of specific criteria. Different criteria are used for different stepwise methods.

The METHOD subcommand has one of the following specifications:

DIRECT   *All variables are entered simultaneously, provided they satisfy the tolerance criterion.* For a discussion of controlling the tolerance criterion, see the *SPSS-X User's Guide,* 3rd Edition. DIRECT is the default method.

WILKS   *The variable that minimizes the overall Wilks' lambda is selected.*

MAHAL   *The variable that maximizes the Mahalanobis' distance between the two closest groups is selected.*

MAXMINF   *The variable that maximizes the smallest F ratio between pairs of groups is selected.*

MINRESID   *The variable that minimizes the sum of unexplained variation between groups is selected.*

RAO   *The variable that produces the largest increase in Rao's V is selected.* Rao's V is a generalized measure of the overall separation between groups.

With all methods, all variables must satisfy the tolerance criterion before they can be entered. With the stepwise methods, all variables must also satisfy the partial F ratio criterion before they can be entered. If you wish to change the default F value (1) for entering variables, specify /FIN=value. To change the F value for removing variables, specify /FOUT=value.

14.18
Requesting Additional Statistics

The STATISTICS subcommand requests additional statistics for DISCRIMINANT. You can specify the STATISTICS subcommand by itself or with one or more keywords.

If you specify the STATISTICS subcommand with no keywords, DISCRIMINANT calculates MEAN, STDDEV, and UNIVF (each defined below). If you include a keyword or keywords on the STATISTICS subcommand, DISCRIMINANT calculates only the statistics you request. The following keywords can be specified on the STATISTICS subcommand:

MEAN   *Means.* Prints total and group means for all independent variables in the analysis. This (along with STDDEV and UNIVF) is the default if you specify the STATISTICS subcommand by itself, with no keywords.

STDDEV   *Standard deviations.* Prints total and group standard deviations for all independent variables in the analysis. This (along with MEAN and UNIVF) is the default if you specify the STATISTICS subcommand by itself, with no keywords.

UNIVF   *Univariate* F *ratios.* Prints *F* for each variable. This is a one-way analysis of variance test for equality of group means on a single discriminating variable. This (along with MEAN and STDDEV) is the default if you specify the STATISTICS subcommand by itself, with no keywords.

COV   *Pooled within-groups covariance matrix.*

CORR   *Pooled within-groups correlation matrix.*

BOXM   *Box's* M *test.* This is a test for equality of group covariance matrices.

GCOV   *Group covariance matrices.*

TCOV   *Total covariance matrix.*

RAW   *Unstandardized canonical discriminant functions.*

TABLE   *Classification results table.*

ALL   *All optional statistics available for DISCRIMINANT.*

14.19
Requesting Classification Plots

Classification plots are useful for examining the relationship of groups to each other and graphically depicting misclassification. The PLOT subcommand requests classification plots. You can specify the PLOT subcommand by itself or with one or more keywords.

COMBINED   *All-groups plot.* The first two functions define the axes. This statistic produces histograms for one-function analyses. This (along with CASES) is the default if you specify the PLOT subcommand by itself, with no keywords.

CASES   *Discriminant scores and classification information.* This (along with COMBINED) is the default if you specify the PLOT subcommand by itself, with no keywords.

SEPARATE   *Separate-groups plots.* These are the same types of plots produced by keyword COMBINED. However, each plot contains cases for one group only. If your model has three groups, three scatterplots are produced, unless you restrict the analysis to compute only one function. For one-function analyses, histograms are produced.

ALL   *All plots available for DISCRIMINANT.*

14.20
A DISCRIMINANT Example

The SPSS-X commands used to produce the figures in this chapter are

```
COMMENT CREDIT RISK DATA FOR DISCRIMINANT
DATA LIST /CASEID 1-2 RISK 3 INCOME 5-7(1) CREDIT 8-9
    AGEHEAD 10-11 CHILDREN 12
VALUE LABELS RISK 1'POOR RISK' 2 'GOOD RISK'
BEGIN DATA
 . . .
END DATA
DISCRIMINANT GROUPS=RISK(1,2)
   /VARIABLES=INCOME CREDIT AGEHEAD CHILDREN
   /STATISTICS=MEAN STDDEV RAW COEFF TABLE /PLOT=CASES COMBINED
```

- The DATA LIST command defines the variables and their location in the file. The VALUE LABELS command assigns value labels to variable RISK.

- The GROUPS subcommand on DISCRIMINANT specifies RISK as the variable that forms the groups. GROUP also defines a range of values for variable RISK (see Section 14.15).

- The VARIABLES subcommand on DISCRIMINANT specifies the variables used in group membership (see Section 14.16).

- The STATISTICS and PLOT subcommands request optional statistics and plots for the analysis (see Sections 14.18 and 14.19).

EXERCISES

Syntax

1. A department store manager wants a discriminant analysis to distinguish between good, poor, and equivocal credit risks (RISK) based on the following variables:

   INCOME CREDIT AGEHEAD CHILDREN JOBTIME RESTIME HOMEOWNR

   The risk variable is coded as 1=poor or equivocal risk and 2=good risk. Write the DISCRIMINANT command necessary to obtain a discriminant analysis.

2. A sociologist wants to discriminate between emotionally expressive (EMOTION= 1) and emotionally reserved (EMOTION=2) people, using the following variables:

   ETHNIC SEX IQ SES EMOTINDX INCOME EDUCATN

   Write the DISCRIMINANT command needed to produce a discriminant analysis.

3. Find the syntax errors in the following DISCRIMINANT commands.

   a. DISCRIMINANT GROUPS=GRADUATE
       /VARIABLES=GPA INCOME YEARS

   b. DISCRIMINANT VARIABLES=V1 V2 V3 /METHOD=WILKS /STATISTICS=COV

Statistical Concepts

1. Consider the discriminant-function coefficients and variable values shown below. For the cases shown, calculate the discriminant scores. (The constant is −10.34.)

```
UNSTANDARDIZED CANONICAL DISCRIMINANT FUNCTION COEFFICIENTS

              FUNC  1

IQ                 .22
EDUC               .95
SAT                .10
TESTSCOR           .35
GRA               1.52

CASE SEQ      IQ      EDUC      SAT    TESTSCORE     GPA    DISCRIMINANT SCORE

      1      115       12      580         59       3.2              ??
      2      121       14      780         45       3.9              ??
      3      127       12      720         52       2.0              ??
```

2. Two discriminant functions, each with four variables, are being considered in a two-group analysis. Histograms of their discriminant scores are shown below. Which function, if either, do you prefer? Why?

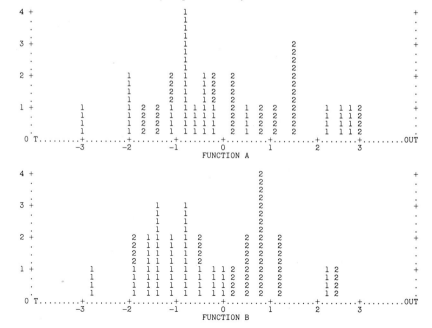

3. Two discriminant functions, one with five variables (Function A), and one with two variables (Function B), have been developed for a data set. Fill in the missing entries in the classification tables and indicate which function you would prefer for classifying new cases. Why do you prefer this function?

FUNCTION A		NO. OF CASES	PREDICTED GROUP MEMBERSHIP 1	2
GROUP EUROPEAN ORIGIN	1	17	16 ??%	?? 5.88%
GROUP ASIAN ORIGIN	2	??	0 0.0%	42 100.0%

PERCENT OF GROUPED CASES CORRECTLY CLASSIFIED: ??%

FUNCTION B		NO. OF CASES	PREDICTED GROUP MEMBERSHIP 1	2
GROUP EUROPEAN ORIGIN	1	17	15 ??%	2 ??%
GROUP ASIAN ORIGIN	2	42	2 ??%	?? ??%

PERCENT OF GROUPED CASES CORRECTLY CLASSIFIED: ??%

4. Consider the classification table shown below.

ACTUAL GROUP (1)		NO. OF CASES	PREDICTED GROUP MEMBERSHIP 1	2	3	4
GROUP FREQUENT PRODUCT USER	1	20	15 75.0%	4 20.0%	1 5.0%	0 0.0%
GROUP OCCASIONAL PRODUCT USER	2	20	0 0.0%	16 80.0%	3 15.0%	1 5.0%
GROUP INFREQUENT PRODUCT USER	3	20	0 0.0%	1 5.0%	18 90.0%	1 5.0%
GROUP NON-USER OF PRODUCT	4	30	0 0.0%	5 16.67%	13 43.33%	12 40.0%

a. What is the overall misclassification rate?

b. Suppose 10% of the population uses the product frequently. If you were primarily interested in identifying these users, would this discriminant analysis be useful to you?

Chapter 15   Identifying Dimensions of Communities: Factor Analysis

What are creativity, love, and altruism? Unlike variables such as weight, blood pressure, and temperature, they cannot be measured on a scale, sphygmomanometer, or thermometer, in units of pounds, millimeters of mercury, or degrees Fahrenheit. Instead, they can be thought of as unifying constructs or labels that characterize responses to related groups of variables. For example, answers of "strongly agree" to items such as he (or she) sends me flowers, listens to my problems, reads my manuscripts, laughs at my jokes, and gazes deeply into my soul, may lead one to conclude that the love "factor" is present. Thus, love is not a single measurable entity but a construct that is derived from measurement of other, directly observable variables. Identification of such underlying dimensions or factors greatly simplifies the description and understanding of complex phenomena, such as social interaction. For example, postulating the existence of something called "love" explains the observed correlations between the responses to numerous and varied situations.

Factor analysis is a statistical technique used to identify a relatively small number of factors that can be used to represent relationships among sets of many interrelated variables. For example, scores on a battery of aptitude tests may be expressed as a linear combination of factors that represent verbal skills, mathematical aptitude, and perceptual speed. Consumer ratings of products in a survey can be expressed as a function of factors such as product quality and utility. Factor analysis helps identify these underlying, not directly observable, constructs.

A huge number of variables can be used to describe a community—degree of industrialization, commercial activity, population, mobility, average family income, extent of home ownership, birth rate, and so forth. However, descriptions of what is meant by the term "community" might be greatly simplified if it were possible to identify underlying dimensions, or factors, of communities. This was attempted by Jonassen and Peres (1960), who examined 82 community variables from 88 counties in Ohio. This chapter uses a subset of their variables (shown in Table 15.0) to illustrate the basics of factor analysis. For detailed discussions of factor analysis, see Cattell (1966), Harman (1967), and Kim and Mueller (1978).

Table 15.0 Community variables

POPSTABL	Population stability
NEWSCIRC	Weekly per capita local newspaper circulation
FEMEMPLD	Percentage of labor force that is female and 14 years or older
FARMERS	Percentage of labor force that is farmers and farm managers
RETAILNG	Per capita dollar retail sales
COMMERCL	Total per capita commercial activity in dollars
INDUSTZN	Industrialization index
HEALTH	Health index
CHLDNEGL	Total per capita expenditures on county aid to dependent children
COMMEFFC	Index of the extent to which a community fosters a high standard of living
DWELGNEW	Percentage of dwelling units built recently
MIGRNPOP	Index measuring the extent of in- and out-migration
UNEMPLOY	Unemployment index
MENTALIL	Extent of mental illness

15.1 THE FACTOR ANALYSIS MODEL

The basic assumption of factor analysis is that underlying dimensions, or factors, can be used to explain complex phenomena. Observed correlations between variables result from their sharing these factors. For example, correlations between test scores might be attributable to such shared factors as general intelligence, abstract reasoning skill, and reading comprehension. The correlations between the community variables might be due to factors like amount of urbanization, the socioeconomic level or welfare of the community, and the population stability. The goal of factor analysis is to identify the not-directly-observable factors based on a set of observable variables.

The mathematical model for factor analysis appears somewhat similar to a multiple regression equation. Each variable is expressed as a linear combination of factors that are not actually observed. For example, the industrialization index might be expressed as

$$INDUSTZN = a(URBANISM) + b(WELFARE) + c(INFLUX) + U_{INDUSTZN}$$

This equation differs from the usual multiple regression equation in that URBANISM, WELFARE, and INFLUX are not single independent variables. Instead, they are labels for groups of variables that characterize these concepts. These groups of variables constitute the factors. Usually, the factors useful for characterizing a set of variables are not known in advance but are determined by factor analysis.

URBANISM, WELFARE, and INFLUX are called *common factors*, since all variables are expressed as functions of them. The U in the equation above is called a *unique factor*, since it represents that part of the industrialization index that cannot be explained by the common factors. It is unique to the industrialization index variable.

In general, the model for the ith standardized variable is written as

$$X_i = A_{i1}F_1 + A_{i2}F_2 + \ldots + A_{ik}F_k + U_i$$

where the F's are the common factors, the U is the unique factor, and the A's are the constants used to combine the k factors. The unique factors are assumed to be uncorrelated with each other and with the common factors.

The factors are inferred from the observed variables and can be estimated as linear combinations of them. For example, the estimated urbanism factor is expressed as

$$\text{URBANISM} = C_1 \text{ POPSTABL} + C_2 \text{ NEWSCIRC} + \ldots + C_{14} \text{ MENTALIL}$$

While it is possible that all of the variables contribute to the urbanism factor, we hope that a only subset of variables characterizes urbanism, as indicated by their large coefficients. The general expression for the estimate of the jth factor F_j is

$$F_j = \sum_{i=1}^{p} W_{ji} X_i = W_{j1} X_1 + W_{j2} X_2 + \ldots + W_{jp} X_p$$

The W_i's are known as factor score coefficients, and p is the number of variables.

15.2
Ingredients of a Good Factor Analysis Solution

Before examining the mechanics of a factor analysis solution, let's consider the characteristics of a successful factor analysis. One goal is to represent relationships among sets of variables parsimoniously. That is, we would like to explain the observed correlations using as few factors as possible. If many factors are needed, little simplification or summarization occurs. We would also like the factors to be meaningful. A good factor solution is both simple and interpretable. When factors can be interpreted, new insights are possible. For example, if liquor preferences can be explained by such factors as sweetness and regional tastes (Stoetzel, 1960), marketing strategies can reflect this.

15.3
STEPS IN A FACTOR ANALYSIS

Factor analysis usually proceeds in four steps.

1 The correlation matrix for all variables is computed, as in Figure 15.4. Variables that do not appear to be related to other variables can be identified from the matrix and associated statistics. The appropriateness of the factor model can also be evaluated. At this step, you should also decide what to do with cases that have missing values for some of the variables (see Chapter 13 for a discussion of missing values).

2 In this step, factor extraction—the number of factors necessary to represent the data and the method of calculating them—must be determined. At this step, you also ascertain how well the chosen model fits the data.

3 This step, the rotation step, focuses on transforming the factors to make them more interpretable.

4 At this step, scores for each factor can be computed for each case. These scores can then be used in a variety of other analyses.

15.4
Examining the Correlation Matrix

The correlation matrix for the 14 community variables is shown in Figure 15.4. Since one of the goals of factor analysis is to obtain "factors" that help explain these correlations, the variables must be related to each other for the factor model to be appropriate. If the correlations between variables are small, it is unlikely that they share common factors. Figure 15.4 shows that almost half the coefficients are greater than 0.3 in absolute value. All variables, except the extent of mental illness, have large correlations with at least one of the other variables in the set.

Figure 15.4   Correlation matrix

```
CORRELATION MATRIX:

             POPSTABL   NEWSCIRC   FEMEMPLD   FARMERS   RETAILNG   COMMERCL   INDUSTZN    HEALTH   CHLDNEGL   COMMEFFC   DWELGNEW   MIGRNPOP
POPSTABL     1.00000
NEWSCIRC      -.17500   1.00000
FEMEMPLD      -.27600    .61600    1.00000
FARMERS        .36900   -.62500    -.63700   1.00000
RETAILNG      -.12700    .62400     .73600   -.51900   1.00000
COMMERCL      -.06900    .65200     .58900   -.30600    .72700    1.00000
INDUSTZN      -.10600    .74200     .78500   -.54500    .78500     .91100    1.00000
HEALTH        -.14900   -.03000     .24100   -.06800    .10000     .12300     .12900    1.00000
CHLDNEGL      -.03900   -.17100    -.58900    .25700   -.55700    -.35700    -.42400   -.40700   1.00000
COMMEFFC      -.00500    .10000     .47100   -.21300    .45200     .28700     .35700    .73200   -.66000   1.00000
DWELGNEW      -.67000    .18800     .41300   -.57900    .16500     .03000     .20300    .29000   -.13800    .31100   1.00000
MIGRNPOP      -.47600   -.08600     .06400   -.19800    .00700    -.06800    -.02400    .08300    .14800    .06700    .50500   1.00000
UNEMPLOY       .13700   -.37300    -.68900    .45000   -.65000    -.42400    -.52800   -.34800    .73300   -.60100   -.26600    .18100
MENTALIL       .23700    .04600    -.23700    .12100   -.19000    -.05500    -.09500   -.27900    .24700   -.32400   -.26600   -.30700


             UNEMPLOY   MENTALIL

UNEMPLOY     1.00000
MENTALIL      .21700    1.00000
```

15.5
Factor Extraction

The goal of the factor extraction step is to determine the factors. In this example, we will obtain estimates of the initial factors from principal components analysis. Other methods for factor extraction are described in Section 15.8. In principal components analysis, linear combinations of the observed variables are formed. The first principal component is the combination that accounts for the largest amount of variance in the sample. The second principal component accounts for the next largest amount of variance and is uncorrelated with the first. Successive components explain progressively smaller portions of the total sample variance, and all are uncorrelated with each other.

It is possible to compute as many principal components as there are variables. If all principal components are used, each variable can be exactly represented by them, but nothing has been gained since there are as many factors (principal components) as variables. When all factors are included in the solution, all of the variance of each variable is accounted for, and there is no need for a unique factor in the model. The proportion of variance accounted for by the common factors, or the *communality* of a variable, is 1 for all the variables, as shown in Figure 15.5a. In general, principal components analysis is a separate technique from factor analysis. That is, it can be used whenever uncorrelated linear combinations of the observed variables are desired. All it does is transform a set of correlated variables to a set of uncorrelated variables (principal components).

To help us decide how many factors we need to represent the data, it is helpful to examine the percentage of total variance explained by each. The total variance is the sum of the variance of each variable. For simplicity, all variables and factors are expressed in standardized form, with a mean of 0 and a standard deviation of 1. Since there are 14 variables and each is standardized to have a variance of 1, the total variance is 14 in this example.

Figure 15.5a contains the initial statistics for each factor. The total variance explained by each factor is listed in the column labeled EIGENVALUE. The next column contains the percentage of the total variance attributable to each factor. For example, the linear combination formed by Factor 2 has a variance of 2.35, which is 16.8% of the total variance of 14. The last column, the cumulative percentage, indicates the percentage of variance attributable to that factor and those that precede it in the table. Note that the factors are arranged in descending order of variance explained. Note also that although variable names and factors are displayed on the same line, there is no correspondence between the two parts of the table. The first two columns provide information about the individual variables, while the last four columns describe the factors.

Figure 15.5a   Initial statistics

```
EXTRACTION  1  FOR ANALYSIS  1, PRINCIPAL-COMPONENTS ANALYSIS (PC)


INITIAL STATISTICS:


VARIABLE     COMMUNALITY  *  FACTOR   EIGENVALUE   PCT OF VAR   CUM PCT
                          *
POPSTABL      1.00000     *    1       5.70658        40.8        40.8
NEWSCIRC      1.00000     *    2       2.35543        16.8        57.6
FEMEMPLD      1.00000     *    3       2.00926        14.4        71.9
FARMERS       1.00000     *    4        .89745         6.4        78.3
RETAILNG      1.00000     *    5        .75847         5.4        83.8
COMMERCL      1.00000     *    6        .53520         3.8        87.6
INDUSTZN      1.00000     *    7        .50886         3.6        91.2
HEALTH        1.00000     *    8        .27607         2.0        93.2
CHLDNEGL      1.00000     *    9        .24511         1.8        94.9
COMMEFFC      1.00000     *   10        .20505         1.5        96.4
DWELGNEW      1.00000     *   11        .19123         1.4        97.8
MIGRNPOP      1.00000     *   12        .16982         1.2        99.0
UNEMPLOY      1.00000     *   13        .10202          .7        99.7
MENTALIL      1.00000     *   14        .03946          .3       100.0
```

Figure 15.5a shows that almost 72% of the total variance is attributable to the first three factors. The remaining eleven factors together account for only 28.1% of the variance. Thus, a model with three factors may be adequate to represent the data.

Several procedures have been proposed for determining the number of factors to use in a model. One criterion suggests that only factors that account for variances greater than 1 (the eigenvalue is greater than 1) should be included. Factors with a variance less than 1 are no better than a single variable, since each variable has a variance of 1. Although this is the default criterion in SPSS-X FACTOR, it is not always a good solution (see Tucker, Koopman, & Linn, 1969).

Figure 15.5b is a plot of the total variance associated with each factor. Typically, the plot shows a distinct break between the steep slope of the large factors and the gradual trailing off of the rest of the factors. This gradual trailing off is called the *scree* (Cattell, 1966) because it resembles the rubble that forms at the foot of a mountain. Experimental evidence indicates that the scree begins at the kth factor, where k is the true number of factors. From the scree plot, it again appears that a three-factor model should be sufficient for the community example.

Figure 15.5b   Scree plot

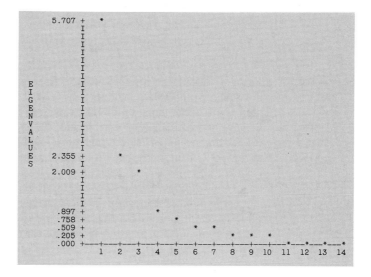

15.6
The Three Factors

Figure 15.6 contains the coefficients that relate the variables to the three factors. The figure shows that the industrialization index can be expressed as

$$INDUSTZN = 0.844F_1 + 0.300F_2 + 0.238F_3$$

Similarly, the health index is

$$HEALTH = 0.383F_1 - 0.327F_2 - 0.635F_3$$

Figure 15.6   Factor matrix

```
FACTOR MATRIX:

                FACTOR  1      FACTOR  2      FACTOR  3
POPSTABL        -.30247        .68597         -.36451
NEWSCIRC         .67238        .28096          .49779
FEMEMPLD         .89461        .01131          .08063
FARMERS         -.68659        .20002         -.40450
RETAILNG         .85141        .24264          .09351
COMMERCL         .72503        .39394          .19896
INDUSTZN         .84436        .29956          .23775
HEALTH           .38347       -.32718         -.63474
CHLDNEGL        -.67430       -.12139          .52896
COMMEFFC         .63205       -.15540         -.64221
DWELGNEW         .45886       -.73940          .18706
MIGRNPOP         .07894       -.74371          .24335
UNEMPLOY        -.78714       -.09777          .30110
MENTALIL        -.30025        .45463          .27134
```

Each row of Figure 15.6 contains the coefficients used to express a standardized variable in terms of the factors. These coefficients are called *factor loadings*, since they indicate how much weight is assigned to each factor. Factors with large coefficients (in absolute value) for a variable are closely related to the variable. For example, Factor 1 is the factor with the largest loading for the INDUSTZN variable. The matrix of factor loadings is called the *factor pattern* matrix.

When the estimated factors are uncorrelated with each other (orthogonal), the factor loadings are also the correlations between the factors and the variables. Thus, the correlation between the health index and Factor 1 is 0.383. Similarly, there is a slightly smaller correlation (−0.327) between the health index and Factor 2. The matrix of correlations between variables and factors is called the *factor structure* matrix. When the factors are orthogonal, the factor structure matrix and the factor pattern matrix are equivalent. As shown in Figure 15.6, such a matrix is labeled the factor matrix in SPSS-X output.

15.7
More on the Factor Matrix

There is yet another interpretation of the factor matrix in Figure 15.6. Whether the factors are orthogonal or not, the factor loadings are the standardized regression coefficients in the multiple regression equation with the original variable as the dependent variable and the factors as the independent variables. If the factors are uncorrelated, the values of the coefficients are not dependent on each other. They represent the unique contribution of each factor and are the correlations between the factors and the variable.

To judge how well the three-factor model describes the original variables, we can compute the proportion of the variance of each variable explained by the three-factor model. Since the factors are uncorrelated, the total proportion of variance explained is just the sum of the variance proportions explained by each factor.

Consider, for example, the health index. Factor 1 accounts for 14.7% of the variance for this variable. This is obtained by squaring the correlation coefficient for Factor 1 and HEALTH (0.383). Similarly, Factor 3 explains 40.3% $((-0.635)^2)$ of the variance. The total percentage of variance in the health index accounted for by this three-factor model is therefore 65.7% (14.7 + 10.7 + 40.3). The proportion of variance explained by the common factors is called the *communality* of the variable.

The communalities for the variables are shown in Figure 15.7, together with the percentage of variance accounted for by each of the retained factors. This table is labeled FINAL STATISTICS since it shows the communalities and factor statistics after the desired number of factors has been extracted. When factors are estimated using the method of principal components, the factor statistics are the same in the tables labeled as initial and final. However, the communalities are different since all of the variances of the variables are not explained when only a subset of factors is retained.

Figure 15.7 Communality of variables

```
FINAL STATISTICS:


VARIABLE     COMMUNALITY  *  FACTOR   EIGENVALUE   PCT OF VAR   CUM PCT
                          *
POPSTABL       .69491     *    1        5.70658       40.8       40.8
NEWSCIRC       .77882     *    2        2.35543       16.8       57.6
FEMEMPLD       .80696     *    3        2.00926       14.4       71.9
FARMERS        .67503     *
RETAILNG       .79253     *
COMMERCL       .72044     *
INDUSTZN       .85921     *
HEALTH         .65699     *
CHLDNEGL       .74921     *
COMMEFFC       .83607     *
DWELGNEW       .79226     *
MIGRNPOP       .61855     *
UNEMPLOY       .71981     *
MENTALIL       .37047     *
```

Communalities can range from 0 to 1, with 0 indicating that the common factors explain none of the variance, and 1 indicating that all the variance is explained by the common factors. The variance that is not explained by the common factors is attributed to the unique factor and is called the *uniqueness* of the variable.

**15.8
Methods for Factor
Extraction**

Several different methods can be used to obtain estimates of the common factors. These methods differ in the criterion used to define "good fit." Principal axis factoring proceeds much as principal components analysis, except that the diagonals of the correlation matrix are replaced by estimates of the communalities. At the first step, squared multiple correlation coefficients can be used as initial estimates of the communalities. Based on these, the requisite number of factors is extracted. The communalities are reestimated from the factor loadings, and factors are again extracted with the new communality estimates replacing the old. This continues until negligible change occurs in the in the communality estimates.

The method of unweighted least squares produces, for a fixed number of factors, a factor pattern matrix that minimizes the sum of the squared differences between the observed and reproduced correlation matrices (ignoring the diagonals). The generalized least-squares method minimizes the same criterion, however, correlations are weighted inversely by the uniqueness of the variables. That is, correlations involving variables with high uniqueness are given less weight than correlations involving variables with low uniqueness.

The maximum-likelihood method produces parameter estimates that are the most likely to have produced the observed correlation matrix if the sample is from a multivariate normal distribution. Again, the correlations are weighted by the inverse of the uniqueness of the variables, and an iterative algorithm is employed.

15.9
Summary of the Extraction Phase

In the factor extraction phase, the number of common factors needed to adequately describe the data is determined. This decision is based on eigenvalues and percentage of the total variance accounted for by different numbers of factors. A plot of the eigenvalues (the scree plot) is also helpful in determining the number of factors.

15.10
The Rotation Phase

Although the factor matrix obtained in the extraction phase indicates the relationship between the factors and the individual variables, it is usually difficult to identify meaningful factors based on this matrix. Often the variables and factors do not appear correlated in any interpretable pattern. Most factors are correlated with many variables. Since one of the goals of factor analysis is to identify factors that are substantively meaningful (in the sense that they summarize sets of closely related variables), the *rotation* phase of factor analysis attempts to transform the initial matrix into one that is easier to interpret.

Consider Figure 15.10a, which is a factor matrix for four hypothetical variables. From the factor loadings, it is difficult to interpret any of the factors, since the variables and factors are intertwined. That is, all factor loadings are quite high, and both factors explain all of the variables.

Figure 15.10a   Hypothetical factor matrix

```
FACTOR MATRIX:

                     FACTOR  1       FACTOR  2

        V1              .50000          .50000
        V2              .50000         -.40000
        V3              .70000          .70000
        V4             -.60000          .60000
```

Figure 15.10b   Rotated hypothetical factor matrix

```
ROTATED FACTOR MATRIX:
                     FACTOR  1       FACTOR  2

        V1              .70684         -.01938
        V2              .05324         -.63809
        V3              .98958         -.02713
        V4              .02325          .84821
```

In the factor matrix in Figure 15.10b, variables V1 and V3 are highly related to Factor 1, while V2 and V4 load highly on Factor 2. By looking at what variables V2 and V4 have in common (such as a measurement of job satisfaction, or a characterization of an anxious personality), we may be able to identify Factor 2. Similar steps can be taken to identify Factor 1. The goal of rotation is to transform complicated matrices like that in Figure 15.10a into simpler ones like that in Figure 15.10b.

Consider Figure 15.10c, which is a plot of variables V1 to V4 using the factor loadings in Figure 15.10a as the coordinates, and Figure 15.10d, which is the corresponding plot for Figure 15.10b. Note that Figure 15.10c would look exactly like Figure 15.10d if the dotted lines were rotated to be the reference axes. When the axes are maintained at right angles, the rotation is called *orthogonal*. If the axes are not maintained at right angles, the rotation is called *oblique*. Oblique rotation is not discussed in this introductory guide.

Figure 15.10c   Prior to rotation

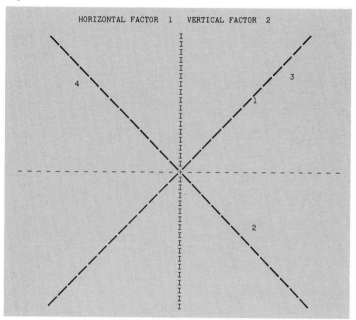

Figure 15.10d   Orthogonal rotation

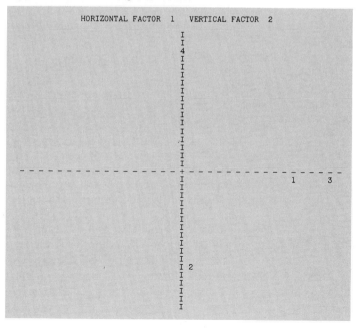

The purpose of rotation is to achieve a simple structure. This means that we would like each factor to have nonzero loadings for only some of the variables. This helps us interpret the factors. We would also like each variable to have nonzero loadings for only a few factors, preferably one. This permits the factors to be differentiated from each other. If several factors have high loadings on the same variables, it is difficult to ascertain how the factors differ.

Rotation does not affect the goodness of fit of a factor solution. That is, although the factor matrix changes, the communalities and the percentage of total variance explained do not change. The percentage of variance accounted for by each of the factors does, however, change. Rotation redistributes the explained variance for the individual factors. Different rotation methods may actually result in the identification of somewhat different factors.

A variety of algorithms are used for orthogonal rotation to a simple structure. The most commonly used method is the *varimax* method, which attempts to minimize the number of variables that have high loadings on a factor. This should enhance the interpretability of the factors.

Consider Figure 15.10e, which shows the factor matrices for the community data before rotation and again after a varimax orthogonal rotation procedure.

Figure 15.10e   Factor matrices for community data

```
FACTOR MATRIX (unrotated):

                 FACTOR  1      FACTOR  2      FACTOR  3

POPSTABL          -.30247        .68597         -.36451
NEWSCIRC           .67238        .28096          .49779
FEMEMPLD           .89461        .01131          .08063
FARMERS           -.68659        .20002         -.40450
RETAILNG           .85141        .24264          .09351
COMMERCL           .72503        .39394          .19896
INDUSTZN           .84436        .29956          .23775
HEALTH             .38347       -.32718         -.63474
CHLDNEGL          -.67430       -.12139          .52896
COMMEFFC           .63205       -.15540         -.64221
DWELGNEW           .45886       -.73940          .18706
MIGRNPOP           .07894       -.74371          .24335
UNEMPLOY          -.78714       -.09777          .30110
MENTALIL          -.30025        .45463          .27134


ROTATED FACTOR MATRIX (varimax):

                 FACTOR  1      FACTOR  2      FACTOR  3

POPSTABL          -.13553        .00916         -.82247
NEWSCIRC           .86634       -.14256          .08920
FEMEMPLD           .78248        .37620          .23055
FARMERS           -.65736       -.04537         -.49077
RETAILNG           .83993        .29454          .01705
COMMERCL           .83432        .11068         -.11000
INDUSTZN           .91325        .15773          .01730
HEALTH            -.05806        .79424          .15101
CHLDNEGL          -.39791       -.75492          .14486
COMMEFFC           .21186        .88794          .05241
DWELGNEW           .17484        .22931          .84208
MIGRNPOP          -.12119       -.00660          .77706
UNEMPLOY          -.57378       -.62483          .01311
MENTALIL           .03133       -.47460         -.37979
```

The unrotated factor matrix is difficult to interpret. Many variables have moderate-size correlations with several factors. After rotation, the number of large and small factor loadings increases. Variables are more highly correlated with single factors. Interpretation of the factors also appears possible. For example, the first factor shows strong positive correlation with newspaper circulation, percentage of females in the labor force, sales, commercial activity, and the industrialization index. It also shows a strong negative correlation with the number of farmers. Thus Factor 1 might be interpreted as measuring something like "urbanism." The second factor is positively correlated with health and a high standard of living and negatively correlated with aid to dependent children, unemployment, and mental illness. This factor describes the affluence or welfare of a community. The last factor is associated with the instability or influx of a community. Thus, communities may be fairly well characterized by three factors—urbanism, welfare, and influx.

15.11
Factor Loading Plots

A convenient means of examining the success of an orthogonal rotation is to plot the variables using the factor loadings as coordinates. In Figure 15.11a, the variables are plotted using Factors 1 and 2 after varimax rotation of the two factors. The plotted numbers represent the number of the variable; for example, 7 represents the seventh variable (INDUSTZN). The coordinates correspond to the factor loadings in Figure 15.10e for the varimax-rotated solution. The coordinates are also listed. In Figure 15.11b, the variables are plotted using Factors 1 and 2 before rotation. (The coordinates are omitted for this plot.)

Figure 15.11a   Varimax-rotated solution

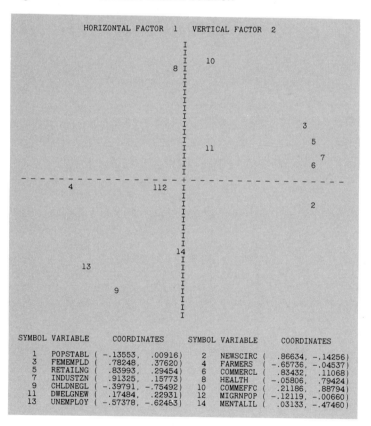

SYMBOL	VARIABLE	COORDINATES	SYMBOL	VARIABLE	COORDINATES
1	POPSTABL	(−.13553, .00916)	2	NEWSCIRC	(.86634, −.14256)
3	FEMEMPLD	(.78248, .37620)	4	FARMERS	(−.65736, −.04537)
5	RETAILNG	(.83993, .29454)	6	COMMERCL	(.83432, .11068)
7	INDUSTZN	(.91325, .15773)	8	HEALTH	(−.05806, .79424)
9	CHLDNEGL	(−.39791, −.75492)	10	COMMEFFC	(.21186, .88794)
11	DWELGNEW	(.17484, .22931)	12	MIGRNPOP	(−.12119, −.00660)
13	UNEMPLOY	(−.57378, −.62463)	14	MENTALIL	(.03133, −.47460)

Figure 15.11b   Unrotated solution

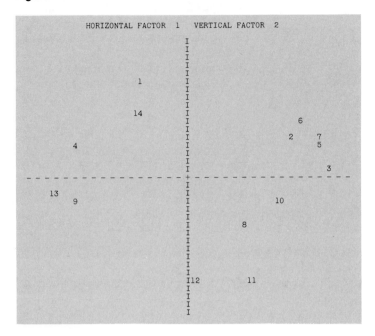

If a rotation has achieved a simple structure, clusters of variables should occur near the ends of the axes and at their intersection. Variables at the end of an axis are those that have high loadings on only that factor. Variables near the origin of the plot have small loadings on both factors. Variables that are not near the axes are explained by both factors. If a simple structure has been achieved, there should be few, if any, variables with large loadings on more than one factor.

15.12
Interpreting the Factors

To identify the factors, it is necessary to group the variables that have large loadings for the same factors. Plots of the loadings, as discussed in Section 15.11, are one way of determining the clusters of variables. Another convenient strategy is to sort the factor pattern matrix so that variables with high loadings on the same factor appear together, as shown in Figure 15.12a. Small factor loadings can be omitted from such a table. In Figure 15.12b, therefore, no loadings less than 0.5 in absolute value are displayed. Note that the mental illness variable, as expected, does not correlate highly with any of the factors.

Figure 15.12a   Sorted loadings

```
ROTATED FACTOR MATRIX:
                 FACTOR  1      FACTOR  2      FACTOR  3

    INDUSTZN       .91325         .15773         .01730
    NEWSCIRC       .86634        -.14256         .08920
    RETAILNG       .83993         .29454         .01705
    COMMERCL       .83432         .11068        -.11000
    FEMEMPLD       .78248         .37620         .23055
    FARMERS       -.65736        -.04537        -.49077

    COMMEFFC       .21186         .88794         .05241
    HEALTH        -.05806         .79424         .15101
    CHLDNEGL      -.39791        -.75492         .14486
    UNEMPLOY      -.57378        -.62483         .01311
    MENTALIL       .03133        -.47460        -.37979

    DWELGNEW       .17484         .22931         .84208
    POPSTABL      -.13553         .00916        -.82247
    MIGRNPOP      -.12119        -.00660         .77706
```

Figure 15.12b   Sorted and blanked loadings

```
ROTATED FACTOR MATRIX:

                FACTOR  1       FACTOR  2       FACTOR  3

   INDUSTZN      .91325
   NEWSCIRC      .86634
   RETAILNG      .83993
   COMMERCL      .83432
   FEMEMPLD      .78248
   FARMERS      -.65736

   COMMEFFC                      .88794
   HEALTH                        .79424
   CHLDNEGL                     -.75492
   UNEMPLOY     -.57378         -.62483
   MENTALIL

   DWELGNEW                                      .84208
   POPSTABL                                     -.82247
   MIGRNPOP                                      .77706
```

15.13
Factor Scores

Since one of the goals of factor analysis is to reduce a large number of variables to a smaller number of factors, it is often desirable to estimate factor scores for each case. The factor scores can be used in subsequent analyses to represent the values of the factors. Plots of factor scores for pairs of factors are useful for detecting unusual observations.

Recall from Section 15.1 that a factor can be estimated as a linear combination of the original variables. That is, for case k, the score for the jth factor is estimated as

$$\hat{F}_{jk} = \sum_{i=1}^{p} W_{ji} X_{ik}$$

where X_{ik} is the standardized value of the ith variable for case k and W_{ji} is the factor score coefficient for the jth factor and the ith variable. Except for principal components analysis, exact factor scores cannot be obtained. Estimates are obtained instead.

There are several methods for estimating factor score coefficients. Each has different properties and results in different scores (see Tucker, 1971; Harman, 1967). The three methods available in SPSS-X FACTOR (Anderson-Rubin, regression, and Bartlett) all result in scores with a mean of 0. The Anderson-Rubin method always produces uncorrelated scores with a standard deviation of 1, even when the original factors are estimated to be correlated. The regression factor scores (the default) have a variance equal to the squared multiple correlation between the estimated factor scores and the true factor values. Regression method factor scores can be correlated even when factors are assumed to be orthogonal. If principal components extraction is used, all three methods result in the same factor scores, which are no longer estimated but are exact.

Figure 15.13 contains the factor score coefficients used to calculate regression method factor scores for the community data.

Figure 15.13   Factor coefficient matrix

```
FACTOR SCORE COEFFICIENT MATRIX:

                FACTOR  1       FACTOR  2       FACTOR  3

   POPSTABL     -.00150          .03191         -.15843
   NEWSCIRC      .05487         -.06095          .03524
   FEMEMPLD      .01729          .14014          .05328
   FARMERS      -.01797          .00113         -.11462
   RETAILNG      .03728          .09460         -.03577
   COMMERCL      .20579         -.11667         -.10723
   INDUSTZN      .77285         -.27024          .00882
   HEALTH       -.02786          .09971         -.00161
   CHLDNEGL      .08404         -.44657          .16521
   COMMEFFC     -.05030          .23211         -.03623
   DWELGNEW     -.05117          .07034          .68792
   MIGRNPOP      .00029         -.03198          .09778
   UNEMPLOY      .03856         -.26435          .05378
   MENTALIL      .01264         -.04224         -.01691
```

To see how factor scores are calculated, consider Table 15.13, which contains standardized values for the original 14 variables for 5 counties and factor score values for the three factors. For each factor, the factor scores are obtained by multiplying the standardized values by the corresponding factor score coefficients. Thus, for Adams county, the value for Factor 1 is −1.328.

$$-.00150 \times -.36 + .05487 \times -.93 + .01729$$
$$\times -1.06 + ... + .01264 \times -.76 = -1.328$$

Table 15.13 Standardized values and factor scores

		County			
Variable	Adams	Butler	Crawford	Cuyahoga	Hamilton
POPSTABL	−0.36	−1.49	2.44	−0.13	−0.30
NEWSCIRC	−0.93	0.39	−0.26	2.04	1.17
FEMEMPLD	−1.06	0.41	0.24	1.30	1.03
FARMERS	2.20	−0.67	0.01	−0.93	−0.90
RETAILNG	−1.41	0.49	0.58	1.15	1.07
COMMERCL	−0.89	−0.30	−0.07	1.58	2.02
INDUSTZN	−1.14	−0.11	0.03	1.53	1.85
HEALTH	−0.25	−0.56	−1.32	−0.36	−1.17
CHLDNEGL	−1.26	0.79	−0.61	0.63	0.99
COMMEFFC	−0.20	0.78	−0.87	−0.78	−1.66
DWELGNEW	−0.52	0.52	−1.09	−0.01	−0.22
MIGRNPOP	−0.98	0.16	−0.60	0.63	1.13
UNEMPLOY	−0.75	−0.36	−0.44	1.56	0.76
MENTALIL	−0.76	−0.77	−0.46	−0.14	0.61

Factor	Scores				
Factor 1	−1.328	−0.089	0.083	1.862	2.233
Factor 2	0.897	0.027	0.197	−1.362	−1.79
Factor 3	−0.830	0.831	−1.290	0.342	0.226

15.14 RUNNING PROCEDURE FACTOR

A variety of extraction and rotation techniques are available in the SPSS-X FACTOR procedure. Only the basics for running the FACTOR procedure are illustrated here; see the *SPSS-X User's Guide,* 3rd ed., for more information.

15.15 Specifying the Variables

The VARIABLES subcommand lists the variables to analyze. It is the only required subcommand. If you do not specify a subsequent EXTRACTION or ROTATION subcommand, the default principal components analysis with varimax rotation is produced. Thus, the command

```
FACTOR VARIABLES=POPSTABL NEWSCIRC FEMEMPLD FARMERS RETAILNG COMMERCL
    INDUSTZN HEALTH CHLDNEGL COMMEFFC DWELGNEW MIGRNPOP UNEMPLOY MENTALIL
```

or, if the variables exist on that order on the active file, the command

```
FACTOR VARIABLES=POPSTABL TO MENTALIL
```

produces the output shown in Figures 15.5a, 15.6, and 15.7.

15.16 Missing Values

FACTOR results are based on the correlation matrix for the variables listed on the VARIABLES subcommand. Use the MISSING subcommand to specify the missing-value treatment for this matrix. The MISSING subcommand, if used, should be placed immediately after the VARIABLES subcommand. If you omit the MISSING subcommand, or include it with no specifications, missing values are deleted listwise.

LISTWISE	*Delete missing values listwise.* Only cases with valid values on all variables on the VARIABLES subcommand are used. This is the default.
PAIRWISE	*Delete missing values pairwise.* Cases with complete data on each pair of variables correlated are used.
MEANSUB	*Replace missing values with the variable mean.* This includes both user-missing and system-missing values.
INCLUDE	*Include user-missing values.* Cases with user-missing values are treated as valid observations. System-missing values are excluded from analysis.

For example, the command

```
FACTOR VARIABLES=IQ GPA TESTSCOR STRESS SAT PSYCHTST
  /MISSING=PAIRWISE
```

requests a default analysis that uses pairwise missing-value treatment in calculating the correlation matrix.

15.17
Requesting Additional Statistics

By default, the statistics listed below under INITIAL, EXTRACTION, and ROTATION are printed. Use the PRINT subcommand to request additional statistics. If you specify PRINT, only those statistics explicitly named are displayed.

UNIVARIATE	*Numbers of valid observations, means, and standard deviations for the variables.*
INITIAL	*Initial communalities, eigenvalues, and percentage of variance explained.* (See Sections 15.5 and 15.7.)
CORRELATION	*Correlation matrix for the variables.*
SIG	*Significance levels of correlations.* These are one-tailed probabilities.
DET	*The determinant of the correlation matrix.*
INV	*The inverse of the correlation matrix.*
AIC	*The anti-image covariance and correlation matrices.*
KMO	*The Kaiser-Meyer-Olkin measure of sampling adequacy and Bartlett's test of sphericity.*
EXTRACTION	*Communalities, eigenvalues, and rotated factor loadings.* (See Sections 15.5 through 15.8.)
REPR	*Reproduced correlations and their residuals.*
ROTATION	*Rotated factor pattern and structure matrices, factor transformation matrix, and factor correlation matrix.* (See Section 15.10.)
FSCORE	*The factor score coefficient matrix.* By default, this is based on a regression solution.
DEFAULT	*INITIAL, EXTRACTION, and ROTATION statistics.* If you use the EXTRACTION subcommand without a subsequent ROTATION subcommand, only the statistics specified by INITIAL and EXTRACTION are displayed by default.
ALL	*All available statistics.*

15.18
Plotting Results

To obtain a scree plot (Section 15.5) or a factor loading plot (Section 15.11), use the PLOT subcommand with the following keywords:

EIGEN	*Scree plot.* Plots the eigenvalues in descending order.
ROTATION(n1 n2)	*Factor loading plot.* The specifications *n*1 and *n*2 refer to the factors used as the axes. Several pairs of factors in parentheses can be specified on one ROTATION specification. A plot is displayed for each pair of factor numbers enclosed in parentheses.

Plots are based on rotated factors. To get an unrotated factor plot, you must explicitly specify NOROTATE on the ROTATION subcommand (see Section 15.22).

The plots in Figures 15.5b and 15.11a can be augmented with two additional factor plots by specifying

```
FACTOR VARIABLES=POPSTABL TO MENTALIL
  /PLOT=EIGEN ROTATION(1 2)(1 3)(2 3)
```

15.19
Formatting the Display

Use the FORMAT subcommand to reformat the display of the factor loading and structure matrices to help you interpret the factors (see Section 15.12). The following keywords may be specified on FORMAT:

SORT   *Order the factor loadings by magnitude.*
BLANK(n) *Suppress coefficients lower in absolute value than* n.
DEFAULT   *Turn off blanking and sorting.*

For example, the command

```
FACTOR VARIABLES=POPSTABL TO MENTALIL
  /FORMAT=SORT BLANK(.5)
```

produced the output in Figure 15.12b.

15.20
Specifying the Extraction Method

To specify the extraction method, use the EXTRACTION subcommand with one of the keywords shown below.

PC   *Principal components analysis.* This is the default.
PAF   *Principal axis factoring.*
ML   *Maximum likelihood.*
ALPHA *Alpha factoring.*
IMAGE *Image factoring.*
ULS   *Unweighted least squares.*
GLS   *Generalized least squares.*

You can specify more than one EXTRACTION subcommand. For example, the command

```
FACTOR VARIABLES=IQ GPA TESTSCOR STRESS SAT PSYCHTST
  /EXTRACTION=ML
  /EXTRACTION=PC
```

produces output based on two extraction methods—maximum likelihood and principal components.

If you use the EXTRACTION subcommand without a subsequent ROTATION subcommand, the factor pattern matrix is not rotated (see Section 15.22).

15.21
Controlling Criteria

Use CRITERIA to control criteria for extractions and rotations that follow the subcommand.

FACTORS(nf)   *Number of factors extracted.* The default is the number of eigenvalues greater than MINEIGEN (see below).
MINEIGEN(eg) *Minimum eigenvalue used to control the number of factors.* The default value is 1.
ITERATE(ni)   *Number of iterations for the factor solution.* The default value is 25.

15.22
Specifying the Rotation Method

Four rotation methods are available in FACTOR: varimax, equamax, quartimax, and oblimin (see Section 15.10). When both the EXTRACTION and ROTATION subcommands are omitted, the factors are rotated using the varimax method. However, if EXTRACTION is specified but ROTATION is not, the factors are not rotated. To specify a rotation method other than these defaults, use the ROTATION subcommand.

VARIMAX   *Varimax rotation.* This is the default if both EXTRACTION and ROTATION are omitted.

EQUAMAX   *Equamax rotation.*

QUARTIMAX   *Quartimax rotation.*

OBLIMIN   *Direct oblimin rotation.*

NOROTATE   *No rotation.* This is the default if EXTRACTION is specified but ROTATION is not.

To obtain a factor loading plot based on unrotated factors, use the PLOT subcommand (see Section 15.18) and specify NOROTATE in the ROTATION subcommand, as in

```
FACTOR VARIABLES=IQ GPA TESTSCOR STRESS SAT PSYCHTST
  /PLOT=EIGEN ROTATION(1,2)
  /ROTATION=NOROTATE
```

15.23
Saving Factor Scores

Use the SAVE subcommand to compute and save factor scores on the active file. The specifications on the SAVE subcommand include the method for calculating factor scores, how many factor scores to calculate, and a *rootname* to be used in naming the factor scores.

First, choose one of the following method keywords (see Section 15.13):

REG   *The regression method.* This is the default.

BART   *The Bartlett method.*

AR   *The Anderson-Rubin method.*

Next, specify within parentheses the number of desired factor scores and a rootname up to seven characters long to be used in naming the scores. The maximum number of scores equals the order of the factor solution. You can use keyword ALL to calculate factor scores for all extracted factors.

FACTOR uses the rootname to name the factor scores sequentially, as in root1, root2, root3, and so on. If you are calculating factor scores for a many-factor solution, make sure that the rootname is short enough to accommodate the number of the highest-order factor score variable. When FACTOR saves the variables on the active file, it automatically supplies a variable label indicating the method used to calculate it, its positional order, and the analysis number.

For example, the following FACTOR command saves factor scores for a study of abortion items:

```
FACTOR VARIABLES=ABDEFECT TO ABSINGLE
  /MISSING=MEANSUB
  /CRITERIA=FACTORS(2)
  /EXTRACTION=ULS
  /ROTATION=VARIMAX
  /SAVE AR (ALL FSULS)
```

FACTOR calculates two factor scores named FSULS1 and FSULS2 using the Anderson-Rubin method and saves them on the active file.

15.24
A FACTOR Example

The following is the basic analysis discussed throughout this chapter:

```
FACTOR VARIABLES=POPSTABL TO MENTALIL
  /FORMAT=SORT
  /PLOT=EIGEN ROTATION(1,2)
  /PRINT=CORRELATION FSCORES
  /ROTATION=VARIMAX
```

- The VARIABLES subcommand specifies the variables for the analysis (see Section 15.15).
- The FORMAT subcommand orders the factor loadings by magnitude (see Section 15.19).
- The PLOT subcommand specifies a scree plot and a factor loading plot (see Section 15.18).
- The PRINT subcommand prints the correlation matrix for the specified variables and the factor score coefficient matrix (see Section 15.17).
- The ROTATION subcommand requests varimax rotation (see Section 15.22).

EXERCISES

Syntax

1. Consider these variables:

   ```
   PCTHOMES PASTSALE DSTRCTYP AVGINCOM PCTBUSNS BUSNSTYP PCTFAMLY
   AVGAGE AVGEDUC PRICE
   ```

   Write the FACTOR command needed to obtain a factor analysis with default output.

2. Consider these variables:

   ```
   DRUGUSE PEERS FAMSTABL NBRHOOD SCHLACHV ALCOHOL ALIENATN RECREATN
   SPORTS SES AGE CRIME
   ```

   Write a command that performs a factor analysis.

3. What is wrong with the FACTOR command shown below?

   ```
   FACTOR EXTRACTION=ML
      /VARIABLES=IQ GPA TESTSCOR SAT EDUCATN SES NBRHOOD
   ```

Statistical Concepts

1. A factor analysis done by a marketing firm produced the factor loadings shown below. Interpret each factor—that is, describe what each factor represents.

	FACTOR 1	FACTOR 2	
MAGAZINE	-.7347	.0398	Type of magazines read
IQ	.0146	.1128	IQ score
OCCSTAT	.0852	.8521	Status of occupation
NBRHOOD	-.0513	-.7952	Type of neighborhood living in
RECREATN	.8707	-.0667	Main recreation interest
EDUCATN	-.0283	.8901	Level of education
INCOME	.1002	.6724	Level of income
POLITACT	.1964	-.0783	Degree of political activity
SPORT	.7095	.0332	Interest in professional sports
CULTURE	-.8948	-.0427	Interest in plays, concerts, etc.

2. Consider the factor pattern matrix shown below:

	FACTOR 1	FACTOR 2	FACTOR 3	
VERBAL	.64453	-.03421	-.03381	Verbal score
MATH	.89116	.07376	.06516	Math score
LOGIC	.91583	-.05229	.08890	Logic score
GPA	.14429	.12238	-.05362	Grade point average
SAT	.18742	.32156	-.12154	Standard aptitude test
SES	.08321	.91842	.14885	Socio-economic status
EDUCATN	.09312	.96593	-.10436	Education level
TESTSCOR	.41127	.34432	-.14892	Test score
STRESS	.08552	.06648	.95422	Stress level
PSYCHTST	.11383	.11524	.89989	Psychology test
IQ	.69877	-.08321	.24661	IQ score

   a. Write the factor models for TESTSCOR and PSYCHTST.
   b. Interpret each factor—that is, describe what each factor represents.

3. Consider the following table:

VARIABLE	COMMUNALITY	FACTOR	EIGENVALUE
AGE	1.00000	1	2.27
MEDHIST	1.00000	2	2.05
BLOODPRS	1.00000	3	1.73
WEIGHT	1.00000	4	.64
IQ	1.00000	5	.15
PSYCHTST	1.00000	6	.10
STRESS	1.00000	7	.07

a. Sketch a scree plot based on the table.

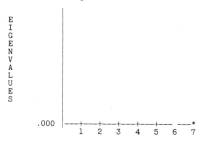

b. Which factors would you use, and why?

4. Below are two factor correlation matrices, one for orthogonal factors before oblique rotation, and the other for the same factors after oblique rotation. Which is the matrix for the factors after rotation?

FACTOR CORRELATION MATRIX:

	FACTOR 1	FACTOR 2	FACTOR 3
FACTOR 1	1.00000	.76000	.34000
FACTOR 2	.76000	1.00000	.28000
FACTOR 3	.34000	.28000	1.00000

FACTOR CORRELATION MATRIX:

	FACTOR 1	FACTOR 2	FACTOR 3
FACTOR 1	1.00000	.00000	.00000
FACTOR 2	.00000	1.00000	.00000
FACTOR 3	.00000	.00000	1.00000

Chapter 16   Stacking Beers: Cluster Analysis

Despite the old adage that opposites attract, it appears instead that likes cluster together. Birds of a feather, yuppies, and many other animate and inanimate objects that share similar characteristics are found together. By studying such clusters, one can determine the characteristics the objects share, as well as those in which they differ. In statistics, the search for relatively homogeneous groups of objects is called *cluster analysis*.

16.1 CLUSTER ANALYSIS

In biology, cluster analysis is used to classify animals and plants. This is called numerical taxonomy. In medicine, cluster analysis is used to identify diseases and their stages. For example, by examining patients who are diagnosed as depressed, one finds that there are several distinct subgroups of patients with different types of depression. In marketing, cluster analysis is used to identify persons with similar buying habits. By examining their characteristics, one may be able to target future marketing strategies more efficiently. See Romesburg (1984) for more examples of the use of cluster analysis.

Although both cluster analysis and discriminant analysis classify objects or cases into categories, discriminant analysis requires you to know group membership for the cases used to derive the classification rule. For example, if you are interested in distinguishing among several disease groups, cases with known diagnoses must be available. Then, based on cases whose group membership is known, discriminant analysis derives a rule for allocating undiagnosed patients. In cluster analysis, group membership for all cases is unknown. In fact, even the number of groups is often unknown. The goal of cluster analysis is to identify homogeneous groups or clusters.

In this chapter, the fundamentals of cluster analysis are illustrated using a subset of data presented in a Consumer Reports (1983) survey of beer. Each of 20 beers is characterized in terms of cost per 12 ounces, alcohol content, sodium content, and the number of calories per 12-ounce serving. The question we pose is: from these variables, is it possible to identify several distinct subgroups of beer?

16.2
Basic Steps

As in other statistical procedures, a number of decisions must be made before one embarks on the actual analysis. Which variables will serve as the basis for cluster formation? How will the distance between cases be measured? What criteria will be used for combining cases into clusters?

Selecting the variables to include in an analysis is always crucial. If important variables are excluded, poor or misleading findings may result. For example, in a regression analysis of salary, if variables such as education and experience are not included, the results may be questionable. In cluster analysis, the initial choice of variables determines the characteristics that can be used to identify subgroups. If one is interested in clustering schools within a city and does not include variables like the number of students or the number of teachers, size is automatically excluded as a criterion for establishing clusters. By excluding all measures of taste or quality from the beer data, only physical characteristics and price will determine which beers are deemed similar.

16.3
How Alike are the Cases?

The concepts of distance and similarity are basic to many statistical techniques. Distance is a measure of how far apart two objects are, and similarity measures closeness. Distance measures are small and similarity measures are large for cases that are similar. In cluster analysis, these concepts are especially important, since cases are grouped on the basis of their "nearness." There are many different definitions of distance and similarity. Selection of a distance measure should be based both on the properties of the measure and on the algorithm for cluster formation. See Section 16.11 for further discussion of distance measures.

To see how a simple distance measure is computed, consider Table 16.3a, which shows the values of calories and cost for two of the beers. There is a 13-calorie and 5-cent difference between the two beers. This information can be combined into a single index or distance measure in many different ways. A commonly used index is the *squared Euclidean distance,* which is the sum of the squared differences over all of the variables. In this example, the squared Euclidean distance is 13^2+5^2, or 194.

Table 16.3a   Values of calories and cost for two beers

	Calories	Cost
Budweiser	144	43
Lowenbrau	157	48

The squared Euclidean distance has the disadvantage that it depends on the units of measurement for the variables. For example, if the cost were given as pennies per ounce instead of per twelve ounces, the distance measure would change. Another disadvantage is that when variables are measured on different scales, as in this example, variables that are measured in larger numbers will contribute more to the distance than variables that are recorded in smaller numbers. For example, the 13-calorie difference contributes much more to the distance score than does the 5-cent difference in cost.

One means of circumventing this problem is to express all variables in standardized form. That is, all variables have a mean of 0 and a standard deviation of 1. This is not always the best strategy, however, since the variability of a particular measure can provide useful information (see Sneath & Sokal, 1973).

Table 16.3b shows the Z scores for calories and cost for Budweiser and Lowenbrau based on the means and standard deviations for all twenty beers. The squared Euclidean distance based on the standardized variables is $(0.38-0.81)^2+(-0.46-(-0.11))^2$, or 0.307. The differences in calories and cost are now weighted equally.

Table 16.3b   *Z* scores for the calories and cost variables

	Calories	Cost
Budweiser	0.38	-0.46
Lowenbrau	0.81	-0.11

16.4
Forming Clusters

Just as there are many methods for calculating distances between objects, there are many methods for combining objects into clusters. A commonly used method for forming clusters is hierarchical cluster analysis, using one of two methods: agglomerative, or divisive. In *agglomerative* hierarchical clustering, clusters are formed by grouping cases into bigger and bigger clusters until all cases are members of a single cluster. *Divisive* hierarchical clustering starts out with all cases grouped into a single cluster and splits clusters until there are as many clusters as there are cases. For a discussion of nonhierarchical clustering methods, see Everitt (1980).

16.5
Agglomerative Clustering

Before we discuss the rules for forming clusters, consider what happens during the steps of agglomerative hierarchical cluster analysis. At the first step all cases are considered separate clusters: there are as many clusters as there are cases. At the second step, two of the cases are combined into a single cluster. At the third step, either a third case is added to the cluster already containing two cases, or two additional cases are merged into a new cluster. At every step, either individual cases are added to clusters or already existing clusters are combined. Once a cluster is formed, it cannot be split; it can only be combined with other clusters. Thus, hierarchical clustering methods do not allow cases to separate from clusters to which they have been allocated. For example, if two beers are deemed members of the same cluster at the first step, they will always be members of the same cluster, although they may be combined with additional cases at a later step.

16.6
Criteria for Combining Clusters

There are many criteria for deciding which cases or clusters should be combined at each step. All of these criteria are based on a matrix of either distances or similarities between pairs of cases. One of the simplest methods is *single linkage*, sometimes called "nearest neighbor." The first two cases combined are those that have the smallest distance (or largest similarity) between them. The distance between the new cluster and individual cases is then computed as the minimum distance between an individual case and a case in the cluster. The distances between cases that have not been joined do not change. At every step, the distance between two clusters is the distance between their two closest points.

Another commonly used method is called *complete linkage*, or the "furthest neighbor" technique. In this method, the distance between two clusters is calculated as the distance between their two furthest points. Other methods for combining clusters available in SPSS-X are described in Section 16.11.

16.7
Back to the Example

Before considering other distance measures and methods of combining clusters, consider Figure 16.7a, which was produced by the SPSS-X PROXIMITIES procedure. (See the *SPSS-X User's Guide,* 3rd ed., for a discussion of this procedure. A distance matrix can also be printed by the CLUSTER procedure, but it's not as nicely labeled.) This figure contains the matrix of squared Euclidean distance coefficients for all possible pairs of the 20 beers, based on standardized calories, sodium, alcohol, and cost. The listing of the original and standardized values for these variables is shown in Figure 16.7b.

Figure 16.7a   The squared Euclidean distance coefficient matrix

```
Squared Euclidean Dissimilarity Coefficient Matrix
    Case      BUDWEISE    SCHLITZ    LOWENBRA    KRONENBO    HEINEKEN    OLD MILW    AUGSBERG    STROHS B

SCHLITZ         .4922
LOWENBRA        .3749      .5297
KRONENBO       7.0040     8.2298     4.8424
HEINEKEN       6.1889     7.0897     4.4835      .8700
OLD MILW       2.5848     1.6534     3.7263    17.0154    15.2734
AUGSBERG       4.0720     1.8735     3.1573    12.1251    11.5371     3.1061
STROHS B       3.3568     1.5561     3.6380    14.8000    12.0038     1.3526     2.0742
MILLER L       3.0662     5.4473     4.9962    11.4721     9.5339     7.4577    13.3723     9.6850
BUDWEISE       3.9181     6.8702     5.8179    11.5391    10.0663     8.9551    15.7993    11.5019
COORS           .2474      .3160      .7568     8.4698     6.8353     1.8432     3.6498     1.9953
COORS LI       2.5940     4.1442     4.4322    12.1519     9.1534     5.4981    11.2604     6.4385
MICHELOB       1.1281     2.8432     1.7663     5.9995     4.9519     6.0530     9.0610     6.8673
BECKS          5.6782     5.3399     4.2859     4.2382     1.6427    11.5628     8.6397     7.0724
KIRIN          8.3245    10.1947     6.6075      .7483      .6064    19.5528    16.0117    16.9620
PABST EX      16.4081    19.7255    20.8463    33.3380    28.0650    17.6015    32.1339    20.5466
HAMMS           .5952      .6788     1.4051    10.0509     7.9746     1.6159     4.3782     1.8230
HEILEMAN       1.9394      .6307     2.1757    11.9216     9.5828     1.2688     1.7169      .3092
OLYMPIA       13.1887    17.6915    16.7104    23.2048    19.8574    19.0673    30.9530    22.3479
SCHLITZ        4.4010     7.4360     6.2635    10.8241     9.1372    10.4511    16.4825    12.7426

    Case      MILLER L    BUDWEISE    COORS      COORS LI    MICHELOB    BECKS       KIRIN       PABST EX

BUDWEISE        .9349
COORS          3.4745     4.5082
COORS LI        .6999     1.5600     2.2375
MICHELOB       1.6931     1.3437     1.6100     1.6536
BECKS         10.2578    10.9762     5.1046     7.8646     5.4275
KIRIN         10.2201    10.3631     9.6179    10.9556     5.9694     4.1024
PABST EX       8.6771     6.9127    15.2083     7.1851    12.2231    24.6793    29.7992
HAMMS          3.3828     4.2251      .1147     1.8315     1.7851     5.6395    10.9812    13.1806
HEILEMAN       7.3607     9.4595     1.0094     4.9491     5.0762     5.9553    13.7962    20.0105
OLYMPIA        4.6046     3.0565    13.4011     5.3477     7.9175    20.5149    19.3851     2.8209
SCHLITZ         .3069      .7793     5.1340     1.5271     1.9902    10.8954     9.0403     9.0418

    Case      HAMMS       HEILEMAN    OLYMPIA

HEILEMAN       1.0802
OLYMPIA       12.3170    20.1156
SCHLITZ        5.1327    10.0114     3.6382
```

Figure 16.7b   Original and standardized values for the 20 beers from procedure LIST

```
ID BEER                        CALORIES SODIUM ALCOHOL COST  ZCALORIE ZSODIUM ZALCOHOL ZCOST

 1 BUDWEISER                      144     15     4.7   .43     .38     .01     .34    -.46
 2 SCHLITZ                        151     19     4.9   .43     .61     .62     .61    -.46
 3 LOWENBRAU                      157     15     4.9   .48     .81     .01     .61    -.11
 4 KRONENBOURG                    170      7     5.2   .73    1.24    -1.2    1.00    1.62
 5 HEINEKEN                       152     11     5.0   .77     .65    -.60     .74    1.90
 6 OLD MILWAUKEE                  145     23     4.6   .28     .42    1.22     .21    -1.5
 7 AUGSBERGER                     175     24     5.5   .40    1.41    1.38    1.40    -.67
 8 STROHS BOHEMIAN STYLE          149     27     4.7   .42     .55    1.83     .34    -.53
 9 MILLER LITE                     99     10     4.3   .43    -1.1    -.75    -.18    -.46
10 BUDWEISER LIGHT                113      8     3.7   .44    -.64    -1.1    -.97    -.39
11 COORS                          140     18     4.6   .44     .25     .46     .21    -.39
12 COORS LIGHT                    102     15     4.1   .46    -1.0     .01    -.45    -.25
13 MICHELOB LIGHT                 135     11     4.2   .50     .09    -.60    -.32     .02
14 BECKS                          150     19     4.7   .76     .58     .62     .34    1.83
15 KIRIN                          149      6     5.0   .79     .55    -1.4     .74    2.04
16 PABST EXTRA LIGHT               68     15     2.3   .38    -2.1     .01    -2.8    -.81
17 HAMMS                          136     19     4.4   .43     .12     .62    -.05    -.46
18 HEILEMANS OLD STYLE            144     24     4.9   .43     .38    1.38     .61    -.46
19 OLYMPIA GOLD LIGHT              72      6     2.9   .46    -2.0    -1.4    -2.0    -.25
20 SCHLITZ LIGHT                   97      7     4.2   .47    -1.2    -1.2    -.32    -.18


NUMBER OF CASES READ =      20     NUMBER OF CASES LISTED =      20
```

The first entry in Figure 16.7a is the distance between Case 1 and Case 2, Budweiser and Schlitz. This can be calculated from the standardized values in Figure 16.7b as

$$D^2 = (0.38 - 0.61)^2 + (0.01 - 0.62)^2$$
$$+ (0.34 - 0.61)^2 + (-0.46 - (-0.46))^2$$
$$= 0.49$$

Since the distance between pairs of cases is symmetric (that is, the distance between Case 3 and Case 4 is the same as the distance between Case 4 and Case 3), only the lower half of the distance matrix is displayed.

16.8
Icicle Plots

Once the distance matrix has been calculated, the actual formation of clusters can commence. Figure 16.8a summarizes a cluster analysis that uses the complete linkage method. This type of figure is sometimes called a vertical icicle plot because it resembles a row of icicles hanging from eaves.

Figure 16.8a   Vertical icicle plot for the 20 beers

```
Vertical Icicle Plot using Complete Linkage

  (Down) Number of Clusters   (Across) Case Label and number

       O    P    M    C    B    S    M    B    K    H    K    A    H    S    O    H    C    S    L    B
       L    A    I    O    U    C    I    E    I    E    R    U    E    T    L    A    O    C    O    U
       Y    B    C    O    D    H    L    C    R    I    O    G    I    R    D    M    O    H    W    D
       M    S    H    R    W    L    L    K    I    N    N    S    L    O    M    M    R    L    E    W
       P    T    E    S    E    I    E    S    N    E    E    B    E    H    M    S    S    I    N    E
       I    L    O    L    I    T    R         K    N    M    A    H    S         I         T    B    I
       A    E    L    S    S    Z         L    E    B    R    N    S    I    B    L    N    Z    R    S
            X    B    I    E              I    E    R    A    N    O    G    W    A         E    A    E
       G    T    G    R    L              I    N    A    G    S    H    O    U    K    U    R
       O    R    L    H    I    L         T    R    R    S    O    L    U    H         E
       L    A    I    T    G    I         E    G    R         L    E    K         E    R
       D         G    H    I    G              H         H    M    E
            L    H         I    T         H              D    I    A
       L    I    T         H              T              S    A    N
       I    G         T    H                             T    N
       G    H         T                                  Y    S
       H    T                                            L    T
       T                                                 E    Y
                                                              L

       1    1    1    1    1    2         1    1              1         1    1
       9    6    3    2    0    0    9    4    5    4    7    8    8    6    7    1    2    3    1
    1 +XXXXXXXXXXXXXXXXXXXXXXXXXXXXXXXXXXXXXXXXXXXXXXXXXXXXXXXXXXXXXXXXXXXXXXXXXXXX
    2 +XXXX XXXXXXXXXXXXXXXXXXXXXXXXXXXXXXXXXXXXXXXXXXXXXXXXXXXXXXXXXXXXXXXXXXXX
    3 +XXXX XXXXXXXXXXXXXXXXXXXXXXX           XXXXXXXXXXXXXXXXXXXXXXXXXXXXXXXXX
    4 +XXXX XXXXXXXXXXXXXXX     XXXXXXX       XXXXXXXXXXXXXXXXXXXXXXXXXXXXXXXXX
    5 +XXXX XXXXXXXXXXXXXXX     XXXXXXX       XXXXXXXXXX     XXXXXXXXXXXXXXX
    6 +XXXX XXXXXXXXXXXXXXX   X XXXXXXX       XXXXXXXXXX     XXXXXXXXXXXXXXX
    7 +XXXX XXXXXXXXXXXXXXX   X XXXXXXX   X   XXXXXXX        XXXXXXXXXXXXXXX
    8 +X  X XXXXXXXXXXXXXXX   X XXXXXXX   X   XXXXXXX        XXXXXXXXXXXXXXX
    9 +X  X X XXXXXXXXXXX     X XXXXXXX   X   XXXXXXX        XXXXXXXXXXXXXXX
   10 +X  X X  X XXXXXXX      X XXXXXXX   X   XXXXXXX        XXXXXXXXXXXXXXX
   11 +X  X X  X XXXXXXX      X XXXXXXX   X   XXXXXXX   XXXX XXXXXXX
   12 +X  X X  X XXXXXXX      X XXXXXXX   X   XXXX   X XXXX XXXXXXX
   13 +X  X X  X X XXXX       X XXXXXXX   X   XXXX   X XXXX XXXXXXX
   14 +X  X X  X X XXXX       X XXXX   X X   XXXX   X XXXX XXXXXXX
   15 +X  X X  X X XXXX     X X X  X   X X   XXXX   X XXXX XXXXXXX
   16 +X  X X  X X XXXX     X X X  X   X X   XXXX   X XXXX   X  XXXX
   17 +X  X X  X X XXXX     X X X  X   X X   XXXX   X XXXX   X  X  X
   18 +X  X X  X X XXXX     X X X  X   X X   X  X   X X  X   X  X  X
   19 +X  X X  X X  X  X    X X X  X   X X   X  X   X X  X   X  X  X
```

The columns of Figure 16.8a correspond to the objects being clustered. They are identified both by a sequential number ranging from 1 to the number of cases and, when possible, by the labels of the objects. Thus, the first column corresponds to beer number 19, Olympia Gold Light, while the last column corresponds to the first beer in the file, Budweiser. In order to follow the sequence of steps in the cluster analysis, the figure is read from bottom to top.

As previously described, all cases are considered initially as individual clusters. Since there are 20 beers in this example, there are 20 clusters. At the first step the two "closest" cases are combined into a single cluster, resulting in 19 clusters. The bottom line of Figure 16.8a shows these 19 clusters. Each case is represented by a single X separated by blanks. The two cases that have been merged into a single cluster, Coors and Hamms, do not have blanks separating them. Instead they are represented by consecutive X's. The row labeled 18 in Figure 16.8a corresponds to the solution at the next step, when 18 clusters are present. At this step Miller Lite and Schlitz Light are merged into a single cluster. Thus, at this point there are 18 clusters, 16 consisting of individual beers and 2 consisting of pairs of beers. At each subsequent step an additional cluster is formed by joining either a case to an already existing multicase cluster, two separate cases into a single cluster, or two multicase clusters.

For example, the row labeled 5 in Figure 16.8a corresponds to a solution that has five clusters. Beers 19 and 16, the very light beers, form one cluster; beers 13, 12, 10, 20, and 9 form the next. These beers, Michelob Light, Coors Light, Budweiser Light, Schlitz Light, and Miller Light, are all light beers, but not as light as the two in the first cluster. The third cluster consists of Becks, Kirin,

Heineken, and Kronenbourg. These are all imported beers. Although no variable in this example explicitly indicates whether beers are domestic or imported, the cost variable (see Figure 16.7b) causes the imported beers to cluster together since they are quite a bit more expensive than the domestic ones. A fourth cluster consists of Augsberger, Heilemans Old Style, Strohs Bohemian Style, and Old Milwaukee. Inspection of Figure 16.8b shows that all of these beers are distinguished by high sodium content. The last cluster consists of five beers, Hamms, Coors, Schlitz, Lowenbrau, and Budweiser. These beers share the distinction of being average. That is, they are neither particularly high nor particularly low on the variables measured. Note from Figure 16.8b that, based on the standard deviations, beers in the same cluster, when compared to all beers, are more homogeneous on the variables measured.

Figure 16.8b Cluster characteristics obtained from TABLES procedure

	CALORIES		COST		ALCOHOL		SODIUM	
	Mean	Standard Deviation	Mean	Standard Deviation	Mean	Standard Deviation	Mean	Standard Deviation
CLUSMEM5								
1	146	8	.44	.02	4.70	.21	17	2
2	155	10	.76	.03	4.97	.21	11	6
3	153	15	.38	.07	4.92	.40	25	2
4	109	16	.46	.03	4.10	.23	10	3
5	70	3	.42	.06	2.60	.42	11	6
TOTAL	132	30	.50	.14	4.44	.76	15	7

Cluster formation continues in Figure 16.8a until all cases are merged into a single cluster, as shown in the first row. Thus, all steps of the cluster analysis are displayed in Figure 16.8a. If we were clustering people instead of beers, the last row would be individual persons, higher up they would perhaps merge into families, these into neighborhoods, and so forth. Often there is not one single, meaningful cluster solution, but many, depending on what is of interest.

16.9
The Agglomeration Schedule

The results of the cluster analysis are summarized in the *agglomeration schedule* in Figure 16.9, which contains the number of cases or clusters being combined at each stage. The first line is Stage 1, the 19-cluster solution. Beers 11 and 17 are combined at this stage, as shown in the columns labeled "Clusters Combined." The squared Euclidean distance between these two beers is displayed in the column labeled "Coefficient." Since this is the first step, this coefficient is identical to the distance measure in Figure 16.7a for Cases 11 and 17. The last column indicates at which stage another case or cluster is combined with this one. For example, at the tenth stage, Case 1 is merged with Cases 11 and 17 into a single cluster. The column entitled "Stage Cluster 1st Appears" indicates at which stage a cluster is first formed. For example, the entry of 4 at Stage 5 indicates that Case 1 was first involved in a merge in the previous step (Stage 4). From the line for Stage 4, you can see that, at this point, Case 1 was involved in a merge with Case 3. From the last column of Stage 5 we see that the new cluster (Cases 1, 2, and 3) is next involved in a merge at Stage 10, where the cases combine with Cases 11 and 17.

Figure 16.9   Agglomeration schedule using complete linkage

```
Agglomeration Schedule using Complete Linkage
```

Stage	Clusters Cluster 1	Combined Cluster 2	Coefficient	Stage Cluster 1st Appears Cluster 1	Cluster 2	Next Stage
1	11	17	.114700	0	0	10
2	9	20	.306900	0	0	8
3	8	18	.309230	0	0	9
4	1	3	.374860	0	0	5
5	1	2	.529700	4	0	10
6	5	15	.606380	0	0	7
7	4	5	.870020	0	6	15
8	9	10	.934910	2	0	11
9	6	8	1.352619	0	3	14
10	1	11	1.405149	5	1	16
11	9	12	1.559990	8	0	12
12	9	13	1.990199	11	0	17
13	16	19	2.820900	0	0	19
14	6	7	3.106110	9	0	16
15	4	14	4.238159	7	0	17
16	1	6	4.378200	10	14	18
17	4	9	12.151939	15	12	18
18	1	4	19.552826	16	17	19
19	1	16	33.338028	18	13	0

The information in Figure 16.9 that is not available in the icicle plot is the value of the distance between the two most dissimilar points of the clusters being combined at each stage. You can get an idea of how different the clusters being combined are by examining these values. Small coefficients indicate that fairly homogeneous clusters are being merged. Large coefficients indicate that clusters containing quite dissimilar members are being combined. The actual value depends on the clustering method and the distance measure used.

These coefficients can also be used for guidance in deciding how many clusters are needed to represent the data. One usually wishes to stop agglomeration as soon as the increase between two adjacent steps becomes large. For example, in Figure 16.9 there is a fairly large increase in the value of the distance measure from a four-cluster to a three-cluster solution (Stages 16 and 17).

16.10
Some Additional Displays and Modifications

The agglomeration schedule and the icicle plot illustrate the results produced by a hierarchical clustering solution. Several variations of these plots may also be useful. For example, when there are many cases, the initial steps of the cluster analysis may not be of particular interest. You might want to display solutions for only certain numbers of clusters. Or you might want to see the results at every *k*th step. Figure 16.10a contains the icicle plot of results at every fifth step.

Figure 16.10a   Icicle plot with results at every fifth step

When there are many cases, all of them may not fit across the top of a single page. In this situation it may be useful to turn the icicle plot on its side. This is called a horizontal icicle plot. Figure 16.10b contains the horizontal icicle plot corresponding to Figure 16.8a.

Figure 16.10b Horizontal icicle plot

```
Horizontal Icicle Plot Using Complete Linkage

                              Number of Clusters

                              1111111111
              C A S E         1234567890123456789
    Label              Seq    ++++++++++++++++++++
OLYMPIA GOLD LIGHT      19    XXXXXXXXXXXXXXXXXXX
                              XXXXXX
                              XXXXXX
PABST EXTRA LIGHT       16    XXXXXXXXXXXXXXXXXXX
                              X
                              X
MICHELOB LIGHT         13    XXXXXXXXXXXXXXXXXXX
                              XXXXXXXX
                              XXXXXXXX
COORS LIGHT            12    XXXXXXXXXXXXXXXXXXX
                              XXXXXXXXX
                              XXXXXXXXX
BUDWEISER LIGHT        10    XXXXXXXXXXXXXXXXXXX
                              XXXXXXXXXXXX
                              XXXXXXXXXXXX
SCHLITZ LIGHT          20    XXXXXXXXXXXXXXXXXXX
                              XXXXXXXXXXXXXXXX
                              XXXXXXXXXXXXXXXX
MILLER LITE             9    XXXXXXXXXXXXXXXXXXX
                              XXX
                              XXX
BECKS                  14    XXXXXXXXXXXXXXXXXXX
                              XXXXX
                              XXXXX
KIRIN                  15    XXXXXXXXXXXXXXXXXXX
                              XXXXXXXXXXXXX
                              XXXXXXXXXXXXX
HEINEKEN                5    XXXXXXXXXXXXXXXXXXX
                              XXXXXXXXXXXXX
                              XXXXXXXXXXXXX
KRONENBOURG             4    XXXXXXXXXXXXXXXXXXX
                              XX
                              XX
AUGSBERGER              7    XXXXXXXXXXXXXXXXXXX
                              XXXXXX
                              XXXXXX
HEILEMANS OLD STYLE    18    XXXXXXXXXXXXXXXXXXX
                              XXXXXXXXXXXXXXXX
                              XXXXXXXXXXXXXXXX
STROHS BOHEMIAN STYL    8    XXXXXXXXXXXXXXXXXXX
                              XXXXXXXXXX
                              XXXXXXXXXX
OLD MILWAUKEE           6    XXXXXXXXXXXXXXXXXXX
                              XXXX
                              XXXX
HAMMS                  17    XXXXXXXXXXXXXXXXXXX
                              XXXXXXXXXXXXXXXX
                              XXXXXXXXXXXXXXXX
COORS                  11    XXXXXXXXXXXXXXXXXXX
                              XXXXXXXXX
                              XXXXXXXXX
SCHLITZ                 2    XXXXXXXXXXXXXXXXXXX
                              XXXXXXXXXXXXXX
                              XXXXXXXXXXXXXX
LOWENBRAU               3    XXXXXXXXXXXXXXXXXXX
                              XXXXXXXXXXXXXX
                              XXXXXXXXXXXXXX
BUDWEISER               1    XXXXXXXXXXXXXXXXXXX
```

Although the composition of clusters at any stage can be discerned from the icicle plots, it is often helpful to display the information in tabular form. Figure 16.10c contains the cluster memberships for the cases at different stages of the solution. From Figure 16.10c, you can easily tell which clusters cases belong to in the two- to five-cluster solutions.

Figure 16.10c   Cluster membership at different stages

```
Cluster Membership of Cases using Complete Linkage

                                        Number of Clusters

    Label                   Case    5    4    3    2

    BUDWEISER                 1      1    1    1    1
    SCHLITZ                   2      1    1    1    1
    LOWENBRAU                 3      1    1    1    1
    KRONENBOURG               4      2    2    2    1
    HEINEKEN                  5      2    2    2    1
    OLD MILWAUKEE             6      3    1    1    1
    AUGSBERGER                7      3    1    1    1
    STROHS BOHEMIAN STYL      8      3    1    1    1
    MILLER LITE               9      4    3    2    1
    BUDWEISER LIGHT          10      4    3    2    1
    COORS                    11      1    1    1    1
    COORS LIGHT              12      4    3    2    1
    MICHELOB LIGHT           13      4    3    2    1
    BECKS                    14      2    2    2    1
    KIRIN                    15      2    2    2    1
    PABST EXTRA LIGHT        16      5    4    3    2
    HAMMS                    17      1    1    1    1
    HEILEMANS OLD STYLE      18      3    1    1    1
    OLYMPIA GOLD LIGHT       19      5    4    3    2
    SCHLITZ LIGHT            20      4    3    2    1
```

16.11
More on Calculating Distances and Similarities

There are many methods for estimating the distance or similarity between two cases. But even before these measures are computed, you must decide whether the variables need to be rescaled. When the variables have different scales, such as cents and calories, and they are not standardized, any distance measure will reflect primarily the contributions of variables measured in the large numbers. For example, the beer data variables were standardized prior to cluster analysis to have a mean of 0 and a standard deviation of 1. Besides standardization to Z scores, variables can be standardized by dividing by just the standard deviation, the range, the mean, or the maximum. See Romesburg (1984) or Anderberg (1973) for further discussion.

Based on the transformed data, it is possible to calculate many different types of distance and similarity measures. Different distance and similarity measures weight data characteristics differently. The choice among the measures should be based on which differences or similarities in the data are important for a particular application. For example, if one is clustering animal bones, what matters may not be the actual differences in bone size but the relationships among the dimensions, since we know that even animals of the same species differ in size. Bones with the same relationship between length and diameter should be judged as similar, regardless of their absolute magnitudes. See Romesburg (1984) for further discussion.

The most commonly used distance measure, the squared Euclidean distance, has been discussed previously. Sometimes its square root, the Euclidean distance, is also used. A distance measure that is based on the absolute values of differences is the *city-block* or *Manhattan* distance. For two cases it is just the sum of the absolute differences of the values for all variables. Since the differences are not squared, large differences are not weighted as heavily as in the squared Euclidean distances. The *Chebychev* distance defines the distance between two cases as the maximum absolute difference in the values over all variables. Thus, it ignores much of the available information.

When variables are binary, special distance and similarity measures are required. Many are based on the familiar measures of association for contingency tables.

16.12
Methods for Combining Clusters

Many methods can be used to decide which cases or clusters should be combined at each step. In general, clustering methods fall into three groups: linkage methods, error sums of squares or variance methods, and centroid methods. All are based on either a matrix of distances or a matrix of similarities between pairs of cases. The methods differ in how they estimate distances between clusters at successive steps. Since the merging of clusters at each step depends on the distance measure, different distance measures can result in different cluster solutions for the same clustering method. See Milligan (1980) for comparisons of the performance of some of the different clustering methods.

One of the simplest methods for joining clusters is *single linkage,* sometimes called "nearest neighbor." The first two cases combined are those with the smallest distance, or greatest similarity, between them. The distance between the new cluster and individual cases is then computed as the minimum distance between an individual case and a case in the cluster. The distances between cases that have not been joined do not change. At every step the distance between two clusters is taken to be the distance between their two closest points.

Another commonly used method is called *complete linkage,* or the "furthest neighbor" technique. In this method the distance between two clusters is calculated as the distance between their two furthest points.

The *average linkage between groups method,* often called UPGMA (unweighted pair-group method using arithmetic averages), defines the distance between two clusters as the average of the distances between all pairs of cases in which one member of the pair is from each of the clusters. For example, if Cases 1 and 2 form cluster A and Cases 3, 4, and 5 form cluster B, the distance between clusters A and B is taken to be the average of the distances between the following pairs of cases: (1,3) (1,4) (1,5) (2,3) (2,4) (2,5). This differs from the linkage methods in that it uses information about all pairs of distances, not just the nearest or the furthest. For this reason it is usually preferred to the single and complete linkage methods for cluster analysis.

The UPGMA method considers only distances between pairs of cases in different clusters. A variant of it, *the average linkage within groups,* combines clusters so that the average distance between all cases in the resulting cluster is as small as possible. Thus, the distance between two clusters is taken to be the average of the distances between all possible pairs of cases in the resulting cluster.

Another frequently used method for cluster formation is *Ward's Method.* For each cluster the means for all variables are calculated. Then for each case the squared Euclidean distance to the cluster means is calculated. These distances are summed for all of the cases. At each step, the two clusters that merge are those that result in the smallest increase in the overall sum of the squared within-cluster distances.

The *centroid method* calculates the distance between two clusters as the distance between their means for all of the variables. One disadvantage of the centroid method is that the distance at which clusters are combined can actually decrease from one step to the next. Since clusters merged at later stages are more dissimilar than those merged at early stages, this is an undesirable property.

In the centroid method, the centroid of a merged cluster is a weighted combination of the centroids of the two individual clusters, where the weights are proportional to the sizes of the clusters. In the *median method,* the two clusters being combined are weighted equally in the computation of the centroid, regardless of the number of cases in each. This allows small groups to have equal effect on the characterization of larger clusters into which they are merged. Squared Euclidean distances should be used with both centroid and median methods.

Some of the above methods, such as single and complete linkage and the average distances between and within clusters, can be used with similarity or distance measures. Other methods require particular types of distance measures. In particular, the median, centroid, and Ward's methods should use squared Euclidean distances. When similarity measures are used, the criteria for combining is reversed. That is, clusters with large similarity-based measures are merged.

16.13
RUNNING
PROCEDURE
CLUSTER

Use the CLUSTER procedure to obtain hierarchical clusters for cases when the number of cases is not too large. (The SPSS-X procedure QUICK CLUSTER can be used when you have many cases. QUICK CLUSTER is described in the *SPSS-X User's Guide*, 3rd ed.) CLUSTER provides several measures of dissimilarity and allows you to specify missing-value treatment.

If you wish to calculate distances for standardized variables, you must standardize the variables first, using the DESCRIPTIVES procedure described in Chapter 4. For example,

```
DESCRIPTIVES CALORIES SODIUM ALCOHOL COST
  /SAVE
CLUSTER ZCALORIE ZSODIUM ZALCOHOL ZCOST
```

first standardizes the variables and assigns the default names ZCALORIE, ZSODIUM, ZALCOHOL, and ZCOST to them. The CLUSTER procedure then uses the standardized variables.

16.14
Specifying the Variables

The first specification on CLUSTER is a list of variables to use in computing similarities or distances between cases, as in

```
CLUSTER ZCALORIE ZSODIUM ZALCOHOL ZCOST
```

The variable list is the only required specification and must precede any optional subcommands. If you do not include any additional specifications you will obtain an analysis using average linkage between groups and squared Euclidean distances.

16.15
Specifying the Clustering
Method

The METHOD subcommand specifies the clustering method. If you do not specify a method, CLUSTER uses the average linkage between groups method (see Section 16.12).

BAVERAGE   *Average linkage between groups (UPGMA). This is the default.*

WAVERAGE   *Average linkage within groups.*

SINGLE   *Single linkage or nearest neighbor.*

COMPLETE   *Complete linkage or furthest neighbor.*

CENTROID   *Centroid clustering (UPGMC). Squared Euclidean distances should be used with this method.*

MEDIAN   *Median clustering (WPGMC). Squared Euclidean distances should be used with this method.*

WARD   *Ward's method. Squared Euclidean distances should be used with this method.*

For example, the command

```
CLUSTER ZCALORIE ZSODIUM ZALCOHOL ZCOST
  /METHOD=SINGLE COMPLETE
```

requests clustering with both the single and complete methods.

16.16
Specifying the Measure

Use the MEASURE subcommand to specify the distance measure to use for clustering cases (see Section 16.3 and 16.11). If you omit MEASURE, CLUSTER uses squared Euclidean distances. You can specify only one distance measure.

MEASURE has the following keywords:

SEUCLID *Squared Euclidean distances.* This is the default. This measure should be used with the centroid, median, and Ward's methods of clustering. The distance between two cases is the sum of the squared differences in values for each variable:

$$\text{Distance}(X, Y) = \sum_i (X_i - Y_i)^2$$

EUCLID *Euclidean distances.* The distance between two cases is the square root of the sum of the squared differences in values for each variable:

$$\text{Distance}(X, Y) = \sqrt{\sum_i (X_i - Y_i)^2}$$

COSINE *Cosine of vectors of variables.* This is a pattern similarity measure:

$$\text{Similarity}(X, Y) = \frac{\sum_i (X_i Y_i)}{\sqrt{\sum_i (X_i^2) \sum_i (Y_i^2)}}$$

BLOCK *City-block or Manhattan distances.* The distance between two cases is the sum of the absolute differences in values for each variable:

$$\text{Distance}(X, Y) = \sum_i \left| X_i - Y_i \right|$$

CHEBYCHEV *Chebychev distance metric.* The distance between two cases is the maximum absolute difference in values for any variable:

$$\text{Distance}(X, Y) = MAX_i \left| X_i - Y_i \right|$$

POWER(p,r) *Distances in an absolute power metric.* The distance between two cases is the *r*th root of the sum of the absolute differences to the *p*th power in values on each variable.

$$\text{Distance}(X, Y) = \left(\sum_i (X_i - Y_i)^p \right)^{\frac{1}{r}}$$

Appropriate selection of integer parameters *p* and *r* yields Euclidean, squared Euclidean, Minkowski, city-block, minimum, maximum, and many other distance metrics.

DEFAULT *Same as SEUCLID.*

16.17
Obtaining Additional Output

CLUSTER automatically displays the clustering method, the similarity or distance measure used for clustering, and the number of cases. Use the PRINT subcommand to obtain additional output. The agglomeration schedule is displayed by default if you do not specify PRINT. If you specify PRINT, you must request SCHEDULE explicitly.

SCHEDULE *Agglomeration schedule.* Display the order in which and distances at which clusters combine to form new clusters as well as the last cluster level at which a case (or variable) joined the cluster (see Figure 16.9). This is the default.

CLUSTER(min,max) *Cluster membership. Min* and *max* specify the minimum and maximum numbers of clusters in the cluster solutions. For each case, CLUSTER displays an identifying label and values indicating which cluster the case belongs to in a given cluster solution (see Figure 16.10c). For example, PRINT=CLUSTER(3,5) displays the clusters to which each case belongs when three, four, and five clusters are produced. Cases are identified by case number plus the value of any string variable specified on the ID subcommand (see Section 16.19).

DISTANCE *Matrix of distances or similarities between items.* The type of matrix produced (similarities or dissimilarities) depends upon the measure selected. With a large number of clustered cases, DISTANCE uses considerable computer processing time.

16.18
Specifying Plots

CLUSTER produces the vertical icicle plot by default. Use the PLOT subcommand to obtain a horizontal icicle plot or a dendrogram. When you specify PLOT, only the requested plots are produced.

VICICLE[(min,max,inc)]   *Vertical icicle plot. Min* and *max* specify the minimum and maximum numbers of cluster solutions to plot, and *inc* specifies the increment to use between cluster levels. Min, max, and inc must be integers. By default, the increment is 1 and all cluster solutions are plotted. For example, PLOT = VICICLE (2,10,2) plots cluster solutions with two, four, six, eight, and ten clusters. VICICLE is the default. (See Figures 16.8a and 16.10a.)

HICICLE[(min,max,inc)]   *Horizontal icicle plot.* Has the same specifications as VICICLE. (See Figure 16.10b.)

DENDROGRAM   *Dendrogram.* The dendrogram is scaled by joining the distances of the clusters.

NONE   *No display output.* Use PLOT=NONE to suppress all plots.

16.19
Identifying Cases

By default, CLUSTER identifies cases by case number. Name a string variable on the ID subcommand to identify cases with string values. For example, the subcommand

```
/ID=BEER
```

produces the beer-name labels in Figures 16.8a, 16.10a, 16.10b, and 16.10c.

16.20
Missing Values

CLUSTER uses listwise deletion as the default missing-value treatment. A case with missing values for any clustering variable is excluded from the analysis. Use the MISSING subcommand to treat user-defined missing values as valid.

INCLUDE   *Include user-missing values.*

LISTWISE   *Delete cases with missing values listwise.* This is the default.

Cases with system-missing values for clustering variables are never included in the analysis.

16.21
A CLUSTER Example

The following is the basic analysis discussed throughout this chapter:

```
DESCRIPTIVES CALORIES SODIUM
  ALCOHOL COST /SAVE
CLUSTER ZCALORIE ZSODIUM ZALCOHOL ZCOST
 /ID=BEER
 /PLOT=HICICLE VICICLE
 /PRINT=SCHEDULE CLUSTER(2,5)
 /METHOD=COMPLETE
```

- CLUSTER specifies variables ZCALORIE, ZSODIUM, ZALCOHOL, and ZCOST for the analysis (see Section 16.14).
- The ID subcommand identifies the cases based on their values for the variable BEER (see Section 16.19).
- The PLOT subcommand specifies both a vertical and a horizontal icicle plot (see Section 16.18).
- The PRINT subcommand prints an agglomeration schedule and a cluster membership for the 2-, 3-, 4-, and 5-cluster solution. (see Section 16.17).
- The METHOD subcommand specifies the complete linkage clustering method (see Section 16.15).

EXERCISES

Syntax

1. Find the error in the following CLUSTER command:

```
CLUSTER V1(1,3)
        V2 V3 /METHOD=MEDIAN /MEASURE=COSINE
```

2. An ornithologist wants a cluster analysis using the following variables for a sample of 85 birds:

```
WINGSPAN BEAKCURV BEAKWDTH MIGRLNTH MATELNTH FSHDIET INSDIET GRNDIET
```

   Write a CLUSTER command for this study.

3. A sociologist studying popular culture wants to see if 60 automobiles can be clustered according to the following variables.

```
WEIGHT LENGTH WIDTH HGHTLEN WINDOWS CHROME DOODADS
```

   Write the commands to perform a cluster analysis using the Euclidean distance and nearest neighbor method.

Statistical Concepts

1. Consider the following four cases:

CASE	OBEDENCE	GUARDING	HUNTING	ONEPERSN
1	1.4	-0.6	-0.9	-0.2
2	-3.1	0.8	2.4	1.9
3	1.5	1.8	-0.3	2.2
4	2.1	2.6	-0.6	2.0

   a. Compute the matrix of squared Euclidean distance coefficients:

```
Squared Euclidean Dissimilarity Coefficient Matrix

    Case          1          2          3

     2           ??

     3           ??         ??

     4           ??         ??         ??
```

   b. Which of these four cases would be combined first into a cluster?

2. Using the vertical icicle plot below and assuming agglomerative clustering, describe the clusters at
   a. Step 7
   b. Step 5
   c. Step 3

```
Vertical Icicle Plot using Complete Linkage

(Down) Number of Clusters   (Across) Case Label and number

        S  B  F  C  C  M  C  E  G  M
        W  L  A  0  0  0  H  D  0  0
        I  U  R  T  L  N  E  A  U  Z
        S  E  M  T  B  T  D  M  D  Z
        S     E  A  Y  E  D  M  D  A
              R  G     R  D     A  R
              S  E     E  A     R  E
                       Y  R        L
                                   L
                       J           A
                       A
                       C
                       K

        1
        0  9  5  4  7  8  6  3  2  1
      1 +XXXXXXXXXXXXXXXXXXXXXXXXXXX
      2 +XXXX  XXXXXXXXXXXXXXXXXXXXX
      3 +XXXX  XXXX  XXXXXXXXXXXXXXX
      4 +XXXX  XXXX  X  XXXXXXXXXXXX
      5 +XXXX  XXXX  X  XXXX  XXXXXX
      6 +X  X  XXXX  X  XXXX  XXXXXX
      7 +X  X  XXXX  X  X  X  XXXXXX
      8 +X  X  X  X  X  X  X  XXXXXX
      9 +X  X  X  X  X  X  X  XXXX  X
```

3. If a program designed to do agglomerative hierarchical clustering produced the
    following icicle plot, would you trust it?

```
        1   1 1     1     1         1   1
        5   2 6 7   1 4   4 6 5 0   9 3 8 2 3 1
     1 +XXXXXXXXXXXXXXXXXXXXXXXXXXXXXXXXXXXXXXXXX
     2 +XXXXXXXXXX  XXXXXXXXXXXXXXXXXXXXXXXXXXXXXX
     3 +XXXXXXXXXX  XXXX  XXXXXXXXXXXXXXXXXXXXXXXX
     4 +XXXX  XXXX  XXXX  XXXXXXXXXXXXXXXXXXXXXXXX
     5 +X  X  XXXX  XXXX  XXXXXXXXXXXXXXXXXXXXXXXX
     6 +X  X  XXXX  XXXX  XXXXXXX  XXXXXXXXXXXXXXXX
     7 +X  X  X  X  XXXX  XXXXXXX  XXXXXXXXXXXX XXXX
     8 +X  X  X  X  XXXX  XXXXXXX  XXXX  XXXXXXX XXXX
     9 +X  X  X  X  X  X  XXXXXXX  XXXX  XXXXXXXXXXXX
    10 +X  X  X  X  X  X  XXXX  X  XXXX  XXXXXXXXXXXX
    11 +X  X  X  X  X  X  XXXX  X  XXXX  XXXXXXX XXXX
    12 +X  X  X  X  X  X  XXXX  X  X  X  XXXXXXX XXXX
    13 +X  X  X  X  X  X  XXXX  X  X  X  XXXXXXX X  X
    14 +X  X  X  X  X  X  XXXX  X  X  X  XXXX X  X  X
    15 +X  X  X  X  X  X  X  X  X  X  X  XXXX X  X  X
```

4. Consider the following icicle plot:

```
Horizontal Icicle Plot Using Complete Linkage

                              Number of Clusters

              C A S E         123456789
Label                  Seq    +++++++++

MOBY DICK               9     XXXXXXXXX
                              XXX
                              XXX
ODYSSEY                 4     XXXXXXXXX
                              X
                              X
GREAT EXPECTATIONS     10     XXXXXXXXX
                              XXXXX
                              XXXXX
OLIVER TWIST            6     XXXXXXXXX
                              XX
                              XX
TOM JONES               5     XXXXXXXXX
                              XXXX
                              XXXX
MADAM BOVARY            7     XXXXXXXXX
                              XXXXXXXX
                              XXXXXXXX
PORTRAIT OF A LADY      8     XXXXXXXXX
                              XXXXXXXXX
                              XXXXXXXXX
ANNA KARENINA           3     XXXXXXXXX
                              XXXXXXX
                              XXXXXXX
BLEAK HOUSE             2     XXXXXXXXX
                              XXXXX
                              XXXXX
CANDIDE                 1     XXXXXXXXX
```

Describe the books in the clusters when you have a three-cluster solution and a
five-cluster solution.

Chapter 17 Grades and Sports: Multivariate Analysis of Variance

Educators and parents alike often ponder why some students are successful in high school and college and others are not. Among the variables that might influence scholastic achievement is participation in varsity sports. In this chapter, we will use data from the 1970 Explorations in Equality of Opportunity survey, which queried over 2,000 people who were originally surveyed in 1955 as high school sophomores, to examine the relationships between academic achievement and participation in varsity sports.*

There are many variables that can be used to characterize a student's academic achievement. Grade point average and performance on achievement tests quickly come to mind. Since these variables are not independent, we will need special statistical procedures for analyzing them together. Before embarking on new techniques, let's review some of the procedures we have already considered for testing hypotheses about means.

17.1
UNIVARIATE TESTS

When we have two groups and wish to test the hypothesis that the two group means are equal, we can use the t test. For example, we can test the null hypothesis that boys and girls do not differ in spelling ability using the T-TEST procedure. When there are more than two groups, we can use the ONEWAY procedure to test the hypothesis that several group means are equal. For example, we can test the null hypothesis that there is no difference in spelling ability for students in the North, South, West, and East.

When cases are classified on the basis of several factors, the ANOVA procedure can be used. For example, if we want to examine spelling abilities in male and female students who live in the four regions of the country, we can use the ANOVA procedure. We can test three hypotheses: that there is no difference between males and females, that there is no difference among the regions of the country, and that there is no interaction between region and sex.

---

* The data were originally collected by Bruce Eckland and were made available by the Inter-University Consortium for Political and Social Research at the University of Michigan. Neither the original source or the collectors of the data nor the Consortium bear any responsibility for the analyses or interpretations presented here.

17.2
SEVERAL DEPENDENT VARIABLES

In all of the previous examples, we are concerned with a single dependent variable, such as spelling ability. What if we are interested in more than just spelling ability? We want to know whether students differ in a variety of academic areas: mathematical achievement, reading comprehension, problem solving, as well as spelling. One strategy is to perform a series of univariate analyses of variance for each of the dependent variables. However, there are several drawbacks to this approach. Multiple univariate analyses ignore the interdependencies among the dependent variables. Information about the correlation structure of the variables is lost. It is possible that groups may not differ significantly on the individual variables, but when considered simultaneously the overall difference is significant. Multiple univariate analyses also do not control for Type I error. That is, the probability of finding significant differences by chance alone greatly increases as the number of comparisons made increases. What we really need in this situation is an analysis of variance procedure for analyzing several dependent variables simultaneously.

17.3
MULTIVARIATE ANALYSIS OF VARIANCE

The extension of analysis of variance to the case of multiple dependent variables is called *multivariate analysis of variance,* or MANOVA. Univariate analysis of variance is just a special case of MANOVA—the case with a single dependent variable. The hypotheses tested with MANOVA are similar to those tested with ANOVA. The difference is that instead of dealing with a single mean, we deal with a set of means. For example, we can test whether average scores on a battery of three tests differ among students in the four regions of the country. For more detailed discussions of multivariate analyses of variance, see Finn (1974), Bock (1975), and Morrison (1967).

17.4
Assumptions

When we have a single dependent variable, two assumptions are needed for the proper application of the ANOVA test: the groups must be random samples from normal populations, and the dependent variable must have the same variance in each of those populations. Similar assumptions are needed for MANOVA. Since we are dealing with several dependent variables, however, we must make assumptions about the joint distribution of the variables—that is, the distribution of the variables considered together. For MANOVA, the dependent variables must come from a multivariate normal population with the same variance-covariance matrix in each group. (A *variance-covariance matrix,* as its name indicates, is a square arrangement of elements, with the variances of the variables on the diagonal, and the covariances of pairs of variables off the diagonal. A variance-covariance matrix can be transformed into a correlation matrix by dividing each covariance by the standard deviations of the two variables.) Later sections of the chapter will present tests for these assumptions.

17.5
Comparing Three Groups

Before we consider more complex generalizations of ANOVA techniques, let's consider a simple one-way analysis of variance and its extension to the case of multiple dependent variables. As you will recall, a one-way analysis of variance is used to test the hypothesis that, in the population, several groups have the same mean. For example, you might want to test the hypothesis that men who do not exercise, men who exercise occasionally, and men who exercise regularly have the same average heart rate. If additional related variables such as blood pressure and respiratory rate are also to be considered, a test that allows comparison of several means is required.

To illustrate this simple MANOVA test and introduce some of the SPSS-X MANOVA output, we will use the previously described high school data set to test hypotheses about grade point averages and composite verbal and math scores for students who do not participate in varsity sports, participate somewhat, and participate a lot.

17.6
Descriptive Statistics

One of the first steps in any statistical analysis, regardless of how simple or complex it may be, is examination of the individual variables. This preliminary screening provides information about a variable's distribution and permits identification of unusual or outlying values.

When multivariate analyses are undertaken, however, it is not sufficient to just look at the characteristics of the variables individually. Information about their joint distribution must also be obtained. Identification of outliers must also be based on the joint distribution of variables. For example, a height of six feet is not very unusual, and neither is a weight of 100 pounds, nor is being a man. A six-foot-tall male who weigh 100 pounds, however, is fairly atypical and needs to be identified, not for just humanitarian reasons, but to ascertain that the values have been correctly recorded, and if so, to gauge the effect of such a lean physique on subsequent analyses.

Figure 17.6a contains descriptive statistics for each of the two variables for students who did not participate in varsity sports, participated somewhat, and participated a lot. From the figure, you can see that the grade point average is 5.169 for the 260 students who did not participate and 5.06 for the 100 students who participated a lot. For the entire sample of 493 students, the grade point average is 5.073.

Figure 17.6a   Student participation in sports

```
Cell Means and Standard Deviations
Variable .. GPA              H.S. Grade Average
     FACTOR          CODE              Mean    Std. Dev.          N    95 percent Conf. Interval

   VARSITY          NONE              5.169     2.095          260      4.913      5.425
   VARSITY          SOME              4.845     1.924          103      4.469      5.221
   VARSITY          A LOT             5.060     1.852          100      4.692      5.428
For entire sample                     5.073     2.007          463      4.890      5.257

Variable .. SCORE            Composite Verbal and Math Scores
     FACTOR          CODE              Mean    Std. Dev.          N    95 percent Conf. Interval

   VARSITY          NONE              7.581     4.196          260      7.068      8.093
   VARSITY          SOME              7.204     4.250          103      6.373      8.035
   VARSITY          A LOT             7.730     3.760          100      6.984      8.476
For entire sample                     7.529     4.113          463      7.153      7.905
```

Another way to visualize the distribution of grade point averages in each of the groups is with box-and-whisker plots, as shown in Figure 17.6b. The upper and lower boundaries of the boxes are the 25th and 75th percentile values. Each box contains the middle 50% of the values for each group. The asterisk (*) inside the box identifies the group median. The larger the box, the greater the spread of the observations. The lines emanating from each box (the whiskers) extend to the smallest and largest observations in a group that are less than one interquartile range from the end of the box. These are marked with an X. Any points outside of this range but less than one-and-a-half interquartile ranges from the end of the box are marked with O's (for *outlying*). Points more than 1.5 interquartile distances away are marked with E's (for *extreme*). If there are multiple points at a single position, the number of points is also displayed.

Figure 17.6b Box plots of grade point averages

```
Box-Plots For Variable .. GPA              H.S. Grade Average

        9     I      X           X           X
              I      I           I           I
       KEY    I      I           I           I
   ---------- I      I           I           I
   * Median   I    +-+-+       +-+-+         I
   - 25%, 75% I    I   I       I   I         I
   X High/Low I    I   I       I   I       +-+-+
   O Outlier  I    I   I       I   I       I   I
   E Extreme  I    I * I       I   I       I * I
              I    I   I       I   I       I   I
              I    I   I       I   I       I   I
              I    I   I       I * I       I   I
              I    I   I       I   I       I   I
              I    +-+-+       +-+-+       +-+-+
              I      I           I           I
              I      I           I           X
              I      I           I
              I      I           X
              I      I
        0     I      X

   Variable-----------------------------------------------
   VARSITY           1           2           3
```

17.7
Tests of Normality

Although the summary statistics presented in Figures 17.6a and 17.6b provide some information about the distributions of the dependent variables, more detailed information about the distributions is often desirable, especially since one of the necessary assumptions for testing hypotheses in MANOVA is that the dependent variables have a multivariate normal distribution. Testing for multivariate normality is not straightforward. If variables have a multivariate normal distribution, however, each one taken individually must be normally distributed. (The opposite is not necessarily true. It is possible that variables that individually have normal distributions when considered together will not necessarily have a multivariate normal distribution.)

Examination of normal probability plots helps us to assess whether individually the variables are normally distributed. Figure 17.7 is a normal plot of the composite verbal and math scores. If the variable has a normal distribution, you would expect the points to cluster around a straight line. In this case, we see some

Figure 17.7 Normal probability plot of composite verbal and math scores

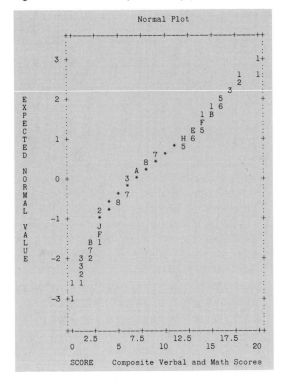

curvature indicating that the distribution is not quite normal. Transformations of the dependent variables can be considered when deviations from normality are substantial.

17.8
Tests of Homogeneity of Variance

One of the assumptions needed for the two-sample multivariate t test is that the variance-covariance matrices of the dependent variables are equal in the two groups. Box's M test, which is based on the determinants of the variance-covariance matrices, provides a test that several covariance matrices are equal. The test is very sensitive to departures from normality, however, and its results should be interpreted with caution. Figure 17.8 shows Box's M test for the varsity data. The significance level for the statistic can be based on either the F or chi-square distribution, and both approximations are given in the output. Given the result of Box's M test, there appears to be no reason to suspect the homogeneity-of-dispersion-matrices assumption.

Figure 17.8   Homogeneity of variance for the varsity data

```
Multivariate test for Homogeneity of Dispersion matrices


Boxs M =                               6.32069
F WITH (6,925086) DF =                 1.04523, P =    .393 (Approx.)
Chi-Square with 6 DF =                 6.27141, P =    .393 (Approx.)
```

17.9
Testing the Hypothesis

When we use analysis of variance to test hypotheses about a single dependent variable, all tests are based on the F-ratio. When we have several dependent variables, a variety of multivariate tests of significance are available. They are all based on the eigenvalues of the hypotheses and error matrices. (The hypothesis matrix contains distances between group means for the dependent variables, while the error matrix is an indicator of how much variability there is in the responses within a groups.) Four commonly used criteria are *Pillai's trace, Wilks' lambda, Hotelling's trace,* and *Roy's largest root.*

When deciding which multivariate test to use, you must consider the power and robustness of the test. The test should detect differences when they exist and not be affected much by departures from the assumptions. For most practical situations, when differences among the groups are spread along several dimensions, the ordering of the test criteria in terms of decreasing power is Pillai's, Wilks', Hotelling's and Roy's. Pillai's trace is also the most robust. That is, the significance level based on it is reasonably correct even when the assumptions are not exactly met. This is important since all of the necessary assumptions are seldom met exactly, and a test that is overly sensitive to the assumptions is of limited use (Olson, 1976).

Figure 17.9 contains the values for the previously described statistics for the varsity example. The first three statistics are all transformed into statistics that have approximately an F-distribution. There is no straightforward transformation for Roy's largest root criterion to a statistic with a known distribution, so only the value of the largest root is displayed. From the column labeled "Sig. of F," you see that the observed significance level is large, about 0.66, for the first three tests. Thus we have no reason to reject the null hypothesis that grade point averages and college aptitude scores differ for the three groups.

Figure 17.9   Statistical values for the varsity data

```
EFFECT .. VARSITY
Multivariate Tests of Significance (S = 2, M = -1/2, N = 228 1/2)

Test Name          Value       Approx. F    Hypoth. DF    Error DF    Sig. of F

Pillais            .00520        .59995         4.00        920.00        .663
Hotellings         .00522        .59794         4.00        916.00        .664
Wilks              .99480        .59895         4.00        918.00        .663
Roys               .00421
Note.. F statistic for WILK'S Lambda is exact.
```

17.10
**Examining Univariate
Differences**

If we had found a significant multivariate difference among the three groups, we could examine each of the dependent variables individually to see which variables contribute to the observed overall difference. Even though we didn't find a difference, let's look at the univariate results to see how this output is arranged. Figure 17.10 shows the results of univariate analyses of variance for each of the dependent variables. Each row of the figure corresponds to a one-way analysis of variance for a dependent variable. As expected, there are no significant differences for either of the variables. The significance levels for the univariate tests have not been adjusted for comparison of several variables, and they should be interpreted with this in mind.

Figure 17.10 Univariate analysis of variance for each dependent variable

```
EFFECT .. VARSITY (CONT.)
Univariate F-tests with (2,460) D. F.

Variable      Hypoth. SS       Error SS      Hypoth. MS       Error MS            F      Sig. of F
GPA              7.79483     1853.70841         3.89742        4.02980       .96715          .381
SCORE           15.62408     7801.73229         7.81204       16.96029       .46061          .631
```

17.11
A Factorial Design

So far we have considered a very simple multivariate design: a one-way analysis of variance. We are now ready to examine a somewhat more complex factorial design. The students represented in our data set are subdivided not only by their participation in varsity sports, but also by whether they are male or female. Since students are classified by varsity participation categories and sex, we have a two-way factorial design with three categories for varsity participation and two categories for sex.

17.12
Examining the Data

The previously described tables and plots are a good first step in examining the data. There are some additional displays that are useful for summarizing the data and looking for violations of the assumptions. Figure 17.12a is a plot of the six cell means for the two variables. From this plot, you can get an idea of the spread of the means. The top row of numbers indicates how many cell means there are in each interval. You can see that, for the grade point average, there are two means close to 5.22 and one mean close to 5.46.

Figure 17.12a Plots of cell means

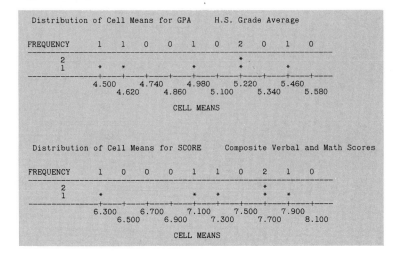

Both univariate and multivariate analyses of variance require equal variances in all of the cells. However, there are many situations in which there is a relationship between the cell means and the variances. Plotting means against standard deviations and variances is useful for uncovering such relationships. Figure 17.12b is a plot of the means versus standard deviations for the grade point variable. There does not appear to be a readily discernable relationship between the two variables in this plot. If patterns were evident, transformations of the dependent variables might be used to stabilize the variances.

Figure 17.12b   Plot of mean vs. standard deviation for the grade point variable

```
            Means VS Std. Devs. for GPA       H.S. Grade
            +-+----+----+----+----+----+----+----+----+
      2.16 +                                          +
  C                                    1
  E   2.08 +                                          +
  L        :1
  L                                              1  :
  S      2 +                                          +
  T
  D        :               1
  .
  D   1.92 +                                          +
  E
  V
  S   1.84 +                                          +
  .
      1.76 :             1          1                 :
           +                                          +
           +-+----+----+----+----+----+----+----+----+
              4.625     4.875     5.125     5.375
            4.5     4.75       5       5.25
                           CELL MEANS
```

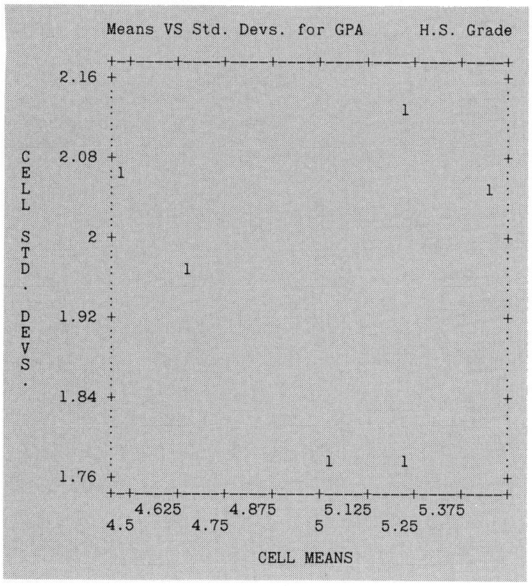

17.13
Testing the Effects

There are three hypotheses that can be tested for a two way factorial design: two hypotheses about the main effects and one hypothesis about the interaction. In our example, we can test whether there are differences among the three varsity categories, the two categories of sex, and whether there is a varsity by sex interaction.

SPSS-X MANOVA displays separate output for each effect. The first effect displayed is the interaction effect. The interaction effect is examined first since if it is significant, it is not advisable to test the main effects (see Chapter 11 for further discussion.)

Figure 17.13a contains the multivariate tests of significance for the VARSITY by SEX interaction. The observed significance level is 0.15, so we will not reject the null hypothesis that there is no interaction effect.

Figure 17.13a   VARSITY by SEX interactions

```
EFFECT .. VARSITY BY SEX
Multivariate Tests of Significance (S = 2, M = -1/2, N = 227 )

Test Name           Value        Approx. F     Hypoth. DF      Error DF      Sig. of F

Pillais             .01471        1.69270         4.00           914.00         .150
Hotellings          .01486        1.68982         4.00           910.00         .150
Wilks               .98533        1.69126         4.00           912.00         .150
Roys                .01177
Note.. F statistic for WILK'S Lambda is exact.
```

Multivariate tests for the SEX main effect are shown in Figure 17.13b. The observed significance level is small, .002, so we will reject the null hypothesis that there is no difference between males and females. Examination of Figure 17.13c, the univariate results, suggests that the differences between the two sexes are primarily due to the differences in grade point averages. The observed significance level for the composite college tests is large.

Figure 17.13b   Multivariate tests for SEX effect

```
EFFECT .. SEX
Multivariate Tests of Significance (S = 1, M = 0, N = 227 )

Test Name            Value        Exact F       Hypoth. DF      Error DF        Sig. of F

Pillais              .02801       6.57021            2.00         456.00          .002
Hotellings           .02882       6.57021            2.00         456.00          .002
Wilks                .97199       6.57021            2.00         456.00          .002
Roys                 .02801
Note.. F statistics are exact.
```

Figure 17.13c   Univariate results for SEX effect

```
EFFECT .. SEX (CONT.)
Univariate F-tests with (1,457) D. F.

Variable     Hypoth. SS       Error SS      Hypoth. MS       Error MS             F       Sig. of F

GPA           25.88464     1795.14752       25.88464        3.92811        6.58959         .011
SCORE         15.86965     7709.85412       15.86965       16.87058         .94067         .333
```

Tests for the VARSITY effect are shown in Figure 17.13d. As before, there are no significant differences among the three categories of varsity participation. You will notice that the statistics for the VARSITY effect are different in Figure 17.13d when compared to Figure 17.9. This is because the number of cases in the various combinations of factor levels is not equal and the analysis of variance results for "unbalanced" designs depends on the other factors in the analysis.

Figure 17.13d   Multivariate tests for VARSITY effect

```
EFFECT .. VARSITY
Multivariate Tests of Significance (S = 2, M = -1/2, N = 227 )

Test Name            Value        Approx. F     Hypoth. DF      Error DF        Sig. of F

Pillais              .00314         .35945           4.00         914.00          .838
Hotellings           .00315         .35811           4.00         910.00          .838
Wilks                .99686         .35878           4.00         912.00          .838
Roys                 .00257
Note.. F statistic for WILK'S Lambda is exact.
```

17.14
RUNNING PROCEDURE MANOVA

The SPSS-X MANOVA procedure can be used to analyze a large variety of multivariate and univariate designs. It can also generate a large assortment of optional output. That's why the procedure has quite a few subcommands and keywords. However, to run simple designs, like the ones discussed in this chapter, you need only a small number of specifications.

17.15
Specifying the Variables

To run the MANOVA procedure, you must indicate which variables are dependent variables, which variables are factors, and which variables (if any) are covariates.

An example of a simple MANOVA command is

```
MANOVA GPA SCORE BY VARSITY(0,2)
```

The first variables listed are the dependent variables. In this example, they are called GPA and SCORE. The keyword BY separates the dependent variables from the factor variables. There is one factor variable, VARSITY, which follows the keyword BY. Each factor name must be followed by two integer values enclosed in parentheses and separated by a comma. These are the lowest and highest values for the factor. The VARSITY factor has three levels coded as 0, 1, and 2. Cases with factor values outside the designated range are excluded from the analysis. For example, the command

```
MANOVA GPA SCORE BY VARSITY(0,1)
```

would include in the analysis only cases which have values of 0 or 1 for the VARSITY variable. MANOVA requires the factor levels to be integers. If you have noninteger factor values they must be recoded to integers. Factors with empty categories must also be recoded, since MANOVA expects cases in all of the groups which fall between the minimum and the maximum factor values.

If you have more than one factor variable, list all of them after the BY keyword. For example,

```
MANOVA GPA SCORE BY VARSITY(0,2) SEX(1,2)
```

specifies that there are two factors: VARSITY and SEX.

If several factors have the same range, you can specify a list of factors followed by a single value range, in parentheses, as in the command

```
MANOVA SALES REVENUE BY TVAD RADIOAD MAGAD NEWSPAD(1,4)
```

If you have covariates in your analysis they are listed after the factors and after the keyword WITH. For example,

```
MANOVA GPA SCORE BY VARSITY(0,2) SEX(1,2) WITH IQ
```

indicates the IQ variable is to be used as a covariate.

17.16
Requesting Optional Output

The PRINT subcommand is used to request optional output. For example,

```
MANOVA GPA COL BY VARSITY(0,2) SEX(1,2)
  /PRINT=CELLINFO(MEANS)
```

requests the display of cell means for GPA and COL for all combinations of values of VARSITY and SEX.

17.17
Requesting Cell Information

You can obtain information about the individual cells (combinations of factors) in the analysis using the CELLINFO keyword on the PRINT subcommand. Following the keyword, in parentheses, you must list the information desired. For example,

```
/PRINT=CELLINFO (MEANS)
```

requests means, standard deviations, and counts for each of the cells. Similarly,

```
/PRINT=CELLINFO (COV)
```

prints variance-covariance matrices for each group. To obtain correlations for each group, specify

```
/PRINT=CELLINFO (COR)
```

You can request more than one set of statistics by specifying more than one keyword within the parentheses. For example,

```
/PRINT=CELLINFO (MEANS,COR)
```

requests both descriptive statistics and correlation matrices for each cell.

17.18
Requesting Homogeneity Tests

The HOMOGENEITY keyword on the PRINT subcommand is used to request tests for homogeneity of variance. As with CELLINFO, you must list the desired tests in parentheses after the keyword. For example, the following PRINT specification was used to generate all the cell information and tests discussed in this chapter:

```
/PRINT=CELLINFO(MEANS)  HOMOGENEITY(BARTLETT,COCHRAN,BOXM)
```

17.19
Specifying Plots

Plots are requested with the PLOT subcommand. For example,

```
/PLOT=BOXPLOTS
```

requests boxplots for each dependent variable. The following keywords may be used for the PLOT subcommand:

CELLPLOTS   *Plot cell statistics, including plots of cell means versus cell variances and cell standard deviations, and a histogram of cell means.*

BOXPLOT   *Plot a boxplot for each dependent variable.*

NORMAL   *Plot a normal plot and a detrended normal plot for each dependent variable.*

STEMLEAF   *Plot a stem-and-leaf display for each dependent variable.*

17.20
Specifying the Model

If you wish to analyze your data as a complete factorial, you don't need additional specifications. A complete factorial is the default. (A complete factorial is a design in which all main effects and all orders of interactions are included.)

If you wish to analyze a model other than a complete factorial, the last subcommand must be a DESIGN specification. For example, if you want to analyze a model which has only main effects you must specify

```
/DESIGN=VARSITY SEX
```

The keyword BY is used on the DESIGN subcommand to indicate interactions. For example,

```
/DESIGN=A,B,C,A BY B,B BY C
```

specifies a model with three main effects and two two-way interactions.

17.21
A MANOVA Example

The following MANOVA command was used to generate some of the figures in this chapter:

```
MANOVA GPA  SCORE  BY VARSITY(0,2)
 /PRINT=CELLINFO(MEANS)  HOMOGENEITY(BOXM)
 /PLOT=CELLPLOTS BOXPLOT NORMAL
```

- MANOVA specifies two dependent variables (GPA and SCORE) and one factor variable (VARSITY). A value range from 0 to 2 is specified for the factor variable (see Section 17.15).
- The PRINT subcommand requests descriptive statistics: the cell means, standard deviations, and counts. PRINT also requests Box's M test (see Sections 17.16 through 17.18).
- The PLOT subcommand requests plots for cell statistics, boxplots for each interval variable, and normal plots for each continuous variable (see Section 17.19).

EXERCISES

Syntax

1. Find the errors in the MANOVA commands below:

    a. `MANOVA ESTEEM SEX(1,2) ATTRACT(1,5) IQ(1,3)`

    b. `MANOVA INCOME PRESTIGE BY AGE(1,4) SEX(1,2) EDUC`

    c. `MANOVA ETHNOCNT POLITICS BY INTEGRTN(1,2) BY RACE(1,2) BY SEX(1,2)`
       `/PRINT=CELLINFO(MEANS)`

2. A researcher wants to obtain a univariate analysis of variance using a full-factorial model and writes the following MANOVA command. Will this produce the analysis she wants?

    ```
    MANOVA ENDURNCE BY SEX(1,2) PROGRAM(1,2) PASTSCOR(1,5)
      /DESIGN=SEX PROGRAM PASTSCOR SEX BY PROGRAM SEX BY PASTSCOR
              PROGRAM BY PASTSCOR
    ```

Statistical Concepts

1. a. Plot the means and variances shown below against each other. Is any relationship evident? If so, how are they related?

Mean	Variance
−2.13	0.28
−0.56	0.02
−11.10	6.51
−1.21	0.09
−6.99	2.65
−3.14	0.65
−18.83	27.12
−9.40	5.02
−5.63	2.08
−4.74	1.47
−15.58	15.8

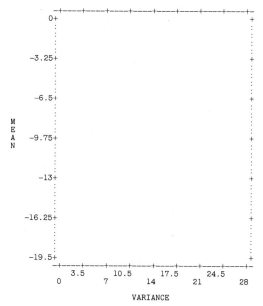

b. Obtain the standard deviations from the variances given in (a) and plot the means shown in (a) against these standard deviations. Is any relationship evident? If so, how are they related?

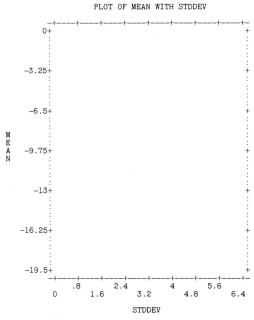

PLOT OF MEAN WITH STDDEV

c. Why are plots like the ones done for (a) and (b) an important part of a MANOVA analysis?

2. A two-sample Hotelling's T^2 test resulted in the output below:

Multivariate Tests of Significance (S = 1, M = 1 , N = 48)

Test Name	Value	Approx. F	Hypoth. DF	Error DF	Sig. of F
Hotellings	21.945	6.997	1.00	46.00	.011

Would you reject the null hypothesis that there is no difference between the two groups?

3. Construct a stem-and-leaf plot from the following exam scores. Do you think these data were taken from a normal population? Why or why not?

100	53	60
91	61	98
18	61	84
27	61	98
41	99	77
100	93	65
71	57	91
71	94	98
82	63	61
52	58	99
76	65	69

4. Use the box-and-whisker plots shown below to answer the following questions:

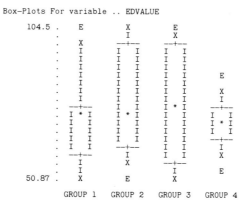

```
Box-Plots For variable .. EDVALUE

  104.5 .     E           X           E
        .                 I           X
        .     X         --+--       --+--
        .     I         I   I       I   I
        .     I         I   I       I   I
        .     I         I   I       I   I
        .     I         I   I       I   I     E
        .     I         I   I       I   I
        .     I         I   I       I   I     X
        .     I         I   I       I * I     I
        .   --+--       I   I       I   I   --+--
        .   I * I       I * I       I   I   I   I
        .   I   I       I   I       I   I   I * I
        .   I   I       I   I       I   I   I   I
        .   I   I       I   I       I   I   --+--
        .   I   I       --+--       I   I     I
        .   --+--         I         I   I     X
        .     I           X         --+--
        .     I                       I       E
  50.87 .     X           E           X

          GROUP 1     GROUP 2     GROUP 3     GROUP 4
```

a. Which group has the most extreme outlier (relative to the rest of the observations)?

b. Which group has the largest spread, not counting outliers?

c. Which group has the largest median?

d. Does the assumption of equal group variances seem reasonable for these data? Why or why not?

5. a. Which of the normal probability plots shown below are inconsistent with the assumption of normality?

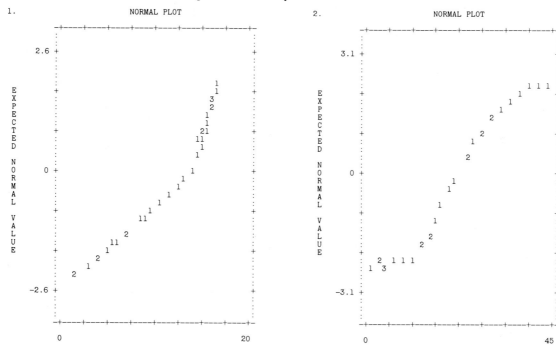

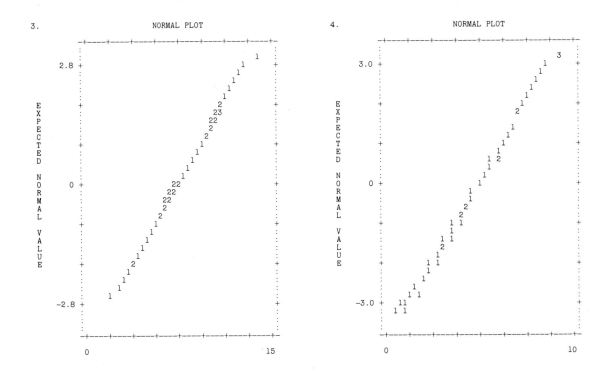

b. Which of the detrended normal probability plots shown below is not consistent with the assumption of normality?

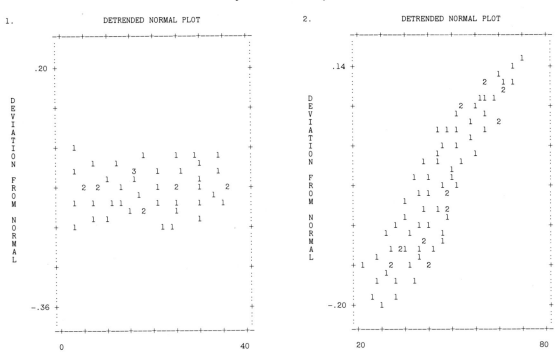

3.

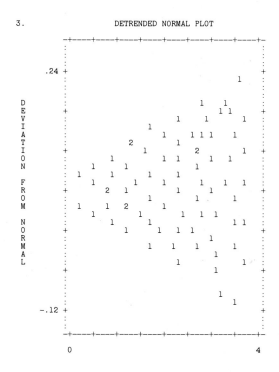

4.

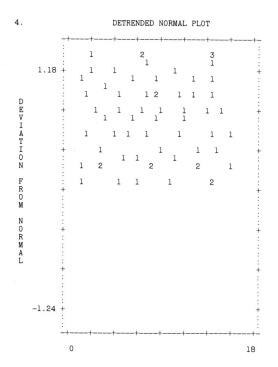

Chapter 18 SPSS-X Command Reference

This chapter is an abbreviated guide to the SPSS-X system. It is designed to accompany this book and therefore does not describe the entire language or the full range of specifications for some of the commands. *SPSS-X User's Guide*, 3rd ed., documents the entire system.

The chapter is divided into four sections: data definition commands; job utility commands; data transformation and modification commands; and procedure commands. The commands are organized alphabetically within each section. In the syntax diagrams, square brackets indicate optional specifications not necessary to the completion of the command. Braces enclose alternative specifications. One of these specifications must be entered to complete the specification correctly. Ellipses are used to indicate optional repetition of an element or elements in the specification. This scheme cannot always exactly describe choices and requirements. If you are in doubt, look at examples in the text. Upper-case specifications should be entered as shown; lower-case specifications show information you must provide. The basic structure and rules for writing SPSS-X commands are discussed in Chapter 2.

18.1 DATA DEFINITION COMMANDS

The data definition commands tell SPSS-X how to read and interpret your data. This involves naming the variables you want to analyze, specifying their location and format within the data for each case, informing SPSS-X of any values that represent missing information, and supplying any labels you want included in your printed output. SPSS-X uses data definition specifications to build a *dictionary* that describes the variables on your file. After you have defined your data, you can save the dictionary and data on an SPSS-X system file and use the system file as input in SPSS-X jobs for additional analysis.

18.2 BEGIN DATA and END DATA Commands

```
BEGIN DATA
lines of data
END DATA
```

If your data are included as lines in your SPSS-X command file, you must use the BEGIN DATA command immediately before the first line of data and the END DATA command immediately after the last line of data to separate lines containing data from lines containing SPSS-X commands. With in-line data, you can omit the FILE subcommand on the DATA LIST command or specify the default FILE=INLINE. The BEGIN DATA command followed by the data lines and the END DATA command should follow the first procedure command.

18.3
DATA LIST Command

```
DATA LIST [FILE=file] [{FIXED}] [RECORDS={1}] [{TABLE  }]
                       {FREE }            {n}   {NOTABLE}
                       {LIST }

              [END=varname]

  /{1     } varlist {col location [(format)]   } [varlist ...]
   {rec #}          {(FORTRAN-like format list}

  [/{2     } ...] [/ ...]
    {rec #}
```

The DATA LIST command has two parts: file definition and variable definition. The file definition portion points SPSS-X to the data file and indicates the format of the file and the number of records per case for fixed-format data files. The variable definition portion names the variables and indicates their location and type.

18.4
File Definition on DATA LIST

You can specify four pieces of information describing the file on the DATA LIST command.

FILE Subcommand. Use the FILE subcommand to specify the file for the data described by the DATA LIST command. If the data are included with the SPSS-X commands, omit the FILE subcommand or explicitly specify the default file INLINE.

FIXED, FREE, and LIST Keywords. Use one of the following keywords to indicate the format of the data:

FIXED   *Fixed-format data.* Each variable is recorded in the same location on the same record for each case in the data. The data file used in Chapter 2 is fixed-format. FIXED is the default.

FREE   *Freefield-format data.* The variables are recorded in the same order for each case, but not necessarily in the same location. You can enter multiple cases on the same record with each value separated by one or more blanks or commas. The data file used in Chapter 12 is freefield format. See Section 18.5 for an example.

LIST   *Freefield data with one case on each record.* The variables are recorded in freefield format as described for keyword FREE except the variables for each case must be recorded on one record. See Section 18.5 for an example.

RECORDS Subcommand. Use the RECORDS subcommand with fixed-format data to specify the number of records per case. By default, SPSS-X assumes one record per case for fixed-format data.

TABLE and NOTABLE Subcommands. TABLE, the default for fixed-format files, displays a table that summarizes your file and variable definitions immediately following the DATA LIST command. An example of the summary table is shown in Chapter 2. To suppress this table, specify subcommand NOTABLE.

18.5
Variable Definition on DATA LIST

Use the variable definition portion of the DATA LIST command to assign a name to each variable you intend to analyze and, depending on the format of your file, to provide information about the location and format of the individual variables. For fixed-format data, specify the record number, name, column location, and type of each variable. The variable definition specifications for fixed-format data are discussed in Chapter 2.

FREE or LIST Formats. For FREE and LIST formats, SPSS-X reads the values sequentially in the order that the variables are named on the DATA LIST command. The values must be separated in your data by at least one blank or comma. For example,

```
DATA LIST FREE/ TREAT1 TREAT2 TREAT3
BEGIN DATA
2.90 2.97 2.67 2.56 2.45 2.62 2.88 2.76
1.87 2.73 2.20 2.33 2.50 2.16 1.27 3.18
2.89 2.39 2.83 2.87 2.39
END DATA
```

defines three treatment variables. The first three values build the first case. The value 2.90 is assigned to variable TREAT1, the value 2.97 is assigned to variable TREAT2, and the value 2.67 is assigned to TREAT3. The second case is built from the next three values in the data, and so forth. Altogether, seven cases are built.

In LIST format, each case is recorded on a separate record. To read this data, specify the keyword LIST, as in:

```
DATA LIST LIST/ TREAT1 TREAT2 TREAT3
BEGIN DATA
2.90 2.97 2.67
2.56 2.45 2.62
2.88 2.76 1.87
2.73 2.20 2.33
2.50 2.16 1.27
3.18 2.89 2.39
2.83 2.87 2.39
END DATA
```

The LIST format requires more records in your data file than the FREE format. However, it is less prone to errors in data entry. Since FREE format reads the data as one long series of numbers, if you leave out a value in the data, the values after the missing value are assigned to the incorrect variable for all remaining cases. Since LIST format reads a case from each record, the missing value will affect only the one case.

You cannot use a blank value to indicate missing information in FREE or LIST formatted data. Rather you must assign a value to the missing information and declare the value missing with the MISSING VALUES command.

18.6
REFERRING TO A FILE IN SPSS-X

SPSS-X can read and write more than one file in a single job. The files include data files, system files, and special files of statistical results. Subcommands that refer to files in SPSS-X are the FILE, OUTFILE, MATRIX, and WRITE subcommands on various procedures.

Not all implementations of SPSS-X use the same method for referring to a file. Some implementations require both host system commands and the use of the FILE HANDLE command within SPSS-X. Others offer extensions to the ability to reference a file directly on a FILE, OUTFILE, MATRIX, or WRITE subcommand. For instance, some implementations permit the specification of just a portion of a file name and supply defaults for the other portions.

For details on the methods you can use to refer to SPSS-X files at your installation, see the documentation available with keyword LOCAL on the INFO command, discussed in Section 18.30.

Examples throughout this manual refer to files by specifying a file handle on the FILE or OUTFILE subcommand of the command being discussed. For example, the GET command uses a FILE subcommand to specify a file, as in

```
GET  FILE=ELECTRIC
```

which gets the SPSS-X system file ELECTRIC.

A file handle cannot exceed eight characters and must begin with an alphabetic character (A–Z) or a $, #, or @. It can also contain numeric characters (0–9), but no embedded blanks are allowed.

On the syntax chart for each command, the file handle is abbreviated to the general term *file*.

18.7
FILE LABEL Command

FILE LABEL label

The FILE LABEL command provides a descriptive label for your data file. The file label can contain up to 60 characters and is specified as a literal (see Section 18.20). It is printed on the first line of each page of output displayed by SPSS-X and is included in the dictionary of the system file. The command

FILE LABEL 'WESTERN ELECTRIC STUDY OF CORONARY HEART DISEASE'

assigns a file label to the data file described in Chapter 2.

18.8
FILE TYPE—END FILE TYPE Structure

For FILE TYPE MIXED

FILE TYPE MIXED [FILE=file] RECORD=[varname] col loc [WILD={NOWARN}]
                                                            {WARN   }

For FILE TYPE GROUPED

FILE TYPE GROUPED [FILE=file] RECORD=[varname] col loc

CASE=[varname] col loc [WILD={WARN }] [DUPLICATE= {WARN }]
                             {NOWARN}   {NOWARN}

[MISSING={WARN }] [ORDERED={YES}]
         {NOWARN}   {NO }

For FILE TYPE NESTED

FILE TYPE NESTED [FILE=file] RECORD=[varname] col loc

[CASE=[varname] col loc] [WILD={NOWARN}] [DUPLICATE={NOWARN}]
                                {WARN }   {WARN }
                                                      {CASE }

[MISSING={NOWARN}]
         {WARN }

The FILE TYPE—END FILE TYPE file definition structure is used to read many types of nonrectangular files. *SPSS-X User's Guide,* 3rd ed., discusses all of the features of this file definition facility for nonrectangular files. Another use of the FILE TYPE—END FILE TYPE structure is to check for duplicate, missing, and wild records in a data file with multiple records for each case. This type of file is a rectangular file defined as a GROUPED file.

With the FILE TYPE—END FILE TYPE structure, each record in your file must contain a unique code identifying the record and a code identifying the case for this record. The records for a single case must be together in your file. By default, SPSS-X assumes that the records are in the same sequence within each case. For example, Figure 18.8 shows the first nine records from the marketing survey data file used in Chapter 7.

Figure 18.8   Marketing survey data with a missing record

```
001H56277544354435327167566266255344376367355423256144376465577730
001W22356652117525535324357512132244231132126543411131122145141140
002H77111547147171741771622421771176511177177177577175123232577577 10
003H66222455311346322133433357121464435353532446533531122235647740
003W66177142311375111353131333377116444367321344352211377272752 2330
004H12132534125477133332343377112433434244133412177144133466355 20
004W11277211211137421137727711331443742773442113222742773642 7731440
005H57254435152577223145366526167422377233166375146266165477 52240
005W33235544277577732214435552522555353775771664442652551465 7753330
```

The first three columns of each record contain the case identifier, and column 4 contains the record identifier. The first two records represent Case 1; the first record is an "H" record type for the husband's record, and the second record is a "W" record type for the wife's record. An error has been introduced into the file: Case 2 has a missing record type W.

You can define this file using FILE TYPE, RECORD TYPE, and END FILE TYPE commands with a DATA LIST command for each record type, as in:

```
FILE TYPE GROUPED FILE=MARKET RECORD=RESPTYP 4 (A) CASE= CASEID 1-3
RECORD TYPE 'H'
DATA LIST    /H1S H1O H1R H2S H2O
  H2R H3S H3O H3R H4S H4O H4R H5S H5O H5R H6S H6O H6R H7S H7O H7R
  H8S H8O H8R H9S H9O H10S H10O H10R H11S H11O H11R H12S H12O H12R
  H13S H13O H13R H14S H14O H14R H15S H15O H15R H16S H16O H16R H17S
  H17O H17R H18S H18O H18R H19S H19O H19R H20S H20O H20R VISUAL 5-65
RECORD TYPE 'W'
DATA LIST    /W1S W1O W1R W2S W2O
  W2R W3S W3O W3R W4S W4O W4R W5S W5O W5R W6S W6O W6R W7S W7O W7R
  W8S W8O W8R W9S W9O W9R W10S W10O W10R W11S W11O W11R W12S W12O W12R
  W13S W13O W13R W14S W14O W14R W15S W15O W15R W16S W16O W16R  W17S
  W17O W17R W18S W18O W18R W19S W19O W19R W20S W20O W20R 5-64
END FILE TYPE
FREQUENCIES VARIABLES=H1S W1S
```

The FILE TYPE command specifies a grouped file type and identifies MARKET as the data file. The FILE TYPE command also specifies the record identifier variable RESPTYP as a string located in column 4, and the case identifier variable CASEID located in columns 1 through 3. The first RECORD TYPE command specifies record type H as the first record for each case. All type H records are defined by the DATA LIST command following this RECORD TYPE command. The second RECORD TYPE command identifies the type W records, and the following DATA LIST command defines this record type. Records with other values on RESPTYP are reported as errors. If a case has a duplicate record type or if a record type is missing for a case, a warning message is printed. The record missing from Figure 18.8 produces the following warning message:

```
>WARNING   518
>A record is missing from the indicated case.  The variables defined on the
>record have been set to the system missing value.

RECORD IDENTIFIER:W
CASE IDENTIFIER :  2
CURRENT CASE NUMBER:      2, CURRENT SPLIT FILE NUMBER:      1.
```

Four types of information are required on the FILE TYPE command for grouped file types.

GROUPED Keyword. GROUPED indicates that the file being described is a grouped file.

FILE Subcommand. FILE names the file to be defined and is required unless your data are included in the command file.

RECORD Subcommand. RECORD names the variable, location, and type of the record identifier. Each record in the file must contain a unique code and the value must be coded in the same location on all records. Specify a variable name, followed by the column location of the variable. If the variable is a string, specify the letter *A* in parentheses after the column location.

CASE Subcommand. CASE names the variable, location, and type of the case identifier. Each case must contain a unique value for this variable. Specify a variable name, followed by the column location of the variable. If the variable is a string, specify an A in parentheses after the column location.

You must include one RECORD TYPE command for each record type containing data that you want to read. The specification on the RECORD TYPE command is the value of the record type variable defined on the RECORD subcommand on the FILE TYPE command. If the record type is a string variable, enclose the value in apostrophes or quotation marks. After each RECORD TYPE command, you must also specify a DATA LIST command describing the variables to be read from that record type. The record types must be specified in the same order as their order within each case.

18.9
GET Command

```
GET FILE=file

[/KEEP={ALL     }] [/DROP=varlist]
       {varlist}

[/RENAME=(old varlist=new varlist)...]

[/MAP]
```

An SPSS-X system file is a self-documented file containing data and descriptive information, called the dictionary. The dictionary contains variable names, their print and write formats, and optional variable labels, value labels, and missing-value indicators. Use the SAVE command to save a system file (Section 18.15) and the GET command to read a system file.

The only required specification on the GET command is the FILE subcommand, which specifies the system file to be read. For example, to read the Western Electric data, specify:

GET FILE=ELECTRIC

Optional subcommands rename variables, select a subset of variables, reorder the variables, and display the names of the variables saved. Separate each subcommand from the other subcommands with a slash. A subcommand acts on the results of all the previous subcommands on the GET command.

18.10
RENAME Subcommand

Use the RENAME subcommand to change the names of variables as they are copied from the system file. Variable names are not changed on the system file. The rename specifications are enclosed in parentheses in the form *old=new,* as in:

GET FILE=ELECTRIC /RENAME=(EDUYR,DBP58=EDUC,BLOODPR)

This command changes the name of variable EDUYR to EDUC, and variable DBP58 to BLOODPR. Use the keyword TO to refer to consecutive variables to be renamed (on the left side of the equals sign) or to generate new variable names (on the right side of the equals sign).

18.11
DROP Subcommand

Use the DROP subcommand to specify variables that you want dropped when SPSS-X reads the system file. For example, to drop the variables CASEID and FAMHXCVR from the Western Electric data, specify:

**GET FILE=ELECTRIC/RENAME=(EDUYR,DBP58=EDUC,BLOODPR)
  /DROP=CASEID,FAMHXCVR**

Note that these variables are not dropped from the system file. Again, you can use the keyword TO to refer to a series of consecutive variables.

18.12
KEEP Subcommand

Use the KEEP subcommand to select a subset of variables and to reorder the variables as they are read from the system file. Specify the variables in the order that you want them copied from the system file. For example, to read only the variables EDUYR (renamed to EDUC), DBP58 (renamed to BLOODPR), and HT58 through DAYOFWK in that order, specify:

```
GET FILE=ELECTRIC/RENAME=(EDUYR,DBP58=EDUC,BLOODPR)
  /KEEP=EDUC,BLOODPR,HT58 TO DAYOFWK
```

Note that the renamed variables are referred to by their new names on the KEEP subcommand. The results of the subcommands are cumulative.

You can reorder all of the variables in your file either by listing the names of all the variables in the order that you want them or by listing the names of the variables that you want at the beginning of the file in the desired order, followed by the keyword ALL. Keyword ALL places all the unnamed variables after the named variables in the same sequence on the active file as they appear in the system file.

18.13
MAP Subcommand

To check the results of the RENAME, DROP, and KEEP subcommands, use the MAP subcommand, as in:

```
GET FILE=ELECTRIC /RENAME=(EDUYR,DBP58=EDUC,BLOODPR)
  /KEEP=EDUC,BLOODPR,HT58 TO DAYOFWK /MAP
```

The MAP subcommand displays the results from the previous subcommands, showing the variables on the active file and their corresponding names on the system file.

18.14
MISSING VALUES
Command

```
MISSING VALUES varlist(value list) [/varlist ...]
```

Keywords for numeric value lists:

LO, LOWEST, HI, HIGHEST, THRU

Very often, your data file lacks complete information on some cases for some variables. Monitoring equipment can malfunction, interviewers can forget to ask a question or record an answer, respondents can refuse to answer, and so forth. Missing does not always mean the same as unknown or absent. For example, if you record the value 9 for "Refused to answer" and the value 0 for "No answer reported," you might want to specify both of these values as missing.

Use the MISSING VALUES command to declare the missing values for certain variables in your file. The values defined as missing are never changed on the data; they are simply flagged in the dictionary. The SPSS-X statistical procedures and transformation commands recognize this flag, and those cases that contain a user-defined missing value are handled specially. All SPSS-X statistical procedures provide options for handling cases with missing values.

The MISSING VALUES command specifies a variable name or variable list and the missing value or values enclosed in parentheses and separated by a comma or blank. You can specify a maximum of three individual values or one value and a range for each variable. For example, to declare the values 0, 98, and 99 as missing for the variable AGE, specify:

```
MISSING VALUES AGE (0,98,99)
```

You can specify a range of values as missing using the keyword THRU to indicate an inclusive range of values. For example, the command

```
MISSING VALUES AGE (0,98,99) /EDUC (0,97 THRU 99)
```

declares the missing values for AGE and the values 0, 97, 98, and 99 as missing for variable EDUC. Use the keyword HIGHEST or LOWEST with THRU to indicate the highest or lowest value of a variable.

You can define missing values for short string variables. To specify a value of a string variable, enclose the value in apostrophes or quotation marks. The command

```
MISSING VALUES STRING1 ('X','Y')
```

specifies the values X and Y as missing for the single-column string variable STRING1. Value ranges cannot be specified for string variables.

18.15
SAVE Command

```
SAVE OUTFILE=file

[/KEEP={ALL     }] [/DROP=varlist]
       {varlist}

[/RENAME=(old varlist=new varlist)...]

[/MAP] [/{COMPRESSED  }]
         {UNCOMPRESSED}
```

An SPSS-X system file is a self-documented file containing data and descriptive information called the dictionary. The dictionary contains variable names, their print and write formats, and optional extended variable labels, value labels, and missing-value indicators. It also contains the file label from the FILE LABEL command and additional documentation supplied on the DOCUMENT command. Use the SAVE command to save a system file and the GET command to read a system file (see Section 18.9).

The only required specification on the SAVE command is the OUTFILE subcommand, which specifies the system file to be saved. For example, to save the Western Electric data, specify:

```
DATA LIST FILE=DATA /CASEID 1-4 FIRSTCHD 6 AGE 17-18 DBP58 20-22
   EDUYR 24-25 CHOL58 27-29 CGT58 31-32 HT58 34-37 (1) WT58 39-40
   DAYOFWK 43 VITAL10 45 FAMHXCVR 47 (A) CHD 49
SAVE OUTFILE=ELECTRIC
```

Optional subcommands rename variables, select a subset of variables, reorder the variables, and display the names of the variables saved. Separate each subcommand from the other subcommands with a slash. A subcommand acts on the results of all the previous subcommands on the SAVE command.

18.16
RENAME Subcommand

Use the RENAME subcommand to change the names of variables as they are copied onto the system file. Variable names are not changed on the active file. The rename specifications are enclosed in parentheses in the form *old=new,* as in:

```
SAVE OUTFILE=ELECTRIC /RENAME=(EDUYR,DBP58=EDUC,BLOODPR)
```

This command changes the name of variable EDUYR to EDUC, and the variable DBP58 to BLOODPR. Use the keyword TO to refer to consecutive variables to be renamed (on the left side of the equals sign) or to generate new variable names (on the right side of the equals sign).

18.17
DROP Subcommand

Use the DROP subcommand to specify variables that you want dropped when SPSS-X writes the system file. The variables are not dropped from the active file. For example, to eliminate variables CASEID and FAMHXCVR from the Western Electric system file, specify:

```
SAVE OUTFILE=ELECTRIC /RENAME=(EDUYR,DBP58=EDUC,BLOODPR)
   /DROP=CASEID,FAMHXCVR
```

You can use the keyword TO to drop a series of consecutive variables.

18.18
KEEP Subcommand

Use the KEEP subcommand to select a subset of variables and to reorder the variables as they are written on the system file. Specify the variables in the order that you want them copied from the active file. For example, to save only the variables EDUYR (renamed to EDUC), DBP58 (renamed to BLOODPR), and HT58 through DAYOFWK in that order, specify:

```
SAVE OUTFILE=ELECTRIC /RENAME=(EDUYR,DBP58=EDUC,BLOODPR)
 /KEEP=EDUC,BLOODPR,HT58 TO DAYOFWK
```

Note that the renamed variables are specified by their new names on the KEEP subcommand. The results of the subcommands are cumulative.

You can reorder all of the variables in your system file either by listing the names of all the variables in the order that you want them or by listing the names of the variables that you want at the beginning of the file in the desired order, followed by the keyword ALL. Keyword ALL places all the unnamed variables after the named variables in the same sequence on the system file as they appear in the active file.

18.19
MAP Subcommand

To check the results of the RENAME, DROP, and KEEP subcommands, use the MAP subcommand, as in:

```
SAVE OUTFILE=ELECTRIC /RENAME=(EDUYR,DBP58=EDUC,BLOODPR)
 /KEEP=EDUC,BLOODPR,HT58 TO DAYOFWK /MAP
```

The MAP subcommand displays the results from the previous subcommands, showing the variables saved on the system file and their corresponding names on the active file.

18.20
VALUE LABELS
Command

```
VALUE LABELS varlist value 'label' value 'label'... [/varlist...]
```

The VALUE LABELS command specifies the variable name or variable list and a list of the values with their associated labels. The labels are specified as literals and must be enclosed in apostrophes or quotation marks, using the same symbol to begin and end the literal. Enter an apostrophe as part of a label by enclosing the literal in quotation marks or by entering the apostrophe twice with no separation. The command

```
VALUE LABELS ANOMIA5 ANOMIA6 ANOMIA7 1 'AGREE' 2 'DISAGREE'
             8 "DON'T KNOW" 9 'NO ANSWER'
```

assigns labels to the values 1, 2, 8, and 9 of variables ANOMIA5, ANOMIA6, and ANOMIA7.

Value labels can be up to 60 characters long and can contain any characters including blanks. However, some procedures print fewer than 60 characters for each label. (See especially the CROSSTABS procedure in Chapter 5.) Additional sets of variable names and value labels can be specified on the same command. A slash is required to separate value labels for one variable list from the next.

To assign value labels to short string variables, enclose the value of string variables in apostrophes. The command

```
VALUE LABELS STRING1 'M' 'MALE' 'F' 'FEMALE'
```

assigns value labels to the values M and F of the string variable STRING1.

If you assign value labels to any variable that already has value labels assigned to it, the new assignment completely replaces the old assignment. Use the ADD VALUE LABELS command to add value labels to a variable with existing labels.

18.21
VARIABLE LABELS Command

```
VARIABLE LABELS varname 'label' [/varname...]
```

Use the VARIABLE LABELS command to assign an extended descriptive label to variables. Specify the variable name followed by at least one blank or comma and the associated label enclosed in apostrophes or quotation marks. A variable label applies to one variable only. Each variable label can be up to 40 characters long and can include blanks and any character. The command

```
VARIABLE LABELS ANOMIA5 'LOT OF AVERAGE MAN GETTING WORSE'
                ANOMIA6 'NOT FAIR TO BRING CHILD INTO WORLD'
                ANOMIA7 'OFFICIALS NOT INTERESTED IN AVERAGE MAN'
```

assigns variable labels to the variables ANOMIA5, ANOMIA6, and ANOMIA7.

18.22
UTILITY COMMANDS

Utility commands tell SPSS-X to print titles and subtitles on your printed output, to edit your commands, to display information from the dictionary describing your data, to include document information on the system file, to assign new print and write formats to variables, and to list the values of cases.

18.23
COMMENT Command

```
COMMENT text
```

Comments help you and others review what you intend to accomplish with the SPSS-X job. You can insert comments by using the COMMENT command or an asterisk (*), or by enclosing the comment within the symbols /* and */ in any command line. Comments are included in the command printback on the display. They are not saved on a system file.

The specification for the COMMENT command is any message you wish, as in:

```
COMMENT   WESTERN ELECTRIC STUDY OF CORONARY HEART DISEASE.
```

Instead of the keyword COMMAND you can use an asterisk, as in:

```
*         WESTERN ELECTRIC STUDY OF CORONARY HEART DISEASE.
```

Alternatively, you can use /* and */ to set off a short comment on a command line, as in:

```
COMPUTE SEXRACE=1   /*CREATE NEW VARIABLE SEXRACE*/
```

If the comment is at the end of the line, the closing */ is optional.

18.24
DISPLAY Command

```
DISPLAY [SORTED] [{NAMES**  }] [/VARIABLES=varlist]
                  {INDEX     }
                  {VARIABLES }
                  {LABELS    }
                  {DICTIONAY }

          [MACROS]
          [DOCUMENTS]
```

**Default if the subcommand is omitted.

Use the DISPLAY command to display information from the dictionary of a system file. This command is very useful for exploring an unfamiliar or forgotten system file or for producing a printed archive document for a system file. The codebooks for the four data files used for the exercises in this book were produced using the DISPLAY command (see Appendix B).

The following keywords can be specified on the DISPLAY command:

NAMES   *Display variable names.* An unsorted list of the variables on the active file is displayed. This is the default.

DOCUMENTS   *Display the text provided by the DOCUMENT command.* No error message is issued if there is no documentary information on the system file.

DICTIONARY   *Display complete dictionary information for variables.*

INDEX   *Display the variable names and positions.*

VARIABLES   *Display the variable names, positions, print and write formats, and missing values.*

LABELS   *Display the variable names, positions, and variable labels.*

Only one of the above keywords can be specified per DISPLAY command, but you can use as many DISPLAY commands as necessary to obtain the desired information.

In addition, you can use keyword SORTED to display information alphabetically by variable name. SORTED can precede keywords NAMES, DICTIONARY, INDEX, VARIABLES, or LABELS, as in:

```
GET FILE=GSS82
DISPLAY DOCUMENTS
DISPLAY SORTED DICTIONARY
```

The first DISPLAY command displays the document information, and the second displays complete dictionary information for variables sorted alphabetically by variable name.

To limit the display to certain variables, follow the keywords NAMES, DICTIONARY, INDEX, VARIABLES, or LABELS with a slash, the VARIABLES subcommand, an optional equals sign, and a list of variables, as in:

```
GET FILE=GSS82
DISPLAY DOCUMENTS
DISPLAY SORTED DICTIONARY/
   VARIABLES=ANOMIA5 TO ANOMIA6
```

18.25
DOCUMENT Command

```
DOCUMENT text
```

Use the DOCUMENT command to save a block of text of any length on your system file. For example, the command

```
DOCUMENT  WESTERN ELECTRIC STUDY OF CORONARY HEART DISEASE.
 A LARGE-SCALE, 20-YEAR, PROSPECTIVE STUDY FOLLOWING
 MEN WITHOUT PREVIOUS INCIDENCES OF CORONARY HEART
 DISEASE.  BASE YEAR:  1958.
```

provides information describing the Western Electric data. The block of text is saved on the system file and can be printed using the DISPLAY command (see Section 18.24).

18.26
EDIT Command

```
EDIT
```

Use the EDIT command to check the syntax of your commands without actually reading the data. The EDIT command has no specifications. EDIT is not allowed in interactive mode; in batch mode, EDIT can appear anywhere in your command file. Commands following EDIT are checked. Commands before EDIT are executed.

Since EDIT checks variable names, if you are using a system file in your job, you must make it available so that SPSS-X can read the dictionary. The data portion of the system file is not read. If you are using DATA LIST to define your input data, you do not need to make the data file available. If your job contains data in the command file, you must remove both the data and the BEGIN DATA and END DATA commands for the EDIT job.

The EDIT facility checks syntax for errors but does not detect errors that could occur when the data are read.

18.27
FINISH Command

```
FINISH
```

The FINISH command has no specifications. In batch mode it is optional and its primary use is to mark the end of a job. In interactive mode it is required to terminate the interactive session.

18.28
FORMATS Command

```
FORMATS varlist(format) [varlist...]
```

SPSS-X assigns a print and write format to each variable in your file. For variables read with a DATA LIST command, the format used to read the variable is assigned as both the print and write format. For numeric variables created with transformation commands, the format F8.2 (eight print positions with two decimal places) is assigned. These print and write formats are stored for each variable on the dictionary of the system file. SPSS-X uses the print format to display the values and the write format to write the values to a file. Three commands in SPSS-X allow you to change the print and write formats: FORMATS, PRINT FORMATS (Section 18.33), and WRITE FORMATS (Section 18.36).

Use the FORMATS command to change both the print and write formats for variables. Specify the variable name or variable list followed by the new format specification in parentheses, as in:

```
FORMATS  SCALE1 (F2.0)
```

This command changes the print and write formats for variable SCALE1 to a two-digit integer. The same command can specify different formats for different variables. Separate the specifications for each variable or list with a slash.

The most common format on a FORMATS command is F, used to alter the F8.2 default format for new variables to a more appropriate length and number of decimal places. Formats specified on the FORMATS command are in effect for the remainder of the SPSS-X job and are saved on a system file if a SAVE command is specified.

18.29
HELP Command

When you run SPSS-X in interactive mode, you have an extensive help system available to you. To use HELP, specify HELP or ? at the SPSS-X> prompt and hit return. A menu of help topics displays on your monitor. Alternatively, for help on a specific command, specify HELP or ? and a command name. For example, to get information on the REGRESSION command, type

```
? REGRESSION.
```

and hit return. To request help from a CONTINUE>, DATA>, or HELP> prompt, you must specify the request with a question mark; you cannot use the keyword HELP.

If a help screen has subtopics, a numbered list for you to choose from is provided. For additional help, type the appropriate number from the list of choices and hit the return key. For example, if a help screen has a topic numbered 2, type "2" at the HELP> prompt and hit return (use the key for numeral "2," not the "PF2" key if you have programmable function keys on your keyboard).

You can also go directly to specific screens from any command prompt by entering "? topic subtopic" at the prompt. For example, from any SPSSX>, CONTINUE>, DATA>, or HELP> prompt, type

```
? REGRESSION STATISTICS.
```

to get help for REGRESSION's STATISTICS subcommand.

In addition to entering subcommand numbers from a command-level screen or typing a complete help request from a command prompt, you can also move from screen to screen using keystrokes. On some systems, the minus ($-$) and plus ($+$) keys are available to help you move through a single branch of the help system. The minus key moves you vertically up from a lower level screen to a higher level screen. For example, if you are at a subcommand screen, the minus key moves you up to its parent command screen. The plus key moves you horizontally across screens at the same hierarchical level. For example, if you are at a subcommand screen, the plus key moves you to a different subcommand screen for the same parent command. On some systems, you may be able to scroll among screens using the directional arrow keys.

The help system also has online syntax charts for each SPSS-X command. To see the syntax for a command, type the keyword SYNTAX after the command name, as in:

```
? REGRESSION SYNTAX.
```

which requests syntax for the REGRESSION command.

Exiting HELP. To exit the HELP system and return to your SPSS-X job, just hit the return key at any blank HELP> prompt.

18.30
INFO Command

```
INFO [OUTFILE = file]
     [OVERVIEW]
     [LOCAL]
     [ERRORS]
     [FACILITIES]
     [PROCEDURES]
     [ALL]
     [procedure name] [/procedure name...]
     [SINCE release number]
```

The INFO command makes available or tells you how to obtain two kinds of documentation not included in this manual or *SPSS-X User's Guide,* 3rd ed., local and update. Local documentation concerns the environment in which you are running SPSS-X. Update documentation includes changes to existing procedures and facilities, new procedures and facilities, and corrections to *SPSS-X User's Guide,* 3rd ed.

You can choose update documentation for facilities (all SPSS-X commands except procedures), for all procedures, or for individual procedures. You can also request documentation produced since a particular release of SPSS-X. To request information via the INFO command, use the following keywords:

OVERVIEW   *Overview of available documentation.* This overview includes a table of contents for the documentation available via the INFO command, along with information about documentation available in print.

LOCAL   *Local documentation.* Includes commands or job control language for running SPSS-X, conventions for specifying files, conventions for handling tapes and other input/output devices, data formats that SPSS-X reads and writes on your computer, and other information specific to your computer and operating system or to your individual installation.

FACILITIES   *Update information for SPSS-X facilities.* This documentation covers all changes, except in procedures, since the publication of this manual and *SPSS-X User's Guide,* 3rd ed. However, unless you use keyword SINCE to specify an earlier release of SPSS-X, you receive updates only for the most current release.

PROCEDURES   *Update information for procedures.* This includes full documentation for procedures new in the current release and update information for procedures that existed prior to the current release.

procedure   *Documentation for the procedure named.* This is the same information as that produced by the PROCEDURES keyword, but limited to the procedure named. Follow every procedure name with a slash.

ALL   *All available documentation.* ALL is equivalent to OVERVIEW, LOCAL, FACILITIES, and PROCEDURES.

Enter as many of these keywords as you wish. If you specify overlapping sets of information, only one copy is printed. The order of specifications is not important and does not affect the order in which the documentation is printed. The following commands produce an overview and documentation for any changes made to system facilities and to the FREQUENCIES and CROSSTABS procedures:

```
INFO  OVERVIEW FACILITIES FREQUENCIES / CROSSTABS
```

Because of possible conflict with procedure names, all keywords in the INFO command must be spelled out in full.

Releases of SPSS-X are numbered by integers, with decimal digits indicating maintenance releases between major releases (so Release 1.1 would be a maintenance release with few changes from Release 1). The release number appears in the heading to each SPSS-X job. Each SPSS-X manual is identified on the title page by the number of the release it documents. This manual documents Release 3.0.

By default, the INFO command produces update information only for the current major release and subsequent maintenance releases. Documentation for earlier releases may also be available, and that fact will be indicated in the INFO overview. To obtain information for earlier releases or to limit the information to maintenance releases since the last major release, use keyword SINCE followed by a release number.

The following command prints documentation for all changes to system facilities and procedures FREQUENCIES and CROSSTABS since Release 3.0 (the release documented in this manual):

```
INFO  OVERVIEW FACILITIES FREQUENCIES / CROSSTABS SINCE 3
```

SINCE is not inclusive—SINCE 3 does not include changes made to the system in Release 3.0, though it does include any changes made in Release 3.1 (if a Release 3.1 occurs). To identify a maintenance release, enter the exact number, with decimal, as in 3.1.

By default, output from the INFO command is included in the display file. If you prefer to send the output to another file, use the OUTFILE subcommand, naming the handle of the file you want to create. The following commands create a file of text comprising an overview, local documentation, changes, and new procedures since Release 3.0:

```
INFO  OUTFILE=SPSSXDOC ALL SINCE 3
```

The characteristics of the output file produced by the INFO command may vary by computer type. As implemented at SPSS Inc., the file includes carriage control, with the maximum length of a page determined by the LENGTH subcommand to the SET command. A printer width of 132 characters is assumed for some examples, though the text is generally much narrower.

18.31
N OF CASES Command

```
N OF CASES n
```

Use the N OF CASES command to read the first *n* cases from your data file. For example, if your data file contains 1,000 cases and you want to use only the first 100 cases to test your SPSS-X commands, specify:

```
DATA LIST FILE=CITY/1 NAME 1-20 (A) TOTPOP 21-30 MEDSAL 31-40
N OF CASES 100
```

You can also use the N OF CASES command to control the reading of cases from an SPSS-X system file. Place the N OF CASES command after the GET command.

N OF CASES controls the number of cases built on the active file. If you use SAMPLE or SELECT IF with N OF CASES, SPSS-X reads as many records as required to build the specified number of cases. Only one N OF CASES can be used in an SPSS-X job, and it is in effect for the entire job.

18.32
NUMBERED Command

{NUMBERED   }
{UNNUMBERED}

It is common practice in some computer environments to reserve columns 73–80 of each input line for line numbers. If your computer system numbers lines this way, SPSS-X includes the line numbers on the printback of commands on the display. The NUMBERED command instructs SPSS-X to check just the first 72 columns for command specifications, and the UNNUMBERED command instructs SPSS-X to check all 80 columns. Neither command has any specifications. If one of the commands is used, it should be the first command in your SPSS-X command file.

The default may vary by installation. Check the local documentation available with the INFO command (Section 18.30) for the default at your installation.

18.33
PRINT FORMATS
Command

PRINT FORMATS varlist(format) [varlist...]

SPSS-X stores a print and write format for each variable in your file (see Section 18.28). Use the PRINT FORMATS command to change the print formats for variables. Specify the variable name or variable list followed by the new format specification in parentheses, as in:

PRINT FORMATS SCALE1 (F2.0)

This command changes the print format for variable SCALE1 to a two-digit integer. The write format does not change. The same command can specify different formats for different variables. Separate the specifications for each variable or variable list with a slash.

The most common formats are F, COMMA, and DOLLAR. Use the F format to provide a more appropriate length and/or number of decimal positions. Use the COMMA format to include commas for large numbers and DOLLAR to include both commas and the dollar sign. When the COMMA or DOLLAR formats are used, include the commas and the dollar sign in your length calculations. The number 32365.67 in F8.2 format prints as 32,365.67 in COMMA9.2 format and $32,365.67 in DOLLAR10.2 format.

Formats specified on the PRINT FORMATS command are in effect for the remainder of the SPSS-X job and are saved on a system file if a SAVE command is specified.

18.34
SUBTITLE Command

SUBTITLE [']text[']

Use the TITLE command (Section 18.35) and the SUBTITLE command to place your own heading at the top of each page of your SPSS-X display. With the SUBTITLE command, you can specify a line up to 60 characters long that prints as the second line at the top of each page, as in:

SUBTITLE 'FREQUENCIES ON ALL VARIABLES'

The subtitle is specified as a literal (see Section 18.20).

18.35
TITLE Command

TITLE [']text[']

The TITLE command specifies the text for the first line of each page of SPSS-X display. The TITLE command can be used by itself or with the SUBTITLE command. The TITLE command follows the same rules as the SUBTITLE command. For example,

```
TITLE 'BANK EMPLOYMENT STUDY'
SUBTITLE 'FREQUENCIES ON ALL VARIABLES'
```

prints two lines at the top of each page of your display.

18.36
WRITE FORMATS Command

WRITE FORMATS varlist (format) [varlist...]

SPSS-X stores a print and write format for each variable in your file (see Section 18.28). Use the WRITE FORMATS command to change the write formats for variables. Specify the variable or variable list followed by the new format specification in parentheses, as in:

```
WRITE FORMATS  SCALE1 (F2.0)
```

This command changes the write format for variable SCALE1 to a two-digit integer. The print format does not change. You can use the same command to specify different formats for different variables. Separate the specifications for each variable or variable list with a slash.

    The most common format is the F format. Use this format to provide appropriate length and/or decimal positions. Formats specified on the WRITE FORMATS command are in effect for the remainder of the SPSS-X job and are saved on a system file if a SAVE command is specified.

18.37
DATA TRANSFORMATION COMMANDS

The ability to transform data before you analyze it or after preliminary analysis is often as important as the analysis itself. You may want to perform simple data-cleaning checks, correct coding errors, or adjust an inconvenient coding scheme. Or you may want to construct an index from several variables or rescale several variables prior to analysis. You may want to perform an analysis on a sample or selected subset of your file, or weight aggregated data to a population. The SPSS-X transformation language provides these and many other possibilities.

18.38
COMPUTE Command

COMPUTE target variable=expression

Use the COMPUTE command to compute a new variable as some combination or transformation of one or more existing variables. The COMPUTE command generates a variable on your active file on a case-by-case basis as an arithmetic or logical transformation of existing variables and constants. To compute a variable, specify the target variable on the left of the equals sign and the expression on the right. For example, the command

```
COMPUTE FAMSCORE=HSSCALE + WSSCALE
```

assigns the sum of existing variables HSSCALE and WSSCALE (the expression) to variable FAMSCORE (the target) for each case.

    The target variable can be an existing variable or a new variable defined by the COMPUTE command itself. If the target variable already exists, the old values are replaced. If the target variable does not exist, it is created by the COMPUTE command and initialized to the system-missing value. The default print and write format of F8.2 is assigned to the new variable. New variables are added to the end of your active file and can be labeled, analyzed, and stored on a new system file along with all other variables.

The expression to the right of the equals sign can be composed of existing variables, arithmetic operators such as $+$ and $-$, arithmetic or statistical functions such as LG10 or MEAN, logical functions such as ANY and SYSMIS, numeric constants, and so forth. The syntax guide above shows the complete list of common arithmetic operators and functions for numeric variables.

If a case is missing on any of the variables used in an expression, SPSS-X nearly always returns the system-missing value since the operation is indeterminate. In the above example, variable FAMSCORE is assigned the system-missing value for any case with a missing value on either HSSCALE or WSSCALE.

18.39
Arithmetic Operations

You can use variables, constants, and functions with arithmetic operators to form complex expressions. The order in which SPSS-X executes the operations on a COMPUTE command is (1) functions; (2) exponentiation; (3) multiplication, division, and unary $-$; (4) addition and subtraction. You can control the order of operations by enclosing in parentheses the operation you want to execute first. The command

```
COMPUTE AVGFAM=(HSSCALE + WSSCALE)/2
```

sums the values of HSSCALE and WSSCALE first and then divides by 2. Without the parentheses, WSSCALE would be divided by 2 first, and the resulting value would be summed with HSSCALE. The order of execution for operations at the same level unspecified by parentheses is left to right. If you are ever unsure of the order of execution, use parentheses to make the order explicit—even if you specify the order SPSS-X would use anyway.

18.40
Numeric Functions

The expression to be transformed by a function is called the *argument*. An argument can be a variable name or a numeric expression, such as $RND(A**2/B)$. Arithmetic functions allow you to round or truncate a variable, take the square root or the log of a variable, and so forth. All arithmetic functions except MOD have single arguments; MOD has two.

Statistical functions allow you to compute statistics such as the mean or variance across variables for each case. You can use the .*n* suffix with all statistical functions to specify the number of valid arguments you consider acceptable. For example, MEAN.2(A,B,C,D) returns the mean of the valid values for variables A, B, C, and D only if at least two of the variables have valid values. If you do not specify a suffix, SPSS-X performs the requested operation when a sufficient number of variables specified in the argument list are valid (one for SUM, MAX, and MIN; two for MEAN, SD, and VARIANCE). You can also use the TO keyword to reference a set of variables in the argument list.

UNIFORM and NORMAL generate pseudo random number variables. The argument for UNIFORM is the upper limit. For example, UNIFORM(1) generates a variable whose values vary uniformly between 0 and 1. The argument for NORMAL is the standard deviation of the desired normal distribution.

18.41
Generating Distributions

You can use SPSS-X to generate cases without an input data file. For example, to create 100 dummy cases with variable X1 as a uniformly distributed random number and X2 as a normally distributed random number, specify:

```
INPUT PROGRAM
LOOP I=1 TO 100
COMPUTE X1=NORMAL(1)
COMPUTE X2=UNIFORM(1)
END CASE
END LOOP
END FILE
END INPUT PROGRAM

FREQUENCIES VARIABLES=X1,X2 /FORMAT=NOTABLE /HISTOGRAM
```

Explanation of these commands is beyond the scope of this manual. However, if you enter the commands exactly as shown, you will get the histograms for both variables. To change the number of cases generated, change the 100 on the LOOP command to the desired number.

18.42
COUNT Command

```
COUNT varname=varlist(value list) [/varname=...]
```

Numeric value list keywords:
  LOWEST LO HIGHEST HI THRU   MISSING   SYSMIS

The COUNT command is a special data transformation utility used to create a numeric variable that, for each case, counts the occurrences of a value (or list of values) across a list of variables. For example,

```
COUNT READER=NEWSWEEK,TIME,USNEWS(2)
```

creates an index (READER) that indicates the number of times the value 2 (those who read each magazine) is recorded for the three variables for a case. Thus, the value of READER will be either 0, 1, 2, or 3. You can enter more than one variable list and more than one value enclosed in parentheses, as in:

```
COUNT READER=NEWSWEEK,TIME,USNEWS (2)
            NYTIMES,WPOST,CHIGTRIB,LATIMES (3,4)
```

You can use the TO keyword to list your variables and the THRU, LOWEST, and HIGHEST keywords in the value list to indicate ranges of values.

The COUNT command ignores the missing-value status of user-missing values. In other words, the COUNT command counts a value even if that value has been previously declared as missing. The variable created by the COUNT command can never be system-missing. You can use the MISSING keyword to count all missing values and the SYSMIS keyword to count only system-missing values. Specify these keywords in parentheses in the value list.

18.43
DO IF—END IF Structure

```
DO IF [(]logical expression[)]

   transformations

[ELSE IF [(]logical expression[)]]

   transformations

[ELSE IF [(]logical expression[)]]
     .
     .
     .
[ELSE]

   transformations

END IF
```

Use the DO IF—END IF structure to conditionally execute a series of transformation commands on the same subset of cases. The DO IF—END IF structure must begin with the DO IF command and end with the END IF command. The structure can be further defined with the ELSE and ELSE IF commands. The DO IF—END IF structure transforms data on subsets of cases defined by the logical expressions on the DO IF and optional ELSE IF commands, as in:

```
DO IF (X EQ 0)
COMPUTE Y=1
ELSE IF (X LT 9)
COMPUTE Y=9
ELSE
COMPUTE Y=2
END IF
```

This structure sets Y equal to 1 when X equals 0; Y equal to 9 when X is less than 9 but not equal to 0; and Y to 2 for all valid values of X greater than 9.

The ELSE IF command can be repeated as many times as desired within the structure. The ELSE command can be used only once and must follow any ELSE IF commands. Logical expressions are required on the DO IF and ELSE IF commands. Do not use logical expressions on the ELSE and END IF commands.

18.44
Logical Expressions

Logical expressions can be simple logical variables or relations, or they can be complex logical tests involving variables, constants, functions, relational operators, logical operators, and nested parentheses to control the order of evaluation. A logical expression returns 1 if the expression is true, 0 if it is false, or system-missing if it is missing. Logical expressions can appear on the IF, SELECT IF, DO IF, ELSE IF, and COMPUTE commands.

You can use the relational operators listed for the IF command (Section 18.45) in any logical expression on any command where logical expressions are allowed. You can also join two or more relations logically using the logical operators AND and OR, as in:

```
IF (X EQ 0 AND Z LT 2) Y=2
```

This command assigns value 2 to variable Y only for cases with X equal to zero and Z less than two. The AND logical operator means that both expressions must be true. The OR logical operator means that either relation can be true. The NOT logical operator reverses the true/false outcome of the expression that immediately follows. For example,

```
IF NOT(X EQ 0) Y=3
```

assigns value 3 to Y for all cases with values other than 0 for variable X.

When arithmetic operators and functions are used in logical expressions, the order of operations is exactly the same as for the COMPUTE command (see Section 18.39). Functions and arithmetic operations are evaluated first, then relational operators, then NOT, then AND, and then OR. With more than one logical operator, AND is evaluated before OR. You can change the order of evaluation with parentheses.

The functions ANY and RANGE are especially useful in constructing logical expressions to test for a series or range of values for a variable. Use ANY to test for a list of values, and RANGE to test for a range of values. For example,

```
DO IF RANGE(Y,20,50)
COMPUTE X=1
ELSE IF ANY(Y,88,99)
COMPUTE X=2
ELSE
COMPUTE X=0
END IF
```

assigns the value 1 to variable X for all cases with values 20 through 50 inclusive for variable Y; value 2 to variable X for cases with the either the value 88 or 99 for variable Y; and value 0 to variable X for cases with all other values for variable Y.

18.45
IF Command

```
IF [(]logical expression[)] target variable=expression
```

Use the IF command to make COMPUTE-like transformations contingent upon logical conditions found in the data. The IF command is followed by a logical expression (Section 18.44) and an assignment expression, which has the same syntax described in Section 18.38 for the COMPUTE command. For example,

```
COMPUTE Y=0
IF (X EQ 0) Y=1
```

computes a new variable Y equal to 0 and changes the variable Y to the value 1 only for cases with value 0 for variable X. The logical expression is X EQ 0 and the assignment expression is Y=1. The parentheses around the logical expression are optional.

18.46
RECODE Command

For numeric variables:

```
RECODE varlist (value list=value)...(value list=value) [INTO varlist]

        [/varlist...]
```

Input Keywords:
LO, LOWEST, HI, HIGHEST, THRU, MISSING, SYSMIS, ELSE

Output Keywords:
COPY, SYSMIS

For string variables:

```
RECODE varlist [('string',['string'...]='string')][INTO varlist]

        [/varlist...]
```

Input Keywords:
CONVERT, ELSE

Output Keyword:
COPY

Use the RECODE command to change one code for a variable to another as the data are read. The variable or variables to be recoded must already exist and must be specified before the value specifications. Each value specification must be enclosed in parentheses and consists of the input value(s) followed by an equals sign and the output value. For example,

```
RECODE ITEM1 (0=1) (1 THRU 3=2) (8,9=0)
```

changes the original value of 0 for ITEM1 to 1, the original values 1 through 3 inclusive to 2, and the values 8 and 9 to 0.

The RECODE command is evaluated left to right. If SPSS-X encounters the current cases's value in an input value list, that case is recoded and the rest of the recode specifications are ignored. All input values not mentioned in the RECODE command are left unchanged. More than one variable can be recoded on the same command by separating each set of specifications with a slash.

Use the keywords THRU, HIGHEST (HI), and LOWEST (LO) to specify ranges of input values. To recode all values not previously mentioned into a single catchall category, use the keyword ELSE as the input value specification on the last recode specification. For example,

```
RECODE AGE (LO THRU 17=0) (ELSE=1)
```

recodes AGE to a dichotomous (two-valued) variable, with 0 representing those below the U.S. voting age and 1 representing potential voters.

Two special keywords, MISSING and SYSMIS, are available to specify missing values. Keyword MISSING is used only as an input value specification and includes the system-missing value and all missing values defined on the MISSING VALUES command. The output value from a MISSING input specification is not automatically missing; use the MISSING VALUES command to declare the new value missing (see Section 18.14). Keyword SYSMIS is used either as an input or output value specification and includes only the system-missing value.

RECODE changes the values of an existing variable; it does not create a new variable. To create a new variable with the recoded values, use the keyword INTO. For example,

```
RECODE AGE (MISSING=9) (18 THRU HI=1) (0 THRU 18=1) INTO VOTER
```

stores the recoded AGE values in target variable VOTER, leaving AGE unchanged. The target variable can be a new variable or an existing variable. If it is an existing variable, the values remain unchanged for cases with values not mentioned in the recode specifications. A new variable has the system-missing value for cases with values not mentioned in the recode specifications and has the default print and write formats of F8.2 (eight digits with 2 decimal places).

To transfer a set of values into a new variable unchanged, use keyword ELSE with the keyword COPY as the output specification, as in:

```
RECODE ITEM1 TO ITEM3 (0=1) (1=0) (2=-1) (ELSE=COPY)
                      INTO DEFENSE WELFARE HEALTH
```

You can use RECODE to change the values of string variables, as in:

```
RECODE STATE ('IO'='IA')
```

Values for string variables must be enclosed in apostrophes or quotation marks. You cannot change a variable from string to numeric or from numeric to string by recoding it into itself; you must use the keyword INTO to specify a new variable, as in:

```
RECODE SEX ('M'=1) ('F'=2) INTO NSEX
```

Use the keyword CONVERT to recode the string representation of numbers to their numeric representation. The command

```
RECODE AJOB (CONVERT) ('-'=11) ('&'=12) INTO JOB
```

first recodes all numbers in string variable AJOB to numbers for target variable JOB and then specifically recodes the minus sign to 11 and the ampersand to 12.

18.47
SAMPLE Command

```
SAMPLE {percentage}
       {n FROM m  }
```

Use the SAMPLE command to select a random sample of cases. To select an approximate percentage of cases, specify a decimal value between 0 and 1, as in:

```
SAMPLE .25
```

This command samples approximately 25% of the cases in the active file. When you specify a proportional sample, you usually do not get the exact proportion specified. If you know exactly how many cases are in the active file, you can get an exact-sized random sample by specifying the number of cases to be sampled from the size of the active file, as in:

```
SAMPLE 50 FROM 200
```

The SAMPLE command permanently samples the active file unless a TEMPO-RARY command precedes it (see Section 18.51). Thus, if you use two SAMPLE commands, the second takes a sample of the first.

18.48
SELECT IF Command

```
SELECT IF [(]logical expression[)]
```

Use the SELECT IF command to select a subset of cases based on logical criteria. The syntax of the logical expression for the SELECT IF command is the same as described in Section 18.44. If the logical expression is true, the case is selected; if it is false or missing, the case is not selected. For example, the command

```
SELECT IF (VSAT GT 600 OR MSAT GT 600)
```

selects the subset of cases with values greater than 600 on VSAT *or* values greater than 600 on MSAT. The remaining cases are not selected for analysis.

The SELECT IF command permanently selects cases unless preceded by a TEMPORARY command (see Section 18.51). If you use multiple SELECT IF commands in your job, they must all be true for a case to be selected.

18.49
SORT CASES Command

```
SORT CASES [BY] varlist[({A})] [varlist...]
                          {D}
```

Use the SORT CASES command to reorder the sequence of cases in your file. The file is reordered according to the values of the variable or variables specified on the SORT CASES command following the optional keyword BY, as in:

```
SORT CASES BY SEX
```

By default, SPSS-X orders the cases in ascending order: cases with the smallest values for the sort variable or variables are at the front of the file. You can specify the default by following the variable name with (A) or (UP). To sort the cases in descending order—cases with the largest values for the sort variable or variables at the front of the file—specify either (D) or (DOWN) after the variable name, as in:

```
SORT CASES BY SEX (D)
```

You can specify several variables as sort variables. The file is sorted on the first variable mentioned, then within that variable on the next variable, and so forth. You can use string variables as sort keys. The sequence of string variables depends on the character set in use at your installation.

18.50
SPLIT FILE Command

```
SPLIT FILE {BY varlist}
           {OFF      }
```

During the analysis of a data file, you may want to perform separate analyses on subgroups of your data. Use the SPLIT FILE command to split your file into subgroups that you can analyze separately using SPSS-X. The subgroups are sets of adjacent cases on your file that have the same value(s) for the variable or set of variables. If the cases are not grouped together according to the variable or variables, use SORT CASES to sort the file in the proper order (see Section 18.49). Specify the split variable or variables following the keyword BY, as in:

```
SORT CASES BY RACE
SPLIT FILE BY RACE
FREQUENCIES VARIABLES=SALNOW /HISTOGRAM
```

These commands sort the file by the values of the variable RACE and specify split-file processing. The FREQUENCIES command produces a histogram of SALNOW for each value of RACE.

Split-file processing is in effect for the entire SPSS-X job unless you use the TEMPORARY command (see Section 18.51). However, split-file definitions are never saved on a system file. You can also turn off split-file processing by specifying the keyword OFF, as in:

```
SPLIT FILE OFF
```

You can change split-file processing by specifying a new SPLIT FILE command.

18.51
TEMPORARY Command

```
TEMPORARY
```

Use the TEMPORARY command to signal the end of permanent data transformations and the beginning of temporary transformations. Temporary transformations are in effect only through the first procedure after the TEMPORARY command. New variables created after the TEMPORARY command are temporary variables, and any modifications made to existing variables are temporary. All of the transformation commands (RECODE, COMPUTE, IF, COUNT, SELECT IF, SAMPLE, and SPLIT FILE), the DO IF control structure, format declaration commands (FORMATS, PRINT FORMATS, and WRITE FORMATS), labeling commands (VARIABLE LABELS and VALUE LABELS), and the MISSING VALUES command are allowed after the TEMPORARY command.

To make transformations temporary for several procedures, you must respecify the TEMPORARY command for each procedure. Otherwise, transformations between procedures are permanent. Since the SAVE command is a procedure, any transformations following a TEMPORARY command and immediately preceding a SAVE command are saved on the system file.

18.52
WEIGHT Command

```
WEIGHT {BY varname}
       {OFF          }
```

Use the WEIGHT command to differentially weight cases for analysis. For example, you can use WEIGHT to apply weights to a sample that has some substratum over- or undersampled to obtain population estimates. Or you can use WEIGHT to replicate a table or aggregated data as shown in Chapter 5. The WEIGHT command uses the value of a variable to weight the case. Specify the variable name following the keyword BY, as in

```
WEIGHT BY WTFACTOR
```

where the variable WTFACTOR has the appropriate weighting values for each case. The variable may be a weighting factor already coded when the data file was prepared, or you may compute the variable with the transformation language in SPSS-X. SPSS-X does not physically replicate cases. Rather, it arithmetically weights cases when a procedure is executed.

Only one variable can be specified, and the variable must be numeric. Weight values need not be integer. However, negative values or missing values are treated the same as a value of zero. Weighting is in effect for the entire job, and a file saved maintains the weighting unless you use the TEMPORARY command (see Section 18.51). In addition, you can turn off weighting with the keyword OFF, as in:

```
WEIGHT OFF
```

To change the weight, use another WEIGHT command specifying a different variable.

18.53
PROCEDURE
COMMANDS

This section describes in general how to use procedures in SPSS-X. These discussions are abbreviated guides to the procedures presented in this book. They do not discuss all of the features of several of the procedures and do not represent the full range of procedures available in SPSS-X. *SPSS-X User's Guide,* 3rd ed., documents all procedures completely.

A *procedure* is defined as any command that actually reads data. This definition distinguishes a procedure from transformations used to define a file, the PRINT and WRITE utilities used to display a file, and GET used to obtain the dictionary from a saved system file.

Procedures in SPSS-X read data from the *active file.* Although you may be defining or manipulating several files during one job, only one file is active at any given point.

Procedures operate on files defined by commands such as DATA LIST, COMPUTE, RECODE, and GET. In fact, procedures execute transformations. Thus, procedures follow blocks of transformations in a job. For example, the commands

```
DATA LIST   /1 SEX 1 SCORE1 TO SCORE10 10-39 GPA 40-42(1)
MISSING VALUES SCORE1 TO SCORE10 (-1)
COMMENT  TRICHOTOMIZE SCORE VARIABLES FOR CROSSTABS
RECODE  SCORE1 TO SCORE10 (0 THRU 33=1)(34 THRU 67=2)(68 THRU 100=3)
VALUE LABELS SCORE1 TO SCORE10 (1) 'LOWER THIRD' (2) 'MIDDLE THIRD'
            (3) 'UPPER THIRD'
CROSSTABS  SCORE1 TO SCORE10 BY SEX
        /CELLS=TOTAL
        /STATISTICS=CHISQ
BEGIN DATA
data records
END DATA
FINISH
```

define variables SEX, SCORE1 to SCORE10, and GPA; flag -1 as missing for variables SCORE1 to SCORE10; recode the values of variables SCORE1 to SCORE10 to range from 1 to 3; and request crosstabular displays of the recoded variables, SCORE1 to SCORE10, by SEX.

You can interleave blocks of transformations and procedures. For example, you can define a file, run a procedure, transform that file, and run another procedure on the transformed file. You can analyze data from more than one file in a single job, but only one file can be analyzed at a time. In the following example, two files are analyzed using two different procedures for each.

```
GET FILE=AGENTS /KEEP JUNE JULY AUG TYPE
FREQUENCIES  VARIABLES=JUNE JULY AUG TYPE
            /FORMAT=LIMIT(20) /HBAR
MEANS  JUNE JULY AUG BY TYPE
GET FILE=ACCTS /KEEP REGION TYPE SIZE
FREQUENCIES  VARIABLES=SIZE /FORMAT=NOTABLE
            /HISTOGRAM
MEANS  SIZE BY REGION TYPE
FINISH
```

The first GET command makes the file referenced by AGENTS the active file. The first FREQUENCIES and MEANS procedures analyze this file. The second GET command replaces the active file with the file referenced by ACCTS, and the second set of procedures analyzes this file.

If you make a syntax error on a procedure command, usually that procedure is skipped and subsequent procedures are executed. However, since some procedures save variables on the active file, a procedure that analyzes variables you intended to save with an earlier procedure is also in error.

18.54
ANOVA

```
ANOVA [VARIABLES=] varlist BY varlist(min,max)...varlist(min,max)
      WITH varlist

  [/MISSING={EXCLUDE**}]
            {INCLUDE }

  [/FORMAT={LABELS**}]
           {NOLABELS}

  [/MAXORDERS={ALL** }]
              {n    }
              {NONE }

  [/COVARIATES={FIRST**}]
               {WITH  }
               {AFTER }

  [/METHOD={EXPERIMENTAL**}]
           {UNIQUE       }
           {HIERARCHICAL }

  [/STATISTICS=[MCA] [REG†] [MEAN] [ALL] [NONE]]
```

**Default if the subcommand is omitted.
†REG (table of regression coefficients) is displayed only if the design is relevant.

Analysis of variance tests the hypothesis that the group means of the dependent variable are equal. The dependent variable must be interval level, and one or more categorical variables define the groups. These categorical variables are termed *factors*. The ANOVA procedure also allows you to include continuous explanatory variables, termed *covariates*. When there are five or fewer factors, the default model is *full factorial,* meaning that all interaction terms are included. If there are more than five factors, only interaction terms up to order five are included.

The only required subcommand on ANOVA is the VARIABLES subcommand, which specifies the variable list to be analyzed. The actual keyword VARIABLES can be omitted.

18.55
VARIABLES Subcommand

The VARIABLES subcommand names the variable list, and the actual keyword VARIABLES is optional. If you use the VARIABLES keyword, an equals sign must precede the variable list.

The simplest ANOVA command contains one *analysis list* with a *dependent variable list* and a *factor variable list*. In the command

```
ANOVA  VARIABLES=PRESTIGE BY REGION(1,9)
```

PRESTIGE is the dependent variable and REGION is the factor, with minimum and maximum values of 1 and 9.

- Value ranges are not specified for dependent variables.
- The factor variable list follows the keyword BY.
- Every factor variable must have a value range indicating its highest and lowest coded values. The values are separated by a comma and are enclosed in parentheses.
- The factor variables must be integers.

The command

```
ANOVA  VARIABLES=PRESTIGE BY REGION(1,9) SEX(1,2)
```

is a two-way analysis of variance with PRESTIGE as the dependent variable, and REGION and SEX as factors. By default, the model effects are the REGION and SEX main effects and the REGION by SEX interaction.

18.56
Specifying Covariates

The *covariate list* follows the keyword WITH, and you do not specify a value range for the covariates. For example, the command

```
ANOVA VARIABLES=PRESTIGE BY REGION(1,9) SEX(1,2) WITH EDUC
```

names EDUC as the covariate.

18.57
COVARIATES
Subcommand

By default, ANOVA assesses the covariates before it assesses the factor main effects.

The COVARIATES subcommand specifies the order for assessing blocks of covariates and factor main effects. The following keywords can be specified on the COVARIATES subcommand:

FIRST   *Process covariates before main effects for factors.* This is the default if you omit the COVARIATES subcommand.

WITH   *Process covariates concurrently with main effects for factors.*

AFTER   *Process covariates after main effects for factors.*

Note that the order of entry is irrelevant when METHOD=UNIQUE (see Section 18.59).

18.58
MAXORDERS
Subcommand

By default, ANOVA examines all the interaction effects up to and including the fifth order.

The MAXORDERS subcommand suppresses the effects of various orders of interaction. The following keywords can be specified on the MAXORDERS subcommand:

ALL   *Examine all the interaction effects up to and including the fifth order.* This is the default if you omit the MAXORDERS subcommand.

n   *Examine all the interaction effects up to and including the n-order effect.* For example, if you specify MAXORDERS=3, ANOVA examines all the interaction effects up to and including the third order. All higher order interaction sums of squares are pooled into the error term.

NONE   *Delete all interaction terms from the model.* All interaction sums of squares are pooled into the error sum of squares.

The keyword NONE suppresses all interaction terms so only main effects and covariate effects appear in the ANOVA table, with interaction sums of squares pooled into the error (residual) sum of squares. For example, to suppress all interaction effects, specify

```
ANOVA VARIABLES=PRESTIGE BY REGION(1,9) SEX,RACE(1,2)
      /MAXORDERS=NONE
```

18.59
METHOD Subcommand

By default, ANOVA uses what is termed the *classic experimental approach* for decomposing sums of squares. Optionally, you can request the *regression approach* or the *hierarchical approach*.

The METHOD subcommand controls the method for decomposing sums of squares. The following keywords can be specified on the METHOD subcommand:

EXPERIMENTAL   *Classic experimental approach.* This is the default if you omit the METHOD subcommand.

UNIQUE   *Regression approach.* UNIQUE overrides the WITH and AFTER keywords on the COVARIATES subcommand. All effects are assessed for their partial contribution, so order is irrelevant. The MCA and MEAN specifications on the STATISTICS subcommand are not available with the regression approach.

HIERARCHICAL   *Hierarchical approach.*

18.60
STATISTICS Subcommand

By default, ANOVA calculates only the statistics needed for analysis of variance. Optionally, you can request a means and counts table, unstandardized regression coefficients, and multiple classification analysis.

The STATISTICS subcommand requests additional statistics for ANOVA. You can specify the STATISTICS subcommand by itself or with one or more keywords.

If you specify the STATISTICS subcommand with no keywords, ANOVA calculates MEAN and REG (each defined below). If you include a keyword or keywords on the STATISTICS subcommand, ANOVA calculates only the additional statistics you request.

Use keyword MEAN to request means and counts for each dependent variable for groups defined by each factor and each combination of factors up to the fifth level.

Use keyword REG to request unstandardized regression coefficients for covariates. The coefficients are computed at the point where the covariates are entered into the equation. Thus, their values depend on the type of design you have specified.

Use keyword MCA to request multiple classification analysis results. In the MCA table, effects are expressed as deviations from the grand mean. The table includes a listing of unadjusted category effects for each factor, category effects adjusted for other factors, category effects adjusted for all factors and covariates, and eta and beta values.

The following keywords can be specified on the STATISTICS subcommand:

MEAN   *Means and counts table.* This statistic is not available with METHOD= UNIQUE.

REG   *Unstandardized regression coefficients.* Prints unstandardized regression coefficients for the covariates.

MCA   *Multiple classification analysis.* The MCA table is not produced when METHOD=UNIQUE.

ALL   *Means and counts table, unstandardized regression coefficients, and multiple classification analysis.*

NONE   *No additional statistics.* This is the default if you omit the STATISTICS subcommand.

18.61
MISSING Subcommand

By default, a case that is missing for any variable named in the analysis list is deleted for all analyses specified by that list.

Use the MISSING subcommand to ignore missing-data indicators and to include all cases in the computations. Two keywords can be specified on the MISSING subcommand:

EXCLUDE   *Exclude missing data.* This is the default if you omit the MISSING subcommand.

INCLUDE   *Include user-defined missing data.*

18.62
FORMAT Subcommand

By default, ANOVA prints variable or value labels if they have been defined.

Use the FORMAT subcommand to suppress variable and value labels. Two keywords can be specified on the FORMAT subcommand:

LABELS   *Print variable and value labels.* This is the default if you omit the FORMAT subcommand.

NOLABELS   *Suppress variable and value labels.*

18.63
Limitations

The following limitations apply to procedure ANOVA:

- A maximum of 5 ANOVA analysis lists.
- A maximum of 5 dependent variables per analysis list.
- A maximum of 10 independent variables per analysis list.
- A maximum of 10 covariates per analysis list.
- A maximum of 5 interaction levels.
- A maximum of 25 value labels per variable displayed in the MCA table.
- The combined number of categories for all factors in an analysis list plus the number of covariates must be less than the sample size.

18.64
CLUSTER

```
CLUSTER varlist [/MISSING={LISTWISE**}]
                         {INCLUDE   }

[/MEASURE={SEUCLID** }]  [/METHOD={BAVERAGE**}[(rootname)] [,...]]
          {EUCLID    }            {WAVERAGE  }
          {COSINE    }            {SINGLE    }
          {POWER(p,r)}            {COMPLETE  }
          {BLOCK     }            {CENTROID  }
          {CHEBYCHEV }            {MEDIAN    }
          {DEFAULT   }            {WARD      }

[/SAVE=CLUSTER({level  })]  [/ID=varname]
              {min,max}

[/PRINT=[CLUSTER({level  })] [DISTANCE] [SCHEDULE**] [NONE]]
                {min,max}

[/PLOT=[VICICLE**[(min[,max[,inc]])]]] [DENDROGRAM] [NONE]]
       [HICICLE[(min[,max[,inc]])]]]

[/MATRIX=[IN({file}] [OUT({file})]]
            {*   }        {*   }
```

**Default if the subcommand is omitted.

The complete syntax chart for CLUSTER is included here. Discussion of CLUSTER appears in Chapter 16. For a more detailed discussion of CLUSTER, please consult the *SPSS-X User's Guide*, 3rd ed.

18.65
CORRELATIONS

```
CORRELATIONS [VARIABLES=] varlist [WITH varlist] [/varlist...]

[/MISSING={PAIRWISE**}   [INCLUDE]]
          {LISTWISE  }

[/PRINT={ONETAIL**}   {SIG** }]
        {TWOTAIL  }   {NOSIG }

[/FORMAT={MATRIX**}]
         {SERIAL  }

[/MATRIX=OUT({*   })]
            {file}

[/STATISTICS=[DESCRIPTIVES]  [XPROD]  [ALL]]
```

**Default if the subcommand is omitted.

Procedure CORRELATIONS produces Pearson product-moment correlations with significance levels and, optionally, univariate statistics, covariances, and cross-product deviations. The only required subcommand on CORRELATIONS is the VARIABLES subcommand, which specifies the variable list to be analyzed. The actual keyword VARIABLES can be omitted. Optional subcommands may be entered in any order, provided they appear after the variable list.

This abbreviated command reference does not discuss the MATRIX subcommand used to write matrices. This feature is not essential to the operation of CORRELATION as described in this book. However, MATRIX is fully discussed in the *SPSS-X User's Guide,* 3rd ed.

18.66
VARIABLES Subcommand

CORRELATIONS prints either a square (symmetric) or rectangular (asymmetric) matrix, depending on how you specify the variable list. Both forms of the specification permit the use of the keyword TO to reference consecutive variables. If you provide a simple list of variables, CORRELATIONS prints the correlations of each variable with every other variable in the list in a square or lower-triangular matrix. The correlation of a variable with itself is always 1.0000 and can be found on the diagonal of the matrix. Each pair of variables appears twice in the matrix (e.g., FOOD with RENT and RENT with FOOD) with identical coefficients, and the upper and lower triangles of the matrix are mirror images.

To obtain the rectangular matrix, specify two variable lists separated by the keyword WITH. SPSS-X then prints a rectangular matrix of variables in the first list correlated with variables in the second list. For example,

```
CORRELATIONS  MECHANIC BUS WITH PUBTRANS
```

produces two correlations, MECHANIC with PUBTRANS and BUS with PUBTRANS, while

```
CORRELATIONS  FOOD RENT WITH COOK TEACHER MANAGER ENGINEER
```

produces eight correlations. The variables listed before the keyword WITH define the rows of the matrix and those listed after the keyword WITH define the columns. Unless a variable is in both lists, there are no identity coefficients or redundant coefficients in the matrix.

You can request more than one matrix on a CORRELATIONS command. Use a slash (/) to separate the specifications for each of the requested matrices. For example,

```
CORRELATIONS  FOOD RENT WITH COOK TEACHER MANAGER ENGINEER
    /FOOD TO ENGINEER /PUBTRANS WITH MECHANIC
```

produces three separate correlation matrices. The first matrix contains eight nonredundant coefficients, the second matrix is a square matrix of all the variables from FOOD to ENGINEER, and the third matrix consists of one coefficient for PUBTRANS and MECHANIC.

If all cases have a missing value for a given pair of variables or if they all have the same value for a variable, the coefficient cannot be computed. Since Pearson correlations always have a value in the range -1.00 to 1.00, a period is printed if a coefficient cannot be calculated.

18.67
PRINT Subcommand

By default, CORRELATIONS prints Pearson correlation coefficients based on a one-tailed test. Below each coefficient, it prints both the number of cases and the significance level.

The PRINT subcommand switches to a two-tailed test and/or suppresses the display of the number of cases and the significance level. The following keywords can be specified on the PRINT subcommand:

ONETAIL   *One-tailed test of significance.* This test is appropriate when the direction of the relationship between a pair of variables can be specified in advance of the analysis. This is the default.

TWOTAIL   *Two-tailed test of significance.* This test is appropriate when the direction of the relationship cannot be determined in advance, as is often the case in exploratory data analysis.

SIG   *Print the number of cases and significance level.* This is the default for all CORRELATIONS matrices.

NOSIG   *Suppress the printing of the number of cases and significance level.*

If you use the keyword WITH in the variable list, the display will be a rectangular matrix with the number of cases suppressed and asterisks indicating significance levels.

    If you specify both FORMAT=SERIAL and PRINT=NOSIG, only FORMAT=SERIAL will be in effect.

18.68
STATISTICS Subcommand

The correlation coefficient, number of cases, and significance level are automatically printed for every combination of variable pairs in the variable list.

    The STATISTICS subcommand provides the following keywords for obtaining additional statistics:

DESCRIPTIVES   *Mean, standard deviation, and number of nonmissing cases for each variable.* Missing values are handled on a variable-by-variable basis regardless of the missing-value option in effect for the correlations.

XPROD   *Cross-product deviations and covariance for each pair of variables.*

ALL   *All additional statistics available in CORRELATIONS.* Includes the mean, standard deviation, and number of nonmissing cases for each variable. Also includes the cross-product deviations and covariance for each pair of variables.

18.69
MISSING Subcommand

By default, CORRELATIONS deletes cases with missing values on a pair-by-pair basis. A case missing for one or both of the pair of variables for a specific correlation coefficient is not used for that coefficient. Since each coefficient is based on all cases that have valid codes on that particular pair of variables, the maximum information available is used in every calculation. This can also result in a set of coefficients based on a varying number of cases.

    The MISSING subcommand controls missing values. The following keywords can be specified on the MISSING subcommand:

PAIRWISE   *Exclude missing values pairwise.* Cases missing for one or both of a pair of variables for a specific correlation coefficient are excluded from the analysis. This is the default.

LISTWISE   *Exclude missing values listwise.* Each variable listed on a command is evaluated separately. Cases missing on any variable named in a list are excluded from all analyses.

INCLUDE   *Include user-defined missing values.* User-missing values are included in the analysis.

The PAIRWISE and LISTWISE keywords are mutually exclusive; however, each can be specified with INCLUDE.

18.70
FORMAT Subcommand

By default, CORRELATIONS includes redundant coefficients in the correlation and prints in matrix format. The FORMAT subcommand has two keywords that control matrix format:

MATRIX   *Print in matrix format with redundant coefficients.* This is the default.

SERIAL   *Print in serial string format with nonredundant coefficients.*

18.71
Limitations   The following limitations apply to CORRELATIONS:

- A maximum of 40 variable lists.
- A maximum of 500 variables total per CORRELATIONS command.
- A maximum of 250 individual elements. Each unique occurrence of a variable name, keyword, or special delimiter counts as 1 toward this total. Variables implied by the TO keyword do not count toward this total.

18.72
CROSTABS   *General mode:*

```
CROSSTABS [TABLES=]varlist BY varlist [BY...] [/varlist...]

[/MISSING={TABLE** }]
          {INCLUDE}

[/FORMAT={LABELS**  }   {AVALUE**}   {NOINDEX**}   {TABLES**}]
         {NOLABELS  }   {DVALUE  }   {INDEX    }   {NOTABLES}
         {NOVALLABS}

[/CELLS={COUNT**}  [ROW    ]  [EXPECTED]  [SRESID  ]]
        {NONE   }  [COLUMN ]  [RESID   ]  [ASRESID ]
                   [TOTAL  ]              [ALL     ]

[/WRITE[={NONE** }]]
         {CELLS  }

[/STATISTICS=[CHISQ]  [LAMBDA]  [BTAU]  [GAMMA]  [ETA ]]
             [PHI  ]  [UC    ]  [CTAU]  [D    ]  [CORR]
             [CC   ]  [NONE  ]                   [ALL ]
```

Integer mode:

```
CROSSTABS VARIABLES=varlist(min,max) [varlist...]

/TABLES=varlist BY varlist [BY...] [/varlist...]

[/MISSING={TABLE** }]
          {INCLUDE}
          {REPORT }

[/FORMAT={LABELS**  }   {AVALUE**}   {NOINDEX**}   {TABLES**}]
         {NOLABELS  }   {DVALUE  }   {INDEX    }   {NOTABLES}
         {NOVALLABS}

[/CELLS={COUNT**}  [ROW    ]  [EXPECTED]  [SRESID  ]]
        {NONE   }  [COLUMN ]  [RESID   ]  [ASRESID ]
                   [TOTAL  ]              [ALL     ]

[/WRITE[={NONE** }]]
         {CELLS  }
         {ALL    }

[/STATISTICS=[CHISQ]  [LAMBDA]  [BTAU]  [GAMMA]  [ETA ]]
             [PHI  ]  [UC    ]  [CTAU]  [D    ]  [CORR]
             [CC   ]  [NONE  ]                   [ALL ]
```

**Default if the subcommand is omitted.

Procedure CROSSTABS produces tables that are the joint distribution of two or more variables that have a limited number of distinct values. The frequency distribution of one variable is subdivided according to the values of one or more variables. The unique combination of values for two variables defines a cell, the basic element of all tables. CROSSTABS can operate in either general or integer mode, similar to FREQUENCIES (Section 18.91) and MEANS (Section 18.114).

This abbreviated command reference does not discuss the WRITE subcommand used to write tables to a procedure output file. This feature is not essential to the operation of CROSSTABS as described in this book. However, WRITE is fully discussed in *SPSS-X User's Guide*, 3rd ed.

Methods for Building Tables. CROSSTABS operates in two different modes: *general and integer. General mode* operates via the TABLES subcommand and requires fewer specifications. (See Section 18.74.) *Integer mode* operates via the TABLES and VARIABLES subcommands and requires that you specify the minimum and maximum values for the variables. This mode builds tables more efficiently. (See Section 18.75.)

18.73
TABLES Subcommand

Use the TABLES subcommand in both general and integer modes. Syntax for TABLES in both is identical.

There is one important difference between the tables request in integer mode and the tables request in general mode. In integer mode, the order of the variables implied on the TABLES subcommand is established by the order of the variables named or implied on the VARIABLES subcommand. In general mode, the order of variables implied on the tables lists is established by their order in the active file.

18.74
General Mode

To run CROSSTABS in general mode, use the TABLES subcommand followed by a list of one or more variables, the keyword BY, and another list of one or more variables. In general mode, you can specify the TABLES subcommand once, only. The actual command keyword TABLES is not required to operate CROSSTABS in general mode.

You can specify a list of one or more variables for each dimension. Separate each list with the keyword BY. The first variable list is the list of *row variables* and the variable list following the first BY keyword is the list of *column variables*. Subsequent variable lists following BY keywords specify orders of *control variables*. For example,

```
CROSSTABS  TABLES=FEAR BY SEX BY RACE
```

crosstabulates FEAR by SEX, controlling for RACE. In each subtable, FEAR is the row variable and SEX is the column variable. The first subtable crosstabulates FEAR by SEX within the first category of RACE. The second subtable also crosstabulates FEAR by SEX, but for the next category of RACE. When you use control variables, a subtable is produced for each value of the control variable. The value of the first control variable changes most quickly and the value of the last control variable changes most slowly.

You can specify more than one variable in each dimension. Use the keyword TO to name a set of adjacent variables in the active file, as in:

```
CROSSTABS  TABLES=CONFINAN TO CONARMY BY SEX TO REGION
```

This command will produce CROSSTABS tables for all the variables between and including CONFINAN and CONARMY by all the variables between and including SEX and REGION. You can use similar variables lists to request higher order CROSSTABS tables. The values of the variables to the right of the last BY keyword change most slowly. Within lists separated by the keyword BY, variables rotate from left to right. For example,

```
CROSSTABS  TABLES=CONFINAN TO CONARMY BY SEX BY RACE,REGION
```

will produce CROSSTABS tables for all the variables between and including CONFINAN and CONARMY by SEX, controlling for RACE, and for all the variables between and including CONFINAN and CONARMY, controlling for

REGION. If there are five variables implied by the first variables list, the command produces 10 crosstabulations. The first table is CONFINAN by SEX by RACE and the second table is CONFINAN by SEX by REGION. The last table produced is CONARMY by SEX by REGION. The number of values encountered for the control variables determines the total number of subtables. If RACE has two values and REGION has three values, the output from the command will have a total of 25 subtables.

Use a slash to separate tables lists on one CROSSTABS command. For example,

```
CROSSTABS  TABLES=FEAR BY SEX/RACE BY REGION
```

specifies two bivariate tables, FEAR by SEX and RACE by REGION. If you omit a slash between tables lists, CROSSTABS includes the variables as if one tables list had been supplied.

18.75
Integer Mode

To run CROSSTABS in integer mode, the values of all the variables must be integers. Two subcommands are required. The VARIABLES subcommand (see Section 18.76) specifies all the variables to be used in the CROSSTABS procedure and the minimum and maximum values for building tables. The TABLES subcommand specifies the tables lists. In integer mode, you can use multiple VARIABLES and TABLES subcommands, provided a variable referenced on a TABLES subcommand has been defined on a previous VARIABLES subcommand.

Integer mode can produce more tables in a given amount of core storage space than general mode, and the processing is faster. The values supplied as variable ranges do not have to be as wide as the range of the variables; thus, you have control from within CROSSTABS over the tabulated ranges of the variables. Some subcommand and keyword specifications are available only in integer mode.

18.76
VARIABLES Subcommand

The VARIABLES subcommand specifies the variables to be used in the crosstabulations. Specify the lowest and highest values in parentheses after each variable. These values must be integers. For example, the command

```
CROSSTABS  VARIABLES=FEAR (1,2) MOBILE16 (1,3)
   /TABLES=FEAR BY MOBILE16
```

produces a table where FEAR has a range from 1 to 2 and MOBILE16 has a range from 1 to 3. Noninteger values are truncated. Cases with values that fall outside the range you specify are not used.

Several variables can have the same range. For example,

```
CROSSTABS  VARIABLES=FEAR SEX RACE (1,2) MOBILE16 (1,3)
   /TABLES=FEAR BY SEX MOBILE16 BY RACE
```

defines 1 as the lowest value and 2 as the highest value for FEAR, SEX, and RACE. Variables may appear in any order. However, the order in which you place them on the VARIABLES subcommand affects their implied order on the TABLES subcommand as described in Section 18.73.

18.77
CELLS Subcommand

By default, CROSSTABS prints only the number of cases in each cell. The CELLS subcommand prints row, column, or total percentages, and also expected values and residuals. These items are calculated separately for each bivariate table or subtable.

You can specify the CELLS subcommand by itself, or with a keyword or keywords. If you specify the CELLS subcommand by itself, CROSSTABS prints cell counts plus ROW, COLUMN, and TOTAL percentages for each cell. If you specify a keyword or keywords, CROSSTABS prints only the cell information you request.

The following keywords can be specified on the CELLS subcommand:

COUNT | *Print cell counts.* This is the default if you omit the CELLS subcommand.
ROW | *Print row percentages.* Print the number of cases in each cell in a row expressed as a percentage of all cases in that row.
COLUMN | *Print column percentages.* Print the number of cases in each cell in a column expressed as a percentage of all cases in that column.
TOTAL | *Print two-way table total percentages.* Print the number of cases in each cell of a subtable expressed as a percentage of all cases in that subtable.
EXPECTED | *Print expected frequencies.* Print the number of cases expected in each cell if the two variables in the subtable were statistically independent.
RESID | *Print residuals.* Print the value of the observed cell count minus the expected value.
SRESID | *Print standardized residuals.* (Haberman, 1978).
ASRESID | *Print adjusted standardized residuals.* (Haberman, 1978).
ALL | *Print all cell information.* Print cell count; row, column, and total percentages; expected values; residuals; standardized residuals; and adjusted standardized residuals.
NONE | *Print no cell information.* Use NONE to write the tables to a procedure file without printed tables. This has the same effect as specifying FORMAT=NOTABLES.

18.78
STATISTICS Subcommand

CROSSTABS can calculate a number of summary statistics for each subtable. Unless you specify otherwise, it calculates statistical measures of association for the cases with valid values included in the subtable. If you specify a range in integer mode that excludes cases, the excluded cases are *not* used in the calculation of the statistics. If you include user-missing values with the MISSING subcommand, cases with user-defined missing values are included in the tables as well as in the calculation of statistics.

The STATISTICS subcommand requests summary statistics. You can specify the STATISTICS subcommand by itself, or with one or more keywords. If you specify STATISTICS by itself, CROSSTABS calculates CHISQ. If you include a keyword or keywords on the STATISTICS subcommand, CROSSTABS calculates all the statistics you request.

The following keywords can be specified on the STATISTICS subcommand:

CHISQ | *Chi-square.* Fisher's exact test is computed using the rounded values of the cell entries when there are fewer than 20 cases in a 2 × 2 table that does not result from missing rows or columns in a larger table; Yates' corrected chi-square is computed for all other 2 × 2 tables. This is the default if you specify the STATISTICS subcommand by itself, with no keywords.
PHI | *Phi for 2 × 2 tables, Cramer's V for larger tables.*
CC | *Contingency coefficient.*
LAMBDA | *Lambda, symmetric and asymmetric.*
UC | *Uncertainty coefficient, symmetric and asymmetric.*
BTAU | *Kendall's tau-b.*
CTAU | *Kendall's tau-c.*
GAMMA | *Gamma.* Partial and zero-order gammas for 3-way to 8-way tables are available in integer mode only. Zero-order gammas are printed for 2-way tables and conditional gammas are printed for 3-way to 10-way tables in general mode.
D | *Somers' d, symmetric and asymmetric.*
ETA | *Eta.* Available for numeric data only.
CORR | *Pearson's r.* Available for numeric data only.
ALL | *All the statistics available for CROSSTABS.*
NONE | *No summary statistics.* This is the default if you omit the STATISTICS subcommand.

18.79
MISSING Subcommand

By default, CROSSTABS deletes cases with missing values on a table-by-table basis. A case missing on any of the variables specified for a table is not used either in the printed table or in the calculation of the statistics. When you separate tables requests with a slash, missing values are handled separately for each list. The number of missing cases is always printed at the end of the table, following the last subtable and after any requested statistics.

The MISSING subcommand controls missing values. The following keywords can be specified on the MISSING subcommand:

TABLE   *Delete cases with missing values on a table-by-table basis.* This is the default if you omit the MISSING subcommand.

INCLUDE   *Include user-defined missing values.*

REPORT   *Report missing values in the tables.* This option includes missing values in tables but not in the calculation of percentages or statistics. It is available only in integer mode.

If the missing values are not included in the range specifications on the VARIABLES subcommand, they are excluded from the table regardless of the keyword you specify on MISSING.

18.80
FORMAT Subcommand

By default, CROSSTABS prints tables and subtables with variable labels and value labels when they are available. The values for the row variables print in order from lowest to highest. CROSSTABS uses only the first 16 characters of the value labels. Value labels for the columns print on two lines with eight characters per line.

The FORMAT subcommand modifies the default tables and subtables. The following keywords can be specified on the FORMAT subcommand:

LABELS   *Print both variable and value labels for each table.* This is the default.

NOLABELS   *Suppress variable and value labels.*

NOVALLABS   *Suppress value labels, print variable labels.*

AVALUE   *Print row variables ordered from lowest to highest.* This is the default.

DVALUE   *Print row variables ordered from highest to lowest.*

NOINDEX   *Suppress a table index.* This is the default.

INDEX   *Prints an index of tables.* The index lists all tables produced by the CROSSTABS command and the page number where each table begins. The index follows the last page of tables produced by the tables list.

TABLES   *Print the crosstabs tables.* This is the default.

NOTABLES   *Suppress printed tables.* If you use the STATISTICS subcommand (see Section 18.78) and specify NOTABLES, only the statistics are printed. If you do not use the STATISTICS subcommand and specify NOTABLES, the CROSSTABS command produces no output.

18.81
Limitations

The following limitations apply to CROSSTABS in *general mode*:

• A maximum of 200 variables total per CROSSTABS command.
• A maximum of 250 nonempty rows or columns printed for each variable.
• A maximum of 20 tables lists per CROSSTABS command.
• A maximum of 10 dimensions per table.
• A maximum of 250 value labels printed on any single table.

The following limitations apply to CROSSTABS in *integer mode*:

- A maximum of 100 variables named or implied with the VARIABLES subcommand.
- A maximum of 100 variables named or implied with the TABLES subcommand.
- A maximum of 200 nonempty rows or columns printed for each variable.
- A maximum of 200 rows per subtable.
- A maximum of 200 columns per table.
- A maximum of 20 tables lists per CROSSTABS command.
- A maximum of 8 dimensions per table.
- No more than 20 rows or columns of missing values can be printed with MISSING= REPORT.
- The largest range that can be implied on the minimum-maximum range specification on the VARIABLES subcommand is 32,766.

18.82
DESCRIPTIVES

```
DESCRIPTIVES [VARIABLES=] varname[(zname)] [varname...]

[/MISSING={VARIABLE**}   [INCLUDE]]
          {LISTWISE  }

[/FORMAT={LABELS**  }  {NOINDEX**}  {LINE**}]
         {NOLABELS }  {INDEX    }  {SERIAL}

[/SAVE]

[/STATISTICS=[DEFAULT**]  [MEAN**]  [MIN**]  [SKEWNESS]]
             [STDDEV** ]  [SEMEAN]  [MAX**]  [KURTOSIS]
             [VARIANCE ]  [SUM   ]  [RANGE]  [ALL]
```

**Default if the subcommand is omitted.

Procedure DESCRIPTIVES (alias CONDESCRIPTIVE) computes univariate summary statistics and standardized variables that are saved on the active file. Although it computes statistics also available in procedure FREQUENCIES (see Section 18.91), DESCRIPTIVES computes descriptive statistics for continuous variables more efficiently because it does not sort values into a frequencies table.

DESCRIPTIVES calculates the mean, standard deviation, minimum, and maximum for *numeric* variables, only. You can request optional statistics and Z-score transformations.

The only required subcommand on DESCRIPTIVES is the VARIABLES subcommand, which specifies the variable list to be analyzed. The actual keyword VARIABLES can be omitted.

18.83
VARIABLES Subcommand

The variables subcommand names the variable list. The actual keyword VARIABLES is optional. If you explicitly specify keyword VARIABLES, an equals sign must precede the variable list. You can use keyword TO in the list to refer to consecutive variables in the active file. The variables must be numeric.

To request the default summary statistics, specify the VARIABLES subcommand and a simple list of variables, as in:

```
DESCRIPTIVES VARIABLES=NTCPRI FOOD RENT
```

You can also use the keyword ALL to specify all variables in the active file.

You can specify only one variable list with DESCRIPTIVES, but there is no limit to the number of variables named or implied on one command. Variables named more than once will appear in the output more than once. If there is insufficient space to process all the requested variables, DESCRIPTIVES truncates the variable list.

18.84
Z Scores

The Z-score variable transformation standardizes variables with different observed scales to the same scale. DESCRIPTIVES generates new variables, each with a mean of 0 and a standard deviation of 1, and stores them on the active file.

18.85
SAVE Subcommand

Use the SAVE subcommand to obtain one Z-score variable for each variable specified on the DESCRIPTIVES variable list. The SAVE subcommand calculates standardized variables and stores them on the active file. The commands

```
DESCRIPTIVES VARIABLES=ALL
   /SAVE
```

produce a table of old variables and new Z-score variables.

DESCRIPTIVES automatically supplies variable names and labels for the new variables. The new variable name is created by prefixing the letter Z to a maximum of seven characters of the variable name. For example, ZNTCPRI is the Z-score variable for NTCPRI. When DESCRIPTIVES creates new Z-score variables, it prints a table containing the source variable name, new variable name, its label, and the number of cases for which it is computed.

If you want Z scores for a subset of the variables listed on DESCRIPTIVES, specify the name of the new variable in parentheses following the source variable on the VARIABLES subcommand, and *do not use the SAVE subcommand.* For example,

```
DESCRIPTIVES VARIABLES=NTCSAL NTCPUR (PURCHZ) NTCPRI (PRICEZ)
```

creates Z-score variables for NTCPUR and NTCPRI.

If you specify new names on the VARIABLES subcommand *and* use the SAVE subcommand, DESCRIPTIVES creates one new variable for each variable on the VARIABLES subcommand, using the default names for variables not explicitly assigned names. For example,

```
DESCRIPTIVES VARIABLES=NTCSAL NTCPUR (PURCHZ) NTCPRI (PRICEZ)
   /SAVE
```

creates PURCHZ and PRICEZ and assigns a default name to the Z-score variable for NTCSAL. When you specify the name of the new variable yourself, you can use any acceptable eight-character variable name, including any of the default variable names, that is not already part of the active file.

If DESCRIPTIVES cannot use the default naming convention because it would produce duplicate names, it uses an alternative naming convention.

DESCRIPTIVES automatically supplies variable labels for the new variables by prefixing *ZSCORE:* to the first 31 characters of the source variable's label. If it uses a name like ZSC001, it prefixes *ZSCORE(varname)* to the first 31 characters of the source variable's label. If the source variable has no label, it uses *ZSCORE(varname)* for the label.

18.86
STATISTICS Subcommand

By default, DESCRIPTIVES prints the mean, standard deviation, minimum, and maximum. If you use the STATISTICS subcommand and any of its keywords, you can specify alternative statistics. When you specify statistics, DESCRIPTIVES prints *only* those statistics you request.

You can use the keyword ALL to obtain all statistics. When requesting the default statistics plus additional statistics, you can specify DEFAULT to obtain the default statistics without having to name MEAN, STDDEV, MIN and MAX.

The following keywords can be specified on the STATISTICS subcommand:

MEAN	*Mean.*
SEMEAN	*Standard error of the mean.*
STDDEV	*Standard deviation.*
VARIANCE	*Variance.*
KURTOSIS	*Kurtosis.* Also prints standard error.
SKEWNESS	*Skewness.* Also prints standard error.
RANGE	*Range.*
MIN	*Minimum.*
MAX	*Maximum.*
SUM	*Sum.*
DEFAULT	*Mean, standard deviation, minimum, and maximum.* These are the default statistics if you omit the STATISTICS subcommand.
ALL	*All the statistics available to DESCRIPTIVES.*

18.87
MISSING Subcommand

By default, DESCRIPTIVES deletes cases with missing values on a variable-by-variable basis. A case missing on a variable will not be included in the summary statistics for that variable, but the case *will* be included for variables where it is not missing.

The MISSING subcommand controls missing values, and three keywords can be specified on it:

VARIABLE	*Exclude missing values on a variable-by-variable basis.* This is the default if you omit the MISSING subcommand.
LISTWISE	*Exclude missing values listwise.* Cases missing on any variable named are excluded from the computation of summary statistics for all variables.
INCLUDE	*Include user-defined missing values.*

The VARIABLE and LISTWISE keywords are mutually exclusive; however, each can be specified with INCLUDE. For example, to include user-missing values in an analysis that excludes missing values listwise, specify

```
DESCRIPTIVES VARIABLES=ALL
  /MISSING=INCLUDE LISTWISE
```

When you use the keyword VARIABLE or the default missing-value treatment, DESCRIPTIVES reports the number of valid cases for each variable. It always displays the number of cases that would be available if listwise deletion of missing values had been selected.

18.88
FORMAT Subcommand

The FORMAT subcommand controls the formatting options available in DESCRIPTIVES, and the following keywords can be specified on it:

LABELS	*Print variable labels.* This is the default if you omit the FORMAT subcommand.
NOLABELS	*Suppress variable labels.*
INDEX	*Print reference indexes.* INDEX prints a positional and an alphabetic reference index following the statistical display. The index shows the page location in the output of the statistics for each variable. The variables are listed by their position in the active file and alphabetically.
NOINDEX	*Suppress reference indexes.* This is the default if you omit the FORMAT subcommand,
LINE	*Print statistics in line format.* LINE prints statistics on the same line as the variable name. It is the default if you omit the FORMAT subcommand.
SERIAL	*Print statistics in serial format.* SERIAL prints statistics below the variable name, permitting larger field widths and more decimal digits for very large or very small numbers. DESCRIPTIVES automatically forces this format if the number of statistics requested does not fit in the column format.

18.89
DISCRIMINANT

```
DISCRIMINANT GROUPS=varname(min,max) /VARIABLES=varlist

[/SELECT=varname(value)]

[/ANALYSIS=varlist(level) [varlist...]]

[/METHOD={DIRECT**}] [/TOLERANCE={0.001}]
          {WILKS     }              {t    }
          {MAHAL     }
          {MAXMINF   }
          {MINRESID  }
          {RAO       }

[/MAXSTEPS={2v}]
           {m }

[/FIN={1.0}] [/FOUT={1.0}] [/PIN={1.0**}]
      {fi }       {fo }          {pi  }

[/POUT={1.0**}] [/VIN={0**}]
       {po  }         {vi }

[/FUNCTIONS={g-1,100.0,1.0**}] [/PRIORS={EQUAL      }]
            {nf , cp ,sig }            {SIZE       }
                                       {value list}

[/SAVE=[CLASS=varname] [PROBS=rootname]

       [SCORES=rootname]]

[/ANALYSIS=...]

[/MISSING={EXCLUDE**}]
          {INCLUDE  }

[/MATRIX=[OUT({*   })] [IN({*   })]]
              {file}        {file}

[/HISTORY={STEP**}  {END**  }]
          {NOSTEP}  {NOEND  }

[/ROTATE={NONE**   }]
         {COEFF    }
         {STRUCTURE}

[/CLASSIFY={NONMISSING  }  {POOLED  }  [MEANSUB]]
           {UNSELECTED  }  {SEPARATE}
           {UNCLASSIFIED}

[/STATISTICS=[MEAN  ]  [COV ]  [FPAIR]  [RAW ]   [ALL]]
             [STDDEV]  [GCOV]  [UNIVF]  [COEFF]
             [CORR  ]  [TCOV]  [BOXM ]  [TABLE]

[/PLOT=[MAP] [SEPARATE] [COMBINED] [CASES] [ALL]]
```

**Default if the subcommand is omitted.

The complete syntax chart for DISCRIMINANT is included here. Discussion of DISCRIMINANT appears in Chapter 14. For a more detailed discussion of DISCRIMINANT, please consult the *SPSS-X User's Guide*, 3rd ed.

18.90
FACTOR

```
FACTOR VARIABLES=varlist† [/MISSING=[{LISTWISE**}] [INCLUDE]]
                                     {PAIRWISE }
                                     {MEANSUB  }
                                     {DEFAULT  }

    [/WIDTH={132}]
            {n  }

    [/MATRIX=[IN({COR=file})] [OUT({COR=file})]]
                 {COR=*    }      {COR=*    }
                 {FAC=file }      {FAC=file }
                 {FAC=*    }      {FAC=*    }

    [/ANALYSIS=varlist...]

    [/PRINT=[DEFAULT**] [INITIAL**] [EXTRACTION**] [ROTATION**]
            [UNIVARIATE**] [CORRELATION] [DET] [INV] [REPR] [AIC] [KMO]
            [FSCORE] [SIG] [ALL]]

    [/PLOT=[EIGEN] [ROTATION (nl,n2)]]

    [/DIAGONAL=value list]

    [/FORMAT=[SORT] [BLANK(n)] [DEFAULT**]]

    [/CRITERIA=[FACTORS(n)] [MINEIGEN({1.0**})] [ITERATE({25**})]
                                      {eig }             {ni }

               [RCONVERGE({0.0001**})] [DELTA({0**})] [{KAISER**}]
                          {rl       }         {d  }    {NOKAISER}

               [ECONVERGE({0.001**})]]
                          {el      }

    [/EXTRACTION={PC**   }] [/ROTATION={VARIMAX** }]
                 {PAF    }             {EQUAMAX  }
                 {ALPHA  }             {QUARTIMAX}
                 {IMAGE  }             {OBLIMIN  }
                 {ULS    }             {NOROTATE }
                 {GLS    }             {DEFAULT  }
                 {ML     }
                 {PA1    }
                 {PA2    }
                 {DEFAULT}

    [/SAVE=[{REG    } ({ALL} rootname)]]
            {BART   }  {n  }
            {AR     }
            {DEFAULT}

    [/ANALYSIS...]

    [/CRITERIA...]      [/EXTRACTION...]

    [/ROTATION...]      [/SAVE...]
```

**Default if the subcommand is omitted.
† Omit VARIABLES with matrix output.

The complete syntax chart for FACTOR is included here. Discussion of FACTOR appears in Chapter 15. For a more detailed discussion of FACTOR, please consult the *SPSS-X User's Guide*, 3rd ed.

18.91
FREQUENCIES

```
FREQUENCIES VARIABLES=varlist[(min,max)] [varlist...]

[/FORMAT=[{CONDENSE}] [{NOTABLE }] [NOLABELS] [WRITE]
          {ONEPAGE }   {LIMIT(n)}

         [{DVALUE}] [DOUBLE] [NEWPAGE] [INDEX]]
          {AFREQ }
          {DFREQ }

[/MISSING=INCLUDE]

[/BARCHART=[MINIMUM(n)] [MAXIMUM(n)] [{FREQ(n)   }]]
                                     {PERCENT(n)}

[/HISTOGRAM=[MINIMUM(n)] [MAXIMUM(n)] [{FREQ(n)   }]
                                      {PERCENT(n)}

           [{NONORMAL}] [INCREMENT(n)]]
            {NORMAL  }

[/HBAR=same as HISTOGRAM]

[/NTILES=n]

[/PERCENTILES=value list]

[/STATISTICS=[DEFAULT] [MEAN] [STDDEV] [MINIMUM] [MAXIMUM]
             [SEMEAN] [VARIANCE] [SKEWNESS] [SESKEW] [RANGE] [MODE]
             [KURTOSIS] [SEKURT] [MEDIAN] [SUM] [ALL] [NONE]]
```

Procedure FREQUENCIES produces a table of frequency counts and percentages for the values of individual variables. Optionally, you can obtain bar charts for discrete variables, histograms for continuous variables, univariate summary statistics, and percentiles. To produce only statistics on interval-level data, see procedure DESCRIPTIVES (Section 18.82).

The only required subcommand on FREQUENCIES is the VARIABLES subcommand, which specifies the variables to be analyzed. Subcommands can be named in any order and are separated from each other by a slash. With the exception of PERCENTILES and NTILES, each subcommand can be used only once per FREQUENCIES command.

18.92
VARIABLES Subcommand

The VARIABLES subcommand names the variables to be analyzed in either *integer* or *general* mode. In integer mode, you specify the dimensions of the table and FREQUENCIES sorts cases into the elements of the table. In general mode, FREQUENCIES dynamically builds the table, setting up one cell for each unique value encountered in the data. You cannot mix integer and general modes on the VARIABLES subcommand.

For general mode, simply list the variable names on the VARIABLES subcommand, as in:

`FREQUENCIES  VARIABLES=POLVIEWS RES16`

The variable and value labels are printed, if available, followed by the value and the number of cases that have the value. The percentage is based on all the observations, and the valid and cumulative percentages are based on those cases that have valid values. The number of valid and missing observations is also provided. General mode tabulates any type of variable, including numeric variables with decimal positions and string variables.

You can use the keyword ALL to name all the variables on the file or the keyword TO to reference a set of consecutive variables on the active file.

For integer mode, specify in parentheses the value range for each variable following the variable name, as in:

```
FREQUENCIES  VARIABLES=POLVIEWS(0,9) RES16(1,6)
```

You must specify a value range for every variable listed. If several variables have the same range, you can specify the range once at the end of the variable list, as in:

```
FREQUENCIES  VARIABLES=SEX(1,2) TVHOURS(0,24) SCALE1 TO SCALE5(1,7)
```

Only observations with values within the range are included in the frequency table. Integer mode truncates values with decimal positions when tabulating. For example, 2.46 and 2.73 are both counted as value 2. Values outside the range are grouped into an out-of-range category and are considered missing. If the variables being tabulated are sparsely distributed within the specified range (that is, there are many empty categories), use the general mode or recode the values to consecutive values with the RECODE command (see Section 18.46).

18.93
General vs. Integer Mode

All optional specifications are available with either integer or general mode. However, you should consider the following points when choosing between the two modes.

- Integer mode usually takes less computation time. However, it is impossible to predict savings on time since the amount of time required for general mode depends upon the range of values and the order in which they are read.
- Integer mode requires less memory than does general mode, except when variables are sparsely distributed.
- In integer mode, you can use the value range specification to eliminate extremely low or high values.
- Since integer mode truncates decimal positions, you can obtain grouped frequency tables for continuous variables without having to recode them to integers. On the other hand, general mode tabulates short strings and does not truncate nonintegers.

18.94
FORMAT Subcommand

The FORMAT subcommand applies to all variables named on the VARIABLES subcommand. You can control the formatting of tables and the order in which values are sorted within the table, suppress tables, produce an index of tables, and write the FREQUENCIES display to another file via keywords on the FORMAT subcommand.

Specify as many formatting options as desired on the FORMAT subcommand. For example,

```
FREQUENCIES  VARIABLES=POLVIEWS PRESTIGE
             /FORMAT=ONEPAGE DVALUE
```

specifies conditional condensed formatting of the tables (keyword ONEPAGE) with values sorted in descending order (keyword DVALUE).

18.95
Table Formats

The following keywords on the FORMAT subcommand control the formatting of tables:

NOLABELS *Do not print variable or value labels.* By default, FREQUENCIES prints variable and value labels defined by the VARIABLE LABELS and VALUE LABELS commands.

DOUBLE *Double-space frequency tables.*

NEWPAGE *Begin each table on a new page.* By default, FREQUENCIES prints as many tables on a page as fit.

CONDENSE *Condensed format.* This format prints frequency counts in three columns. It does not print value labels and percentages for all cases, and it rounds valid and cumulative percentages to integers.

ONEPAGE *Conditional condensed format.* Keyword ONEPAGE uses the condensed format for tables that would require more than one page with the default format. All other tables are printed in default format. If you specify both CONDENSE and ONEPAGE, all tables are printed in condensed format.

18.96
Order of Values

By default, frequency tables are printed in ascending order of values. You can override this order with one of three sorting options on the FORMAT subcommand.

AFREQ *Sort categories in ascending order of frequency.*

DFREQ *Sort categories in descending order of frequency.*

DVALUE *Sort categories in descending order of values.*

18.97
Suppressing Tables

You might be using FREQUENCIES to obtain univariate statistics not available in other procedures, or to print histograms or bar charts, and thus may not be interested in the frequency tables themselves. Or you might want to suppress tables for variables with a large number of values. Two options are available for suppressing tables.

LIMIT(n) *Do not print tables with more categories than the specified value.*

NOTABLE *Suppress all frequency tables.*

If you specify both NOTABLE and LIMIT, NOTABLE overrides LIMIT and no tables are printed.

18.98
Index of Tables

To obtain both a positional index of frequency tables and an index arranged alphabetically by variable name, use the INDEX keyword on the FORMAT subcommand.

INDEX *Index of tables.*

18.99
Bar Charts and Histograms

You can request both bar charts and histograms on one FREQUENCIES command. Use the BARCHART subcommand to produce bar charts for all variables named on the VARIABLES subcommand and the HISTOGRAM subcommand to produce histograms for all variables. Or use the HBAR subcommand to produce bar charts for variables that fit on one page (11 individual categories for the default page length) and histograms for other variables. You can specify only one of these three subcommands on each FREQUENCIES command. If you specify more than one, FREQUENCIES assumes HBAR.

18.100
BARCHART Subcommand

No specifications are required for the BARCHART subcommand. In the default bar chart format, all tabulated values are plotted, and the horizontal axis is scaled in frequencies. The scale is determined by the frequency count of the largest single category plotted. You can specify minimum and maximum bounds for plotting and can request a horizontal scale labeled with percentages or frequencies.

MIN(n) *Lower bound.* Values below the specified minimum are not plotted.

MAX(n) *Upper bound.* Values above the specified maximum are not plotted.

PERCENT(n) *Horizontal axis scaled in percentages.* The *n* specifies the preferred maximum and is not required. If you do not specify an *n* or your *n* is too small, FREQUENCIES chooses 5, 10, 25, 50 or 100, depending on the percentage for the largest category.

FREQ(n) *Horizontal axis scaled in frequencies.* While FREQ is the default scaling method, you can use this keyword to specify a maximum frequency *(n)* for the scale. If you do not specify an *n* or your *n* is too small, FREQUENCIES chooses 10, 20, 50, 100, 200, 500, 1000, 2000, and so forth, depending on the frequency count for the largest category.

You can enter optional specifications in any order, as in

```
FREQUENCIES  VARIABLES=SIBS
             /BARCHART=PERCENT MAX(10)
```

which requests a bar chart on SIBS with values through 10 plotted and the horizontal axis scaled in percentages.

18.101
HISTOGRAM Subcommand

No specifications are required for the HISTOGRAM subcommand. In the default histogram format, all tabulated values are included, and the horizontal axis is scaled by frequencies. The scale is determined by the frequency count of the largest category plotted. The number of intervals plotted is 21 (or fewer if the range of values is less than 21).

You can use all of the formatting options available with BARCHART (MIN, MAX, PERCENT, and FREQ) on the HISTOGRAM subcommand. In addition, you can specify the interval width and superimpose a normal curve on the histogram.

INCREMENT(n) *Interval width.* By default, values are collected into 21 intervals for plotting. You can override the default by specifying the actual interval width. For example, if a variable ranges from 1 to 100 and you specify INCREMENT(2), the width of each interval is 2, producing 50 intervals.

NORMAL *Superimpose the normal curve.* The normal curve is based on all valid values for the variable and includes values excluded by MIN and MAX. The default is NONORMAL.

You can enter the optional specifications in any order, as in

```
FREQUENCIES  VARIABLES=PRESTIGE
             /HISTOGRAM=NORMAL INCREMENT(4)
```

which produces a histogram of PRESTIGE with a superimposed normal curve and an interval width of four.

18.102
HBAR Subcommand

The HBAR subcommand produces either bar charts or histograms, depending upon the number of values encountered in the data. If a bar chart for a variable fits on a page, HBAR produces a bar chart; otherwise, it produces a histogram. For the default page length of 59, a barchart is displayed for variables with fewer than 12 categories. Histograms are displayed for all other variables specified on the VARIABLES subcommand. All specifications for HISTOGRAM and BARCHART also work with HBAR.

18.103
Percentiles and Ntiles

You can use either the PERCENTILES or NTILES subcommands to print percentiles for all variables specified on the VARIABLES subcommand. If two or more PERCENTILES and NTILES subcommands are specified, FREQUENCIES prints one table with the values for all requested percentiles.

18.104
PERCENTILES Subcommand

Percentiles are the values below which a given percentage of cases fall. Use the PERCENTILES subcommand followed by an optional equals sign and a list of percentiles between 0 and 100 to print the values for each percentile. For example, to request the values for percentiles 10, 25, 33.3, 66.7, and 75 for variable PRESTIGE, specify:

```
FREQUENCIES   VARIABLES=PRESTIGE
            /PERCENTILES=10 25 33.3 66.7 75
```

18.105
NTILES Subcommand

*N*tiles are the values that divide the sample into groups of equal numbers of cases. To print the values for each *n*tile, use the NTILES subcommand followed by an optional equals sign and one integer value specifying the number of subgroups. For example, to request quartiles for PRESTIGE, specify:

```
FREQUENCIES VARIABLES=PRESTIGE /NTILES=4
```

SPSS-X prints one less percentile than the number specified on the NTILES subcommand. If a requested percentile cannot be calculated, SPSS-X prints a period (.) as the value associated with that percentile.

18.106
STATISTICS Subcommand

The STATISTICS subcommand specifies univariate statistics for all variables named on the VARIABLES subcommand. In integer mode, only cases with values in the specified range are used in the computation of statistics.

MEAN *Mean.*

SEMEAN *Standard error of the mean.*

MEDIAN *Median.* The median is defined as the value below which half the cases fall. If there is an even number of cases, the median is the average of the (nth/2) and (nth/2+1) cases when the cases are sorted in ascending order. The median is not available if you specify AFREQ or DFREQ on the FORMAT subcommand.

MODE *Mode.*

STDDEV *Standard deviation.*

VARIANCE *Variance.*

SKEWNESS *Skewness.*

SESKEW *Standard error of the skewness statistic.*

KURTOSIS *Kurtosis.*

SEKURT *Standard error of the kurtosis statistic.*

RANGE *Range.*

MINIMUM *Minimum.*

MAXIMUM *Maximum.*

SUM *Sum.*

DEFAULT *Mean, standard deviation, minimum, and maximum.* You can use DEFAULT jointly with other statistics.

ALL *All available statistics.*

NONE *No statistics.*

You can specify as many keywords as you wish on the STATISTICS subcommand. For example,

```
FREQUENCIES  VARIABLES=PRESTIGE POLVIEWS
             /STATISTICS=MEDIAN DEFAULT
```

prints the median and the default statistics (the mean, standard deviation, minimum, and maximum). If you use the STATISTICS subcommand with no specifications, the default statistics are printed.

18.107
MISSING Subcommand

FREQUENCIES recognizes three types of missing values: user-missing, system-missing, and in integer mode, out-of-range values. Both user- and system-missing values are included in frequency tables. They are labeled as missing and are not included in the valid and cumulative percentages. Missing values are not used in the calculation of descriptive statistics, nor do they appear in bar charts and histograms.

To treat user-missing values as valid values, use the MISSING subcommand, which has one specification, INCLUDE. For example,

```
MISSING VALUES  SATFAM TO HAPPY(8,9)
FREQUENCIES  VARIABLES=SATFAM HAPPY (0,9)
             /BARCHART
             /MISSING=INCLUDE
```

includes values 8 and 9 (which were previously defined as missing with the MISSING VALUES command) in the bar charts.

18.108
Limitations

The following limitations apply to FREQUENCIES:

• A maximum of 500 variables total per FREQUENCIES command.
• A maximum value range of 32,767 for a variable in integer mode.
• A maximum of 32,767 observed values over all variables.

18.109
LIST

```
LIST [VARIABLES={ALL    }] [/FORMAT=[{WRAP  }] [{UNNUMBERED}]]
                {varlist}                {SINGLE}   {NUMBERED  }


     [/CASES=[FROM {1}] [TO {eof}] [BY {1}]]
                  {n}       {n  }      {n}
```

The LIST procedure displays the values of variables for cases in the active file in an automatic format. The simplest LIST command is the command alone implying all variables, as in:

```
DATA LIST  FILE=HUBDATA RECORDS=3
 /1 MOHIRED YRHIRED 12-15 DEPT82 19
 /2 SALARY79 TO SALARY82 6-25
 /3 NAME 25-48 (A)
LIST
```

LIST uses the dictionary print formats assigned when the variables are defined on a DATA LIST, PRINT FORMATS, or FORMATS command, or the formats assigned when the variables are created with transformation commands.

LIST may require more than one line to display each case, depending on the page width. Values for each case are always displayed with a blank space between the variables.

Each execution of LIST begins at the top of a new page. If SPLIT FILE is in effect (Section 18.50), each split also begins at the top of a new page.

18.110
VARIABLES Subcommand

The default specification for the VARIABLES subcommand is keyword ALL. You can limit the listing to specific variables using the VARIABLES subcommand, as in:

```
DATA LIST  FILE=HUBDATA RECORDS=3
  /1 EMPLOYID 1-5 MOHIRED YRHIRED 12-15 DEPT79 TO DEPT82 SEX 16-20
  /2 SALARY79 TO SALARY82 6-25 HOURLY81 HOURLY82 40-53(2) PROMO81 72
     AGE 54-55 RAISE82 66-70
  /3 JOBCAT 6 NAME 25-48 (A)
LIST VARIABLES=MOHIRED YRHIRED DEPT82 NAME
```

Variables named must already exist. Because LIST is a procedure, variables named cannot be scratch or system variables. You can use the TO convention for naming consecutive variables, as in:

```
LIST VARIABLES=MOHIRED YRHIRED DEPT82 SALARY79 TO SALARY82 NAME
```

If you specify more variables than can be printed on one line, the line wraps. If all the variables fit on a single line, SPSS-X prints a heading using the variable name and prints a single line per case. When the variable name is longer than the print width, SPSS-X centers numeric variables in the column.

18.111
CASES Subcommand

Use the CASES subcommand to limit the number and pattern of cases listed. Subcommand CASES must be followed by at least one of the following keywords:

FROM n *The case number of the first case to be listed.* The specification CASES FROM 100 starts listing cases at the 100th sequential case. If LIST is preceded by SAMPLE or SELECT IF, the first case listed is the 100th case selected. The default is 1, which means listing begins with the first selected case.

TO n *Upper limit on the cases to be listed.* The specification CASES TO 1000 limits listing to the 1000th selected case or the end of the file, whichever comes first. The default is to list until the end of the file. If LIST encounters the CASE subcommand followed by a single number, TO is assumed. For example, CASES 100 is interpreted as CASES TO 100.

BY n *Increment used to choose cases for listing.* The specification CASES BY 5 lists every fifth selected case. The default is 1, which means every case is listed.

You need only specify one of these keywords, but you can specify any two or all three, as in:

```
LIST VARIABLES=MOHIRED YRHIRED DEPT82 SALARY79 TO SALARY82 NAME
  /CASES FROM 50 TO 100 BY 5
```

If SPLIT FILE is in effect, case selections specified via the CASE subcommand are restarted for each split.

18.112
FORMAT Subcommand

The default specifications for the FORMAT subcommand are WRAP and UNNUMBERED. If the page width cannot accommodate your entire variable list, keyword WRAP wraps the listing in multiple lines per case.

When the list requires more than one line per case, SPSS-X prints the name of the first variable listed in that line. To locate the values of a particular variable, consult the table produced before the listing.

If there is enough space, keyword WRAP implies one line per case. To tell SPSS-X to use the single-line format only, specify the keyword SINGLE, as in:

```
LIST VARIABLES=MOHIRED YRHIRED DEPT82 SALARY79 TO SALARY82 NAME
  /CASES FROM 50 TO 100 BY 5 /FORMAT=SINGLE
```

If there is not enough room within the line width, SPSS-X issues an error message and does not execute the listing. Therefore, use SINGLE only when you want one line per case or nothing.

If you want LIST to number the cases that are being listed, specify keyword NUMBERED, as in:

```
LIST VARIABLES=MOHIRED YRHIRED DEPT82 SALARY79 TO SALARY82 NAME
  /CASES FROM 50 TO 100 BY 5 /FORMAT=SINGLE,NUMBERED
```

18.113
MANOVA

```
MANOVA dependent varlist [BY factor list (min,max) [factor list...]

                            [WITH covariate list]]

[/WSFACTORS=name (levels) name...]

[/TRANSFORM [(varlist [/varlist])]=[ORTHONORM] [{CONTRAST}]]
      [{DEVIATIONS (refcat) }]                 {BASIS   }
       {DIFFERENCE          }
       {HELMERT             }
       {SIMPLE (refcat)     }
       {REPEATED            }
       {POLYNOMIAL [(metric)]}
       {SPECIAL (matrix)    }

[/WSDESIGN=effect effect...]

[/MEASURE=newname newname...]

[/RENAME={newname} {newname}...]
         {*       } {*      }
[/MISSING=[LISTWISE] [INCLUDE]]

[/{PRINT  }= [CELLINFO ([MEANS] [SSCP] [COV] [COR] [ALL])]]
  {NOPRINT}

     [HOMOGENEITY ([BARTLETT] [COCHRAN] [BOXM] [ALL])]

     [DESIGN ([ONEWAY] [OVERALL] [DECOMP] [BIAS] [SOLUTION]
              [REDUNDANCY] [COLLINEARITY] [ALL])]

     [ERROR ([SSCP] [COV] [COR] [STDDEV] [ALL])]

     [SIGNIF ([MULTIV] [EIGEN] [DIMENR] [UNIV] [HYPOTH]
              [AVERF] [AVONLY] [HF] [GG] [EFSIZE]
              [SINGLEDF] [BRIEF] [STEPDOWN] [ALL] [NONE])]

     [PARAMETERS ([ESTIM] [ORTHO] [COR] [NEGSUM] [ALL])]
                 [EFSIZE] [OPTIMAL]]

[/PLOT=[CELLPLOTS] [STEMLEAF] [ZCORR] [NORMAL] [BOXPLOTS]]
       [ALL]

[/PCOMPS [COR] [NCOMP(n)] [MINEIGEN(eigencut)]
         [COV] [ROTATE(rottype)] [ALL]]

[/DISCRIM [RAW] [STAN] [ESTIM] [COR] [ALL]
          [ROTATE(rottype)] [ALPHA({.25})]]
                                   { a}

[/OMEANS [VARIABLES(varlist)] [TABLES ({factor name    })]]
                                       {factor BY factor}
                                       {CONSTANT        }
[/PMEANS [VARIABLES(varlist)] [TABLES ({factor name    })]]
                                       {factor BY factor}
          [PLOT]                       {CONSTANT        }

[/RESIDUALS [CASEWISE] [PLOT]]
[/METHOD=[MODELTYPE ({MEANS      })]
                    {OBSERVATIONS}

     [ESTIMATION ({QR      } {NOLASTRES} {NOBALANCED} {CONSTANT  })]
                 {CHOLESKY} {LASTRES  } {BALANCED  } {NOCONSTANT}
```

```
        [SSTYPE ({UNIQUE    })]]
                {SEQUENTIAL}

   [/MATRIX=[IN({file})]  [OUT({file})]]
               {*   }        {*   }


   [/ANALYSIS [({CONDITIONAL  })]=dependent varlist
               {UNCONDITIONAL}   [WITH covariate varlist]
                                 [/dependent varlist...]]


   [/PARTITION (factorname)[=({1,1...   })]]
                             {df,df...}


                               {DEVIATION [(refcat)]    }
                               {SIMPLE [(refcat)]        }
                               {DIFFERENCE               }
   [/CONTRAST (factorname)={HELMERT                  }]
                               {REPEATED                 }
                               {POLYNOMIAL[(({1,2,3...})]}
                               {              {metric  } }
                               {SPECIAL (matrix)         }


   [/CRITERIA=[ZETA ({1.0E-8})]  [EPS ({1.0E-8})]]]
                      {zeta  }          {eps  }


              {WITHIN             }    {W }
   [/ERROR={RESIDUAL           } or {R }]
              {WITHIN + RESIDUAL}    {WR}
              {n                  }


   [/POWER=[T({.05})] [F({.05})] [{APPROXIMATE}]]
              {  a}      {  a}     {EXACT      }


   [/CINTERVAL=[{INDIVIDUAL}][(({.95}) ]] [UNIVARIATE ({BONFER })]
               {JOINT     }    {  a}                   {SCHEFFE}

                                       [MULTIVARIATE ({ROY     })]]
                                                      {PILLAI  }
                                                      {BONFER  }
                                                      {HOTELLING}
                                                      {WILKS   }


          {[CONSTANT...]                                      }
          {[effect effect...]                                 }
          {[POOL (varlist)...]                                }
          {[effects BY effects...]                            }
   [/DESIGN={[effects {WITHIN} effects...]                    }]
          {         {W     }                                  }
          {[effect + effect...]                               }
          {[factor (level)... [WITHIN factor (partition)...]] }
          {[MUPLUS...]                                        }
          {[MWITHIN...]                                       }
          {[{terms-to-be-tested} {AGAINST} {WITHIN  }    {W }]}
          {{term=n             } {VS     } {RESIDUAL} or {R }}
          {                                 {WR      }    {RW}}
          {                                 {n       }       }
```

The complete syntax chart for MANOVA is included here. Discussion of MANOVA appears in Chapter 17. For a more detailed discussion of MANOVA, please consult the *SPSS-X User's Guide*, 3rd ed.

18.114
MEANS

General mode:

```
MEANS [TABLES=]varlist BY varlist [BY...] [/varlist...]

[/MISSING={TABLE**   }]
          {INCLUDE   }
          {DEPENDENT}

[/FORMAT={LABELS**  }  {NAMES**}  {VALUES**}  {TABLE**}]
         {NOLABELS  }  {NONAMES}  {NOVALUES}  {TREE   }
         {NOCATLABS}

[/CELLS=[DEFAULT**]  [MEAN**   ]  [ALL]]
        [COUNT**  ]  [STDDEV**]
        [SUM      ]  [VARIANCE]

[/STATISTICS=[ANOVA] [LINEARITY] [ALL] [NONE] ]
```

Integer mode:

```
MEANS VARIABLES=varlist({min,max         }) [varlist...]
                        {LOWEST,HIGHEST}

/{TABLES    }=varlist BY varlist [BY...] [/varlist...]
 {CROSSBREAK}

[/MISSING={TABLE**   }]
          {INCLUDE   }
          {DEPENDENT}

[/FORMAT={LABELS**  }  {NAMES**}  {VALUES**}]
         {NOLABELS  }  {NONAMES}  {NOVALUES}
         {NOCATLABS}

[/CELLS=[DEFAULT**]  [MEAN**   ]  [ALL]]
        [COUNT**  ]  [STDDEV**]
        [SUM      ]  [VARIANCE]

[/STATISTICS=[ANOVA] [LINEARITY] [ALL] [NONE] ]
```

**Default if the subcommand is omitted.

MEANS (alias BREAKDOWN) calculates means and variances for a criterion or dependent variable over subgroups of cases defined by independent or control variables. This operation is similar to crosstabulation, where each mean and standard deviation summarize the distribution of a complete row or column of a contingency table.

You can specify the subcommands in MEANS in any order, provided the VARIABLES subcommand precedes the TABLES or CROSSBREAK subcommands in integer mode.

Methods for Building Tables. MEANS operates in two different modes: general and integer. *General mode* operates via the TABLES subcommand and requires fewer specifications. It also offers an optional tree format for the output. (See Section 18.116.) *Integer mode* operates via the TABLES and VARIABLES subcommands and requires that you specify the minimum and maximum values for the variables. This mode builds tables more efficiently. (See Section 18.117.)

18.115
TABLES Subcommand

Use the TABLES subcommand with MEANS in both general and integer modes. There is one important difference between the tables request in integer mode and the tables request in general mode. In integer mode, the order of the variables implied on the TABLES subcommand is established by the order of the variables named or implied on the VARIABLES subcommand. In general mode, the order of variables implied on the tables lists is established by their order in the active file.

18.116
General Mode   To run MEANS in general mode, use the TABLES subcommand followed by one or more dependent variables, the keyword BY, and one or more independent variables. The actual command keyword TABLES is not required to operate MEANS in general mode.

A maximum of six dimensions can be specified on an analysis list: one dependent variable and up to five independent variables separated by the keyword BY. For example,

```
MEANS   TABLES=RAISE81 BY DEPT81 BY GRADE81S
```

breaks down RAISE81 by DEPT81 and by GRADE81S within DEPT81. The first variable always becomes the dependent or criterion variable. The independent variables are entered into the table in the order in which they appear following the TABLES subcommand, proceeding from left to right. The values of the last variable change most quickly. MEANS prints subpopulation statistics for each category of the first independent variable. However, for subsequent variables, it prints statistics only for each category of the variable within a category of the preceding independent variable.

You can specify more than one dependent variable and more than one independent variable in each dimension. Use the keyword TO to name a set of adjacent variables in the active file, as in:

```
MEANS   TABLES=RAISE79 TO RAISE81 BY DEPT TO AGE
```

This command will produce MEANS tables for all the variables between and including RAISE79 and RAISE81 by all the variables between and including DEPT and AGE. You can also use variable lists to request higher-order breakdowns. The variables to the right of the last BY change most quickly. Within lists separated with a BY, variables rotate from left to right. For example,

```
MEANS   TABLES=VAR1 TO VAR3 BY VAR4 VAR5 BY VAR6 TO VAR8
```

produces 18 tables. The first table is VAR1 by VAR4 by VAR6 and the second is VAR1 by VAR4 by VAR7. The combinations of VAR1 and VAR5 follow the combinations of VAR1 and VAR4. The last table produced is VAR3 by VAR5 by VAR8.

Use multiple TABLES subcommands, or a slash to separate tables lists on one TABLES subcommand. For example,

```
MEANS   TABLES=RAISE82 BY GRADE/SALARY BY DEPT
```

specifies two tables, RAISE82 by GRADE and SALARY by DEPT. If you omit a slash between tables lists, MEANS includes the variables as if one analysis list had been supplied.

18.117
Integer Mode   To run MEANS in integer mode, the values of all the independent variables must be integers. Two subcommands are required. The VARIABLES subcommand (see Section 18.118) specifies all the variables to be used in the MEANS procedure and the minimum and maximum values for building tables. The TABLES subcommand specifies the tables lists. Repeated VARIABLES and TABLES subcommands are allowed.

In integer mode, the TABLES subcommand names the tables list and has the same syntax as the TABLES subcommand in general mode. You can use multiple TABLES subcommands or name multiple tables lists separated by slashes on one TABLES subcommand. Variables named on the TABLES subcommand must have been previously named or implied on the VARIABLES subcommand.

Integer mode can produce more tables in a given amount of core storage space than general mode, and the processing is faster. In addition, integer mode has an alternate CROSSBREAK display format (see Section 18.119).

18.118
VARIABLES Subcommand

The VARIABLES subcommand is followed by a list of variables. This list identifies variables to be included on the TABLES subcommand. Specify the lowest and highest values in parentheses after each variable. These values must be integers. You can *not* use LOWEST, LO, HIGHEST, HI with independent variables. For example, the command

```
MEANS   VARIABLES=DEPT81(1,4) EEO81(1,9) RAISE81(LO,HI)
  /TABLES=RAISE81 BY DEPT81 BY EEO81
```

produces a table where RAISE81 has a range from the lowest to the highest value, DEPT81 has a range from 1 to 4, and EEO81 has a range from 1 to 9. The final variable or set of variables and their range must be followed by a slash.

You do not have to specify an explicit range for dependent variables because they are usually continuous and are not assumed to be integers. However, you must provide bounds. Use keywords LOWEST (or LO) and HIGHEST (or HI) for criterion variables. You can also use explicit bounds to eliminate outliers from the calculation of the summary statistics. Explicit numeric bounds must be specified as integers. For example, (0,HI) excludes nonnegative values.

Several variables can have the same range. For example,

```
MEANS   VARIABLES=DEPT80 DEPT81 DEPT82 (1,3) GRADE81S (1,4)
            SALARY82 (LO,HI)
   /TABLES=SALARY82 BY DEPT80 TO DEPT82 BY GRADE81S
```

defines 1 as the lowest value and 3 as the highest value for DEPT80, DEPT81, and DEPT82. Variables may appear in any order. However, the order in which you place them on the VARIABLES subcommand affects their implied order on the TABLES subcommand.

18.119
CROSSBREAK Subcommand

To print tables in a crosstabular form when using integer mode, use the CROSSBREAK subcommand in place of the TABLES subcommand. It has exactly the same specification field as the TABLES subcommand.

Tables printed in crossbreak form resemble CROSSTABS tables, but their contents are considerably different. The cells contain means, counts, and standard deviations for the dependent variable. The first independent variable defines the rows and the second independent variable defines the columns. The CROSSBREAK format is especially suited to breakdowns with two control variables. The CROSSBREAK subcommand prints separate subtables for each combination of values when you specify three or more dimensions.

18.120
CELLS Subcommand

By default, MEANS prints the means, standard deviations, and cell counts in each cell. Use the CELLS subcommand to modify cell information.

You can specify the CELLS subcommand by itself, or with a keyword or keywords. If you specify the CELLS subcommand with no keywords, MEANS prints ALL cell information (defined below). If you specify a keyword or keywords, MEANS prints only the information you request.

The following keywords can be specified on the CELLS subcommand:

DEFAULT   *Print the means, standard deviations, and cell counts in each cell.* This is the default if you omit the CELL subcommand.

MEAN   *Print cell means.*

STDDEV   *Print cell standard deviations.*

COUNT   *Print cell frequencies.*

SUM   *Print cell sums.*

VARIANCE   *Print variances.*

ALL   *Print the means, counts, standard deviations, sums, and variances in each cell.* This is the default if you specify the CELLS subcommand with no keyword(s).

18.121
STATISTICS Subcommand

MEANS automatically computes means, standard deviations, and counts for subpopulations. Optionally, you can obtain a one-way analysis of variance for each table as well as a test of linearity. The STATISTICS subcommand computes additional statistics. Statistics you request on the STATISTICS subcommand are computed *in addition to* the default statistics or those you request on the CELLS subcommand.

You can use the STATISTICS subcommand by itself or with a keyword or keywords. If you use the STATISTICS subcommand with no keyword, MEANS computes ANOVA (defined below). If you specify a keyword, MEANS computes the additional statistics you request.

The following keywords can be specified on the STATISTICS subcommand:

ANOVA   *Analysis of variance.* Prints a standard analysis of variance table and calculates *ETA* and *ETA²*. This is the default if you specify the STATISTICS subcommand with no keyword.

LINEARITY *Test of linearity.* Calculates the sums of squares, degrees of freedom, and mean square associated with linear and nonlinear components, as well as the *F* ratio, Pearson's *r*, and *r²*. ANOVA *must* be requested to obtain LINEARITY. LINEARITY is ignored if the control variable is a short string.

ALL   *Both ANOVA and LINEARITY.*

NONE   *No additional statistics.* This is the default if you omit the STATISTICS subcommand.

If you specify a two-way or higher-order breakdown, the second and subsequent dimensions are ignored in the analysis of variance table. To obtain a two-way and higher analysis of variance, use procedure ANOVA (see Section 18.54).

18.122
MISSING Subcommand

By default, MEANS deletes cases with missing values on a tablewide basis. A case missing on any of the variables specified for a table is not used. Every case contained in a table will have a complete set of nonmissing values for all variables in that table. When you separate tables requests with a slash, missing values are handled separately for each list.

The MISSING subcommand controls missing values, and the following keywords can be specified on it:

TABLE   *Delete cases with missing values on a tablewide basis.* This is the default if you omit the MISSING subcommand.

INCLUDE   *Include user-defined missing values.* Handles user-defined missing values as if they were not missing.

DEPENDENT *Exclude cases with missing values for the dependent variable only.* A case is included if it has a valid value for the dependent variable, although it may have missing values for the independent variables. Missing values are ignored for control variables.

18.123
FORMAT Subcommand

By default, MEANS prints variable and value labels and the names and values of independent variables. All tables print in report format.

The FORMAT subcommand controls table formats, and the following keywords can be specified on it:

LABELS	*Print both variable and value labels for each table.* This is the default if you omit the FORMAT subcommand.
NOLABELS	*Suppress variable and value labels.*
NOCATLABS	*Suppress value (category) labels.*
NAMES	*Print the names of independent variables.* This is the default if you omit the FORMAT subcommand.
NONAMES	*Suppress names of independent variables.*
VALUES	*Print the values of independent variables.* This is the default if you omit the FORMAT subcommand.
NOVALUES	*Suppress values of independent variables.* This is useful when there are category labels.
TABLE	*Print each table in report format.* This is the default if you omit the FORMAT subcommand.
TREE	*Print each table in tree format.* This option is available for general mode only.

18.124
Limitations

The following limitations apply to MEANS in general mode:

• A maximum of 200 variables total per MEANS command.
• A maximum of 250 tables.
• A maximum of 6 dimensions per table.
• A maximum of 30 tables lists per MEANS command.
• A maximum of 200 value labels printed on any single table.

The following limitations apply to MEANS in integer mode:

• A maximum of 100 variables named or implied on the VARIABLES subcommand.
• A maximum of 100 variables named or implied on the TABLES subcommand.
• A maximum of 100 tables.
• A maximum of 6 dimensions per table.
• A maximum of 30 tables lists per MEANS command.
• A maximum of 200 nonempty rows and columns in a CROSSBREAK table.

18.125
NONPAR CORR

```
NONPAR CORR [VARIABLES=] varlist [WITH varlist] [/varlist...]

[/MISSING={PAIRWISE**}]
            {INCLUDE   }
            {LISTWISE  }

[/PRINT={ONETAIL**}  {SIG**}  {SPEARMAN**}]
          {TWOTAIL  }  {NOSIG}  {KENDALL    }
                                 {BOTH       }

[/FORMAT={MATRIX**}]
          {SERIAL  }

[/MATRIX=OUT({*   })]
             {file}

[/SAMPLE]
```

**Default if the subcommand is omitted.

NONPAR CORR computes two rank-order correlation coefficients, Spearman's rho and Kendall's tau-*b*, with their significance levels. You can obtain either or both coefficients.

The only required subcommand on NONPAR CORR is the VARIABLES subcommand, which specifies the list of variables to be analyzed (see Section 18.126). The actual keyword VARIABLES can be omitted. You can specify NONPAR CORR's optional subcommands in any order, separated by slashes. However, you must first specify the variables to be used in the analysis before you can specify any of the optional subcommands.

This abbreviated command reference does not discuss the MATRIX subcommand used to write matrices. This feature is not essential to the operation of NONPAR CORR as described in this book. However, MATRIX is fully discussed in *SPSS-X User's Guide,* 3rd ed.

18.126
VARIABLES Subcommand

The VARIABLES subcommand names the variable list. The actual keyword VARIABLES is optional. If you explicitly specify keyword VARIABLES, an equals sign must precede the variable list. You can use keyword TO in the list to refer to consecutive variables in the active file. The variables must be numeric.

Depending on how you specify the variable list, NONPAR CORR prints either a lower-triangular or a rectangular matrix. If you provide a simple list of variables, NONPAR CORR prints the correlations of each variable with every other variable in the list in a lower-triangular matrix. For example, the command

```
NONPAR CORR VARIABLES=PRESTIGE SPPRES PAPRES16 DEGREE PADEG MADEG
```

produces a triangular matrix. The correlation of a variable with itself (the diagonal) and redundant coefficients are not printed. The default coefficients produced by NONPAR CORR are Spearman correlations. The number of cases upon which the correlations are based and the one-tailed significance level are printed for each correlation. To obtain Kendall coefficients, you must use the PRINT subcommand (see Section 18.127).

To obtain the rectangular matrix, specify two variable lists separated by keyword WITH. NONPAR CORR then prints a rectangular matrix of variables in the first list correlated with variables in the second list. For example,

```
NONPAR CORR VARS=PRESTIGE SPPRES PAPRES16 WITH DEGREE PADEG MADEG
```

produces nine correlations. The variables listed before keyword WITH define the rows of the matrix, and those listed after keyword WITH define the columns. Unless a variable is in both lists, there are no identity coefficients in the matrix.

You can request more than one matrix on a NONPAR CORR command. Use a slash to separate the specifications for each of the requested matrices. For example,

```
NONPAR CORR VARIABLES=SPPRES PAPRES16 PRESTIGE/
            SATCITY WITH SATHOBBY SATFAM
```

produces two correlation matrices. The first matrix contains three coefficients in triangular form. The second matrix is rectangular and contains two coefficients.

If all cases have a missing value for a given pair of variables, or if they all have the same value for a variable, the coefficient cannot be computed. Because Spearman's rho and Kendall's tau-*b* coefficients always have a value in the range -1.00 to $+1.00$, NONPAR CORR prints a decimal point if a correlation cannot be computed.

18.127
PRINT Subcommand

By default, NONPAR CORR prints Spearman correlation coefficients. Below each coefficient it prints the number of cases and the significance level. The significance level is based on a one-tailed test.

Use the PRINT subcommand to request the Kendall correlation coefficient or both Spearman and Kendall coefficients. Both coefficients are based on ranks. You can also use PRINT to switch to a two-tailed test and to suppress the display of the number of cases and significance level.

The following keywords are available on PRINT:

SPEARMAN *Spearman's rho.* Only Spearman coefficients are displayed. This is the default.

KENDALL *Kendall's tau*-b. Only Kendall coefficients are displayed.

BOTH *Kendall and Spearman coefficients.* Both coefficients are displayed.

SIG *Print the number of cases and significance level.* This is the default.

NOSIG *Suppress the printing of the number of cases and significance level.*

ONETAIL *One-tailed test of significance.* This is the default.

TWOTAIL *Two-tailed test of significance.*

If you specify both FORMAT=SERIAL (Section 18.130) and PRINT=NOSIG, only FORMAT=SERIAL will be in effect.

18.128
SAMPLE Subcommand

NONPAR CORR must store cases in memory to build matrices. You may not have sufficient computer resources to store all the cases to produce the coefficients requested. The SAMPLE subcommand allows you to select a random sample of cases when there is not enough space to store all the cases. To request a random sample, simply specify the subcommand, as in:

```
NONPAR CORR VARIABLES=PRESTIGE SPPRES PAPRES16 DEGREE PADEG MADEG
  /SAMPLE
```

The SAMPLE subcommand has no additional specifications.

18.129
MISSING Subcommand

By default, NONPAR CORR deletes cases with missing values on a pair-by-pair basis. A case missing on one or both of the pair of variables for a specific correlation coefficient is not used for that coefficient. Because each coefficient is based on all cases that have valid codes on that particular pair of variables, the maximum information available is used in every calculation. This also results in a set of coefficients based on a varying number of cases.

Use the MISSING subcommand to specify alternative missing-value treatments. The following keywords are available:

PAIRWISE *Exclude missing values pairwise.* Cases missing for one or both of a pair of variables for a specific correlation coefficient are excluded from the analysis. This is the default.

LISTWISE *Exclude missing values listwise.* Cases missing on any variable named in a list are excluded from all analyses. Each variable list on a command is evaluated separately. If you specify multiple variable lists, a case missing for one matrix might be used in another matrix. This option decreases the amount of memory required and significantly decreases computational time.

INCLUDE *Include user-defined missing values.* User-missing values are treated as if they are not missing.

Only one of these keywords can be specified on MISSING.

18.130
FORMAT Subcommand

The FORMAT subcommand controls the format of the correlation matrix. The following keywords are available:

MATRIX *Print correlations in matrix format.* This is the default.

SERIAL *Print correlations in serial string format.*

18.131
Limitations   The following limitations apply to NONPAR CORR:

- A maximum of 25 variable lists.
- A maximum of 100 variables total per NONPAR CORR command.

18.132
NPAR TESTS

```
NPAR TESTS [CHISQUARE=varlist[(lo,hi)]/] [/EXPECTED={EQUAL      }]
                                                     {f1,f2,...fn}

           [/K-S({UNIFORM[,lo,hi]})=varlist]
                 {NORMAL[,m,sd] }
                 {POISSON[,m]   }

           [/RUNS({MEAN  })=varlist]
                  {MEDIAN}
                  {MODE  }
                  {value }

           [/BINOMIAL[(p)]=varlist[({v1,v2})]]]
                                   {value}

           [/MCNEMAR=varlist [WITH varlist [(PAIRED)]]]

           [/SIGN=varlist [WITH varlist [(PAIRED)]]]

           [/WILCOXON=varlist [WITH varlist [(PAIRED)]]]

           [/COCHRAN=varlist]

           [/FRIEDMAN=varlist]

           [/KENDALL=varlist]

           [/MEDIAN[(value)]=varlist BY var (v1,v2)]

           [/M-W=varlist BY var (v1,v2)]

           [/K-S=varlist BY var (v1,v2)]

           [/W-W=varlist BY var (v1,v2)]

           [/MOSES[(n)]=varlist BY var (v1,v2)]

           [/K-W=varlist BY var (v1,v2)]

           [/MISSING={ANALYSIS**}  [INCLUDE]]
                     {LISTWISE }

           [/SAMPLE]

           [/STATISTICS=[DESCRIPTIVES]  [QUARTILES] [ALL]]
```

**Default if the subcommand is omitted.

Procedure NPAR TESTS is a collection of nonparametric tests that make minimal assumptions about the underlying distributions of data. In addition to the nonparametric tests available in NPAR TESTS, the *k*-sample chi-square and Fisher's exact test are available in procedure CROSSTABS (see Section 18.72).

Each NPAR TESTS subcommand names a specific test, followed by a variable list. You can use the keyword TO to reference contiguous variables in the active file. The form of the variable list differs with the data organization required for the test. You can request any or all of the available tests, separated by slashes, on one NPAR TESTS command. Some tests require additional parameters, and the CHISQUARE test has an optional subcommand.

18.133
One-Sample Tests

A one-sample test uses the entire set of observations for the variable being tested. Specify the name of the test and one or more variables to be tested. Each variable in the list produces one test.

18.134
CHISQUARE Subcommand

Subcommand CHISQUARE tabulates a variable into categories and computes a chi-square statistic based on the differences between observed and expected frequencies. By default, the CHISQUARE test assumes equal expected frequencies. To specify expected frequencies, use the associated EXPECTED subcommand. The general form is:

NPAR TESTS CHISQUARE = *varlist* [(lo,hi)]
      /EXPECTED = *f1, f2, ... fn*

The range following the variable list is optional. If you do not specify a range, each distinct value encountered is defined as a category. If you do specify a range, integer-valued categories are established for each value within the inclusive range. Noninteger values are truncated, and cases with values outside the bounds are excluded. For example,

NPAR TESTS CHISQUARE = RANK (1,4)

uses only the values 1 through 4 for the chi-square test of the variable RANK.

EXPECTED Subcommand. To specify expected frequencies, percentages, or proportions, use a value list on the EXPECTED subcommand. You must specify a value greater than zero for each observed category of the data. The values listed after the EXPECTED subcommand are summed. Each value is then divided by this sum to calculate the proportion of cases expected in the corresponding category. For example,

NPAR TESTS CHISQUARE = RANK (1,4) /**EXPECTED = 3 4 5 4**

specifies expected proportions of 3/16, 4/16, 5/16, and 4/16 for categories 1, 2, 3, and 4, respectively. You can specify the same expected proportion for two or more consecutive categories with an asterisk (*), as in:

NPAR TESTS CHISQUARE = A (1,5) /EXPECTED = 12, **3*16**, 18

This command tests the observed frequencies for variable A against the hypothetical distribution of 12/78 occurrences of category 1; 16/78 occurrences each of categories 2, 3, and 4; and 18/78 occurrences of category 5.

The EXPECTED subcommand applies to all variables named on the preceding CHISQUARE subcommand. If you want to specify different expected proportions for each variable, use multiple combinations of the CHISQUARE and EXPECTED subcommands. If you want to test the same variable against different proportions, you can also use multiple combinations.

18.135
K-S Subcommand
(One-Sample Test)

Subcommand K-S compares the cumulative distribution function for a variable with a specified distribution, which may be uniform, normal, or Poisson. The Kolmogorov-Smirnov Z is computed from the largest difference (in absolute value) between the observed and theoretical distribution functions. The general form is:

NPAR TESTS K-S (*dis* [*parameters*]) = *varlist*

where *dis* is one of the three distributions: UNIFORM, NORMAL, or POISSON.

Each of these distributions has optional parameters:

UNIFORM *Uniform distribution.* The optional parameters are the minimum and maximum values (in that order). If you do not specify them, K-S uses the observed minimum and maximum values.

NORMAL *Normal distribution.* The optional parameters are the mean and standard deviation (in that order). If you do not specify them, K-S uses the observed mean and standard deviation.

POISSON *Poisson distribution.* The one optional parameter is the mean. If you do not specify it, K-S uses the observed mean. A word of caution about testing against a Poisson distribution: if the mean of the test distribution is large, evaluating the probabilities is a very time-consuming process. If a mean of 100,000 or larger is used, K-S uses a normal approximation to the Poisson distribution.

For example, the command

```
NPAR TESTS  K-S (UNIFORM) = A
```

compares the distribution for variable A with a uniform distribution which has the same range as variable A, while the command

```
NPAR TESTS  K-S (NORMAL,0,1) = B
```

compares the distribution for variable B with a normal distribution which has a mean of 0 and standard deviation of 1.

K-S assumes that the test distribution is entirely specified in advance. When parameters of the test distribution are estimated from the sample, the distribution of the test statistic changes. NPAR TESTS does not provide any correction for this.

18.136
RUNS Subcommand

Subcommand RUNS performs the runs test to determine the randomness of observations for dichotomous variables. A run is defined as a sequence of one of the values which is preceded and followed by the other data value (or the end of the series). For example, the following sequence

| 1 1 | 0 0 0 | 1 | 0 0 0 0 | 1 | 0 | 1 |

contains seven runs (vertical bars are used to separate the runs). The general form of the RUNS subcommand is:

```
NPAR TESTS  RUNS (cutpoint) = varlist
```

You must specify a cutting point to dichotomize the variable. Use either the observed mean, median, or mode or a specified value, where one category comes from cases with values below the point and the other category comes from cases with values equal to or greater than the point. To specify the *cutpoint*, use either the keywords MEAN, MEDIAN, MODE, or a value. Even if the variable is already dichotomized, you still must specify a cutting point. For example, if the variable has values 0 and 1, you can use 1 as the cutting point.

18.137
BINOMIAL Subcommand

Subcommand BINOMIAL compares the observed frequency in each category of a dichotomous variable with expected frequencies under a binomial distribution. BINOMIAL tabulates a variable into two categories based on the way you specify a cutting point. The general form is:

```
NPAR TESTS  BINOMIAL[(p)] = varlist(value or value1,value2)
```

where p is the proportion of cases expected in the *first* category. The proportion is compared to the test proportion and the significance test is performed. The default test proportion is .5, but you can specify any other proportion. If the proportion is .5, BINOMIAL computes a two-tailed probability. If it is anything else, BINOMIAL computes a one-tailed probability.

If you name one value in parentheses following the variable list, it is used as a cutting point. All cases equal to or less than the cutting point form the first category; all remaining cases form the second category. If you specify two values in parentheses following the variable list, all cases with *value1* are in the first category and all cases with *value2* are in the second category. The frequencies in these categories are compared to the proportion you specify for *p*, or to .5 if you do not specify *p*.

18.138
Tests for Two Related Samples

Tests for two related samples compare pairs of variables. Specify the name of the test and two or more variables to be tested. If you specify a simple variable list, a test is performed for each variable paired with every other variable on the list. To obtain tests for specific pairs of variables, use two variable lists separated by keyword WITH. Each variable in the first list will be tested with each variable in the second list. For example,

```
NPAR TESTS  SIGN = A WITH B C
```

produces sign tests for A with B and A with C. No test is performed for B with C.

(PAIRED) Keyword. Keyword (PAIRED) used in conjunction with WITH provides additional control over which variables are paired together. When you specify (PAIRED), the first variable in the first list is paired with the first variable in the second list, the second variable in the first list is paired with the second variable in the second list, and so on. You must name or imply the same number of variables in both lists. For example,

```
NPAR TESTS  MCNEMAR = A B WITH C D (PAIRED)
```

pairs A with C and B with D. You must specify (PAIRED) after the second variable list. You cannot use (PAIRED) if keyword WITH is not specified.

18.139
MCNEMAR Subcommand

Subcommand MCNEMAR tabulates a 2 × 2 table for each pair of dichotomous variables. If your data are not dichotomous, recode them. The test is not performed for variables with more than two values. A chi-square statistic is computed for cases with different values for the two variables. If fewer than 30 cases change values from the first variable to the second variable, the binomial distribution is used to compute the significance level. The general form is:

NPAR TESTS MCNEMAR = *varlist*

18.140
SIGN Subcommand

Subcommand SIGN counts the positive and negative differences between each pair of variables and ignores zero differences. Under the null hypothesis for large sample sizes, the test statistic Z is approximately normally distributed with mean 0 and variance 1. The binomial distribution is used to compute an exact significance level if 25 or fewer differences are observed. The general form is:

NPAR TESTS SIGN = *varlist*

18.141
WILCOXON Subcommand

Subcommand WILCOXON computes the differences between the pair of variables, ranks the absolute differences, sums the positive and negative ranks, and computes the test statistic Z from the positive and negative rank sums. Under the null hypothesis, Z is approximately normally distributed with mean 0 and variance 1 for large sample sizes. The general form is:

NPAR TESTS WILCOXON = *varlist*

18.142
Tests for *k* Related Samples

Tests for *k* related samples compare sets of variables and have the following general form:

NPAR TESTS *testname* = *varlist*

Specify the name of the test and two or more variables to be tested. The *k* variables in the list produce one test for *k* related samples. The COCHRAN (see Section 18.143), FRIEDMAN (see Section 18.144), and KENDALL (see Section 18.145) tests are available for *k* related samples.

18.143
COCHRAN Subcommand

Subcommand COCHRAN tabulates a 2 × *k* contingency table (category vs. variable) for dichotomous variables and computes the proportions for each variable. If your data are not dichotomous, recode them. Cochran's *Q* statistic has approximately a chi-square distribution. The general form is:

NPAR TESTS COCHRAN = *varlist*

18.144
FRIEDMAN Subcommand

Subcommand FRIEDMAN *ranks k* variables from 1 to *k* for each case, calculates the mean rank for each variable over all the cases, and then calculates a test statistic with approximately a chi-square distribution. The general form is:

NPAR TESTS FRIEDMAN = *varlist*

18.145
KENDALL Subcommand

Subcommand KENDALL ranks *k* variables from 1 to *k* for each case, calculates the mean rank for each variable over all the cases, and then calculates Kendall's *W* and a corresponding chi-square statistic, correcting for ties. *W* ranges between 0 and 1, with 0 signifying no agreement and 1 signifying complete agreement. The general form is:

NPAR TESTS KENDALL = *varlist*

This test assumes that each case is a judge or rater. If you want to perform this test with variables as judges and cases as entities, you must first transpose your data matrix.

18.146
Tests for Two Independent Samples

Tests for two independent samples compare two groups of cases on one variable. Specify the name of the test and one or more variables to be tested. Each variable in the list produces one test. The variable following the keyword BY splits the file into two groups or samples. All cases with *value1* are in the first group, and all cases with *value2* are in the second group.

18.147
MEDIAN Subcommand (Two-Sample Test)

Subcommand MEDIAN tabulates a 2 × 2 contingency table with counts of the number of cases greater than the median and less than or equal to the median for the two groups. You can specify a value as a cutting point or use the median calculated from the data. If the total number of cases is greater than 30, a chi-square statistic is computed. Fisher's exact procedure (one-tailed) is used to compute the significance level for 30 or fewer cases. The general form is:

NPAR TESTS MEDIAN [(*value*)] = *varlist* BY *var*(*value1*,*value2*)

where the value following the MEDIAN subcommand is the test median. If the test median is not specified, the calculated median is used. For the two-sample median test, the variable following the BY keyword must have only two values (*value1* and *value2*). Otherwise, a *k*-sample test is performed (see Section 18.153).

18.148
M-W Subcommand

Subcommand M-W ranks all the cases in order of increasing size and computes the test statistic U, the number of times a score from Group 1 precedes a score from Group 2. If the samples are from the same population, the distribution of scores from the two groups in the ranked list should be random; an extreme value of U indicates a nonrandom pattern. For samples with fewer than 30 cases, the exact significance level for U is computed using the algorithm of Dineen and Blakesly (1973). For larger samples, U is transformed into a normally distributed Z statistic. The general form is:

NPAR TESTS M-W = *varlist* BY *var(value1,value2)*

18.149
K-S Subcommand
(Two-Sample Test)

Subcommand K-S computes the observed cumulative distributions for both groups and the maximum positive, negative, and absolute differences. The Kolmogorov-Smirnov Z is then computed along with the two-tailed probability level based on the Smirnov (1948) formula. The one-tailed test can be used to determine whether the values of one group are generally larger than the values of the other group. The general form is:

NPAR TESTS K-S = *varlist* BY *var(value1,value2)*

18.150
W-W Subcommand

Subcommand W-W combines observations from both groups and ranks them from lowest to highest. If the samples are from the same population, the two groups should be randomly scattered throughout the ranking. A runs test is performed using group membership as the criterion. If there are ties involving observations from both groups, both the minimum and maximum number of runs possible are calculated. If the total sample size is 30 cases or fewer, the exact one-tailed significance level is calculated. Otherwise, the normal approximation is used. The W-W general form is:

NPAR TESTS W-W = *varlist* BY *var(value1,value2)*

18.151
MOSES Subcommand

Subcommand MOSES arranges the scores from the groups in a single ascending sequence. The span of the control group is computed as the number of cases in the sequence containing the lowest and highest control score. The exact significance level can be computed for the span. Chance outliers can easily distort the range of the span. To minimize this problem, you can specify that a certain number of outliers be trimmed from each end of the span. No adjustments are made for tied observations. The general form is:

NPAR TESTS MOSES [(*n*)] = *varlist* BY *var(value1,value2)*

where n is the number of cases trimmed from each end. If you do not specify n, MOSES automatically trims 5% of the cases from each end. *Value1* corresponds to the control group.

18.152
Tests for *k* Independent
Samples

Tests for k independent samples compare k groups of cases on one variable. Specify the name of the test and one or more variables to be tested. Each variable in the list produces one test. The variable following the keyword BY splits the file into k groups. *Value1* and *value2* specify minimum and maximum values for the grouping variable.

18.153
MEDIAN Subcommand
(*k*-Sample Test)

Subcommand MEDIAN tabulates a $2 \times k$ contingency table with counts of the number of cases greater than the median and less than or equal to the median for the *k* groups. A chi-square statistic for the table is computed. The general form is:

NPAR TESTS MEDIAN [(value)] = *varlist* BY *var*(*value1*,*value2*)

The value following the MEDIAN subcommand is the test median. If the test median is not specified, the calculated median is used. The values specified for the variable that groups the cases determines whether a two-sample or *k*-sample test is performed. If you use a variable that has more than two values and *value1* is smaller than *value2*, a *k*-sample median test is performed. For example, in

NPAR TESTS MEDIAN = A BY B (1,3) /MEDIAN = A BY B (3,1)

the first test is a *k*-sample median test with three groups, while the second is a two-sample median test for Groups 1 and 3.

18.154
K-W Subcommand

Subcommand K-W ranks all cases from the *k* groups in a single series, computes the rank sum for each group, and computes the Kruskal-Wallis *H* statistic, which has approximately a chi-square distribution. The general form is:

NPAR TESTS K-W = *varlist* BY *var*(*value1*,*value2*)

Every value in the range *value1* to *value2* forms a group.

18.155
STATISTICS Subcommand

In addition to the statistics provided for each test, you can also obtain two types of summary statistics for variables named on each of the subcommands. Use the STATISTICS subcommand to request the following statistics for NPAR TESTS:

DESCRIPTIVES *Univariate statistics.* Prints the mean, maximum, minimum, standard deviation, and number of nonmissing cases for each variable named on the combined subcommands.

QUARTILES *Quartiles and number of cases.* Prints values corresponding to the 25th, 50th, and 75th percentiles for each variable named on the combined subcommands.

ALL *All statistics available on NPAR TESTS.*

18.156
MISSING Subcommand

By default, NPAR TESTS deletes cases with missing values on a test-by-test basis. For subcommands where you can specify several tests, it evaluates each test separately for missing values. For example,

NPAR TESTS MEDIAN = A B BY GROUP (1,5)

specifies two tests, A by GROUP and B by GROUP. A case missing for GROUP is excluded from both tests, but a case missing for A is not excluded from the test for B if it is not missing for B.

Use the MISSING subcommand to specify alternative missing-value treatments. The following keywords can be specified:

ANALYSIS *Exclude missing values on a test-by-test basis.* This is the default.

LISTWISE *Exclude missing values listwise.* Cases missing on any variable named on any subcommand are excluded from all analyses.

INCLUDE *Include user-missing values.* User-defined missing values are treated as if they were not missing.

The ANALYSIS and LISTWISE keywords are mutually exclusive; however, each can be specified with INCLUDE.

18.157
SAMPLE Subcommand

NPAR TESTS must store cases in memory. You may not have sufficient computer resources to store all the cases to produce the tests requested. The SAMPLE subcommand allows you to select a random sample of cases when there is not enough space to store all the cases. The SAMPLE subcommand has no additional specifications.

Because sampling would invalidate a runs test, this option is ignored when you use the RUNS subcommand.

18.158
Limitations

The following limitations apply to NPAR TESTS:

• A maximum of 100 subcommands.
• A maximum of 500 variables total per NPAR TESTS command.
• A maximum of 200 values for subcommand CHISQUARE.

18.159
ONEWAY

```
ONEWAY  varlist BY varname(min,max)

[/POLYNOMIAL=n]  [/CONTRAST=coefficient list] [/CONSTRAST=...]

[/RANGES={LSD         }({0.05 }) ] [/RANGES=...]
         {DUNCAN      } {alpha}
         {SNK         }
         {TUKEYB      }
         {TUKEY       }
         {LSDMOD      }
         {SCHEFFE     }
         {ranges values}

[/MISSING={ANALYSIS**} [{EXCLUDE**}]]
         {LISTWISE  }  {INCLUDE  }

[/HARMONIC={NONE** or PAIR}]
           {ALL           }

[/FORMAT={NOLABELS**}]
         { LABELS   }

[/MATRIX =[NONE**] [IN({*   })] [OUT({*   })]]
                      {file}        {file}

[/STATISTICS=[NONE        **]]
             [DESCRIPTIVES]
             [EFFECTS     ]
             [HOMOGENEITY ]
             [ALL         ]
```

**Default if the subcommand is omitted.

Procedure ONEWAY produces a one-way analysis of variance for an interval-level variable by one independent variable. You can test for trends across categories, specify contrasts, and use a variety of range tests. Procedure ONEWAY requires a dependent variable list and the independent variable with its range of integer values. All ONEWAY subcommands are optional and may be entered in any order, provided they appear after the variable list.

This abbreviated command reference does not discuss the MATRIX subcommand used to read and write matrices. This feature is not essential to the operation of ONEWAY as described in this book. However, MATRIX is fully discussed in the *SPSS-X User's Guide*, 3rd ed.

18.160
Specifying the Design

A ONEWAY analysis list contains a dependent variable list and one independent (grouping) variable with its minimum and maximum values. Use only one analysis list per ONEWAY command. Dependent variables must be numeric. The independent variable follows the keyword BY, and you must include a value range specifying the highest and lowest values to be used in the analysis. These values are separated by a comma and are enclosed in parentheses.

While you can specify any number of categories for the independent variable, contrasts and multiple comparison tests are not available for more than 50 groups. ONEWAY deletes empty groups for the analysis of variance and range tests. The independent variable must have integer values. Noninteger values encountered in the independent variable are truncated.

18.161
POLYNOMIAL Subcommand

The POLYNOMIAL subcommand partitions the between-groups sum of squares into linear, quadratic, cubic, or higher-order trend components. Specify this subcommand after the analysis specification, as in:

```
ONEWAY  WELL BY EDUC6 (1,6)
  /POLYNOMIAL = 2
```

The value specified in the POLYNOMIAL subcommand denotes the highest degree polynomial to be used. This value must be a positive integer less than or equal to 5 and less than the number of groups. Use only one POLYNOMIAL subcommand per ONEWAY command.

When you use the POLYNOMIAL subcommand with balanced designs, ONEWAY computes the sum of squares for each order polynomial from weighted polynomial contrasts, using the group code as the metric. These contrasts are orthogonal; hence the sum of squares for each order polynomial is statistically independent. If the design is unbalanced and there is equal spacing between groups, ONEWAY also computes sums of squares using the unweighted polynomial contrasts. These contrasts are not orthogonal. The deviation sums of squares are always calculated from the weighted sums of squares (Speed, 1976).

18.162
CONTRAST Subcommand

The CONTRAST subcommand specifies a priori contrasts to be tested by the t statistic. The specification for the CONTRAST subcommand is a vector of coefficients, with each coefficient corresponding to a category of the grouping variable. For example, the command

```
ONEWAY  WELL BY EDUC6(1,6)
  /CONTRAST = -1 -1 -1 -1 2 2
```

contrasts the combination of the first four groups with the combination of the last two groups.

You can also specify fractional weights, as in:

```
  /CONTRAST = -1 0 0 0 .5 .5
```

This subcommand contrasts Group 1 and the combination of Groups 5 and 6.

For most applications, the coefficients should sum to zero. Those sets that do not sum to zero are used, but a warning message is printed. In addition, you can use the repeat notation $n * c$ to specify the same coefficient for a consecutive set of means. For example,

```
  /CONTRAST = 1 4*0 -1
```

specifies a contrast coefficient of 1 for Group 1, 0 for Groups 2 through 5, and -1 for Group 6. You must specify a contrast for every group implied by the range specification in the analysis list, even if a group is empty. However, you do not have to specify trailing zeros. For example,

```
/CONTRAST = -1 2*0 1 2*0
/CONTRAST = -1 0 0 1 0 0
/CONTRAST = -1 2*0 1
```

all specify the same set of contrast coefficients for a six-group analysis.

You can specify only one set of contrast coefficients per CONTRAST subcommand and no more than 50 coefficients per set. Output for each contrast list includes the value of the contrast, the standard error of the contrast, the t statistic, the degrees of freedom for t, and the two-tailed probability of t. Both pooled- and separate-variance estimates are printed.

18.163
RANGES Subcommand

The RANGES subcommand specifies any of seven different tests appropriate for multiple comparisons between means. Each RANGES subcommand specifies one test. For example,

```
ONEWAY  WELL BY EDUC6 (1,6)
  /POLYNOMIAL = 2
  /CONTRAST = 2*-1,2*1
  /CONTRAST = 2*0, 2-*1, 2*1
  /CONTRAST = 2*-1,2*0,2*1
  /RANGES = SNK
  /RANGES = SCHEFFE (.01)
```

produces two range tests. RANGES subcommands cannot be separated by CONTRAST or POLYNOMIAL subcommands. The available tests are

LSD   *Least-significant difference.* Any alpha between 0 and 1 can be specified. The default is 0.05.

DUNCAN   *Duncan's multiple range test.* The default alpha is 0.05. Only 0.01, 0.05, and 0.10 are used. DUNCAN uses 0.01 if the alpha specified is less than 0.05; 0.05 if the alpha specified is greater than or equal to 0.05 but less than 0.10; and 0.10 if the alpha specified is greater than or equal to 0.10.

SNK   *Student-Newman-Keuls.* Only 0.05 is available as the alpha value.

TUKEYB   *Tukey's alternate procedure.* Only 0.05 is available as the alpha value.

TUKEY   *Honestly significant difference.* Only 0.05 is available as the alpha value.

LSDMOD   *Modified LSD.* Any alpha between 0 and 1 can be specified. The default alpha is 0.05.

SCHEFFE *Scheffé's test.* Any alpha between 0 and 1 can be specified. The default alpha is 0.05.

Range tests always produce multiple comparisons between all groups. Nonempty group means are sorted in ascending order. Asterisks in the matrix indicate significantly different group means. In addition to this output, homogeneous subsets are calculated for balanced designs and for all designs that use either the Duncan (DUNCAN) or the Student-Newman-Keuls (SNK) procedure to calculate multiple range tests.

18.164
User-Specified Ranges

You can specify any other type of range by coding specific range values. You can specify up to $k - 1$ range values in ascending order, where k is the number of groups and where the range value times the standard error of the combined subset is the critical value. If fewer than $k - 1$ values are specified, the last value specified is used for the remaining ones. You can also specify n repetitions of the same value with the form $n * r$. To use a single critical value for all subsets, specify one range value, as in:

```
ONEWAY  WELL BY EDUC6(1,6)
  /RANGES=5.53
```

18.165
HARMONIC Subcommand

The HARMONIC subcommand determines the sample size estimate to be used when the N's are not equal in all groups. Either only the sample sizes in the two groups being compared are used, or an average sample size of all groups is used.

The default keyword for HARMONIC is NONE, which uses the harmonic mean of the sizes of just the two groups being compared. To use the harmonic mean of *all* group sizes, specify keyword ALL. If ALL is used, ONEWAY calculates homogeneous subsets for SCHEFFE, TUKEY, TUKEYB, and LSD-MOD tests on unbalanced designs. Specify only one keyword on the HARMONIC subcommand.

NONE *Harmonic mean of the sizes of the two groups being compared.* You may also use keyword PAIR as an alias for NONE.

ALL *Harmonic mean of group sizes as sample sizes for range tests.* If the harmonic mean is used for unbalanced designs, ONEWAY determines homogeneous subsets for all range tests.

18.166
STATISTICS Subcommand

By default ONEWAY calculates the analysis of variance table. It also calculates any statistics specified by the CONTRASTS and RANGES subcommands.

Use the STATISTICS subcommand to request additional statistics. The default keyword for STATISTICS is NONE, for no additional statistics. You can specify any one or all of the following statistics:

NONE *No optional statistics.* This is the default.

DESCRIPTIVES *Group descriptive statistics.* Prints the number of cases, mean, standard deviation, standard error, minimum, maximum, and 95% confidence interval for each dependent variable for each group.

EFFECTS *Fixed- and random-effects statistics.* Prints the standard deviation, standard error, and 95% confidence interval for the fixed-effects model, and the standard error, 95% confidence interval, and estimate of between-component variance for the random-effects model.

HOMOGENEITY *Homogeneity-of-variance tests.* Prints Cochran's C, the Bartlett-Box F, and Hartley's F max.

ALL *All statistics available for ONEWAY.*

18.167
MISSING Subcommand

The MISSING subcommand controls missing values. Its default keywords are ANALYSIS and EXCLUDE. ANALYSIS excludes cases with missing values on an analysis-by-analysis basis. Use keyword LISTWISE to delete cases on a variable-by-variable basis. EXCLUDE determines that user-missing values are not used in the analysis. Use keyword INCLUDE to treat user-missing values as valid.

ANALYSIS *Exclude missing values on a pair-by-pair basis.* A case missing on either the dependent variable or grouping variable for a given analysis is not used for that analysis. Also, a case outside the range specified for the grouping variable is not used. This is the default.

LISTWISE *Exclude missing values listwise.* Cases missing on any variable named are excluded from all analyses.

EXCLUDE *Exclude user-missing values.* This is the default.

INCLUDE *Include user-missing values.* User-defined missing values are included in the analysis.

Keywords ANALYSIS and LISTWISE are mutually exclusive. Each can be used with either INCLUDE or EXCLUDE.

18.168
FORMAT Subcommand

By default, ONEWAY identifies groups as GRP1, GRP2, GRP3, etc. Use the FORMAT subcommand to identify the groups by their value labels. The FORMAT subcommand has only two keywords, NOLABELS and LABELS. NOLABELS is the default.

NOLABELS *Suppress value labels.* This is the default.

LABELS *Use the first eight characters from value labels for group labels.* The value labels are those defined for the independent variable.

18.169
Limitations

The following limitations apply to ONEWAY:

- A maximum of 100 dependent variables and 1 independent variable.
- An unlimited number of categories for the independent variable. However, contrasts and range tests are not performed if the actual number of nonempty categories exceeds 50.
- Only 1 POLYNOMIAL subcommand.
- A maximum of 10 CONTRAST subcommands and 10 RANGES subcommands.
- Any alpha values between 0 and 1 are permitted for the LSD, LSDMOD, and SCHEFFE range tests. SNK, TUKEY, and TUKEYB use an alpha value of 0.05, regardless of what is specified. DUNCAN uses an alpha value of 0.01 if the alpha specified is less than 0.05; 0.05 if the alpha specified is greater than or equal to 0.05 but less than 0.10; 0.10 if the alpha specified is greater than or equal to 0.10; or 0.05 if no alpha is specified.

18.170
PLOT

```
PLOT [HSIZE = {80**}]  [/VSIZE = {40**}]
              {n   }               {n   }

 [/CUTPOINT = {EVERY({1**})}]
              {      {n  } }
              {value list  }

 [/SYMBOLS = {ALPHANUMERIC**                        }]
             {NUMERIC                               }
             {'symbols'[,'overplot symbols']        }
             {X'hexsymbs'[,'overplot hexsymbs']}
             {DEFAULT                               }

 [/MISSING = [{PLOTWISE**}] [INCLUDE]]
              {LISTWISE  }

 [/FORMAT = {DEFAULT**          }]
            {CONTOUR[({10})]}
            {        {n } }
            {OVERLAY            }
            {REGRESSION         }

 [/TITLE = 'title']

 [/HORIZONTAL = ['title'] [STANDARDIZE] [REFERENCE(value list)]
                [MIN(min)] [MAX(max)] [UNIFORM]]

 [/VERTICAL = ['title'] [STANDARDIZE] [REFERENCE(value list)]
              [MIN(min)] [MAX(max)] [UNIFORM]]

 /PLOT = varlist WITH varlist [(PAIR)] [BY varname] [;varlist...]

 [/PLOT=...]
```

**Default if the subcommand is omitted.

Procedure PLOT produces two-dimensional line-printer plots. You can request simple scatterplots, scatterplots with a control variable and/or regression statistics, contour plots, and overlay plots.

The only required subcommand on PLOT is the PLOT subcommand. There are two types of optional subcommands: global subcommands (HSIZE, VSIZE, CUTPOINT, SYMBOLS, and MISSING) and local subcommands (FORMAT, TITLE, HORIZONTAL, and VERTICAL).

You can specify each of the global subcommands only once, and each must be prior to the first occurrence of the PLOT subcommand. You can use the PLOT subcommand and accompanying local subcommands more than once within a PLOT command. However, local subcommands apply only to the *immediately following* PLOT subcommand. A PLOT subcommand must be the last subcommand you specify. Use a slash to separate every subcommand from the next.

This abbreviated command reference does not discuss the character overstrike capabilities on the SYMBOLS subcommand. This feature is not essential to the operation of PLOT as described in this book. However, these features are fully discussed in the *SPSS-X User's Guide,* 3rd ed.

18.171
PLOT Subcommand

Use the PLOT subcommand to specify the variables to plot. Specify the variables for the vertical (Y) axis, then the keyword WITH, then the variables for the horizontal (X) axis.

By default, PLOT creates separate plots for all combinations formed by each variable on the left side of the WITH keyword with each variable on the right. However, you can choose to plot only corresponding pairs of variables by using the keyword PAIR in parentheses. In the following,

```
/PLOT = Yl Y2  WITH  Xl X2
```

```
/PLOT = Yl Y2  WITH  Xl X2 (PAIR)
```

the first PLOT subcommand specifies four plots, showing Y1 with X1, Y1 with X2, Y2 with X1, and Y2 with X2. The second PLOT subcommand specifies only two plots, showing Y1 with X1 and Y2 with X2.

Use semicolons to separate multiple plot lists. For example,

```
/PLOT = BONUS WITH TENURE SALNOW;SALNOW WITH SALBEG
```

requests three scatterplots. The first request produces plots of BONUS with TENURE and BONUS with SALNOW. The second request produces the plot of SALNOW with SALBEG.

In the output, an information table precedes the plots you request on a PLOT subcommand. This table shows the number of cases used, the size of the plot, and a list of symbols and frequencies.

18.172
Control and Contour Variables

Use the BY keyword on a PLOT subcommand's variable list to specify a control variable or a contour variable for a set of plots. You can specify only one such variable on any plot list. Producing a contour plot requires the FORMAT subcommand (see Section 18.177).

PLOT uses the first character of the control variable's value label as the plot symbol. If no value labels are supplied, PLOT uses the first character of the actual value. For the numeric value 28, the symbol would be 2; for the string value MALE, the symbol would be M. PLOT does not check uniqueness of symbols, but you can use the VALUE LABELS command to create appropriate value labels that prevent ambiguity.

18.173
TITLE Subcommand

You can provide a title for a plot with the TITLE subcommand. Enclose your own descriptive title for a plot in apostrophes on the TITLE subcommand. The default title of a plot uses either the names of the variables for a bivariate plot or the type of plot requested on the FORMAT subcommand (see Section 18.175). The command

```
PLOT TITLE='Plot of Beginning Salary on Current Salary'
 /PLOT=SALNOW WITH SALBEG
```

requests a title that overrides the default.

A title can contain up to 60 characters. A title longer than the horizontal width specified on the HSIZE subcommand (see Section 18.180) will be truncated.

18.174
VERTICAL and HORIZONTAL Subcommands

You can specify axis labels with the HORIZONTAL and VERTICAL subcommands. These two subcommands also control minimum and maximum values plotted, standardization of axes, provisions for reference lines, and whether the axes have uniform scales on different plots. Adjusting minimum and maximum values is especially useful when you want to focus on a subset of a larger plot. The minimum and maximum value specifications function like a TEMPORARY SELECT IF transformation (see Section 18.48). PLOT excludes values outside the specified range from the immediately following PLOT subcommand. PLOT scales the axes to include the specified values. However, to ensure that integers or simple decimals are on the axes, PLOT may extend the scales slightly beyond the specified minimum and maximum.

You can also use the VERTICAL or HORIZONTAL subcommand to designate a label for each axis, to choose the positions of reference lines, and to specify standardization of values.

The VERTICAL and HORIZONTAL subcommands have the same keyword specifications:

'label'	*Label of axis.* You can specify a label of up to 40 characters. The default is the variable label for the variable on the axis. If there is no variable label, PLOT uses the variable name. If you specify a label longer or wider than the plot frame size (see Section 18.180), the label will be truncated.
MIN(min)	*Minimum value included on axis.* The default is the minimum observed value. With the MIN option, only data values greater than or equal to *min* are plotted. The axis scale includes this value.
MAX(max)	*Maximum value included on axis.* The default is the maximum observed value. With the MAX option, only data values less than or equal to *max* are plotted. The axis scale includes this value.
UNIFORM	*Uniform values on axis.* This option specifies that all plots will have scales with the same values on the (vertical or horizontal) axis. Uniform scales also result if you specify both MIN and MAX. If you specify UNIFORM but not MIN and MAX, PLOT determines the minimum and maximum across all variables for the axis.
REFERENCE(value list)	*Reference lines for axis.* For either axis, this option specifies values at which to draw reference lines perpendicular to the axis.
STANDARDIZE	*Standardize variables on axis.* With this option, PLOT standardizes variables to have a mean of 0 and a standard deviation of 1. This option is useful if you want to overlay plots of variables that otherwise would have different scales.

The command

```
PLOT TITLE='Annual Salary by Age, XYZ Corporation  1983'
    /VERTICAL='Annual salary before taxes' MIN (500) MAX (75000)
        REFERENCE(25000,50000)
    /HORIZONTAL='Age of employee' MIN (18) MAX (65)
        REFERENCE (33,48)
        /PLOT=INCOME WITH AGE
```

produces a bivariate scatterplot with labeled axes that include values of INCOME between 500 and 75,000 and values of AGE between 18 and 65. The keyword REFERENCE requests reference lines at 25,000 and 50,000 on the vertical axis and at 33 and 48 on the horizontal axis.

18.175
FORMAT Subcommand

Procedure PLOT produces four main types of plots: scatterplots, contour plots, overlay plots, and regression plots. The FORMAT subcommand specifies the plot type for the immediately following PLOT subcommand.

18.176
Bivariate Scatterplots

The default plot is a bivariate scatterplot. To obtain a bivariate scatterplot, you can omit the FORMAT subcommand or specify FORMAT=DEFAULT.

18.177
Contour Plots

A contour plot is similar to a control plot in that symbols on either plot indicate values of the control variable for the cases represented at the positions of the symbols. However, the control variable for a contour plot is a continuous variable. You specify a contour variable after the BY keyword on the PLOT subcommand (see Section 18.172).

The CONTOUR keyword on the FORMAT subcommand requests a recoding of the control variable into n equal-width intervals corresponding to n plotting symbols. When more than one contour level occurs at a print position, PLOT prints the symbol for the highest level. You can specify a maximum of 35 contour levels for each contour plot. If you do not specify the number of levels the number defaults to 10.

The command

```
PLOT FORMAT=CONTOUR(10)
  /TITLE 'SOLUBILITY OF AMMONIA IN WATER'
  /HORIZONTAL='ATMOSPHERIC PRESSURE'
  /VERTICAL='TEMPERATURE'
  /PLOT=TEMP WITH PRESSURE BY CONCENT
```

requests a contour plot with ten levels of the variables named on the PLOT subcommand. Labels are specified for the HORIZONTAL and VERTICAL axes. The boundary values of each level of the control variable appear below the plot.

18.178
Overlay Plots

The OVERLAY keyword on the FORMAT subcommand tells SPSS-X to put all plots specified on the following PLOT subcommand in one frame. You can overlay only bivariate plots (simple scatterplots and regression plots), not control or contour plots. PLOT selects a unique symbol for each plot to be overlaid, plus a symbol to represent multiple plots in one print position.

You can overlay plots by specifying groups of variables on either side of the keyword WITH. The command

```
PLOT FORMAT=OVERLAY
  /TITLE 'MARRIAGE AND DIVORCE RATES  1900-1983'
  /VERTICAL='RATES PER 1000 POPULATION'
  /HORIZONTAL='YEAR' REFERENCE (1918,1945) MIN (1900) MAX (1983)
  /PLOT=MARRATE DIVRATE WITH YEAR
```

requests two plots to be overlaid in one frame. The TITLE specification provides a title for the plot. The VERTICAL subcommand provides a label for the vertical axis. The HORIZONTAL subcommand provides a label, specifies that reference lines be drawn perpendicular to points 1918 and 1945, and specifies 1900 and 1983 as minimum and maximum data values to plot. The PLOT subcommand specifies the variables for the overlay.

18.179
Regression Plots

With the REGRESSION keyword, PLOT calculates and prints statistics for the regression of the vertical-axis variable on the horizontal-axis variable. PLOT produces a scatterplot and marks regression-line intercepts with the letter R. For example, the command

```
PLOT TITLE='SALARY REGRESSION'
 /VERTICAL='CURRENT ANNUAL SALARY'
 /HORIZONTAL= 'ANNUAL STARTING SALARY'
 /FORMAT=REGRESSION
 /PLOT=SALNOW WITH SALBEG
```

requests a fully labeled regression plot of SALNOW with SALBEG.

You can also request regression plots with control variables. For example, the command

```
PLOT FORMAT=REGRESSION
 /PLOT=A B C WITH D; Y WITH X BY Z
```

requests regression statistics for three bivariate plots and one control plot. In a control plot, you do not get separate regression statistics for each control category. Instead, regression statistics are pooled over all categories.

18.180
HSIZE and VSIZE
Subcommands

Use the HSIZE and VSIZE subcommands to specify dimensions for your plots. The HSIZE and VSIZE subcommands must precede all PLOT subcommands and can be specified only once. All plots requested on one PLOT command are drawn to the same specified size.

The default size of your plot depends on current page size. With a typical computer page, the default width is 80 positions and the default length is 40 lines. You can override the defaults by using the VSIZE and HSIZE subcommands. The VSIZE subcommand specifies the vertical frame size (length) of the plot, and the HSIZE subcommand specifies the horizontal frame size (width). For example,

```
PLOT VSIZE=30/HSIZE=70
 /PLOT= Y WITH X
```

requests a length of 30 print lines and a width of 70 print positions. The specified size does *not* include print lines for the plot frames or for auxiliary information such as titles, axis scale numbers, regression statistics, or the symbol table.

18.181
HSIZE and VSIZE with
HORIZONTAL and VERTICAL

When you specify HSIZE or VSIZE in conjunction with a HORIZONTAL or VERTICAL minimum value, PLOT uses the minimum value as the starting point of the axis. To provide equal-interval, integer scale values, PLOT may extend an axis beyond the minimum and maximum values specified on the HORIZONTAL or VERTICAL subcommand. For example, the command

```
PLOT VSIZE=30 /HSIZE=70
 /FORMAT=OVERLAY
 /TITLE 'MARRIAGE AND DIVORCE RATES  1900-1983'
 /VERTICAL='RATES PER 1000 POPULATION'
 /HORIZONTAL='YEAR' REFERENCE (1918,1945) MIN (1900) MAX (1983)
 /PLOT=MARRATE DIVRATE WITH YEAR
```

produces a plot whose area is 30 lines by 70 characters. The values on the horizontal axis starts at 1900, and the maximum value on the horizontal axis is slightly greater than 1983.

18.182
Controlling Plot Symbols

Two subcommands, CUTPOINT and SYMBOLS, control the frequencies that plotted symbols represent and the characters for the symbols in plots.

Use the CUTPOINT subcommand to adjust the frequencies represented by each plot symbol in bivariate plots (simple scatterplots and regression plots). The SYMBOLS subcommand lets you specify which characters represent a given frequency value in bivariate scatter and regression plots, overlay, and contour plots. Both CUTPOINT and SYMBOLS must precede the first PLOT subcommand and can be specified only once on a PLOT command. All requested plots use the same cutpoint values and symbols.

You cannot use SYMBOLS specifications for scatterplots with control variables or for regression plots with control variables. For these plots, procedure PLOT assigns the symbols. However, you can determine what the symbols will be by giving the control variables appropriate names or value labels (see Section 18.172). Table 18.182 summarizes the subcommands affecting plot symbols.

Table 18.182 Subcommands for symbol control

Plot type	Meaning of each symbol	Subcommand(s) for controlling symbols
Bivariate scatter or regression	Frequency of cases	CUTPOINT SYMBOLS
Control	Value of control variable	None (see Section 18.172)
Overlay	Identity of overlaid plot	SYMBOLS
Contour	Level of contour variable	SYMBOLS FORMAT (for number of levels)

18.183
SYMBOLS Subcommand

Use the SYMBOLS subcommand to specify the plotting symbols. The SYMBOLS subcommand applies to bivariate, overlay, and contour plots. It does not apply to control plots. You can use only one SYMBOL subcommand on a PLOT command. The available keywords are:

ALPHANUMERIC   *Alphanumeric plotting symbols.* PLOT uses the characters 1–9, A–Z, and * as plot symbols. Thus, * represents 36 or more cases at a print position. This is the default symbol set.

NUMERIC   *Numeric plotting symbols.* PLOT uses the characters 1–9 and * as plot symbols. Thus, * represents 10 or more cases at a print position.

'symbols'[,'ovprnt']   *List of plot symbols.* You can provide your own list of symbols enclosed in apostrophes. Optionally, you can specify a second list of overprinting symbols separated from the first list by a comma or space. The overprinting symbols can be either hexadecimal representations (preceded by an X) or keyboard characters.

X'hexsym'[,'ovprnt']   *List of hexadecimal plot symbols.* Indicate hexadecimal symbols by specifying X before the hexadecimal representation list enclosed in apostrophes. Optionally, you can specify a second list of overprinting symbols separated from the first list by a comma or space. The overprinting symbols can be either hexadecimal representations or keyboard characters.

18.184
CUTPOINT Subcommand

By default, frequency plots use successive symbols in print positions corresponding to 1, 2, 3... cases, respectively. To define your own set of frequency values for the successive symbols, use the CUTPOINT subcommand. You can specify the desired interval width on the EVERY keyword, or you can use a value list in parentheses to specify cutpoints:

EVERY(n) *Frequency intervals of width* n. The default is an interval size of 1, meaning that each individual frequency up to 35 has a different symbol. The last default frequency interval includes all frequencies greater than 35. If you specify SYMBOLS as well as EVERY, the last symbol specified will represent all frequencies greater than those for the next-to-last symbol.

(value list) *Cutpoints at the values specified.*

You can specify only one CUTPOINT subcommand on a PLOT command, and it applies only to bivariate plots, not to control, overlay, or contour plots. If you specify

```
PLOT  CUTPOINT=EVERY(4)
 /PLOT = Y WITH X
```

1 will represent 1 to 4 cases at a print position, 2 will represent 5 to 8 cases, and so forth. If you specify

```
PLOT  CUTPOINT= (4, 10, 25)
 /PLOT = Y WITH X
```

1 will represent 1 to 4 cases at a print position, 2 will represent 5 to 10 cases, 3 will represent 11 to 25 cases, and 4 will represent 26 or more cases.

18.185
MISSING Subcommand

Use the MISSING subcommand to change or make explicit the treatment of cases with missing values. You can use only one MISSING subcommand on a PLOT command. Three specifications are available:

PLOTWISE *Exclude cases with missing values plotwise.* For each plot within a single frame, cases are deleted that have missing values on any variable for that plot. This is the default.

LISTWISE *Exclude cases with missing values listwise.* Cases with missing values on any variable named on any PLOT subcommand are deleted from all plots specified on the PLOT command.

INCLUDE *Include user-defined missing values as valid.*

If you specify

```
PLOT MISSING = LISTWISE
 /FORMAT=REGRESSION
 /PLOT = Y WITH A; Z WITH B
```

PLOT excludes cases with missing values on any of the variables Y, A, Z, and B.

For overlay plots, plotwise deletion applies to each subplot requested, not to the full list specified on the PLOT subcommand. With the command

```
PLOT FORMAT=OVERLAY
 /PLOT = INCOME82 TAXES82 WITH YEAR82
```

cases with missing values on INCOME82 or YEAR82 will be deleted from that subplot only, and cases with missing values on TAXES82 or YEAR82 will be deleted from the other subplot. The complete overlay plot may have a different number of cases for each subplot that is overlaid. The number of cases plotted in each subplot is stated below the plot frame.

18.186
Limitations

There are no limitations on the number of plots requested or on the number of variables specified on a PLOT command. The following limitations apply to the optional subcommands:

• A maximum of 60 characters for a title specified on the TITLE subcommand.
• A maximum of 36 symbols per SYMBOLS subcommand.
• A maximum of 35 cutpoints per CUTPOINT subcommand.
• A maximum of 10 reference points on each HORIZONTAL or VERTICAL subcommand.
• A maximum of 40 characters per label on each HORIZONTAL or VERTICAL subcommand.

18.187
REGRESSION

```
REGRESSION [MATRIX=[IN({file})] [OUT({file})]]
                       {*    }        {*    }

[/WIDTH={132**}]
        {n    }

[/SELECT={ (ALL)**               }]
         {varname relation value}

[/MISSING={LISTWISE**       }] [INCLUDE]]
          {PAIRWISE         }
          {MEANSUBSTITUTION }

[/DESCRIPTIVES=[DEFAULTS] [MEAN] [STDDEV] [CORR] [COV]
               [VARIANCE] [XPROD] [SIG] [N] [BADCORR]
               [ALL] [NONE**]]

[/VARIABLES={varlist    }]
            { (COLLECT)**}
            {ALL        }

[/CRITERIA=[DEFAULTS**] [TOLERANCE({0.0001**})] [MAXSTEPS(n)]
                                   {value   }

           [PIN({0.05**})] [POUT({0.10**})]
                {value }         {value }

           [FIN({3.84 })] [FOUT({2.71 })]]
                {value}         {value}

[/STATISTICS=[DEFAULTS**] [R**] [COEFF**] [ANOVA**] [OUTS**]
             [ZPP] [LABEL] [CHA] [CI] [F] [BCOV] [SES] [LINE]
             [HISTORY] [XTX] [COND] [END] [TOL] [ALL]]

[/ {NOORIGIN**}]
   {ORIGIN    }

[/REGWGT=varname]

/DEPENDENT=varlist

[/METHOD=]{STEPWISE [varlist]          } [...] [/...]
          {FORWARD [varlist]           }
          {BACKWARD [varlist]          }
          {ENTER [varlist]             }
          {REMOVE varlist              }
          {TEST(varlist)(varlist)...   }

[/RESIDUALS=[DEFAULTS] [ID(varname)] [DURBIN] [{SEPARATE}]]
                                              {POOLED  }
            [HISTOGRAM({ZRESID     })] [OUTLIERS({ZRESID     })]
                       {tempvarlist}             {tempvarlist}

            [NORMPROB({ZRESID     })] [SIZE({LARGE})]]
                      {tempvarlist}          {SMALL}

[/CASEWISE=[DEFAULTS] [{OUTLIERS({ 3   })}]
                      {         {value} }
                      {ALL             }

           [PLOT({ZRESID })] [{DEPENDENT PRED RESID}]]
                 {tempvar}    {tempvarlist         }

[/SCATTERPLOT=[SIZE({SMALL})] (varname,varname)...]
                    {LARGE}

[/PARTIALPLOT=[{ALL    }] [SIZE({SMALL})]]
              {varlist}         {LARGE}

[/SAVE=tempvar(newname) tempvar(newname)...]
```

**Default if the subcommand is omitted.
Temporary variables for residuals analysis are: PRED, ADJPRED, SRESID, MAHAL, RESID, ZPRED, SDRESID, COOK, DRESID, ZRESID, SEPRED, LEVER.

Procedure REGRESSION calculates a multiple regression equation and associated statistics and plots. Several methods for variable selection as well as statistics for analysis of residuals and influential observations are available. Several types of plots can be displayed.

Only two subcommands are required. The DEPENDENT subcommand lists the dependent variable(s). The METHOD subcommand keywords specify the method to be used for variable selection. All other subcommands either have default values or are optional.

This abbreviated command reference does not discuss the MATRIX subcommand used to read and write matrices, the COLLECT and PREVIOUS keywords used with the VARIABLES subcommand or the TEST keyword used with the METHOD subcommand, the PARTIALPLOT and SAVE subcommands for additional analysis of residuals and for saving residuals on the active file, or the REGWGT subcommand for estimating weighted least squares models. These features are not essential to the operation of REGRESSION as described in this book. However, they are fully discussed in *SPSS-X User's Guide,* 3rd ed.

18.188
DEPENDENT Subcommand

Specify the dependent variable or variables with the DEPENDENT subcommand. If you name more than one dependent variable, REGRESSION uses the same independent variables and methods for each dependent variable named. All methods are executed for the first dependent variable, then the second, and so on. None of the variables named on the DEPENDENT subcommand is treated as an independent variable in any model associated with that DEPENDENT subcommand. Each DEPENDENT subcommand initiates a new regression model, and you can specify more than one DEPENDENT subcommand.

You can name more than one variable on a DEPENDENT subcommand, as in:

```
REGRESSION VARIABLES=IQ TO ACHIEVE
          /DEPENDENT=ACHIEVE IQREPORT /STEPWISE
```

REGRESSION first uses ACHIEVE as the dependent variable, then IQREPORT as the dependent variable. IQREPORT is not used as an independent variable when ACHIEVE is the dependent variable, and ACHIEVE is not used as an independent variable when IQREPORT is the dependent variable.

You can also use multiple DEPENDENT subcommands, as in:

```
REGRESSION  VARIABLES=IQ TO ACHIEVE
           /DEPENDENT=ACHIEVE /STEPWISE
           /DEPENDENT=IQREPORT /ENTER ACHIEVE,SES,IQ
```

Variable IQREPORT is an independent variable in the first model, and ACHIEVE is an independent variable in the second model.

18.189
METHOD Subcommand

Use the METHOD subcommand to specify the method or combination of methods you want to use to build a multiple regression equation. The actual keyword METHOD may be omitted. A variable list must follow the METHOD subcommand if you specify REMOVE as the method for building the regression equation. Otherwise, the variable list following the METHOD subcommand is optional. All variables which pass the tolerance criterion are candidates for entry (see Section 18.195).

The following keywords are available on the METHOD subcommand:

FORWARD   *Forward entry.* Variables enter the equation one at a time. At each step, the independent variables not yet in the equation are examined for entry. The variable with the smallest probability-of-*F* value enters, provided that this value is smaller than the entry criterion PIN (see Section 18.195) and the variable passes the tolerance tests.

BACKWARD *Backward elimination.* At each step, the independent variables already in the equation are examined for removal. Variables are removed from the equation one at a time. The variable with the largest probability-of-*F* value is removed, provided that this value is larger than the removal criterion POUT (see Section 18.195). If no variables are in the equation prior to the BACKWARD specification, REGRESSION first enters all independent variables passing the tolerance criterion and then examines them for removal.

STEPWISE   *Stepwise selection.* If there are independent variables already in the equation, the variable with the largest probability of *F* is examined for removal. If the probability of *F* is larger than the removal criterion POUT, the variable is removed. The equation is recomputed, and the rest of the variables are examined for removal. Once no more independent variables need to be removed, all independent variables not in the equation are examined for entry. The variable with the smallest probability of *F* is entered if this value is smaller than the entry criterion PIN and the variable passes the tolerance tests. Once a variable enters, variables in the equation are again examined for removal. This process continues until no variables in the equation need to be removed and no variables not in the equation are eligible for entry, or until the maximum number of steps has been reached (see Section 18.195).

ENTER   *Forced entry.* The ENTER keyword enters all variables that satisfy the tolerance criterion. Variables are entered one at a time in order of decreasing tolerance but are treated as a single block for statistics computed for changes in the equation. If the ENTER keyword is accompanied by a list of variables, those variables are candidates for entry. Specification of ENTER without a variable list enters *all* independent variables that pass the tolerance criterion. If the order of entry of independent variables is of interest, then either control the order of entry by specifying one ENTER subcommand for each independent variable or specify one of the three equation methods already discussed.

REMOVE   *Forced removal.* The REMOVE keyword removes all named variables from the equation as a single block. The REMOVE keyword *must* have an accompanying variable list.

You can specify multiple METHOD subcommands within the same equation. For example, you might want to see how the independent variables would enter in stepwise fashion but ultimately want all the variables in the equation, as in:

```
REGRESSION VARIABLES=IQ TO ACHIEVE
           /DEPENDENT=ACHIEVE  /STEPWISE  /ENTER
```

18.190
VARIABLES Subcommand

The VARIABLES subcommand is optional and lists the variables to be used in the analyses. If omitted, all variables named on the DEPENDENT and METHOD subcommands for each analysis are used. When used, the VARIABLES subcommand must precede the DEPENDENT subcommand and the METHOD subcommand, as in

```
REGRESSION VARIABLES=IQ TO ACHIEVE
           /DEPENDENT=ACHIEVE  /STEP
```

Only one VARIABLES subcommand is allowed.

18.191
MISSING Subcommand

By default, analyses are performed using only cases with nonmissing values on all variables specified for the analysis. Use the MISSING subcommand and one of the following keywords to specify alternative missing-value treatments.

LISTWISE	*Delete cases with missing values listwise.* This is the default.
PAIRWISE	*Delete cases with missing values pairwise.* Each correlation coefficient is computed using cases with complete data for the pair of variables correlated, regardless of whether the cases have missing values for any other variables named on the VARIABLES subcommand.
MEANSUBSTITUTION	*Replace missing values with the variable mean.* All cases are used in the analyses with the substitutions treated as valid observations.
INCLUDE	*Include cases with user-missing values.* All user-missing values are treated as valid values. System-missing values are not used.

When residuals and predicted values are requested (see Sections 18.198–18.202), they are created missing or valid based on whether any values they require are missing or not. Predicted values are valid if all values of the independent variables entered in the equation are valid. Residual values are valid if all values of the independent variables entered in the equation are valid and if the values of the dependent variable are valid.

18.192
DESCRIPTIVES Subcommand

By default, REGRESSION does not display descriptive statistics. However, you can obtain descriptive statistics by using the DESCRIPTIVES subcommand. DESCRIPTIVES provides univariate statistics (such as the mean and standard deviation) as well as bivariate statistics (such as the correlation coefficient).

You can use the following keyword specifications for the DESCRIPTIVES subcommand to display statistics for all variables used in the analysis:

NONE	*Do not display descriptive statistics.* This is the default if the DESCRIPTIVES subcommand is omitted.
DEFAULTS	*MEAN, STDDEV, and CORR.* If you specify DESCRIPTIVES with no specifications, these are the defaults.
MEAN	*Variable means.*
STDDEV	*Variable standard deviations.*
VARIANCE	*Variable variances.*
CORR	*Correlation matrix.*
SIG	*One-tailed significance levels of the correlation coefficients.*
BADCORR	*Display the correlation matrix only if some coefficients cannot be computed.*
COV	*Covariance matrix.*
XPROD	*Cross-product deviations from the mean.*
N	*Numbers of cases used to compute correlation coefficients.* Used with pairwise or mean substitution missing-value treatments.

18.193
SELECT Subcommand

Use the SELECT subcommand to select a subset of your cases for computing the regression equation. Only selected cases contribute to the correlation coefficients and to the regression equation. Residuals and predicted values are calculated and reported for both selected and unselected cases (see Section 18.198).

The general form of the SELECT subcommand is

/SELECT= varname relation value

where the *relation* is EQ, NE, LT, LE, GT, or GE.

Do not use a variable from a temporary transformation as a selection variable. The file is read more than once if you request residuals processing. If the selection variable is the result of a temporary recode specification, the value of the variable will change when the file is read a second time.

18.194
Equation Control Subcommands

Three optional subcommands can be placed between the VARIABLES subcommand and the DEPENDENT subcommand. Use the CRITERIA subcommand to change the entry and removal criteria SPSS-X uses in developing the equation. Use the STATISTICS subcommand to control the statistics displayed. Use the ORIGIN subcommand to request regression through the origin. All equation control modifiers are in effect for subsequent equations unless overridden by appropriate subcommands.

18.195
CRITERIA Subcommand

All variables are tested for *tolerance* prior to entry into an equation. The tolerance of a variable is the proportion of its variance not accounted for by other independent variables in the equation. The *minimum tolerance* of a variable is the smallest tolerance any variable already in the analysis would have if that variable were included in the analysis. A variable must pass both tolerance and minimum tolerance tests in order to enter a regression equation.

If a variable passes the tolerance criterion, it is further tested depending on the equation method specified (see Section 18.189). To control the criteria used for variable selection, use the following keywords:

DEFAULTS   *PIN(0.05), POUT(0.1), and TOLERANCE(0.0001)*. If you do not specify a CRITERIA subcommand, these are the defaults. If you have changed the criteria for an equation, use the keyword DEFAULTS to restore these defaults.

PIN(value)   *Probability of* F-*to-enter*. The default value is 0.05.

POUT(value)   *Probability of* F-*to-remove*. The default value is 0.10.

FIN(value)   F-*to-enter*. If no value is specified, the default is 3.84.

FOUT(value)   F-*to-remove*. If no value is specified, the default is 2.71.

TOLERANCE(value) *Tolerance*. The default value is 0.0001.

MAXSTEPS(n)   *Maximum number of steps*. For the STEPWISE method, the default is twice the number of independent variables. For the FORWARD and BACKWARD methods, the default maximum is the number of variables meeting the PIN and POUT or FIN and FOUT criteria. The MAXSTEPS value applies to the total model. The default value for the total model is the sum of the maximum number of steps over each method in the model.

A CRITERIA subcommand must appear before the DEPENDENT subcommand that initiates the equation and after the VARIABLES subcommand. The criteria remain in effect for all subsequent regression analyses until modified. For example, in the command

```
REGRESSION  VARIABLES=SALARY TO VERBAL
            /CRITERIA=PIN(.1) POUT(.15) TOL(.001)
            /DEPENDENT=VERBAL /FORWARD
            /CRITERIA=DEFAULTS
            /DEPENDENT=VERBAL /STEPWISE
```

the first CRITERIA subcommand relaxes the default criteria for entry and removal, while the second CRITERIA subcommand reestablishes the defaults.

18.196
STATISTICS Subcommand

Use the STATISTICS subcommand to display a number of statistics for the regression equation. The STATISTICS subcommand must appear before the DEPENDENT subcommand. It remains in effect for all new equations until overridden by another STATISTICS subcommand.

There are four types of STATISTICS keywords: global specifications, summary statistics for the equation, statistics for the independent variables, and step summary statistics.

Global Specifications. The keywords are

DEFAULTS   *R, ANOVA, COEFF, and OUTS.* In the absence of any STATISTICS subcommand, these are the defaults.

ALL   *Print all summary statistics except LABEL, F, LINE, and END.*

Summary Statistics for the Equation. The keywords are

R   *Multiple R.* Print the multiple R, R^2, adjusted R^2, and standard error of the estimate. In the absence of a STATISTICS subcommand, these statistics are displayed.

ANOVA   *Analysis of variance table.* Print the analysis of variance table for the model, F value for multiple R, and significance level of F. In the absence of a STATISTICS subcommand, these statistics are displayed.

CHA   *Change in R^2.* Print the change in R^2 between steps, F value for change in R^2, and significance level of F.

BCOV   *Variance-covariance matrix for unstandardized regression coefficients.* Print a matrix with the following elements: variances of the regression estimates on the diagonal, the covariances of the regression estimates below the diagonal, and correlations of the regression estimates above the diagonal.

XTX   *Sweep matrix.* Print the current status of the sweep matrix.

COND   *Condition number bounds.* Print the lower and upper bounds for the condition number of the submatrix of the sweep matrix that contains independent variables already entered. (See Berk, 1977.)

Statistics for the Independent Variables. The keywords are

COEFF   *Regression coefficients.* Print the unstandardized regression coefficient (B), the standard error of B, standardized regression coefficient (beta), t value for B, and two-tailed significance level of t for each variable in the equation. In the absence of a STATISTICS subcommand, these statistics are displayed.

OUTS   *Coefficients and statistics for variables not yet in the equation.* Print the standardized regression coefficient (beta) if the variable were to enter the equation at the next step, t value for B, significance level of t, partial correlation with the dependent variable controlling for all variables in the equation, and minimum tolerance. The default.

ZPP   *Correlation, part, and partial correlation.* Print the zero-order correlation of each independent variable in the equation with the dependent variable, the partial correlation for each independent variable, and the partial correlation with the dependent variable controlling for the other independent variables in the equation.

CI   *95% confidence interval for the unstandardized regression coefficient.*

SES   *Approximate standard error of beta.* (See Meyer & Younger, 1976.)

TOL   *Tolerance and minimum tolerance.*

LABEL   *Variable labels.*

F   F *value for B and its significance level.* Displayed instead of the t value. Significance of t is the same as the significance of F in this case.

Step Summary Statistics. The keywords are

LINE   *Print a single summary line of output for each step performed. Print full output on completion of each method.* This option differs from END, which prints the full output only on completion of the model.

HISTORY   *Print a final summary report.* Includes summary statistics computed at each step.

END   *Print one line per step (STEPWISE, FORWARD, or BACKWARD) or one line per block (ENTER, REMOVE) and full output only on completion of the model.* This option differs from LINE, which prints the full output on completion of each method block.

18.197
ORIGIN Subcommand

Use the ORIGIN subcommand to specify regression through the origin. Place the ORIGIN subcommand between the VARIABLES subcommand and the DEPENDENT subcommand. ORIGIN is in effect for all subsequent analyses unless you specify the keyword NOORIGIN. For example,

```
REGRESSION  VARIABLES=GNP TO M1
            /ORIGIN
            /DEPENDENT=GNP /FORWARD
```

requests a regression analysis through the origin using GNP as the dependent variable and the forward-selection method.

18.198
Analysis of Residuals

Use the following subcommands for analysis of residuals: RESIDUALS, CASEWISE, SCATTERPLOT, PARTIALPLOT, and SAVE. Any or all of these keywords can be specified in any order to obtain an analysis of residuals. For each analysis, REGRESSION can calculate 12 temporary variables containing several types of residuals, predicted values, and related measures. Optionally, these variables can be added to the active file for analysis using other SPSS-X procedures.

18.199
Temporary Variables

The following temporary variables are available for the analysis of residuals:

PRED   *Unstandardized predicted values.*
RESID   *Unstandardized residuals.*
DRESID   *Deleted residuals.*
ADJPRED   *Adjusted predicted values.*
ZPRED   *Standardized predicted values.*
ZRESID   *Standardized residuals.*
SRESID   *Studentized residuals.*
SDRESID   *Studentized deleted residuals.* (See Hoaglin & Welsch, 1978.)
SEPRED   *Standard errors of the predicted values.*
MAHAL   *Mahalanobis' distances.*
COOK   *Cook's distances.* (See Cook, 1977.)
LEVER   *Leverage values.* (See Velleman & Welsch, 1981.)

18.200
RESIDUALS Subcommand

Several measures and plots based on the residuals and predicted values for the regression equation can be displayed. Specifications for the RESIDUALS subcommand are

DEFAULTS	*SIZE(LARGE), DURBIN, NORMPROB(ZRESID), HISTOGRAM(ZRESID), and OUTLIERS(ZRESID).* If you specify the RESIDUALS subcommand without any keywords, these defaults are used.
SIZE(plotsize)	*Plot sizes.* The default is LARGE if the display width is at least 120 (see Section 18.203) and the page length is at least 58. Use SIZE(SMALL) to override the default.
HISTOGRAM(varlist)	*A histogram of the temporary variable or variables named.* The default variable is ZRESID. Other variables that can be plotted include PRED, RESID, ZPRED, DRESID, ADJPRED, SRESID, and SDRESID.
NORMPROB(varlist)	*A normal probability* (P-P) *plot of standardized values.* The default variable is ZRESID. Other variables that can be plotted are PRED, RESID, ZPRED, DRESID, ADJPRED, SRESID, and SDRESID.
OUTLIERS(varlist)	*The 10 worst outliers based on values of the variables specified.* The default variable is ZRESID. Other variables that can be used include RESID, SRESID, SDRESID, DRESID, MAHAL, and COOK.
DURBIN	*Durbin-Watson test statistic.*
ID(varname)	*Use the values from this variable to label casewise or outlier plots.* Any variable in your file can be named. If ID(varname) is not specified, cases are identified by case number. ID also labels the list of cases obtained from the CASEWISE subcommand (see Section 18.201).
POOLED	*Display pooled plots and statistics for selected and nonselected cases.* The default is SEPARATE, so that if SELECT is in effect, separate copies of the summary statistics and all plots are produced for selected and nonselected cases.

The RESIDUALS subcommand must follow the last method keyword. All calculations and plots requested on the RESIDUALS subcommand are based on the regression equation produced as a result of the last method specified. For example,

```
/RESID=DEFAULT SIZE(SMALL) ID(COUNTRY)
```

requests residual statistics and plots. DEFAULT implies a normal probability plot of standardized residuals, a histogram of standardized residuals, a table showing the 10 worst outliers based on the values of the standardized residual, the Durbin-Watson statistic, and large plot sizes. SIZE(SMALL) overrides the large plot sizes. ID(COUNTRY) names COUNTRY as a variable to identify the cases on outlier plots.

18.201
CASEWISE Subcommand

You can display a casewise plot of any of the temporary residuals variables accompanied by a listing of the values of the dependent variable and the values of as many of the other temporary variables as can be displayed in the available page width (see Section 18.203). Candidate variables for display include the 12 temporary residual variables, the dependent variable, and the ID variable (see Section 18.200). The widest page allows a maximum of eight of these to be displayed. For example,

```
/CASEWISE=DEFAULT ALL SRE MAH COOK SDR
```

displays the dependent variable SAVINGS and the six temporary variables PRED, RESID, SRESID, SDRESID, MAHAL, and COOK for all cases, and plots the standardized residuals in the casewise plot.

The CASEWISE subcommand has the following specifications:

DEFAULTS *OUTLIERS(3), PLOT(ZRESID), DEPENDENT, PRED, and RESID*. If you specify CASEWISE without any keywords, these defaults are used.

OUTLIERS(value) *Limit plot to outliers defined by this value.* The plot contains those cases whose absolute value is at least as large as the value you specify. The default value is 3 for standardized residuals (ZRESID). To display all cases, specify the keyword ALL. However, this is not recommended for large files because it results in a line being printed for each case.

PLOT(varname) *Plot the values of this temporary variable in the casewise plot.* The default variable is ZRESID. You can also specify RESID and DRESID, both of which are standardized for the plot, or the already standardized SRESID and SDRESID.

varlist *Display the values of these variables.* Some combination of the 12 temporary variables can be specified, although not all 12 can be displayed. The defaults are DEPENDENT (for the dependent variable), PRED, and RESID.

18.202
SCATTERPLOT Subcommand

Use the SCATTERPLOT subcommand to display a series of scatterplots of the temporary variables and the variables in the regression equation. Whenever you specify a temporary variable in a scatterplot, you must precede the name with an asterisk (*) to distinguish the temporary variable name from a standard variable name. Specifications are

SIZE(plotsize) *Plot sizes.* The default is SMALL for scatterplots. Keyword LARGE requires substantially more computer memory and should be used when detail is required.

(varname,varname) *Plot the variables specified.* If the variable is one of the temporary variables, precede the keyword with an asterisk. Temporary variables that can be plotted include PRED, RESID, ZPRED, ZRESID, DRESID, ADJPRED, SRESID, and SDRESID. These variables, as well as MAHAL, COOK, MAHAL, and SEPRED, can be saved on the active file and plotted later using the SCATTERGRAM procedure. Otherwise, the name can be any variable specified on the VARIABLES subcommand. Specify as many pairs in parentheses as you want plots.

The first variable named in each set of parentheses is plotted along the vertical axis. The second variable is plotted along the horizontal axis. Plotting symbols are used to represent multiple points occurring at the same print position.

All scatterplots are standardized. That is, specifying *RESID is the same as specifying *ZRESID, and *PRED is the same as *ZPRED. For example,

```
/SCATTERPLOT (*RES,*PRE)(*RES,SAVINGS)
```

specifies two scatterplots—the plot of the residuals against the predicted values and the plot of the residuals against the values of the dependent variable. To obtain unstandardized scatterplots, save residuals variables on the active file for subsequent processing with procedure SCATTERGRAM.

18.203
WIDTH Subcommand

You can control the width of output from REGRESSION. The default width is 132 characters, but you can specify any width from 72 to 132. The width you choose affects the volume of regression statistics displayed and the amount of information displayed in a casewise residuals plot. This is especially true when the width is quite narrow. The WIDTH subcommand can appear anywhere. If you specify more than one WIDTH subcommand, SPSS-X uses the width from the last WIDTH subcommand specified.

18.204
T-TEST

Independent samples:

```
T-TEST GROUPS=varname ({1,2**     }) /VARIABLES=varlist
                       {value     }
                       {value,value}

  [/MISSING={ANALYSIS**}  [INCLUDE]]
           {LISTWISE  }

  [/FORMAT={LABELS**}]
          {NOLABELS}
```

Paired samples:

```
T-TEST PAIRS=varlist [WITH varlist [(PAIRED)]] [/varlist ...]

  [/MISSING={ANALYSIS**}  [INCLUDE]]
           {LISTWISE  }

  [/FORMAT={LABELS**}]
          {NOLABELS}
```

**Default if the subcommand is omitted.

T-TEST compares sample means by calculating Student's *t* and tests the significance of the difference between the means. It tests either independent samples (different groups of cases) or paired samples (different variables). T-TEST subcommands can be used in any order.

18.205
Independent Samples

An independent-samples test divides the cases into two groups and compares the group means on a single variable. This test requires the GROUPS and VARIABLES subcommands. You can specify only one independent-samples test per T-TEST command.

18.206
GROUPS Subcommand

The GROUPS subcommand names the variable and the criterion for dividing the cases into two groups. You can name only one variable. You can use any of three different methods to define the two groups. In the first method, a single value in parentheses groups all cases with a code equal to or greater than the value into one group and the remaining cases into the other group. For example, the command

```
T-TEST GROUPS=WORLD(2) /VARIABLES=NTCPUR
```

groups together all cases with the value of WORLD greater than or equal to 2. The remaining cases go into the other group.

Alternatively, if you specify two values in parentheses, one group includes cases with the first value on the grouping variable, and the other includes cases with the second value, as in:

```
T-TEST  GROUPS=WORLD(1,3) /VARIABLES=NTCPUR
```

In this example, cases with values other than 1 or 3 for variable WORLD are not used.

If the grouping variable has only two values, coded 1 and 2, respectively, you do not have to specify a value list. For example, the command

```
T-TEST  GROUPS=SEX /VARIABLES=GRADES
```

groups all cases having the value 1 for SEX into one group and cases having the value 2 for SEX into the other group. All other cases are not used.

18.207
VARIABLES Subcommand

The VARIABLES subcommand names the variables being analyzed. You can use only numeric variables. The command

```
T-TEST  GROUPS=WORLD(1,3) /VARIABLES=NTCPRI NTCSAL NTCPUR
```

compares the means of the two groups defined by WORLD for the variables NTCPRI, NTCSAL, and NTCPUR, while

```
T-TEST  GROUPS=WORLD(1,3) /VARIABLES=NTCPRI TO MCLOTHES
```

compares the means of the groups defined by WORLD for all variables between and including NTCPRI and MCLOTHES.

18.208
PAIRS Subcommand

A typical application of a paired-samples test is the comparison of pre- and post-course test scores for students in a class. To obtain a paired-samples *t* test, use the PAIRS subcommand, as in:

```
T-TEST  PAIRS=WCLOTHES MCLOTHES
```

You can name only numeric variables. If you specify a list of variables, each variable is compared with every other variable. For example, the command

```
T-TEST PAIRS=TEACHER CONSTRUC MANAGER
```

compares TEACHER with CONSTRUC, TEACHER with MANAGER, and CONSTRUC with MANAGER.

    You can use the keyword WITH to request a test comparing every variable to the left of the keyword with every variable to the right of the keyword. For example,

```
T-TEST  PAIRS=TEACHER MANAGER WITH CONSTRUC ENGINEER
```

compares TEACHER with CONSTRUC, TEACHER with ENGINEER, MANAGER with CONSTRUC, and MANAGER with ENGINEER. TEACHER is not compared with MANAGER, and CONSTRUC is not compared with ENGINEER.

    You can use the slash to separate analysis lists, as in

```
T-TEST  PAIRS=WCLOTHES MCLOTHES/NTCPRI WITH NTCPUR NTCSAL
```

which specifies two analysis lists.

(PAIRED) Keyword. Use the keyword (PAIRED) for testing paired samples. If you specify the keyword (PAIRED) in addition to the keyword WITH on the PAIRS subcommand, as in

```
T-TEST  PAIRS=TEACHER MANAGER WITH CONSTRUC ENGINEER (PAIRED)
```

TEACHER is paired with CONSTRUC and MANAGER is paired with ENGINEER. You must name or imply the same number of variables on each side of the keyword WITH. If the number of variables is not equal, SPSS-X will generate as many T-TESTS as it can and will then issue a warning indicating the number of variables is not equal.

18.209
Independent and Paired Designs

You can request both independent- and paired-samples tests on a single T-TEST command. To do so, specify the GROUPS, VARIABLES, and PAIRS subcommands.

```
T-TEST GROUPS= WORLD(1,3) /VARIABLES=NTCPRI NTCSAL NTCPUR
       /PAIRS=WCLOTHES MCLOTHES
```

18.210
One-Tailed Significance Levels

By default, the probability is based on the two-tailed test. This is appropriate when significant differences in either direction are of interest. When theoretical considerations predict that the difference will be in a given direction (such as the Group 1 mean will be higher than the Group 2 mean), a one-tailed test is appropriate. To calculate the one-tailed probability, divide the two-tailed probability by 2.

18.211
MISSING Subcommand

By default, T-TEST deletes cases with missing values on an analysis-by-analysis basis. For independent-samples tests, cases missing on either the grouping variable or the analysis variable are excluded from the analysis of that variable. For paired-samples tests, a case missing on either of the variables in a given pair is excluded from the analysis of that pair. The following keyword options are available using the MISSING subcommand:

ANALYSIS *Delete cases with missing values on an analysis-by-analysis basis.* This is the default if you omit the MISSING subcommand.

LISTWISE *Exclude missing values listwise.* A case missing for any variable specified on either the GROUPS or the VARIABLES subcommand is excluded from any independent sample analysis. A case missing for any variable specified on the PAIRS subcommand is excluded from any paired sample analysis.

INCLUDE *Include user-defined missing values.* User-missing values are included in the analysis.

The ANALYSIS and LISTWISE keywords are mutually exclusive; however, each can be specified with INCLUDE.

18.212
FORMAT Subcommand

By default, T-TEST prints variable labels. You can suppress variable labels by specifying NOLABELS on the FORMAT subcommand:

LABELS *Print variable labels.* This is the default if you omit the FORMAT subcommand.

NOLABELS *Suppress variable labels.*

18.213
Limitations

The following limitation applies to procedure T-TEST:

- A maximum of 1 GROUPS and 1 VARIABLES subcommand per T-TEST command. Otherwise, T-TEST is constrained only by the amount of work space available on your computer.

Appendix A Answers to Selected Exercises

Chapter 1

Data Analysis

1. a. The codes are not mutually exclusive. For example, someone eating out once per day can be coded as a 1, 2, 3, or 4. The codes also do not cover all possible events.
    b. It would be best to record the actual number of meals eaten out per week.

2. Age requires at least two columns in the file. Since ages of 40 can occur, 40 is a bad choice for the missing value code. A negative number, such as -1, would be acceptable since negative ages are impossible.

    Entering the actual occupation instead of a code can make processing difficult since each unique combination of seven characters will be considered a separate occupation. For example, HOUSEWI and HOMEMAK are different. Seven characters may also be insufficient to distinguish between occupations. College students, janitors, and professors may all end up identified as COLLEGE.

    Since several colors begin with the same letter, for example, black, blue, and burgundy, the first letter is not a unique identifier. Also note that COLOR is coded in column 9. This is in the middle of the code for occupation.

3. a. The case is the person answering the survey.
    b. Name, sex, age, candidate, registered to vote, and employment status.

Chapter 2

Syntax

1. a. This variable name is too long. Only eight characters are allowed in a variable name.
    b. This variable name begins with an illegal character. Variable names must begin with one of the 26 letters A–Z or @.
    c. This variable name has an illegal blank. Embedded blanks are not allowed in variable names.
    d. This is a valid variable name.

2. a. The RECORDS subcommand specifies one record per case but the /2 points SPSS-X to the second record.
    b. There is a wrong columns specification. KIDAGE1 TO KIDAGE3 30–36 tells SPSS-X to divide seven columns among three variables. The number of columns must be an integer multiple of the number of variables specified.
    c. You cannot specify duplicate variable labels. A variable label can apply to one variable only.
    d. The value label NEW YORK is not enclosed in apostrophes or quotation marks.
    e. No variable name is specified.
    f. The missing values must be enclosed by parentheses.

3. a.

	NAME	AGE	GPA
1	WILLIAM JOHNSON	19	3.76
2	CAROLYN STEVENS	18	3.81
3	WAYNE ROBERTSON	20	3.59
4	LEONARD GILMORE	19	3.79
5	VIVIAN SMITHFIELD	21	3.80

   b. WILLIAM JOHNSON

   c. LEONARD GILMORE

   d. 4

4. There are eight syntax errors.

   a. The A following NAME 1–20 must be in parentheses.

   b. The second line of the DATA LIST cannot begin in column 1.

   c. The variable name HAIRCOLOR has too many characters.

   d. The variable name WEIGH on the VARIABLE LABELS command is incorrect.

   e. A slash (/) must be used to separate the label HAZEL from the variable name HAIRCOLOR.

   f. HAIRCOLOR on the VALUE LABELS command is an invalid variable name.

   g. The variable name AGE on the MISSING VALUES command is not defined on the DATA LIST command.

   h. The order of the variables on the LIST command is incorrect given the order in which they are defined on the DATA LIST command.

5. The variable AGE must contain only numeric values given the way it is defined on the DATA LIST command. Case 8 contains an alphanumeric code for AGE. The most simple solution is to change the value in the data to some numeric code, such as −1. Since DK stands for DON'T KNOW, the numeric values used to replace DK would probably be set to missing using the MISSING VALUES command.

   For larger data sets, changing all of the alphanumeric codes may not be practical. In this situation, the variable could be specified as a string on the DATA LIST command. Then, the nonnumeric codes could be modified using the RECODE command.

Chapter 3

Syntax

1. a. False. Slashes can go anywhere between the subcommands.

   b. False. Frequently, commands can be made more readable with blanks around equals signs.

   c. True. The keyword is NOTABLE with no intervening blank.

   d. False. As long as the second and any subsequent continuation lines of a command in batch mode begins with at least one blank, the command is free format.

   e. False. Commas and blanks are interchangeable when separating variable names in a list.

   f. False. The order you enter the variable names is up to you and affects only the order in which the output is displayed.

   g. False. Keyword NOTABLE (when spelled correctly) eliminates the frequency tables.

   h. True. Bar charts are requested for variables FIRSTCHD and DAYOFWK.

2. a. Incorrect. The BARCHART subcommand is missing and MISSING=INCLUDE would have generated a bar for the missing value.

   b. Incorrect. MISSING=INCLUDE would have generated a bar for the missing value.

   c. Correct. This command creates the bar chart plus a frequency table also displayed in descending order of frequency.

3. a. False. The FREQUENCIES syntax is fine.

   b. False. The three lines of information following the GET command indicate that the file was located and read correctly.

   c. False. The message following the GET command shows that the file was recognized as an SPSS-X system file.

   d. True. The error message points directly to the variable name as having caused the problem. The DISPLAY command gives you all dictionary information on a system file including the variable names (see Chapter 18).

Statistical Concepts

1. a. Bar chart.
   b. Bar chart.
   c. Histogram.
   d. Histogram.
   e. Bar chart.
   f. Histogram.
   g. Histogram.

2. a. True.
   b. True.
   c. False.
   d. False.
   e. False.
   f. True.

3.

VALUE LABEL	VALUE	FREQUENCY	PERCENT	VALID PERCENT	CUM PERCENT
	1	23	46.0	47.9	47.9
	2	12	24.0	25.0	72.9
	3	10	20.0	20.8	93.8
	4	3	6.0	6.3	100.0
MISSING	9	2	4.0	MISSING	
	TOTAL	50	100.0	100.0	

4. Histogram A provides the best summary of the data. B has too many intervals and C has too few.

5. HT58   STATURE, 1958 -- TO NEAREST 0.1 INCH

```
    COUNT   MIDPOINT   ONE SYMBOL EQUALS APPROX.         1.00 OCCURRENCES

        0      59
        0      60
        1      61   *
        0      62
        3      63   ***
        8      64   ********
       12      65   ************
       25      66   *************************
       32      67   ********************************
       48      68   ************************************************
       29      69   *****************************
       28      70   ****************************
       21      71   *********************
       14      72   **************
        8      73   ********
        6      74   ******
        3      75   ***
        1      76   *
        1      77   *
        0      78
        0      79
              I....+....I....+....I....+....I....+....I....+....I
              0        10        20        30        40        50
                         HISTOGRAM FREQUENCY

   VALID CASES    240      MISSING CASES    0
```

6. a.

VALUE LABEL	VALUE	FREQUENCY	PERCENT	VALID PERCENT	CUM PERCENT
	1.00	6	24.0	24.0	24.0
	2.00	3	12.0	12.0	36.0
	3.00	6	24.0	24.0	60.0
	4.00	2	8.0	8.0	68.0
	5.00	4	16.0	16.0	84.0
	8.00	1	4.0	4.0	88.0
	9.00	2	8.0	8.0	96.0
	10.00	1	4.0	4.0	100.0
	TOTAL	25	100.0	100.0	

b.

```
    COUNT   VALUE   ONE SYMBOL EQUALS APPROX.         .20 OCCURRENCES

       6    1.00    *******************************
       3    2.00    ***************
       6    3.00    *******************************
       2    4.00    **********
       4    5.00    *********************
       0    6.00
       0    7.00
       1    8.00    *****
       2    9.00    **********
       1   10.00    *****
              I........I........I........I........I........I........I
              0        2        4        6        8        10
                         HISTOGRAM FREQUENCY
```

c.

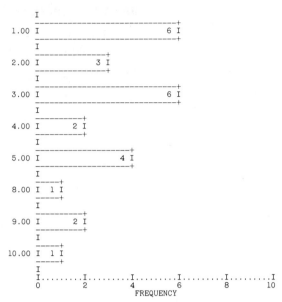

d. The histogram is preferable since codes of 6 and 7 are included, even if they do not occur in the data.

7. a. False.
    b. False.
    c. False.
    d. True.

Chapter 4

Syntax

1. a. All of the following three answers are correct:

```
COMPUTE PCTINT = INTEREST/INCOME * 100
COMPUTE PCTINT = INTEREST * 100 / INCOME
COMPUTE PCTINT = 100 * INTEREST / INCOME
```

b. The two ways to create the square of variable X are:

```
COMPUTE XSQ = X*X
COMPUTE XSQ = X**2
```

c. `COMPUTE  DIS = SQRT(A**2+B**2) + 2`

d. `COMPUTE  SMALL=MIN(A,B,C)`

2. a. 13: 3 times 4 (12) plus 2 (14) minus 1.
    b. 19: 2 plus 3 (5) times 4 (20) minus 1.
    c. 15: 2 plus 3 (5), 4 minus 1 (3), and multiply.
    d. 11: 4 minus 1 (3) times 3 (9) plus 2.
    e. 13: same order as for 2.a.

3. a. 2: the square root of 4.
    b. 9: the sum of 2 plus 3 plus 4.
    c. 3: the average of 2, 3, and 4.
    d. 4: the sum of 2, 3, and 4 (9) plus 7 (16), and take the square root.

Statistical Concepts

1. a. Mild case is the mode.
    b. Moderately severe is the median.
    c. Doesn't make sense since scale is not interval.

2. a. Black is the mode.
    b. No ordering so median does not make sense.
    c. No ordering so mean does not make sense.

3. a. Nominal.
   b. Ratio.
   c. Ordinal.
   d. Ratio.
   e. Interval.
   f. Nominal.

4. The 78th observation.

5. a. 0.267
   b. 0.267 since the mean, median, and mode are identical for a normal distribution.
   c. 0.012
   d. 0

6. The average of the standardized scores must be zero so a mistake must have occurred.

7. 72% of the sample are females.

8. a. False.
   b. False.
   c. True.

9. The median is not influenced by extreme values so it would reflect the low pay levels of the employees. The mean is affected by extremes, so a single salary with seven digits would inflate the mean.

10.
MEAN	1.700	MEDIAN	2.000	MODE	2.000
STD DEV	1.059	VARIANCE	1.122	RANGE	4.000
MINIMUM	.000	MAXIMUM	4.000		

11.
Case	Standard score	Original score
1	1	12
2	0	10
3	−2	6

12.
Student	Score	Standardized score
1	70	0
2	58	−1.00
3	94	2.00

13. a.
VARIABLE	STD DEV	VARIANCE	VALID N
VARA	6.529	42.622	10

   b.
VARIABLE	RANGE	MINIMUM	MAXIMUM	VALID N
VARB	19.000	.000	19.000	10

   c.
VARIABLE	MEAN	SUM	VALID N
VARC	8.500	85.000	10

14. All statistics except the total sample size stay the same.

Chapter 5

Syntax

1. a. False. The CROSSTABS command produces one 2 × 2 table for ADDRESS by LOCATION.
   b. True. The variable specified before the first BY keyword becomes the row variable.
   c. False. The variable LOCATION is the column variable.
   d. False. The VARIABLES subcommand is never used in general mode in CROSSTABS.
   e. True.
   f. False. Keyword ROW requests row percentages only. Use keyword TOTAL to request total percentages.
   g. True. Keyword ROW requests row percentages only.
   h. False. No statistics are requested. Use the STATISTICS subcommand to request statistics.

2. a. Incorrect. When you use integer mode, you must specify a range for each variable named with the VARIABLES subcommand. Keyword TOTAL requests total percentages but these are not shown in the output.

    b. Correct. To use integer mode, use the VARIABLES subcommand followed by the variables and the ranges you want to use in the tables. Separate the VARIABLES subcommand and the TABLES subcommand with a slash.

    c. Incorrect. The VARIABLES subcommand is specified correctly but needs a slash following the range. The TABLES subcommand requests a table with the variables reversed.

    d. Incorrect. The ranges should be specified with the VARIABLES subcommand.

3. a. Ages less than or equal to 40 years are coded as 1; ages 41–65 are coded as 2.

    b. Ages 18–29 are coded as 1; ages 30–49 are coded as 2; and ages 50–65 are coded as 3.

    c. Ages 18, 19 and 20 are coded as 1; ages 21–30 are coded as 2; ages 41–50 are coded as 3; and ages 51–65 are coded as 4. Ages 31–40 keep their original values.

    d. Ages 60–65 are coded as 1; all other ages are coded as 2.

    e. Ages 60–65 are coded as 1; all other ages keep their original values.

4. VARA is the frequency count for each cell. VARB is the row variable and VARC is the column variable.

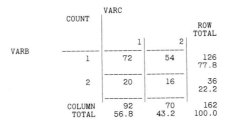

```
                              VARC
                COUNT
                                                    ROW
                                                  TOTAL
                                1        2
        VARB    ------- ------- -------
                  1      72       54       126
                                           77.8
                        ------- -------
                  2      20       16        36
                                           22.2
                        ------- -------
                COLUMN   92       70       162
                TOTAL   56.8     43.2     100.0
```

Statistical Concepts

1. a. False.
    b. True.
    c. False.
    d. False.

2. a. No.
    b. No.
    c. Yes.
    d. Yes (no for symmetric).
    e. Yes.

3. None.

4. They are easier to interpret, and values from different tables can be compared.

5. This is not a good strategy since calculating many statistics and reporting only the ones with large values distorts significance levels.

6. GPA is the independent variable. PERFORM is the dependent variable. Look at row percentages.

7.
```
                        DEPTH
              COUNT
              ROW PCT  SMALL    MEDIUM   LARGE      ROW
              COL PCT                              TOTAL
                         1|       2|       3|
        CURE  --------+--------+--------+--------+
                1       29       10       30        69
         NO            42.0     14.5     43.5      60.5
                       65.9     50.0     60.0
                      +--------+--------+--------+
                2       15       10       20        45
        YES            33.3     22.2     44.4      39.5
                       34.1     50.0     40.0
                      +--------+--------+--------+
              COLUMN    44       20       50       114
              TOTAL    38.6     17.5     43.9     100.0
```

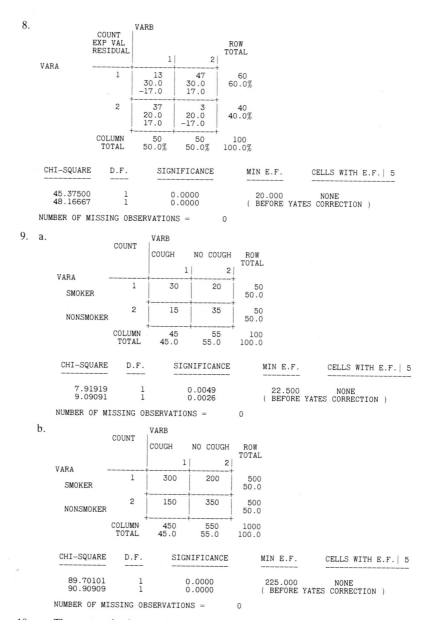

8.

```
                        VARB
            COUNT
            EXP VAL                           ROW
            RESIDUAL                          TOTAL
                             1|        2|
    VARA    --------+--------+--------+
                1   |   13   |   47   |   60
                    |  30.0  |  30.0  |  60.0%
                    | -17.0  |  17.0  |
                +--------+--------+
                2   |   37   |    3   |   40
                    |  20.0  |  20.0  |  40.0%
                    |  17.0  | -17.0  |
                +--------+--------+
            COLUMN     50       50      100
            TOTAL    50.0%    50.0%   100.0%
```

CHI-SQUARE	D.F.	SIGNIFICANCE	MIN E.F.	CELLS WITH E.F.	5
45.37500	1	0.0000	20.000	NONE
48.16667	1	0.0000	(BEFORE YATES CORRECTION)

NUMBER OF MISSING OBSERVATIONS =   0

9. a.

```
                        VARB
            COUNT
                    |COUGH   |NO COUGH| ROW
                    |        |        | TOTAL
                             1|        2|
    VARA    --------+--------+--------+
                1   |   30   |   20   |   50
    SMOKER          |        |        |  50.0
                +--------+--------+
                2   |   15   |   35   |   50
    NONSMOKER       |        |        |  50.0
                +--------+--------+
            COLUMN     45       55      100
            TOTAL    45.0     55.0    100.0
```

CHI-SQUARE	D.F.	SIGNIFICANCE	MIN E.F.	CELLS WITH E.F.	5
7.91919	1	0.0049	22.500	NONE
9.09091	1	0.0026	(BEFORE YATES CORRECTION)

NUMBER OF MISSING OBSERVATIONS =   0

b.

```
                        VARB
            COUNT
                    |COUGH   |NO COUGH| ROW
                    |        |        | TOTAL
                             1|        2|
    VARA    --------+--------+--------+
                1   |  300   |  200   |  500
    SMOKER          |        |        |  50.0
                +--------+--------+
                2   |  150   |  350   |  500
    NONSMOKER       |        |        |  50.0
                +--------+--------+
            COLUMN    450      550     1000
            TOTAL    45.0     55.0    100.0
```

CHI-SQUARE	D.F.	SIGNIFICANCE	MIN E.F.	CELLS WITH E.F.	5
89.70101	1	0.0000	225.000	NONE
90.90909	1	0.0000	(BEFORE YATES CORRECTION)

NUMBER OF MISSING OBSERVATIONS =   0

10. a.   The expected values are in the table below:

```
                        VARB
            COUNT
            EXP VAL |SMOKER  |NONSMOKE| ROW
                    |        |R       | TOTAL
                             1|        2|
    SEX     --------+--------+--------+
                1   |   45   |   55   |  100
    MALE            |  37.5  |  62.5  |  50.0%
                +--------+--------+
                2   |   30   |   70   |  100
    FEMALE          |  37.5  |  62.5  |  50.0%
                +--------+--------+
            COLUMN     75      125      200
            TOTAL    37.5%    62.5%   100.0%
```

CHI-SQUARE	D.F.	SIGNIFICANCE	MIN E.F.	CELLS WITH E.F.	5
4.18133	1	0.0409	37.500	NONE
4.80000	1	0.0285	(BEFORE YATES CORRECTION)

NUMBER OF MISSING OBSERVATIONS =   0

b. There is one degree of freedom for this table.

c. The chi-square value without Yates' correction is 4.80.

Chapter 6

Syntax

1. The correct syntax is

    ```
    MEANS TABLES=SALNOW BY SEX BY JOBCAT
        /MISSING=DEPENDENT
    ```

2. The CROSSBREAK subcommand on MEANS requires the VARIABLES subcommand. The correct syntax is

    ```
    MEANS VARIABLES=EDLEVEL(LO,HI) SEX MINORITY (0,1)
        /CROSSBREAK=EDLEVEL BY SEX BY MINORITY
    ```

3. a. This MEANS command produces two tables: SALNOW BY SEX and SALNOW BY MINORITY.

    b. This is the correct MEANS command to produce the output shown.

    c. This MEANS command specifies MINORITY as the dependent variable on which to calculate means.

4. a. The correct form of the IF command is either

    ```
    IF (JOBCAT EQ 2 OR JOBCAT EQ 4 OR JOBCAT 6) TRAINEE=1
    ```
    or
    ```
    IF (ANY(JOBCAT,2,4,6)) TRAINEE=1
    ```

    b. The THEN is incorrect. The parentheses around the logical expression are optional. The correct form of the command is

    ```
    IF EDLEVEL LE 12 AND SALNOW LE 10000 LOW=1
    ```

    c. The correct form of the command is

    ```
    IF (AGE GE 20 OR AGE LE 55) OLDYOUNG=1
    ```
    Or you can use the RANGE function, as in:
    ```
    IF RANGE(AGE,20,55) OLDYOUNG=1
    ```

5. The complete table of data values for the five cases is:

JOBCAT	AGE	SALNOW	EDLEVEL	TRAINEE	ACHIEVER	LOW
6	28.50	16080	16	1.00	1.00	.00
5	40.33	41400	16	.00	1.00	.00
1	54.33	8880	12	.00	.00	1.00
2	32.33	22000	17	1.00	.00	.00
3	30.92	19020	19	.00	.00	.00

Statistical Concepts

1. a. MEANS
    b. CROSSTABS
    c. FREQUENCIES
    d. MEANS
    e. CROSSTABS

2. CROSSTABS prints numbers (and percentages) of cases that fall in each cell of the table, while MEANS prints statistics for a dependent variable for combinations of values of the independent variables.

3. a. False.
    b. False.

4. a.
```
              D E S C R I P T I O N   O F   S U B P O P U L A T I O N S
    Criterion Variable    DBP58      AVERAGE DIAST BLOOD PRESSURE 58
       Broken Down by     FAMHXCVR   FAMILY HISTORY OF CHD
                 by       VITAL10    STATUS AT TEN YEARS

    Variable         Value  Label              Mean      Std Dev    Cases
    For Entire Population                       88.7908   13.0499    239

    FAMHXCVR     Y          YES                 91.6935   13.0039    62
       VITAL10         0    ALIVE               90.4000   12.0593    45
       VITAL10         1    DEAD                95.1176   15.0868    17

    FAMHXCVR     N          NO                  87.7740   12.9490    177
       VITAL10         0    ALIVE               86.6015   11.1137    133
       VITAL10         1    DEAD                91.3182   17.0304    44

       Total Cases =  240
       Missing Cases =  1 OR  0.4 PCT.
```
  b. Yes.
  c. No.

5. The table is not interpretable since the mean makes no sense for a nominal variable.

Chapter 7

Syntax

1. a. Group 1 has cases where the value for SHOESIZE is less than 8. Group 2 has cases where the value for SHOESIZE is equal to or greater than 8.
   b. Group 1 has cases where the value for SHOESIZE equals 1. Group 2 has cases where the value for SHOESIZE equals 9.
   c. Group 1 has cases where the value for SHOESIZE equals 1. Group 2 has cases where the value for SHOESIZE equals 2.

2. a. Correct.
   b. Incorrect. You must specify the independent-samples test before the paired-samples test, as in:

      ```
      T-TEST  GROUPS=SEX/VARIABLES=WEIGHT/PAIRS=TEST1 TEST2
      ```
   c. Incorrect. A paired-samples test requires at least two variables.
   d. Correct.
   e. Incorrect. Use one, two, or no values to specify the groups.

3.    ```
      T-TEST  GROUPS=TYPE(1,2)/ VARIABLES=RECALL

      T-TEST  PAIRS=SELF ACTUAL/
      ```

Statistical Concepts

1. a. False.
   b. False.
   c. True.
   d. False.
   e. True.
   f. False.
   g. False.
   h. True.

2. a. Since the researcher is interested in detecting only levels which are too high, a one-tailed test is appropriate.
   b. The company would prefer a two-tailed test since larger differences are required to attain statistically significant results.
   c. 0.041

3. It is possible, but unlikely.
      ```

4. a. FREQUENCIES.
   b. Histograms, skewness, and kurtosis.

5. a. That the means of the two populations are equal.
   b. That the means of the two populations are equal.

6. a. Paired.
   b. Paired.
   c. Independent.
   d. Paired.
   e. Paired.

7. a. When the two populations have different variances.
   b. When the two populations have similar variances.

8.

a.

- T - T E S T -

```
GROUP 1 - TYPE    EQ      1.
GROUP 2 - TYPE    EQ      2.
                                                      *  POOLED VARIANCE ESTIMATE  * SEPARATE VARIANCE ESTIMATE
                                                      *                            *
VARIABLE        NUMBER              STANDARD  STANDARD *   F   2-TAIL *  T  DEGREES OF 2-TAIL *  T   DEGREES OF 2-TAIL
                OF CASES    MEAN    DEVIATION  ERROR   * VALUE  PROB. * VALUE  FREEDOM   PROB. * VALUE  FREEDOM    PROB.
------------------------------------------------------*------------*---------------------------*-------------------------
RECALL   COMMERCIAL RECALL SCORE                       *             *                            *
        GROUP 1    66     17.1087    2.804    0.345    *             *                            *
                                                       *  2.57 0.000 *  2.12  146    0.036       *  2.02  103.96   0.046
        GROUP 2    82     16.3093    1.750    0.193    *             *                            *
                                                       *             *                            *
```

b.

- T - T E S T -

```
VARIABLE   NUMBER            STANDARD  STANDARD *(DIFFERENCE) STANDARD  STANDARD *      2-TAIL *  T  DEGREES OF 2-TAIL
           OF CASES   MEAN   DEVIATION  ERROR   *  MEAN     DEVIATION   ERROR   * CORR. PROB. * VALUE  FREEDOM   PROB.
-------------------------------------------------*----------------------------------*------------------*---------------------------
SELF    SELF-REPORTED ARRESTS                     *                                  *                *
                   8.9620   6.458    0.727        *                                  *                *
                                                  *  -0.2912    5.216    0.587       * 0.654 0.000    * -0.50   78      0.621
                   9.2532   6.248    0.703        *                                  *                *
ACTUAL    ACTUAL ARRESTS                          *                                  *                *
```

Chapter 8

Syntax

1. PLOT PLOT = INCOME WITH AGE

3. PLOT PLOT = INCOME WITH AGE BY SEX

5. The PLOT subcommand was omitted.

Statistical Concepts

1. a. MEANS
   b. CROSSTABS
   c. PLOT
   d. CROSSTABS
   e. MEANS
   f. PLOT

2. a. Unrelated; d. Nonlinear (curvilinear) relationship.

Chapter 9

Syntax

1. CORRELATIONS MONEY INVEST SALARY WEALTH
   /PRINT=TWOTAIL

3. a. PLOT must be the last subcommand.
    b. The keyword PLOT is omitted from the specifications.
    c. The second PLOT belongs after the slash, and WITH should be used instead of BY.
    d. The second of the three PLOT keywords in this command is unwanted.

Statistical Concepts

1. a. Positive; c. Negative; e. Negative; g. Positive.

3. The correlation coefficient is meaningless, since product code does not measure anything at the interval level.

5. The correlation coefficient is appropriate only when variables are measured at the interval or ratio level and when the relationship between them is linear. When he computes a large number of correlation coefficients, some of them will be large enough to be statistically significant because of sampling variation alone.

9. The intercept is 10,000 and the slope is 500. The predicted income for a 40-year-old is $30,000.

12. You can't tell which correlation is larger.

Chapter 10

Syntax

1. a. ONEWAY INCOME BY EDUCATION(1,6)/ RANGES=LSD/ RANGES=SCHEFFE/
    b. ONEWAY INCOME BY EDUCATION(1,6)/
    c. ONEWAY INCOME BY EDUCATION(1,6)/ RANGES SCHEFFE/
        or
        ONEWAY INCOME BY SEX(1,2)/ RANGES SCHEFFE/

2. ONEWAY WELL BY EDUC6 (1,6)

Statistical Concepts

1. a. This is not true since the interval 4.89 to 13.23 either does or does not include the population mean. Ninety-five percent of the intervals obtained by repeated sampling would be expected to include the population mean.
    b. True.

2.

		ANALYSIS OF VARIANCE		
SOURCE	D.F.	SUM OF SQUARES	MEAN SQUARES	F RATIO
BETWEEN GROUPS	3	184.00	61.33	2.83
WITHIN GROUPS	36	780.84	21.69	
TOTAL	39	964.84		

3. No. The total sum of squares must be the sum of the between and within-groups sums of squares. The mean square must be the sum of squares divided by the degrees of freedom.

4. Group 1 is different from Groups 3, 4, and 5.

5. Group 1 is different from Groups 3, 4, 5, and 6. Group 2 is different from Groups 4, 5, and 6. Group 3 is different from Group 6.

6. Group 1 cannot be significantly different from itself.

7. No. Multiple comparison procedures are more stringent (require larger differences for significant differences) than t tests.

Chapter 11

Syntax

1. ANOVA DIAS BY RACE (1,4) CHD (0,1)

2. a. ANOVA SCORE BY REGION (1,4) SEX (1,2)
    b. ANOVA SCORE BY REGION (1,4) SEX (1,2)

    c. ANOVA SCORE BY RACE (1,3) SEX (1,2)

    d. ANOVA SCORE1 SCORE2 BY RACE (1,3) SEX (1,2)

    e. ANOVA SCORE1 BY RACE (1,3)/ SCORE2 by SEX (1,2)

3. a. 12 cells.

   b. 9 cells.

   c. 6 cells.

Statistical Concepts

1. Neither statement is true.

2.

```
          * * * A N A L Y S I S   O F   V A R I A N C E * * *

               VAR A
          BY   FACTOR1
               FACTOR2

                                    SUM OF                MEAN
        SOURCE OF VARIATION         SQUARES      DF       SQUARE       F

        MAIN EFFECTS                 524.61       5       104.92      1.03
           FACTOR1                    310.11       3       103.37      1.02
           FACTOR2                    214.50       2       107.25      1.05

        2-WAY INTERACTIONS           104.17       6        17.36      0.17
           FACTOR1 FACTOR2            104.17       6        17.36      0.17

        EXPLAINED                     628.78      11        57.17      0.56

        RESIDUAL                     4988.02      49       101.80

        TOTAL                        5616.80      60
```

3. Yes.

Chapter 12

Syntax

1. a. Expected values cannot be zero.

   b. NPAR TESTS K–W TUMOR BY DIET (0,1)/

   c. NPAR TESTS M–W TUMOR BY DIET (0,1)/

2. NPAR TESTS M–W TUMOR BY DIET (0,1)

3.

VARA	VARB	VARC
14	3	267
18	9	122
1	7	537
19	-3	711
13	0	5

Statistical Concepts

1. a. Ordinal.

   b. Ordinal.

   c. Ordinal.

   d. Nominal.

   e. Ordinal.

2. a. Rank correlation coefficient.

   b. Mann-Whitney test.

   c. Kruskal-Wallis one-way ANOVA

   d. Sign test and Wilcoxon test.

3. a. Two independent samples come from populations having the same distribution.

   b. k samples come from the same population.

    c. The distribution of two paired variables is the same.

    d. The probability of observations falling into the categories are equal to those specified by the researcher.

4. The parametric test is more powerful. It will find true differences more often than the nonparametric test.

Chapter 13

Syntax

1. a. The method subcommand (STEP) precedes the DEPENDENT subcommand.

    b. The VARIABLES subcommand precedes the DESCRIPTIVES subcommand.

    c. There is no DEPENDENT subcommand.

    d. The SCATTERPLOT subcommand precedes the method subcommand.

2.
```
REGRESSION  DESCRIPTIVES=MEAN STDDEV/
    VARIABLES=X1, X2, Y/    DEPENDENT=Y/ STEP
```

3. a. Analysis 1: X dependent; Y, A, B, and C independent.

    b. Analysis 2: Y dependent; X, A, B, and C independent.

    c. Analysis 3: X dependent; A, B, and C independent.

    d. Analysis 4: Y dependent; A, B, and C independent.

4. Equation 4.b computes the correlation matrix once while Equation 4.a computes the correlation matrix twice. Therefore, Equation 4.b is preferred.

5. You have to specify explicitly the variables to be removed.

6. Temporary residual variables must be preceded by an asterisk on the SCATTERPLOT subcommand.

7.
```
a. REGRESSION  . . ./ SCATTERPLOT (*RES,X1)/
b. REGRESSION  . . ./ RESIDUALS = HIST/
c. REGRESSION  . . ./ RESIDUALS = OUTLIERS ID(ID)/
d. REGRESSION  . . ./ CASEWISE = PLOT DEP PRED ALL/
```

Statistical Concepts

1. This hypothesis is of interest because it specifies that there is no linear relationship between the dependent variable and the independent variable.

2. You are checking the assumption of independence of errors when you examine a casewise serial plot.

3. a. $\beta_1 = \beta_2 = \ldots \beta_k = 0$

    b. The coefficients for the variables entered at this step are zero, or the increase in R^2 for the population is zero.

4. Multiple R^2 cannot decrease as additional variables are entered into an equation.

5. No. The band must be narrowest at the mean, $\overline{X}$.

6. You can make the best predictions of the mean of Y at the mean of the X's. The best predictions of values of Y are at $\overline{X}$.

7. a. The assumption of equality of variance appears violated. As the predicted vaues increase in magnitude so does the spread of the residuals.

    b. Since there is a definite pattern to the residuals the assumption of linearity appears to be violated.

    c. There appears to be a pattern to the residuals. Groups of negative residuals are followed by groups of positive residuals, suggesting that the observations are not independent.

    d. The assumption of normality appears to be violated since the histogram of residuals is definitely not normal.

    e. The normal probability plot suggests that the normality assumption is violated.

8. The variable SEX would be the next to enter since it has the largest F value and the value exceeds 3.84.

9. The variable WORK would be removed next since it has the smallest F value and the F value is less than 3.

10. When several variables are very highly correlated, inclusion of all of them in a regression model can lead to computational difficulties and unstable coefficients. In this case the squared multiple correlation between X4 and the other independent variables, X1 and X3, is greater than 0.9999.

11.
```
ANALYSIS OF VARIANCE
                   DF       SUM OF SQUARES     MEAN SQUARE
  REGRESSION        1           28.90000        28.90000
  RESIDUAL          3           20.30000         6.76667

  F =      4.27094      SIGNIF F =  .1307
```

12.
```
CASEWISE PLOT OF STANDARDIZED RESIDUAL

  *: SELECTED   M: MISSING

            -3.0            0.0            3.0
   CASE # X   0:.............:.............:0    Y      *PRED      *RESID
       1 1    .              .  *          .     7     6.0000      1.0000
       2 2    .              .  *          .     9     7.7000      1.3000
       3 3    .         *    .             .     6     9.4000     -3.4000
       4 4    .            * .             .    10    11.1000     -1.1000
       5 5    .              .   *         .    15    12.8000      2.2000
   CASE # X   0:.............:.............:0    Y      *PRED      *RESID
            -3.0            0.0            3.0
```

13.
```
------------------ VARIABLES IN THE EQUATION ------------------

  VARIABLE          B          SE B        BETA        T    SIG T

  WORK          23.77950    21.55603      .06583     1.103   .2705
  MINORITY    -939.85580   252.80301     -.12368    -3.718   .0002
  SEX        -1617.52918   240.70102     -.25615    -6.720   .0000
  EDLEVEL      630.05377    40.77734      .57734    15.451   .0000
  AGE           33.43079    15.42695      .12517     2.167   .0307
  (CONSTANT) -2183.78652   775.23833                -2.817   .0051
```

Appendix B Codebooks

B.1
THE WESTERN
ELECTRIC STUDY

The Western Electric study was undertaken in 1957 to prospectively study factors related to the incidence of coronary heart disease in men who were initially disease-free. Participants were selected through random sampling of 5397 men who were 40 to 55 years of age and employed for at least two years at the Western Electric Company's Hawthorne Works in the Chicago area. The procedures according to which participants were selected, examined, and followed are described in Paul, et al. (1963). A sample of 240 men from the Western Electric study is included on the tape. Chapters 1, 2, and 3 describe the data.

```
                  LIST OF VARIABLES ON THE ACTIVE FILE

   NAME                                                    POSITION

   CASEID    CASE IDENTIFICATION NUMBER                       1
                  PRINT FORMAT: F4
                  WRITE FORMAT: F4

   FIRSTCHD  FIRST CHD EVENT                                  2
                  PRINT FORMAT: F1
                  WRITE FORMAT: F1

             VALUE     LABEL

                1     NO CHD
                2     SUDDEN  DEATH
                3     NONFATALMI
                5     FATAL    MI
                6     OTHER    CHD

   AGE       AGE AT ENTRY                                     3
                  PRINT FORMAT: F2
                  WRITE FORMAT: F2

   DBP58     AVERAGE DIAST BLOOD PRESSURE 58                  4
                  PRINT FORMAT: F3
                  WRITE FORMAT: F3

   EDUYR     YEARS OF EDUCATION                               5
                  PRINT FORMAT: F2
                  WRITE FORMAT: F2

   CHOL58    SERUM CHOLESTEROL 58 -- MG PER DL                6
                  PRINT FORMAT: F3
                  WRITE FORMAT: F3

   CGT58     NO OF CIGARETTES PER DAY IN 1958                 7
                  PRINT FORMAT: F2
                  WRITE FORMAT: F2

   HT58      STATURE, 1958 -- TO NEAREST 0.1 INCH             8
                  PRINT FORMAT: F5.1
                  WRITE FORMAT: F5.1

   WT58      BODY WEIGHT, 1958 -- LBS                         9
                  PRINT FORMAT: F3
                  WRITE FORMAT: F3

   DAYOFWK   DAY OF DEATH                                    10
                  PRINT FORMAT: F1
                  WRITE FORMAT: F1
                  MISSING VALUES:  9

             VALUE     LABEL

                1     SUNDAY
                2     MONDAY
                3     TUESDAY
                4     WEDNSDAY
                5     THURSDAY
                6     FRIDAY
                7     SATURDAY
                9 M   MISSING
```

```
VITAL10    STATUS AT TEN YEARS                              11
               PRINT FORMAT: F1
               WRITE FORMAT: F1

           VALUE    LABEL

               0    ALIVE
               1    DEAD

FAMHXCVR   FAMILY HISTORY OF CHD                            12
               PRINT FORMAT: A1
               WRITE FORMAT: A1

           VALUE    LABEL

               N    NO
               Y    YES

CHD        INCIDENCE OF CORONARY HEART DISEASE              13
               PRINT FORMAT: F1
               WRITE FORMAT: F1
```

B.2
THE BANK DATA FILE

The bank data file (Roberts, 1979) contains information about 474 employees hired by a midwestern bank between 1969 and 1971. The study is described in Chapters 6 and 13.

```
            LIST OF VARIABLES ON THE ACTIVE FILE

     NAME                                              POSITION

     ID        EMPLOYEE CODE                              1
                 PRINT FORMAT: F4
                 WRITE FORMAT: F4

     SALBEG    BEGINNING SALARY                           2
                 PRINT FORMAT: F5
                 WRITE FORMAT: F5
                 MISSING VALUES:  0

     SEX       SEX OF EMPLOYEE                            3
                 PRINT FORMAT: F1
                 WRITE FORMAT: F1
                 MISSING VALUES:  9

               VALUE    LABEL

                   0    MALES
                   1    FEMALES

     TIME      JOB SENIORITY                              4
                 PRINT FORMAT: F2
                 WRITE FORMAT: F2
                 MISSING VALUES:  0

     AGE       AGE OF EMPLOYEE                            5
                 PRINT FORMAT: F6.2
                 WRITE FORMAT: F6.2
                 MISSING VALUES:    .00

     SALNOW    CURRENT SALARY                             6
                 PRINT FORMAT: F5
                 WRITE FORMAT: F5
                 MISSING VALUES:  0

     EDLEVEL   EDUCATIONAL LEVEL                          7
                 PRINT FORMAT: F2
                 WRITE FORMAT: F2
                 MISSING VALUES:  0

     WORK      WORK EXPERIENCE                            8
                 PRINT FORMAT: F6.2
                 WRITE FORMAT: F6.2

     JOBCAT    EMPLOYMENT CATEGORY                        9
                 PRINT FORMAT: F1
                 WRITE FORMAT: F1
                 MISSING VALUES:  0

               VALUE    LABEL

                   1    CLERICAL
                   2    OFFICE TRAINEE
                   3    SECURITY OFFICER
                   4    COLLEGE TRAINEE
                   5    EXEMPT EMPLOYEE
                   6    MBA TRAINEE
                   7    TECHNICAL

     MINORITY  MINORITY CLASSIFICATION                   10
                 PRINT FORMAT: F1
                 WRITE FORMAT: F1
                 MISSING VALUES:  9

               VALUE    LABEL

                   0    WHITE
                   1    NONWHITE
```

```
            SEXRACE    SEX & RACE CLASSIFICATION                    11
                         PRINT FORMAT: F8.2
                         WRITE FORMAT: F8.2

                       VALUE    LABEL

                        1.00    WHITE MALES
                        2.00    MINORITY MALES
                        3.00    WHITE FEMALES
                        4.00    MINORITY FEMALES
```

B.3
THE PRODUCTS
DATA FILE

The products data file contains information on ratings of 19 products by a convenience sample of 100 couples enrolled in an evening MBA program (Davis and Ragsdale, 1983). The goals of the study were to study husband and wife agreement in product purchases. The study is described further in Chapter 7.

For each of the 19 products, the following information is available: husband's rating of the product; husband's prediction of the wife's rating; wife's rating of the product; wife's prediction of the husband's rating; husband's assessment of his relative influence on the decision to buy; and wife's assessment of her relative influence.

```
              LIST OF VARIABLES ON THE PRODUCTS SYSTEM FILE

          NAME                                                POSITION

          H1S        VTR HUSB SELF                                1

                     How likely are you to buy a video-tape unit
                     for in-home education, languages, and so
                     forth?

                           PRINT FORMAT: F1
                           WRITE FORMAT: F1

                       VALUE    LABEL

                         1      DEFINITELY
                         2      VERY LIKELY
                         3      SOMEWHAT LIKELY
                         4      INDIFFERENT
                         5      SOMEWHAT UNLIKELY
                         6      VERY UNLIKELY
                         7      DEFINITELY NOT

          H2S        POP-TOP CANS HUSB SELF                        2
                     Pop-top cans for canned vegetables, soups,
                     or hash.
                           PRINT FORMAT: F1
                           WRITE FORMAT: F1

          H3S        ALARM HUSB SELF                               3
                     A home burglar alarm system that operates
                     via your telephone.
                           PRINT FORMAT: F1
                           WRITE FORMAT: F1

          H4S        TELLER HUSB SELF                              4
                     Automatic tellers in supermarkets that
                     enable deposits or withdrawals from your
                     checking and savings accounts.
                           PRINT FORMAT: F1
                           WRITE FORMAT: F1

          H5S        BIG TV HUSB SELF                              5
                     A big TV that projects a picture on a
                     large screen.
                           PRINT FORMAT: F1
                           WRITE FORMAT: F1

          H6S        PLUMB HUSBAND SELF                            6
                     Do-it-yourself plumbing fixtures.
                           PRINT FORMAT: F1
                           WRITE FORMAT: F1

          H7S        WASHDRY HUSB SELF                             7
                     A combination washer and dryer.
                           PRINT FORMAT: F1
                           WRITE FORMAT: F1

          H8S        AIR HUSB SELF                                 8
                     An energy-saving window air-conditioner.
                           PRINT FORMAT: F1
                           WRITE FORMAT: F1

          H9S        COUNS HUSB SELF                               9
                     Investment counseling via closed-circuit TV.
                           PRINT FORMAT: F1
                           WRITE FORMAT: F1

          H10S       CANDY HUSB SELF                              10
                     A natural candy bar with no sugar or
                     preservatives.
                           PRINT FORMAT: F1
                           WRITE FORMAT: F1
```

H11S	PHONE HUSB SELF	11

A hands-free telephone--talk and listen up
to 20 feet.
PRINT FORMAT: F1
WRITE FORMAT: F1

H12S	PAINT HUSB SELF	12

A rental service for paintings and lithographs.
PRINT FORMAT: F1
WRITE FORMAT: F1

H13S	AIRFARE HUSB SELF	13

Economy airfare (no food or liquor served)
between Chicago and New York.
PRINT FORMAT: F1
WRITE FORMAT: F1

H14S	SHOP SERV HUSB SELF	14

A shop-at-home service using closed-circuit
TV and your telephone.
PRINT FORMAT: F1
WRITE FORMAT: F1

H15S	ELECT AUTO HUSB SELF	15

An electric-powered automobile--250 miles
without a recharge.
PRINT FORMAT: F1
WRITE FORMAT: F1

H16S	SAUNA HUSB SELF	16

An easy-to-install sauna.
PRINT FORMAT: F1
WRITE FORMAT: F1

H17S	AUTO-TRAIN HUSB SELF	17

An auto-train service between Chicago and
Denver.
PRINT FORMAT: F1
WRITE FORMAT: F1

H18S	CHEESE BOARD HUSB SELF	18

A disposable cheese board containing an
assortment of French dinner cheeses.
PRINT FORMAT: F1
WRITE FORMAT: F1

H19S	RAINCOAT HUSB SELF	19

A disposable fashion raincoat.
PRINT FORMAT: F1
WRITE FORMAT: F1

H20S	VACUUM HUSB SELF	20

A vacuum system with outlets in every
room of the house.
PRINT FORMAT: F1
WRITE FORMAT: F1

W1S	VTR WIFE SELF	21

PRINT FORMAT: F1
WRITE FORMAT: F1

W2S	POP-TOP CANS WIFE SELF	22

PRINT FORMAT: F1
WRITE FORMAT: F1

W3S	ALARM WIFE SELF	23

PRINT FORMAT: F1
WRITE FORMAT: F1

W4S	TELLER WIFE SELF	24

PRINT FORMAT: F1
WRITE FORMAT: F1

W5S	BIG TV WIFE SELF	25

PRINT FORMAT: F1
WRITE FORMAT: F1

W6S	PLUMB WIFE SELF	26

PRINT FORMAT: F1
WRITE FORMAT: F1

W7S	WASHDRY WIFE SELF	27

PRINT FORMAT: F1
WRITE FORMAT: F1

W8S	AIR WIFE SELF	28

PRINT FORMAT: F1
WRITE FORMAT: F1

W9S	COUNS WIFE SELF	29

PRINT FORMAT: F1
WRITE FORMAT: F1

W10S	CANDY WIFE SELF	30

PRINT FORMAT: F1
WRITE FORMAT: F1

W11S	PHONE WIFE SELF	31

PRINT FORMAT: F1
WRITE FORMAT: F1

W12S	PAINT WIFE SELF	32

PRINT FORMAT: F1
WRITE FORMAT: F1

W13S	AIRFARE WIFE SELF	33

PRINT FORMAT: F1
WRITE FORMAT: F1

```
W14S      SHOP SERV WIFE SELF                          34
              PRINT FORMAT: F1
              WRITE FORMAT: F1

W15S      ELECT AUTO WIFE SELF                         35
              PRINT FORMAT: F1
              WRITE FORMAT: F1

W16S      SAUNA WIFE SELF                              36
              PRINT FORMAT: F1
              WRITE FORMAT: F1

W17S      AUTO-TRAIN WIFE SELF                         37
              PRINT FORMAT: F1
              WRITE FORMAT: F1

W18S      CHEESE BOARD WIFE SELF                       38
              PRINT FORMAT: F1
              WRITE FORMAT: F1

W19S      RAINCOAT WIFE SELF                           39
              PRINT FORMAT: F1
              WRITE FORMAT: F1

W20S      VACUUM WIFE SELF                             40
              PRINT FORMAT: F1
              WRITE FORMAT: F1

H10       VTR HUSB SPOUSE                              41

          How likely is your spouse to buy a video-tape
          unit for in-home education, languages, and
          so forth?

              PRINT FORMAT: F1
              WRITE FORMAT: F1

          VALUE     LABEL

              1       DEFINITELY
              2       VERY LIKELY
              3       SOMEWHAT LIKELY
              4       INDIFFERENT
              5       SOMEWHAT UNLIKELY
              6       VERY UNLIKELY
              7       DEFINITELY NOT

H20       POP-TOP CANS HUSB SPOUSE                     42
              PRINT FORMAT: F1
              WRITE FORMAT: F1

H30       ALARM HUSB SPOUSE                            43
              PRINT FORMAT: F1
              WRITE FORMAT: F1

H40       TELLER HUSB SPOUSE                           44
              PRINT FORMAT: F1
              WRITE FORMAT: F1

H50       BIG TV HUSB SPOUSE                           45
              PRINT FORMAT: F1
              WRITE FORMAT: F1

H60       PLUMB HUSB SPOUSE                            46
              PRINT FORMAT: F1
              WRITE FORMAT: F1

H70       WASHDRY HUSB SPOUSE                          47
              PRINT FORMAT: F1
              WRITE FORMAT: F1

H80       AIR HUSB SPOUSE                              48
              PRINT FORMAT: F1
              WRITE FORMAT: F1

H90       COUNS HUSB SPOUSE                            49
              PRINT FORMAT: F1
              WRITE FORMAT: F1

H100      CANDY HUSB SPOUSE                            50
              PRINT FORMAT: F1
              WRITE FORMAT: F1

H110      PHONE HUSB SPOUSE                            51
              PRINT FORMAT: F1
              WRITE FORMAT: F1

H120      PAINT HUSB SPOUSE                            52
              PRINT FORMAT: F1
              WRITE FORMAT: F1

H130      AIRFARE HUSB SPOUSE                          53
              PRINT FORMAT: F1
              WRITE FORMAT: F1

H140      SHOP SERV HUSB SPOUSE                        54
              PRINT FORMAT: F1
              WRITE FORMAT: F1

H150      ELECT AUTO HUSB SPOUSE                       55
              PRINT FORMAT: F1
              WRITE FORMAT: F1

H160      SAUNA HUSB SPOUSE                            56
              PRINT FORMAT: F1
              WRITE FORMAT: F1

H170      AUTO-TRAIN HUSB SPOUSE                       57
              PRINT FORMAT: F1
              WRITE FORMAT: F1
```

```
H180       CHEESE BOARD HUSB SPOUSE                          58
               PRINT FORMAT: F1
               WRITE FORMAT: F1

H190       RAINCOAT HUSB SPOUSE                              59
               PRINT FORMAT: F1
               WRITE FORMAT: F1

H200       VACUUM HUSB SPOUSE                                60
               PRINT FORMAT: F1
               WRITE FORMAT: F1


W10        VTR WIFE SPOUSE                                   61
               PRINT FORMAT: F1
               WRITE FORMAT: F1

W20        POP-TOP CANS WIFE SPOUSE                          62
               PRINT FORMAT: F1
               WRITE FORMAT: F1

W30        ALARM WIFE SPOUSE                                 63
               PRINT FORMAT: F1
               WRITE FORMAT: F1

W40        TELLER WIFE SPOUSE                                64
               PRINT FORMAT: F1
               WRITE FORMAT: F1

W50        BIG TV WIFE SPOUSE                                65
               PRINT FORMAT: F1
               WRITE FORMAT: F1

W60        PLUMB WIFE SPOUSE                                 66
               PRINT FORMAT: F1
               WRITE FORMAT: F1

W70        WASHDRY WIFE SPOUSE                               67
               PRINT FORMAT: F1
               WRITE FORMAT: F1

W80        AIR WIFE SPOUSE                                   68
               PRINT FORMAT: F1
               WRITE FORMAT: F1

W90        COUNS WIFE SPOUSE                                 69
               PRINT FORMAT: F1
               WRITE FORMAT: F1

W100       CANDY WIFE SPOUSE                                 70
               PRINT FORMAT: F1
               WRITE FORMAT: F1

W110       PHONE WIFE SPOUSE                                 71
               PRINT FORMAT: F1
               WRITE FORMAT: F1

W120       PAINT WIFE SPOUSE                                 72
               PRINT FORMAT: F1
               WRITE FORMAT: F1

W130       AIRFARE WIFE SPOUSE                               73
               PRINT FORMAT: F1
               WRITE FORMAT: F1

W140       SHOP SERV WIFE SPOUSE                             74
               PRINT FORMAT: F1
               WRITE FORMAT: F1

W150       ELECT AUTO WIFE SPOUSE                            75
               PRINT FORMAT: F1
               WRITE FORMAT: F1

W160       SAUNA WIFE SPOUSE                                 76
               PRINT FORMAT: F1
               WRITE FORMAT: F1

W170       AUTO-TRAIN WIFE SPOUSE                            77
               PRINT FORMAT: F1
               WRITE FORMAT: F1

W180       CHEESE BOARD WIFE SPOUSE                          78
               PRINT FORMAT: F1
               WRITE FORMAT: F1

W190       RAINCOAT WIFE SPOUSE                              79
               PRINT FORMAT: F1
               WRITE FORMAT: F1

W200       VACUUM WIFE SPOUSE                                80
               PRINT FORMAT: F1
               WRITE FORMAT: F1

H1R        VTR HUSB INFLUENCE                                81

           Who would have more influence in deciding
           to buy this product?

               PRINT FORMAT: F1
               WRITE FORMAT: F1

           VALUE     LABEL

               1     HUSB DECIDE
               2     HUSB MORE INFLUENCE
               3     HUSB/WIFE EQUAL
               4     WIFE MORE INLUENCE
               5     WIFE DECIDE
```

```
H2R      POP-TOP CANS INFLUENCE                        82
                PRINT FORMAT: F1
                WRITE FORMAT: F1

H3R      ALARM HUSB INFLUENCE                          83
                PRINT FORMAT: F1
                WRITE FORMAT: F1

H4R      TELLER HUSB INFLUENCE                         84
                PRINT FORMAT: F1
                WRITE FORMAT: F1

H5R      BIG TV HUSB INFLUENCE                         85
                PRINT FORMAT: F1
                WRITE FORMAT: F1

H6R      PLUMB HUSB  INFLUENCE                         86
                PRINT FORMAT: F1
                WRITE FORMAT: F1

H7R      WASHDRY HUSB INFLUENCE                        87
                PRINT FORMAT: F1
                WRITE FORMAT: F1

H8R      AIR HUSB INFLUENCE                            88
                PRINT FORMAT: F1
                WRITE FORMAT: F1

H9R      COUNS HUSB INFLUENCE                          89
                PRINT FORMAT: F1
                WRITE FORMAT: F1

H10R     CANDY HUSB INFLUENCE                          90
                PRINT FORMAT: F1
                WRITE FORMAT: F1

H11R     PHONE HUSB INFLUENCE                          91
                PRINT FORMAT: F1
                WRITE FORMAT: F1

H12R     PAINT HUSB INFLUENCE                          92
                PRINT FORMAT: F1
                WRITE FORMAT: F1

H13R     AIRFARE HUSB INFLUENCE                        93
                PRINT FORMAT: F1
                WRITE FORMAT: F1

H14R     SHOP SERV HUSB INFLUENCE                      94
                PRINT FORMAT: F1
                WRITE FORMAT: F1

H15R     ELECT AUTO HUSB INFLUENCE                     95
                PRINT FORMAT: F1
                WRITE FORMAT: F1

H16R     SAUNA HUSB INFLUENCE                          96
                PRINT FORMAT: F1
                WRITE FORMAT: F1

H17R     AUTO-TRAIN HUSB INFLUENCE                     97
                PRINT FORMAT: F1
                WRITE FORMAT: F1

H18R     CHEESE BOARD HUSB INFLUENCE                   98
                PRINT FORMAT: F1
                WRITE FORMAT: F1

H19R     RAINCOAT HUSB INFLUENCE                       99
                PRINT FORMAT: F1
                WRITE FORMAT: F1

H20R     VACUUM HUSB INFLUENCE                        100
                PRINT FORMAT: F1
                WRITE FORMAT: F1

W1R      VTR WIFE INFLUENCE                           101
                PRINT FORMAT: F1
                WRITE FORMAT: F1

W2R      POP-TOP CANS INFLUENCE                       102
                PRINT FORMAT: F1
                WRITE FORMAT: F1

W3R      ALARM WIFE INFLUENCE                         103
                PRINT FORMAT: F1
                WRITE FORMAT: F1

W4R      TELLER WIFE INFLUENCE                        104
                PRINT FORMAT: F1
                WRITE FORMAT: F1

W5R      BIG TV WIFE INFLUENCE                        105
                PRINT FORMAT: F1
                WRITE FORMAT: F1

W6R      PLUMB WIFE  INFLUENCE                        106
                PRINT FORMAT: F1
                WRITE FORMAT: F1

W7R      WASHDRY WIFE INFLUENCE                       107
                PRINT FORMAT: F1
                WRITE FORMAT: F1

W8R      AIR WIFE INFLUENCE                           108
                PRINT FORMAT: F1
                WRITE FORMAT: F1
```

```
W9R        COUNS WIFE INFLUENCE                         109
               PRINT FORMAT: F1
               WRITE FORMAT: F1

W10R       CANDY WIFE INFLUENCE                         110
               PRINT FORMAT: F1
               WRITE FORMAT: F1

W11R       PHONE WIFE INFLUENCE                         111
               PRINT FORMAT: F1
               WRITE FORMAT: F1

W12R       PAINT WIFE INFLUENCE                         112
               PRINT FORMAT: F1
               WRITE FORMAT: F1

W13R       AIRFARE WIFE INFLUENCE                       113
               PRINT FORMAT: F1
               WRITE FORMAT: F1

W14R       SHOP SERV WIFE INFLUENCE                     114
               PRINT FORMAT: F1
               WRITE FORMAT: F1

W15R       ELECT AUTO WIFE INFLUENCE                    115
               PRINT FORMAT: F1
               WRITE FORMAT: F1

W16R       SAUNA WIFE INFLUENCE                         116
               PRINT FORMAT: F1
               WRITE FORMAT: F1

W17R       AUTO-TRAIN WIFE INFLUENCE                    117
               PRINT FORMAT: F1
               WRITE FORMAT: F1

W18R       CHEESE BOARD WIFE INFLUENCE                  118
               PRINT FORMAT: F1
               WRITE FORMAT: F1

W19R       RAINCOAT WIFE INFLUENCE                      119
               PRINT FORMAT: F1
               WRITE FORMAT: F1

W20R       VACUUM WIFE INFLUENCE                        120
               PRINT FORMAT: F1
               WRITE FORMAT: F1

CASEID                                                  121
               PRINT FORMAT: F3
               WRITE FORMAT: F3

VISUAL     PICTURE ACCOMPANIED QUESTION                 122
               PRINT FORMAT: F1
               WRITE FORMAT: F1

           VALUE     LABEL

             0     NO PICTURES
             1     PICTURES

HSSCALE    HUSBAND SELF SCALE                           123

           The sum of scores for all twenty products.

               PRINT FORMAT: F8.2
               WRITE FORMAT: F8.2

HRSCALE    HUSBAND INFLUENCE SCALE                      124
               PRINT FORMAT: F8.2
               WRITE FORMAT: F8.2

HOSCALE    HUSBAND SPOUSE SCALE                         125
               PRINT FORMAT: F8.2
               WRITE FORMAT: F8.2

WSSCALE    WIFE SELF SCALE                              126
               PRINT FORMAT: F8.2
               WRITE FORMAT: F8.2

WOSCALE    WIFE SPOUSE SCALE                            127
               PRINT FORMAT: F8.2
               WRITE FORMAT: F8.2

WRSCALE    WIFE INFLUENCE SCALE                         128
               PRINT FORMAT: F8.2
               WRITE FORMAT: F8.2

FAMSCORE   FAMILY BUYING SCORE                          129
           The sum of husband's and wife's total
           scores.
               PRINT FORMAT: F8.2
               WRITE FORMAT: F8.2

SSDIFF     HUSBAND-WIFE DIFFERENCE SCALE                130
           Husband's total scores minus wife's total
           scores.
               PRINT FORMAT: F8.2
               WRITE FORMAT: F8.2

RRDIF      HUSB-WIFE RELATIVE INFLUENCE SCALE           131
           Husband's influence score minus wife's
           influence score.
               PRINT FORMAT: F8.2
               WRITE FORMAT: F8.2
```

B.4
THE GENERAL
SOCIAL SURVEY
FILE

The General Social Surveys have been conducted since 1972 to study social indicators (Davis, 1982). Each survey is an independently drawn sample of English-speaking persons 18 years of age or over, living in non-institutional arrangements within the continental United States. The data described below are a subset of variables from the 1982 survey dealing with patterns of social interaction.

```
DOCUMENTS      ENTERED 07/13/82
               THIS SYSTEM FILE CONTAINS DATA FOR THE 1972-1982
               GENERAL SOCIAL SURVEYS, CONDUCTED BY THE NATIONAL
               OPINION RESEARCH CENTER.
         (Entered 08 FEB 83)

               LIST OF VARIABLES ON THE ACTIVE FILE

         NAME                                              POSITION

         PRESTIGE  RESP'S OCCUPATIONAL PRESTIGE SCORE          1
                      PRINT FORMAT: F2
                      WRITE FORMAT: F2
                      MISSING VALUES:  0

                   VALUE    LABEL

                      0 M   DK,NA,NAP

         AGE                                                   2
                      PRINT FORMAT: F2
                      WRITE FORMAT: F2
                      MISSING VALUES:  0, 98, 99

                   VALUE    LABEL

                      0 M   NAP
                     98 M   DK
                     99 M   NA

         EDUC      HIGHEST YEAR SCHOOL COMPLETED               3
                      PRINT FORMAT: F2
                      WRITE FORMAT: F2
                      MISSING VALUES:  97, 98, 99

                   VALUE    LABEL

                     97 M   NAP
                     98 M   DK
                     99 M   NA

         SEX                                                   4
                      PRINT FORMAT: F2
                      WRITE FORMAT: F2

                   VALUE    LABEL

                      1      MALE
                      2      FEMALE

         SOCREL    SPEND EVE WITH RELATIVES                    5
                   How often do you spend a social evening
                   with relatives?
                      PRINT FORMAT: F2
                      WRITE FORMAT: F2
                      MISSING VALUES:  -1, 8, 9

                   VALUE    LABEL

                     -1 M   NAP
                      1      ALMOST  DAILY
                      2      SEV TIMES A WEEK
                      3      SEV TIMES A MNTH
                      4      ONCE A MONTH
                      5      SEV TIMES A YEAR
                      6      ONCE A YEAR
                      7      NEVER
                      8 M   DK
                      9 M   NA

         SOCOMMUN  SPEND EVE WITH NEIGHBOR                     6
                   How often do you spend a social evening
                   with someone who lives in your neighborhood?
                      PRINT FORMAT: F2
                      WRITE FORMAT: F2
                      MISSING VALUES:  -1, 8, 9

                   See SOCREL for value labels.

         SOCFREND  SPEND EVE WITH FRIENDS                      7
                   How often do you spend a social evening
                   with friends who live outside the
                   neighborhood?
                      PRINT FORMAT: F2
                      WRITE FORMAT: F2
                      MISSING VALUES:  -1, 8, 9

                   See SOCREL for value labels.
```

```
SOCBAR     SPEND EVE AT BAR                                      8
           How often do you go to a bar or tavern?
               PRINT FORMAT: F2
               WRITE FORMAT: F2
               MISSING VALUES:  -1, 8, 9

           See SOCREL for value labels.

SOCPARS    SPEND EVENING WITH PARENTS                            9
           How often do you spend a social evening
           with your parents?
               PRINT FORMAT: F2
               WRITE FORMAT: F2
               MISSING VALUES:  -1, 8, 9

           VALUE     LABEL

               -1 M  NOT APPROPRIATE (no such relatives)
                1    ALMOST  DAILY
                2    SEV TIMES A WEEK
                3    SEV TIMES A MNTH
                4    ONCE A MONTH
                5    SEV TIMES A YEAR
                6    ONCE A YEAR
                7    NEVER
                8 M  DK
                9 M  NA

SOCSIBS    SPEND EVENING WITH SIBLINGS                          10
           How often do you spend a social evening
           with a brother or sister?
               PRINT FORMAT: F2
               WRITE FORMAT: F2
               MISSING VALUES:  -1, 8, 9

           See SOCPARS for value labels.

ANOMIA5    LOT OF AVERAGE MAN GETTING WORSE                     11
           In spite of what some people say, the
           lot (situation/condition) of the average
           man is getting worse, not better.
               PRINT FORMAT: F2
               WRITE FORMAT: F2
               MISSING VALUES:  0, 8, 9
               VALUE     LABEL

                1    AGREE
                2    DISAGREE
                8 M  DK
                9 M  NA

ANOMIA6    NOT FAIR TO BRING CHILD INTO WORLD                   12
           It's hardly fair to bring a child into
           the world with the way things look for
           the future.
               PRINT FORMAT: F2
               WRITE FORMAT: F2
               MISSING VALUES:  0, 8, 9

           See ANOMIA5 for value labels.

ANOMIA7    OFFICIALS NOT INTERESTED IN AVERAGE MAN              13
           Most public officials (people in public
           office) are not really interested in the
           problems of the average man.
               PRINT FORMAT: F2
               WRITE FORMAT: F2
               MISSING VALUES:  0, 8, 9

           See ANOMIA5 for value labels.

TVHOURS    HOURS PER DAY WATCHING TV                            14
           On the average day, about how may hours
           do you personally watch television?
               PRINT FORMAT: F2
               WRITE FORMAT: F2
               MISSING VALUES:  -1, 98, 99

           VALUE     LABEL

               -1 M  NAP
               98 M  DK
               99 M  NA
```

Bibliography

Anderberg, M. R. *Cluster analysis for applications.* New York: Academic Press, 1973.

Anderson, R., and S. Nida. Effect of physical attractiveness on opposite and same-sex evaluations. *Journal of Personality,* 46:3 (1978), 401–413.

Beard, C. M., V. Fuster, and L. R. Elveback. Daily and seasonal variation in sudden cardiac death, Rochester, Minnesota, 1950–1975. *Mayo Clinic Proceedings,* 57 (1982), 704–706.

Berk, K. N. Comparing subset regression procedures. *Technometrics,* 20 (1978), 1–6.

————. Tolerance and condition in regression computation. *Journal of the American Statistical Association,* 72 (1977), 863–866.

Black and Sherba. Contracting to problem solve to lose weight. *Behavior Therapy,* 14 (1983), 105–109.

Blalock, H. M. *Social statistics.* New York: McGraw-Hill, 1979.

Bock, R. D. *Multivariate statistical methods in behavioral research.* New York: McGraw-Hill, 1975.

Borgatta, E. F., and G. W. Bohrnstedt. Level of measurement once over again. *Sociological methods and research,* 9:2 (1980), 147–160.

Cattell, R. B. The meaning and strategic use of factor analysis. In *Handbook of Multivariate Experimental Psychology,* ed. R. B. Cattell. Chicago: Rand McNally, 1966.

Cedercreutz, C. Hypnotic treatment of 100 cases of migraine. In F. H. Frankel and H. S. Zamansky, eds. *Hypnosis at Its Bicentennial.* New York: Plenum, 1978.

Churchill, G. A., Jr. *Marketing research: methodological foundations.* Hinsdale, Il.: Dryden Press, 1979.

Conover, W. J. Some reasons for not using the Yates continuity correction on 2×2 contingency tables. *Journal of the American Statistical Association,* 69 (1974), 374–376.

Consumer Reports, July 1983.

Cook, R. D. Detection of influential observations in linear regression. *Technometrics,* 19 (1977), 15–18.

Daugirdas, J. T. *Unpublished data.*

Davis, J. A. *General Social Surveys, 1972–1982: Cumulative Codebook.* Chicago: National Opinion Research Center, 1982.

Davis, H., and E. Ragsdale. Unpublished working paper. Chicago: University of Chicago, Graduate School of Business, 1983.

Dineen, L. C., and B. C. Blakesley. Algorithm AS 62: A generator for the sampling distribution of the Mann-Whitney U statistic. *Applied Statistics,* 22 (1973), 269–273.

Everitt, B. S. *Cluster analysis.* 2nd ed. London: Heineman Educational Books Ltd., 1980.

Everitt, B. S. *The analysis of contingency tables.* London: Chapman and Hall, 1977.

Fienberg, S. E. *The analysis of cross-classified categorical data.* Cambridge: MIT Press, 1977.

Finn, J. D. *A general model for multivariate analysis.* New York: Holt, Rinehart, and Winston, 1974.

Frane, J. W. Some simple procedures for handling missing data in multivariate analysis. *Psychometrika,* 41 (1976), 409–415.

————. A note on checking tolerance in matrix inversion and regression. *Technometrics,* 19 (1977), 513–514.

Goodman, L. A., and W. H. Kruskal. Measures of association for cross-classification. *Journal of the American Statistical Association,* 49 (1954), 732–764.

Greeley, A. M., W. C. McCready and G. Theisen. *Ethnic drinking subcultures.* New York: Praeger Publishers, 1980.

Haberman, S. J. *Analysis of qualitative data,* Vol. 1. London: Academic Press, 1978.

Hansson, R. O., and K. M. Slade. Altruism toward a deviant in city and small town.

Harman, H. H. *Modern factor analysis.* 2nd ed. Chicago: University of Chicago Press, 1967. *Journal of Applied Social Psychology,* 7:3 (1977), 272–279.

Hoaglin, D. C., and R. E. Welsch. The hat matrix in regression and ANOVA. *American Statistician,* 32 (1978), 17–22.

Hocking, R. R. The analysis and selection of variables in linear regression. *Biometrics,* 32 (1976), 1–49.

Jonassen, C. T., and S. H. Peres. *Interrelationships of dimensions of community systems.* Columbus: Ohio State University Press, 1960.

Kim, J. O., and C. W. Mueller. *Introduction to factor analysis.* Beverly Hills: Sage Press, 1978.

King, M. M., et al. Incidence and growth of mammary tumors induced by 7,12-dimethylbenz(a) anthracene as related to the dietary content of fat and antioxident. *Journal of the National Cancer Institute,* 63:3 (1979), 657–663.

Kleinbaum, D. G., and L. L. Kupper. *Applied regression analysis and other multivariable methods.* North Scituate, Massachusetts: Duxbury Press, 1978.

Lachenbruch, P. A. *Discriminant analysis.* New York: Hafner Press, 1975.

Lee, E. T. *Statistical methods for survival data analysis.* Belmont, California: Lifetime Learning Publications, 1980.

Loether, H. J., and D. G. McTavish. *Descriptive and inferential statistics: an introduction.* Boston: Allyn and Bacon, 1976.

Mantel, N. Comment and a suggestion on the Yates continuity correction. *Journal of the American Statistical Association,* 69 (1974), 378–380.

Meyer, L. S., and M. S. Younger. Estimation of standardized coefficients. *Journal of the American Statistical Association,* 71 (1976), 154–157.

Milligan, G. W., and P. D. Isaac. The validation of four ultrametric clustering algorithms. *Pattern Recognition,* 12 (1980), 41-50.

Morrison, D. F. *Multivariate statistical methods.* New York: McGraw-Hill, 1967.

Neter, J., and W. Wasserman. *Applied linear statistical models.* Homewood, Illinois: Richard D. Irwin Inc., 1974.

Olson, C. L. On choosing a test statistic in multivariate analysis of variance. *Psychological Bulletin,* 83 (1976), 579-586.

Overall, J. E., and C. Klett. *Applied multivariate analysis.* New York: McGraw-Hill, 1972.

Paul, O., et al. A longitudinal study of coronary heart disease. *Circulation,* 28 (1963), 20–31.

Rabkin, S. W., F. A. Mathewson and R. B. Tate. Chronobiology of cardiac sudden death in men. *Journal of the American Medical Association,* 244:12, (1980), 1357–1358.

Roberts, H. V. *An analysis of employee compensation.* Rpt. 7946, Center for Mathematical Studies in Business and Economics, University of Chicago: October 1979.

———. Statistical bases in the measurement of employment discrimination. In E. Robert Livernash, ed., *Comparable worth: issues and alternatives.* Washington, D.C.: Equal Employment Advisory Council, 1980, 173–195.

Romesburg, H. C. *Cluster analysis for researchers.* Belmont, California: Lifetime Learning Publications, 1984.

Siegel, S. *Nonparametric statistics for the behavioral sciences.* New York: McGraw-Hill, 1956.

Sigall, H., and N. Ostrove. Beautiful but dangerous: effects of offender attractiveness and nature of the crime on juridic judgment. *Journal of Personality and Social Psychology,* 31 (1975), 410–414.

Smirnov, N. V. Table for estimating the goodness of fit of empirical distributions. *Annals of mathematical statistics,* 19 (1948), 279–281.

Sneath, P. H. A., and R. R. Sokal. *Numerical taxonomy.* San Francisco: W.H. Freeman and Co., 1973.

Snedecor, G. W., and W. G. Cochran. *Statistical methods.* Ames, Iowa: Iowa State University Press, 1967.

Somers, R. H. A new symmetric measure of association for ordinal variables. *American Sociological Review,* 27 (1962), 799–811.

Speed, M. F. Response curves in the one way classification with unequal numbers of observations per cell. *Proceedings of the Statistical Computing Section,* American Statistical Association, 1976.

SPSS Inc. *SPSS-X user's guide.* Chicago: SPSS Inc., 1987.

SPSS Inc. *SPSS-X Statistical Algorithms.* Chicago: SPSS Inc., 1983.

Stevens, S. S. On the theory of scales of measurement. *Science,* 103 (1946), 677–680.

Stoetzel, J. A factor analysis of liquor preference of French consumers. *Journal of Advertising Research,* 1:1 (1960), 7-11.

Tatsuoka, M. M. *Multivariate analysis.* New York: John Wiley and Sons, 1971.

Theil, H. *Economics and information theory.* Chicago: Rand McNally, 1967.

Tucker, L. R. Relations of factor score estimates to their use. *Psychometrika,* 36 (1971), 427-436.

Tucker, R. F., R. F. Koopman, and R. L. Linn. Evaluation of factor analytic research procedures by means of simulated correlation matrices. *Psychometrika,* 34 (1969), 421-459.

Velleman, P. F., and R. E. Welsch. Efficient computing of regression diagnostics. *American Statistician,* 35 (1981), 234–242.

Winer, B. J. *Statistical principles in experimental design.* New York: McGraw-Hill, 1971.

Wynder, E. L. Nutrition and cancer. *Federal Proceedings,* 35 (1976), 1309–1315.

Wyner, G. A. Response errors in self-reported number of arrests. *Sociological Methods and Research,* 9:2 (1980), 161–177.

Index